Exploring
Leadership

Exploring
Leadership

⌄

For College Students
Who Want to
Make a Difference

Third Edition

Susan R. **Komives**
Nance **Lucas**
Timothy R. **McMahon**

◇

JOSSEY-BASS
A Wiley Imprint
www.josseybass.com

Published by Jossey-Bass
A Wiley Imprint
One Montgomery Street, Suite 1200, San Francisco, CA 94104-4594—www.josseybass.com

Jossey-Bass books and products are available through most bookstores. To contact Jossey-Bass directly call our Customer Care Department within the U.S. at 800-956-7739, outside the U.S. at 317-572-3986, or fax 317-572-4002.

Wiley also publishes its books in a variety of electronic formats and by print-on-demand. Some material included with standard print versions of this book may not be included in e-books or in print-on-demand. If the version of this book that you purchased references media such as CD or DVD that was not included in your purchase, you may download this material at http://booksupport.wiley.com. For more information about Wiley products, visit www.wiley.com.

Library of Congress Cataloging-in-Publication Data
Komives, Susan R., 1946-
  Exploring leadership : for college students who want to make a difference / Susan R. Komives, Nance Lucas, Timothy R. McMahon.—Third edition.
      pages cm
  Includes bibliographical references and index.
  ISBN 978-1-118-39947-7 (pbk.), ISBN: 978-1-118-41748-5 (ebk.), ISBN: 978-1-118-42181-9 (ebk.), ISBN: 978-1-118-44356-9 (ebk.)
  1. Student activities—United States. 2. Leadership—Study and teaching (Higher)—United States. 3. Interpersonal relations—United States. I. Title.
  LB3605.K64 2013
  378.1′980973—dc23

                                                                    201300101

Printed in the United States of America
FIRST EDITION
PB Printing   10 9 8 7 6 5 4

CONTENTS

If you purchased a new copy of this book, you will find a unique code to use to take the Clifton StrengthsQuest in the back of this book. Go to The Gallup Organization website http://strengths.gallup.com where you can enter your code and access your assessment. If you purchased a used copy or rented or borrowed a copy of this book, the code may already have been used, and you can purchase a new code directly from https://www.gallupstrengthscenter.com/Purchase/

Clifton StrengthsQuest is a 30-minute online assessment which has helped more than eight million people around the world discover their talents. After taking take the self-assessment, you'll receive a customized report that lists your top five talent themes, along with action items for development and suggestions about how you can use your talents to achieve academic, career, and personal success.

PREFACE

What comes to mind when you hear the word leadership? Do you think of international or national figures like Mark Zuckerberg, Marissa Mayer, Hillary Clinton, Jan Brewer, Cory Booker, Barack Obama, Kofi Annan, Aung San Suu Kyi, Mohandas Gandhi, Nelson Mandela, Elaine Chao, Bud Selig, or Harry Potter? Our brains somehow immediately translate the word "leadership" to mean "leader." You probably just did the same thing. You probably imagined a company president, a prime minister, your professor, your supervisor at work, or the person standing at a podium with a gavel. However, the premise of this book is that leadership is a relational and ethical process of people together attempting to accomplish positive change. In other words, leadership is about relationships. And you can be part of the leadership process, whether as a formal leader or as an active, committed group member.

> Purpose of This Book

Chances are that you are reading this book because you want to learn more about leadership. You may be taking a leadership course, attending a workshop, learning to be a resident assistant, or just reading for your own development. Somehow, you want to be more effective in accomplishing change, making a difference, or working with others. Perhaps you have just accepted a new leadership role, selected a career in which you will be called on to assume leadership responsibilities, or will be working on a

team making complex decisions. Maybe you have had many leadership experiences, or maybe you have never thought of yourself
as a leader at all. Indeed, you may have thought of leadership as
emphasizing leaders—not followers or group members.

A popular sentiment wisely reminds us that all of us are
smarter than one of us. The wisdom, common purpose, inclusivity, sense of community, and personal empowerment embedded
in that statement are profound. Leadership is not something
possessed by only a select few people in high positions. We are
all involved in the leadership process, and we are all capable
of being effective leaders. Through collaboration with others,
you can make a difference from any place within a group or
organization, whether as the titled leader or as an active member.

> Scope of the Book and Treatment of Topics

Our rapidly changing world needs each of us to do what we
can to make a difference in our own communities. Each of us is
a member of many communities—our family, neighborhood,
religious group, workplace, classroom, residence hall floor, or
sports team. In this book, we will ask you to examine yourself
and your communities: where you live, where you work, whom
you care for, what interests you, and how you want to develop.
Together, we will explore how you see yourself in relation to
others and how you prefer to interact with others in various
group settings. Our aim in this book is to help you use your own
college context and your experience as a college student as the
frame within which to understand leadership. The students who
helped us with this book said, "Most students skip the preface!"

We are glad you did not do that. You will understand the book better for having read this section.

The three of us have, for many years, taught leadership courses, advised students in formal leadership roles, mentored student leaders and group members, supervised student workers, sought to bring students into campus governance, served as leaders ourselves both in formal positions and as members of teams and groups, and read and researched leadership. When we developed the first edition of this book, we were keenly aware that when we taught a leadership course, we shared a frustration that the scholarship and literature in leadership studies did not connect with most students. Business majors often find themselves in the literature because so much of it comes from their major. Psychology and sociology majors usually relate to it because the leadership field is interdisciplinary and draws heavily from their fields of study. But many students have trouble relating to the leadership literature, much of which is written for corporate chief executive officers (CEOs). Some students find the leader-focused approaches to be self-centered, and some say, "I'm not a leader. I just want to make a difference."

Leadership can be viewed from various frames: political science addresses power and influence, business management sees leadership as good management and effectiveness in outcomes or emphasizes supervisor-subordinate relationships, anthropology views cultural influences and such factors as symbols and norms, history looks to the influence and experience of key figures during significant times or when leading major social movements, and psychology or sociology looks at individuals and groups as they interact, including social status and social capital. One book cannot do justice to all these diverse perspectives, but we challenge you to explore how your field or fields of study approach leadership.

The primary perspectives or frames we use in this book are a combination of psychological and educational approaches; we emphasize learning about yourself and understanding yourself in the context of others. Being aware of your personal values, beliefs, strengths, and commitments builds a strong foundation for your position as a member in the world's many communities. Self-awareness is central to being able to understand others and interact effectively in groups, organizations, and communities.

We believe that you can learn to understand yourself and others, that organizations are most effective when they are learning environments and function as caring communities, and that our rapidly changing world will require people leading together toward meaningful change. The belief that leadership is grounded in learning together must be modeled in our educational environments. Yet the world does not always work this way. You constantly will be challenged to understand how things are, see how they could be, and be a part of change if necessary.

Throughout the book, you will find essays and stories from students from across the country. We think you will find their thoughts and experiences interesting. We encourage you to explore the philosophy of leadership these students may hold by what they share in their stories.

› Summary of the Contents

Because personal awareness and personal development are central to learning leadership, the focus of this book is as much on you, others, and your relationships with others as it is on understanding leadership theory, styles, practices, and applications.

We organized the book around four major themes: leadership for a changing world (Part One), with an emphasis on the Relational Leadership Model; relationships as the foundation of leadership (Part Two); the context of leadership in communities, groups, and organizations (Part Three); understanding change and how to make a difference using leadership while thriving personally and with others (Part Four). This third edition includes a number of revisions and updates to the original chapters from previous editions focusing on lessons from positive psychology, including self-assessments embedded in this edition.

In Chapter One, we introduce the concepts in this book with specific attention to the variety among groups of students with different experiences who learn leadership for different purposes and practice it in various settings. In Chapter Two, we show how the study and understanding of leadership has evolved through recent times and how rapidly changing times lead to new leadership approaches. In Chapter Three, we present the Relational Leadership Model (RLM). This model emphasizes the nature of relationships that are the building blocks in working with others to make a difference and accomplish change.

In Part Two (Chapters Four, Five, and Six), we ask you to explore yourself, others, yourself in relation to others, and the nature of leading with integrity. Understanding self includes understanding your values, character, and the strengths you use in interacting, deciding, and learning. Self-awareness is an essential foundation for understanding leadership and helps you respond to the differences and commonalties you have with others. This chapter focuses on the concept of leading from your strengths and talents. We recommend you wait until reading

Chapter Four to use the Clifton StrengthsQuest code to explore your strengths further. Please note that although we have a dedicated chapter on leading with integrity, the treatment of values, ethics, and character is a theme throughout this book.

Part Three (Chapters Seven, Eight, and Nine) examines the various settings in which leadership is needed; for example, in groups and teams. It explores the core elements of communities and emphasizes collaborative processes. It also examines aspects of complex organizations and how these may raise distinct issues for the practice of relational leadership, and it presents the need for organizational renewal in all the contexts of leadership.

Part Four (Chapters Ten, Eleven, and Twelve) presents material on the nature of change, the change process, the immunity to change, and being change agents. It explores such applications and strategies as service learning, coalition building, Appreciative Inquiry, and activism. This part also contains another widely used model of leadership development, the Social Change Model of Leadership Development. Chapter Twelve closes the circle and brings you back to where you started, with the most foundational aspects of self-awareness and the importance of staying renewed in the leadership process so that you might thrive personally and nurture thriving in groups and teams.

> Leadership Can Be Learned

This book (and perhaps the course you are taking as well) is designed to expose you to key concepts of leadership and to provide activities that will encourage you to learn leadership. You will need to practice these new concepts and skills and help your classmates and peers practice them as well. If you want to learn to play the piano, you might imagine playing with gusto, but you know it will take practice to do that. If you want to learn to play tennis, you can imagine hitting a cross-court backhand, but you know you have to hit many of them to perfect that stroke. Likewise, if you imagine a group coming to agreement after much conflict and going forward with shared vision and a sense of respectful community, then you have to learn a lot about yourself and practice the skills of listening and collaborating. You would not drop piano lessons when the first scale you learn gets boring or sell your tennis racket when you develop a sore muscle. Likewise, you do not give up on practicing leadership because you find it hard or challenging. Practicing together will help each person learn leadership.

If you are using this book, along with the *Facilitation and Activity Guide* and *The Student Workbook*, as a textbook for a class, you will find it is designed to help your class become a learning community. After an introduction to leadership, the book focuses on you. Learning activities are designed to help you reflect on yourself and show you how to listen to and learn from others. This will not always be easy or painless. Research shows that the frequency with which you talk with others about sociocultural issues like politics, religion, and complex issues outside of the classroom also enhances your leadership, since you are actively practicing listening, understanding others, and clarifying your own perspectives (Dugan & Komives, 2010). The classroom provides an opportunity to practice the difficult skills of building learning communities in which to experience collaborative leadership.

Many students tell us they dislike group projects, but unless you learn the skills required for working effectively with others and building common purpose with others, including handling frustration when things do not go well, you have not practiced collaborative leadership. Most great things were not accomplished by an individual acting alone. Even when one person is singled out for credit, there were usually many others who contributed or collaborated to make that accomplishment possible.

As you read and discuss this book, we encourage you to think about yourself. Do not distance yourself from the pages, but connect with the concepts and ask yourself: In what ways could this help me be more effective? Not everything will resonate with you all the time, but think about your life right now and the many roles and responsibilities you anticipate acquiring as you go forward. We invite you to deepen your leadership journey as you explore yourself in various contexts. Each step of the way will enhance your sense of self-awareness and help you realize that you are leading when you are actively working with others toward a shared purpose. You do make a difference.

We are still on our own leadership journey and know this is a lifelong activity. As we change and as times change, we will always need to be sensitive to the relational process of leadership. We hope you will enhance your own abilities to be effective in this leadership journey.

ACKNOWLEDGMENTS

Susan, Nance, and Tim acknowledge our co-authorship and, more important, our friendship that has endured and even transcended the writing processes in all three editions of *Exploring Leadership*. We began our journey as colleagues with ideas for a book scribbled on a notepad, and we landed as authors who discovered how to play to our unique strengths in making these three editions of our book possible. In applying the Relational Leadership Model in our work together, we used the components to guide us through the trials and tribulations of writing collaboratively. We are proud to have started this journey as colleagues and to have experienced our transformation as enduring friends. We treasure each other and we have learned from each other. We also learned from the many people who assisted us along the way.

During the first two editions of the book we have been gratified to see the growth in campus efforts on student leadership development and in the plethora of leadership education resources (Komives, 2011). We are proud to have contributed to the movement to challenge college students to take an active role in their communities.

We recognize the tremendous support we have received from others and feel truly blessed to have such an array of loving and giving families, friends, and colleagues. This edition stands on the shoulders of those who assisted in previous editions. For the first edition of *Exploring Leadership* we continue to offer special appreciation to Marcy Levy Shankman, Elizabeth McGovern, Mike Sarich, Reena Meltzer, Carrie Goldstein, Mary Campbell, and Alice Faron. The second edition was greatly

shaped by Julie Owen and other colleagues who worked with
the instructor manual, including Jennifer Armstrong, Kristan
Cilente Skendall, Krystal Clark, Keith Edwards, Jeff Grim, Paige
Haber-Curran, Anthony Kraft, Karol Martinez, Jim Neumeister,
Darren Pierre, Jessica Porras, Terry Zacker, and Seth Zolin. We
also thank Jen Edwards Serra and Paige Haber-Curran, both
Maryland master's students at the time. For this edition we are
again grateful to Julie Owen, who is an exceptionally informed
critic and wise leadership visionary. Special thanks to talented
leadership educators Wendy Wagner and Daniel Ostick, who
assembled a marvelous team to develop our student workbook
and a fine instructor and activities manual. Appreciation to
Craig Slack and Josh Hiscock, whose guidance of the National
Clearinghouse for Leadership Programs continued to promote
the Relational Leadership Model and nurture a new generation
of leadership educators. We are all grateful to Denny Roberts,
whose contributions to student leadership development are
legendary and has most recently helped all leadership educators
explore global dimensions of learning leadership.

Susan: I offer special thanks to my husband, Ralph, for his
unfailing support and phenomenal Macintosh graphics skills.
I am particularly grateful to my two University of Maryland
leadership teams: leadership identity research team (Julie Owen,
Susan Longerbeam, Felicia Mainella, and Laura Osteen—then
Maryland doctoral students), for our amazing leadership identity
development project (LID); and co-researcher, John Dugan, and
the Multi-Institutional Study of Leadership team (MSL), whose
research guides the principles and emphases in this edition.

Nance: I am grateful to family members and mentors who
taught me about leadership through their example, especially my

late Aunt Dee, who *has* the most profound influence on my life. And thanks to the late Don Clifton for his scholarly contributions on understanding and practicing leadership using talents and strengths. I am indebted to the late Don and Nancy de Laski, who inspired me to continue on a path for greater meaning and purpose in life through their own examples and through their generosity. It was through their gifts that the Center for Consciousness and Transformation (CCT) was founded in New Century College, providing opportunities for students and others to learn about and embody many of the principles, practices, and concepts found in *Exploring Leadership*. I would like to acknowledge an early career mentor, Joel Rudy, who encouraged me to pursue a scholarly path in leadership, and one of my current mentors, Jack Censer at George Mason University, who provided me with recent numerous opportunities to expand my work and reach in leadership. Special appreciation goes to New Century College faculty and staff at George Mason University for their encouragement of my involvement in this book-writing venture and to the CCT faculty and staff for their inspiration, passion, and dedication to the mission. A special thank you to Martha Souder for assisting the authors in the important behind-the-scenes tasks that were critical to completing our manuscript. A heartfelt thank you goes out to my many undergraduate and graduate students for influencing my philosophy of leadership. I recognize a constant thought partner and sister of choice in Karen Silien, who was my inspiration in all editions of our book and who provided inspiration and guidance since cofounding the National Leadership Symposium with me in 1989 and through years of best friendship. And finally, deep-felt gratitude and love to my partner Pam Patterson for her unyielding encouragement, collaborations, wisdom, and love that provided anchoring and centering throughout the writing process and beyond.

Tim: I thank my father, Jim, and brother, Tom, for their ongoing support, while remembering my late mother, Irene. I especially thank Curt Kochner for sharing ideas, laughter, and experiences over many years in the last, best place—notably the memorable trek along the Beaten Path Trail; and longtime friend and college roommate Rick Howser for all the great times at Wrigley and in Chicago. Thanks to all those who helped shape my ideas about leadership over the years—especially Kathy Allen, Gary Althen, Steve Axley, George Bettas, Laura Blake-Jones, Pam Boersig, Bruce Clemetsen, John Duncan, Pat Enos, Chris Esparza, Tina Gutierez-Schmich, Will Keim, Barbara Maxwell, Laurie Jones-Neighbors, Richard Preuhs, Denny Roberts, Larry Roper, Karen Roth, Dave Strang, and Mia Tuan. I want to thank all of my Oregon friends and colleagues in CoDaC and the Holden Center for their ongoing collegiality and support and my friends, on Facebook and otherwise, who have encouraged my photography of migratory waterfowl. Your kind words have kept me going.

We are all grateful to Jossey-Bass's student leadership team, particularly our editor, Erin Null, and team leader, Paul Foster, whose support of student leadership has led to major contributions since the last edition. Their vision to move into more books, workbooks, assessments for students. and online seminars for leadership educators supports this work. Special appreciation to our editorial team for their work on establishing the Gallup partnership on the Clifton StrengthsQuest.

THE AUTHORS

Susan R. Komives is professor emerita and former director of the student affairs graduate program at the University of Maryland, College Park. She is former president of the Council for the Advancement of Standards in Higher Education (CAS) as well as the American College Personnel Association (ACPA); and former vice president for student development at Stephens College and the University of Tampa. She is author or coauthor of 11 books or monographs and over 50 articles or book chapters, and she has delivered more than 400 keynote speeches. She was cofounder and publications editor of the National Clearinghouse for Leadership Programs, a senior scholar with the James MacGregor Burns Academy of Leadership, and a member of the Board of Directors of the International Leadership Association. She was a member of the ensemble that developed The Social Change Model of Leadership Development and was principal investigator (PI) of a team whose research resulted in a grounded theory of Leadership Identity Development. She is co-PI of the Multi-Institutional Study of Leadership. She is the 2011 recipient of the University of Maryland Board of Regent's Award for Faculty Teaching and the National Association of Student Personnel Administrators (NASPA) Shaffer Award for Academic Excellence as a graduate faculty member. A 2006 recipient of both the ACPA and NASPA outstanding research and scholarship awards, she is the 2012 recipient of the ACPA Life Time Achievement Award. Komives received her bachelor of science degree (1968) in mathematics and chemistry from Florida State University, as well as her master of science degree

(1969) in higher education administration. Her doctorate in educational administration and supervision (1973) is from the University of Tennessee.

Nance Lucas is the associate dean and associate professor of New Century College at George Mason University and executive director of the Center for Consciousness & Transformation. Her teaching and scholarship interests focus on positive psychology and leadership, well-being, ethics, and character development. She is coauthor of *Exploring Leadership: For College Students Who Want To Make A Difference* (1st and 2nd editions) and contributing author of *Leadership Reconsidered* and *The Social Change Model of Leadership Development* and past coeditor of the *Journal of Leadership and Organizational Studies* for special issues and a member of the journal's editorial board. Nance served as the creator and convener of the 1997 Global Leadership Week Program (a worldwide leadership program initiative spanning five continents), cofounder of the National Leadership Symposium, cofounder of the National Clearinghouse for Leadership Programs, and a past chair of the National InterAssociation Leadership Project. She served on the W. K. Kellogg Foundation Leadership Studies Project Ethics Focus Group, W. K. Kellogg Foundation College Age Youth Leadership Program Review Team, and the Kellogg Forum on Higher Education National Dialogue Series Planning Team. At George Mason University, she is the cofounder of the Mason Institute for Leadership Excellence, the Leadership Legacy Program, and MasonLeads. Dr. Lucas is an affiliate faculty member with The Gallup Organization and the Higher Education Program at George Mason University. Prior to her appointment at Mason, Nance had previous appointments at the University of Maryland and

Ohio University. She received a Ph.D. in higher education with a concentration in leadership studies and ethics at the University of Maryland, College Park. Her master's degree in college student personnel and bachelor of arts degree in industrial and organizational psychology are from the Pennsylvania State University.

Timothy R. McMahon is a curriculum transformation specialist in the Center on Diversity and Community and a director of special projects at the Holden Center, both at the University of Oregon. Prior to that he served as a faculty consultant in the Teaching Effectiveness Program at Oregon. He also co-teaches graduate courses in the College of Education at Oregon State University. Prior to coming to Oregon he worked at Western Illinois University as a faculty member in the Department of Counselor Education and College Student Personnel. Tim also has professional experience in student affairs at Western Illinois University, the University of Iowa, Washington State University, Lakeland College, and the University of Wisconsin-River Falls. He has made numerous national presentations on topics related to leadership education and has also taught undergraduate leadership and diversity courses. He is co-author of *Exploring Leadership: For College Students Who Want To Make A Difference* (1st and 2nd editions). Tim's current professional interests include leadership, chaos and systems theory, diversity, and issues related to teaching and learning. McMahon received a bachelor of science degree (1973) in astronomy and a master of education degree (1975) in higher education administration from the University of Illinois. He received his doctorate (1992) in college student services administration from Oregon State University.

Exploring
Leadership

˅

PART I

Leadership for a Changing World

More than ever, today's times demand that diverse people work flexibly and respectfully together. The chapters in this section establish a foundation for understanding how leadership has been perceived over time and how today's rapidly changing, networked world calls for new approaches to leadership. This section ends with exploration of a model of relational leadership and its elements of being purposeful, inclusive, ethical, and empowering. These four elements are embedded within an overall process orientation, which is the fifth component of the Relational Leadership Model.

The leadership process is not about things—it is about people. As you read this section, challenge yourself to think how it relates to you and to those you have worked with in groups or communities. Identify the strengths you bring to engage in this approach and try to see what new awareness or skill you might need to be more effective in working with others.

The writings of the Chinese philosopher Lao Tzu are wise guides to understanding yourself and others. In the book *Tao of Leadership*, Heider (1985) adapts Lao Tzu's proverbs. Lao Tzu advises us:

> The superficial leader cannot see how things happen, even though the evidence is everywhere. This leader is swept up by drama, sensation, and excitement. All this confusion is blinding. But the leader who returns again and again to awareness-of-process has a deep sense of how things happen. (p. 69)

The model presented in this section promotes a relational process to leadership.

Chapter 1

An Introduction to Leadership

You will most likely find yourself—your interests and your attitudes—reflected on every page of this book, incorporating such characteristics as your age, gender, race, ethnicity, sexual orientation, generational status, social class, ability, or academic major. You can find ideas that apply to your interests whether you are majoring in engineering or English or are planning a career in journalism, agriculture, education, engineering, or law. Any number of other majors pertain to leadership as well.

Your habits are also reflected here. You might like details or you might only focus on the big picture. You might think best by speaking aloud or by turning thoughts over in your head before saying anything. However you work and think best, your perspective is distinctly yours and is represented in these pages.

Your unique experiences have shaped your view of yourself as a leader or member of a group. Think of the various leadership roles you have held or observed. Think about the various

ways you have led formally, led informally, or been an active
participant in various groups. Think about the leadership
exhibited by the people you have admired or abhorred in the
national or international news, in your home community,
on campus, at work, or in the career field you are choosing.
Think ahead to the places and relationships in which you
could become more active—your classes, class projects, student
employment position, residence hall, honor societies, student
government, fraternity or sorority, athletic teams, alternative
spring break program, study abroad experience, internship site,
PTA meetings, your family, friendship groups, your off-campus
work, community service settings, your church or temple—the
possibilities are endless.

You draw on your personal characteristics, experiences,
and the settings in which you might be involved for different
leadership purposes. Some readers may want to further personal
development; others may want to enhance a career skill, still
others to accomplish social change. Whatever your purpose, your
journey through the leadership process will make a difference in
all aspects of your life.

> Book Overview

As noted in the Preface, *Exploring Leadership* introduces you to
the concepts of leader, follower, and leadership by embracing the
philosophy that when engaging others in accomplishing change,
everyone can be a leader. In Part One we describe the social construction of leadership over time and present a relational leadership model suitable for contemporary groups. Since the model

is based in relationships, in Part Two we explore understanding yourself and others and the critical importance of ethical practices in your engagement with others. Appreciating and applying your strengths and those of others is the basis of those chapters. In Part Three we examine the team, group, and organizational contexts in which leadership is exhibited, using the perspective of those groups being viewed as communities. Part Four examines how leadership is critical to change and the importance of all involved thriving together as they engage each other in healthy, relational approaches.

> Chapter Overview

In this chapter, we introduce key concepts and models that will be developed throughout the book, and we provide an overview of what we mean by leader, follower, and leadership. We show that new views on leadership are needed—views that call for ethical collaborations—and we describe ways to understand these new views. We assert our belief that leadership develops best when organizations and the individuals in them are open to learning together.

> Foundational Principles

We encourage you to critique and analyze the perspectives and frames we present in this book. You will probably agree and connect with some ideas and disagree with others. But try to figure out why you agree or disagree. Go back and read the Preface if you did not already, to more fully understand the approach this book explores. Exercising critical thinking is a key to furthering your understanding about leadership. We encourage you to learn about leadership from different perspectives. To do that, you will need to identify the principles that are important to you and relate those beliefs to these perspectives. Also acknowledge those concepts and ideas that you disagree with and why. The foundational principles in this book are as follows:

1. *Leadership is a concern of all of us.* As individuals and groups, we have a responsibility to contribute effectively as members of organizations, local communities, nations, and in the world community. Members of communities (work, learning, living, and ideological communities) are citizens of those various groups and have a responsibility to develop shared leadership and participatory governance.

2. *Leadership is viewed and valued differently by various disciplines and cultures*; it is the critical question in each field. There are profound issues that need leadership in every field of study and every career. A multidisciplinary approach to leadership develops a shared understanding of differences and commonalities in leadership principles and practices across professions and cultures.

3. *Conventional views of leadership have changed.* Leadership is not static; it must be practiced flexibly. The rapid pace of change leads people to continually seek new ways of relating to shared problems.

4. *Leadership can be exhibited in many ways.* These ways of leading can be analyzed and adapted to varying situations. Different settings might call for different types of leadership.

Pluralistic, empowering leadership values the inclusion of diverse people and diverse ideas, working toward common purposes.

5. *Leadership qualities and skills can be learned and developed.* Today's leaders are made, not born. Leadership effectiveness begins with self-awareness and self-understanding and grows to understanding of others. Identifying your core values and strengths and maximizing those in your leadership are key components in your leadership development.

6. *Leadership committed to ethical action is needed to encourage change and social responsibility.* Leadership happens through relationships among people engaged in change. As a relational process, leadership requires the highest possible standards of credibility, authenticity, integrity, and ethical conduct. Ethical leaders model positive behaviors that influence the actions of others.

Leadership development is greatly enhanced when you understand how important relationships are in leadership; that is, when you see the basic relational foundation of the leadership process. Three basic principles are involved:

- *Knowing.* You must know—yourself, how change occurs, and how and why others may view things differently than you do.
- *Being.* You must be—ethical, principled, authentic, open, caring, and inclusive.
- *Doing.* You must act—in socially responsible ways, consistently and congruently, as a participant in a community, and on your commitments and passions.

It is unrealistic to think that certain traditional leadership behaviors are required if you are to be an effective leader or

collaborator in this time of rapid change. Leadership cannot
be reduced to a number of easy steps. It is realistic, however,
to develop a way of thinking—a personal philosophy of
leadership—and identify core values that can help you work
with others toward change. In today's complex times, we need a
set of principles to guide our actions.

> Rapidly Changing Times

At the current speed of change and with the complexity of
today's problems, we can easily feel overwhelmed; we gasp for air
as we navigate our fast-paced days with our many responsibilities.
Your clock radio may awaken you to the news of protestors at
US embassies somewhere in the world and the latest horrific
crimes in your community. Your new system upgrade on your
computer will not support some of your favorite programs. You
go to class to learn something you hope you can apply to real
life, but you find the material irrelevant. Just as you settle in
to write a paper for class, one of your children falls and breaks
her leg, changing your plans for days to come. You get to your
job in the student activities office and find that the work you
left unfinished yesterday is needed in fifteen minutes, instead of
in two days as you had thought. You are troubled that student
hazing, cheating, date rape, incivility, and other problems exist
on campus. And the problems continue.

We no longer have simple problems with right and wrong
answers but are increasingly faced with complex dilemmas and
paradoxes. For example, we may want to be civil yet affirm freedom of speech, or we may want to find community and common
purpose but also value individuality and individual differences.

Developing a personal approach to leadership that joins one person with others in an effort to accomplish a shared goal is difficult. It requires being intentional and thoughtful. A critical process to leading in rapidly changing, complex times is examining our own assumptions and realizing that others might see things differently. Gaining new insight means learning to identify and understand paradigms.

> Understanding Paradigms

In every aspect of our lives, change is more rapid, confusing, and unpredictable than ever before. Daily newspapers bring awareness of complex local issues, and the nightly news flashes images of conflict at home and abroad. The conventional ways of thinking about and organizing our shared experiences do not seem helpful anymore. Instead of individual determinism, competition, and predictable structures, we seem to need quickly responding, nimble systems; collaboration; and a new awareness of shared values that honor our diversity.

These different perspectives might be called different worldviews, frames, or paradigms. Paradigms are patterns and ways of looking at things in order to make sense of them. Some paradigms are clear and help us function well. For example, you have fairly clear paradigms about playing baseball, going to class the first day, going to the airport, or attending the first meeting of an organization you wish to join. Consider going to that first class. You may sit in a preferred spot, expect to greet the person sitting beside you, get a syllabus, learn what text to buy, and perhaps even get out a bit early. That paradigm might be shattered if you arrived to find no chairs, or a professor who said, "I have not yet organized this class. What do you want to learn?" It is hard then to figure out what will happen; the rules no longer work; your established paradigms do not help fill in the gaps. Indeed, you might judge this class to be more exciting or more terrifying because it is unpredictable.

Some paradigms change suddenly, but we can adjust to the new paradigm. Following the World Trade Center bombings in 2001, airport security became more complex. You now have to remove your shoes, jacket, jewelry, and place your computer on the conveyer to be screened.

There are widely divergent paradigms for what it means to be a good leader. For some, a good-leader paradigm signals a verbal, self-confident person clearly in charge and directing followers with confidence. Some would see a good leader as someone who delegates and involves others in the group's decisions and actions. Still others think beyond "good leader" to consider "good leadership." Some imagine a good leadership paradigm as a group of colleagues sharing in leadership, with each contributing to the group outcome and no one dominating others. Deliberately thinking about leadership paradigms may help identify what was previously unclear or even unseen and what now might be very obvious.

As times change, standard approaches to a topic may no longer be effective. An awareness of needing new ways to approach problems may signal a paradigm shift. There was a time in our country's history when the predominant paradigm held that women were not capable of understanding issues sufficiently to vote; at other times, the prevailing paradigm has held that education should be a privilege of only the elite, or that corporations could do anything to enhance their profits, or that smokers could light up anywhere they pleased. A paradigm shift means a shift in the previously held patterns or views. Instead of rushing home to see your favorite 10 p.m. show on television, you know you can grab it off of Netflix or Hulu or record it yourself or watch it "On Demand" when you choose to do so. When your grandfather says, "We had no TV when I was a boy, and all our social life revolved around the church," he is observing a paradigm shift in how we spend leisure time, brought on by technology and transportation.

There have been numerous shifts in how people acquire information over time. Think of the changes from early, sagelike scholars imparting wisdom to small groups of students sitting at their feet to the volume-filled libraries we could borrow from to the electronic retrieval systems that allow us to acquire information on the Web. Instead of going to the library to borrow a book, we now download articles from a website. How reasonable is it in these changing times to use an old paradigm of measuring the quality of universities by the number of volumes in their libraries when any student can access thousands of volumes through interlibrary loan, buy the e-book in seconds, or enroll in an online class and not have to be present physically in a classroom?

A paradigm shift, however, does not necessarily mean completely abandoning one view for another. The new paradigm or view often emerges "alongside the old. It is appearing inside and around the old paradigm ... building on it, amplifying it and extending it ... not replacing it" (Nicoll, 1984, p. 5). We encourage you to examine the conventional authority paradigm of command and control as a method of leadership and seek to identify other paradigms that may be emerging, through your own experiences as well as from reading this book. Hierarchical structures, like bureaucracies, will continue to exist and, when done well, identify a division of tasks and labor that helps an organization meet its goals. The method of relating within those structures, however, may change to be more relational and crossfunctional. The "what" may be the same, but the "how" is shifting.

If old patterns or paradigms no longer work well, those who see things differently and hold new paradigms begin to employ new approaches, and paradigm shifts emerge. We are fully engaged now in the current paradigm that values collaborative processes among authentic people in organizations. Yes, there are bad or toxic leaders in some groups (Erickson, Shaw, & Agabe, 2007; Kellerman, 2004; Lipman-Blumen, 2005), but group expectations have largely shifted to expect ethical processes among people of integrity.

> Examining the Paradigms

Leadership has long been presented as an elusive, complex phenomenon. Thousands of books and articles have been written about leaders and leadership, seeking to identify traits, characteristics, situations, and behaviors that signal leadership effectiveness. A simple Google search of the word "leadership" identifies more than 515,000,000 sources. We present an overview of several significant leadership approaches in the next chapter so you can see how these paradigms have emerged and how leadership has been socially constructed over time. This impressive number of publications provides some insight, but leadership is perhaps best described as using your personal philosophy of how to work effectively with others toward meaningful change.

Research in leadership studies is largely centered on the individual leader rather than the process of leadership. Most approaches examine what a leader does with followers to accomplish some purpose. Only recently has the literature focused extensively on followers or group members themselves. The conventional way of looking at people in groups (whether work groups or friendship groups) is first to identify a leader (or leaders) and then describe their followers. However, "understanding the relational nature of leadership and followership opens up richer forms of involvement and rewards in groups, organizations, and society at large" (Hollander, 1993, p. 43).

Prior to the 1990s, most leadership literature focused on how managers function in organizational settings and assumes that the manager is also a leader. Therefore, much attention has been focused on the leader's behaviors to get followers to do what the leader wants. This kind of leader usually holds a positional role like chairperson, president, or supervisor. This emphasis on positional leaders frequently promotes a passive approach to followers, often ignoring the role or effect followers have in the organization, including the way followers affect the positional leader. This approach clearly does not adequately describe the leadership relationship among people in groups or teams. Concepts of transforming leadership value how these followers could become leaders themselves (Burns, 1978), how these followers begin to identify as leadership themselves, and how the process of leadership works among these people.

We must reconstruct our view of leadership to see that "leadership is not something a leader possesses so much as a process involving followership" (Hollander, 1993, p. 29). Further, followership is really leadership in action among people in the group. In this book, *we view leadership as a relational and ethical process of people together attempting to accomplish positive change.*

STUDENT ESSAY

Before my time at DePaul, I thought that in order to be a leader, you had to be loud, aggressive, demanding, and have a winner-take-all kind of attitude. While I did see myself as competitive and very driven, I did not have the qualities of someone that one would expect to see as a captain of a sports team or leading student government. Because of this distinction I had made years before, I had always seen myself as a follower rather than a leader.

Holding an executive position in a student organization has helped me re-evaluate my definition of leadership. Being able to lead does not mean being loud. It means having the ability to communicate, understand, and create bonds. My position at Globe Med DePaul required me to facilitate discussions about ourselves, our communities, and the world we live in. It meant I had to get people to sit down, talk, share, and be respectful. It meant creating dialogue and an atmosphere that people would want to contribute to.

These experiences made me realize that leadership is not just about *leading*. It's about respecting, understanding, creating, and compromising. Anyone can be a leader in their own right as long as they play to their own strengths. I have found my place as a leader on my campus. I can only hope others use their own college experience to do the same.

Samantha Grund-Wickramasekera is a junior and political science major at DePaul University. She is an Albert G. Schmitt scholar, an executive member of her Globe Med chapter, and plays on the women's club soccer team.

Some leadership approaches, such as participative leader-ship, acknowledge that followers must be meaningfully involved in everything from setting goals to decision making. Followers must be active participants. Often, these approaches do not go far enough to genuinely engage followers while sharing power with them. This difference signals a paradigm shift from control-ling follower behavior to empowering followers to be central to an organization's outcomes. Indeed, followers quickly see through and reject those leaders who ask for advice and input but rarely change their opinions. Followers usually embrace positional lead-ers who introduce issues to the group for discussion and decision. And followers are usually willing to self-manage a leadership pro-cess where decision making is vested in the group or team.

> The Search for a New Conceptualization of Followers

Since childhood, we have heard the lesson "Follow the leader." You may have been a lunch line leader or a bus patrol in elementary school. We have been taught that someone is in charge, so we let that person take the lead and we follow. The predominant paradigm is that if we are the leader, we expect others to cooperate and follow our lead. The leadership literature includes a range of perspectives on followers, largely based on the role of the leader. On one extreme, if the leader is viewed as hierarchically apart from the group, then followers matter less and are expected to be more compliant with the leader's views. On the other extreme, when the leader is embedded in the group, it is a shared leadership process and followers are perceived as colleagues. In this example, leadership is an *outcome* of people working together on a common agenda or change initiative.

Followership

Most organizations are hierarchies designed with manager or leader roles and follower or staff roles. In work settings these followers are sometimes referred to as subordinates. To honor and recognize the important role of the follower, the term *followership* started being used in conjunction with the term *leadership* (Kelley, 1988, 1992). Followership skills are those skills and processes practiced by members of groups. However, not all followers are alike. One taxonomy, presented in Figure 1.1, presents approaches to being a follower by considering both the individuals' commitment to performing in the group and their interest in group relationships. Imagine Maria, who is passive and unengaged in her group. She will do what is asked of her but is a passive participant; she is a subordinate. James does not

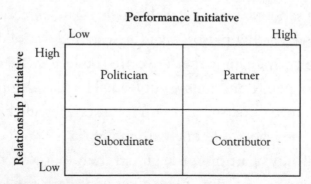

Figure 1.1   Follower Types
Source: Adapted from Porter, Rosenbach, & Pittman (2005), p. 149. Used with permission.

engage much with other members of the group, but he is diligent about getting his tasks done and meeting his obligations; he is a contributor. Tonya uses her interpersonal skills and really knows how to network with others, but she does not always get her work done or show commitment to the group's task; she is a politician. Carl both embraces the task and wants to do good work, as well as join others in a successful team effort; he is a partner.

USAF Lieutenant Colonels Sharon Latour and Vicki Rast (2004) summarize their review of followership research and define effective followers as "individuals with high organizational commitment who are able to function well in a change-oriented team environment. Additionally, they are independent, critical thinkers with highly developed integrity and competency" (p. 6). They posit that dynamic followership is a prerequisite for effective leadership. (Chaleff, 1995; Riggio, Chaleff, & Lipman-Blumen, 2008) went a step further and encouraged followers to be courageous. Followers have special responsibilities to speak truth to leaders and to take risks when the leadership practices being used are not effective for the organization. The child abuse scandal of 2011 at Pennsylvania State University has many lessons for leadership and, for one, illustrated how important people in all levels of the organization were to bring needed information to those in control. For another, the case shows how hard it can be to speak truth to power. We explore this situation further in Chapter Six.

Just as there are skills or capacities to develop in leadership, many assert there are skills and capacities to develop to be an effective follower. Clearly there is a reciprocal relationship between the leader and the follower. Some authors advise followers how to be effective with their positional leaders. Lussier and Achua (2004) suggest that as a follower you should

- Offer support to the leader
- Take initiative
- Play counseling and coaching roles to the leader, when appropriate
- Raise issues and/or concerns when necessary
- Seek and encourage honest feedback from the leader
- Clarify your role and expectations
- Show appreciation
- Keep the leader informed
- Resist inappropriate influence of the leader (p. 237)

Latour and Rast (2004) promote several categories of important follower competencies (see Table 1.1). These authors clarify that followership skills help develop leadership skills and are essential perspectives for teamwork.

Because most of the followership models are presented in the context of a hierarchical authority figure interacting in some way to influence followers, these models may not transfer well to nonhierarchical groups or community contexts in which public leadership seeks to address shared issues (Luke, 1998). Nonhierarchical groups are groups that function as colleagues such a project groups, often without a designated leader, using processes of shared authority and power. Using public leadership as the context, Luke (1998) illustrates how the leader-follower dynamic differs in the public sector:

> In an interconnected world, this model is simply inaccurate. One individual may be the leader who galvanizes and stimulates initial

Table 1.1 **Follower Competencies**

Competency	Description
Displays loyalty	Shows deep commitment to the organization, adheres to the boss's vision and priorities, disagrees agreeably, aligns personal and organizational goals
Functions well in change-oriented environments	Serves as a change agent, demonstrates agility, moves fluidly between leading and following
Functions well on teams	Collaborates, shares credit, acts responsibly toward others
Thinks independently and critically	Dissents courageously, takes the initiative, practices self-management
Considers integrity of paramount importance	Remains trustworthy, tells the truth, maintains the highest performance standards, admits mistakes

Source: Latour & Rast (2004), p. 111. Used with permission.

action. Then other leaders and autonomous stakeholders will refine the initial burst of vision, agree on directions for action, and pursue specific initiatives aimed at solving the program. Public leadership does not engage followers; rather, it involves collaborations, audiences, and other self-organizing groups ... effective leaders are forced to become "leader-followers" simultaneously. Public leadership shifts, changes, and is shared at different times by different people in different organizations. (pp. 32–33)

We need to reconceptualize how we view followers and the nature of relationships in groups. It seems woefully inadequate to call group members by the term *followers*, implying they are following someone or something, unable to think for themselves, or remaining indifferent to the group's goals, when actually they are creating and shaping the context themselves.

What New Term for Followers?

Leadership scholars have been searching for a new term to more adequately describe followers for many years. Followers have been called members, employees, associates, or subordinates. Addressing this topic in the early years of relational leadership, Kouzes and Posner (1993) suggest calling them the *constituents*. "A constituent is someone who has an active part in the process of running an organization and who authorizes another to act on his or her behalf. A constituent confers authority on the leader, not the other way around" (p. xix). Although the concept is usually found in describing how constituents from their voting districts authorize political leaders, it is useful in other situations as well.

Imagine the senior class council discussing changes the provost's office is planning in the commencement ceremony; the president of the senior class is likely to be empowered by her constituents and expected to carry the wishes of the council to the provost for consideration. She would be speaking on behalf of others, not just carrying a personal opinion forward.

Crum (1987) likes the term *co-creator*, elevating the empowered, collaborative, transformational role of group members. "When we choose co-creation, we end separation, the root cause of conflict ... They know through responsible participation that they can empower each other and ultimately their institutions and society, thereby creating a life that is meaningful and satisfying for everyone" (p. 175). Positional leaders who see group members as co-creators will take important decisions to the group and ask, "What do we want to do about this?"

Rost (1991) believes that the traditional meaning of the word *follower* is too embedded in all of our minds to adequately shift to a new meaning. He implores us to see that we have moved from an industrial worldview to a postindustrial era. In the industrial view, people in the organization are merely resources—like steel or other raw materials—whereas in the postindustrial view, people are essential because they bring information and wisdom and the capacity to adapt. Rost now encourages use of the term *collaborator* for the role of people in this new way of working together. He clarifies, "I now use the word followers when I write about leadership in the industrial paradigm. I use the word collaborators when I write about leadership in the postindustrial paradigm ... no amount of reconstruction is going to salvage the word [follower]" (Rost, 1993, p. 109).

In this book, we use the term *participant* to refer to people involved in groups in this new paradigm. Participants are involved in the leadership process, actively sharing leadership with other group members, including with the titled leader. Participants include the informal or formal positional leader in a group, as well as all active group members who seek to be involved in group change. Participants are active, engaged, and intentional.

> A Word About Leaders

The word *leader* is used in this book in two primary ways. One use of the term refers to a person in a leadership position who has been elected, selected, or hired to assume responsibility for a group working toward change; this leader has defined responsibilities for decision making and action. Such a positional leader usually has a title of some kind, such as supervisor, general, team captain, chairperson, or vice president. Clearly, being in such a position does not mean that the person knows how to lead, is a good leader, or is looked to as a leader by others. We all have known committee chairs, supervisors, or organization officers who did not seem to know what they were doing, let alone know how to lead anyone or anything toward change. When we use *leader* to mean a positional leader, we will say so.

The other meaning of leader—and the one that we generally use—is entirely different. It refers to any person who actively engages with others to accomplish change. Whether as the positional leader or participant-collaborator-group member, a person can be a leader by taking initiative and making a difference in moving the group forward toward positive change. This philosophy shifts your paradigm from seeing the concept of leader as only the person in charge to all those who are actively engaged with each other to accomplish the group's purposes. You can be that kind of leader.

> Purposes of Leadership

Why leadership? What purpose does your leadership serve? Leadership should attempt to accomplish something or change something. Leadership is purposeful and intentional. On a more profound level, leadership should be practiced in such a way as to be socially responsible. This kind of social responsibility is involved in the outcomes or content of the group's purpose (that is, what the group wants to accomplish), as well as in the group's process (that is, how the group goes about their task).

We are concerned about leadership that advances the welfare and quality of life for all. The outcomes of this ethical leadership approach on a broad scale—on your campus or in your community—would contribute to the public good. On a small scale, like in a club, this leadership would seek to incorporate the common good. The concept of common good does not mean the majority view, but it does mean shared purposes and common vision. This commitment to the public good or common good is a valuing of the role of social responsibility.

Social responsibility is a personal commitment to the well-being of people, our shared world, and the public good. It is "a way of being in the world that is deeply connected to others and the environment" (Berman & La Farge, 1993, p. 7). Being socially responsible also means you are willing to confront unfair and unjust treatment of others wherever it may appear—in classes, at work, or in your organizations. It means functioning within your organizations in ways that value relationships and acting ethically with honor and integrity toward your responsibilities and each other.

> Socially responsible leadership means operating with an awareness of the ways in which the group's decisions and actions affect others. Socially responsible leaders are concerned about the well-being of group members and about the impact of the group's decisions on the community. (Wagner, 2009, p. 33)

To illustrate,

> A socially responsible outdoor adventure club will always make sure it leaves campsites as clean as it found them. A sorority would make sure that its traditions and ways of socializing are welcoming to students from a diversity of social classes, ethnicities, and religious backgrounds. A socially responsible approach to leadership will

influence the group's purposes, decision making, and how members work together. (Wagner, 2009, p. 33)

Somehow, too many people have developed into observers instead of activists in their daily lives. They act as if they are spectators instead of citizens and active participants. Instead of complaining or doing nothing, we need to become engaged in the processes of improving our shared experience, whether at work, in clubs, in class, on a residence hall floor, on an intramural team, or in any of our other communities. Civic engagement is a heightened sense of responsibility for all those communities.

Civic Engagement and Civic Responsibility

Civic engagement is not as narrow as what ninth graders learn about in government class. Civic responsibility is the sense of personal responsibility individuals should feel to uphold their obligations as part of any community. Certainly, civic responsibility may mean voting in campus, local, state, or national elections. Yet civic responsibility means far more. It means noticing that key campus parking lot lights are broken and stopping by an office to report them instead of merely thinking, "I sure hope someone doesn't get assaulted in the dark." Civic engagement means attending your academic department's brown-bag lunch seminar to support your friends who planned the event and to be part of this learning community. Civic responsibility means saying, "If I am a member of this community, I have a responsibility to work with others to keep it functioning and make it better."

Making a Difference

In the 1990s, over 75% of 18 to 22-year-old students said they could name people they admired—people who made a difference (Levine, 1993). These admired people were local heroes: parents, the neighbor who started a local recycling movement, a minister, or the people who drove hundreds of miles to stuff sandbags to reinforce the levees in the Midwest floods or to rebuild houses after a hurricane on the Gulf coast. These were not major world leaders or rich corporate executives. These real heroes were average people who, together with others, made a difference in their communities, sometimes overcoming seemingly insurmountable odds to do so. The nightly CBS news began identifying a weekly hero—average Americans who made extraordinary contributions. On May 29, 1995, the cover of *Newsweek* magazine featured two youths active in service to their neighborhood with the caption, "Everyday Heroes: Yes, You Can Make a Difference." The community service movement in the 1990s solidified the practice of people helping others in their local communities and shaped the millennial generation to be people who wanted to make a difference with their lives. A driving question at the turn of the century became how can people (and companies) do well and, concurrently, do good?

> Leadership Viewed from Different Frames

Leadership cannot be touched, smelled, or tasted, but it can be understood by how it is seen, heard, thought, and felt. Leadership is, therefore, a socially constructed phenomenon. To understand social construction, think of the fact of most people being one of two sexes—a woman or a man; however, the concepts of feminine or masculine are socially constructed and perpetuate roles and expectations that may constrain individuals. Many phenomena are given meaning by how they are constructed. Seeing, hearing, thinking, and feeling are all perceptual processes. People interpret their perceptions and draw meaning from them.

Many disciplines provide their own framework for viewing social constructions such as leadership. As we noted in the preface, leadership is explored in many academic majors—including anthropology, history, sociology, psychology, political science, education, and business—as well as through literature or the arts. Leadership comes in various forms and relates to different disciplines and majors in different ways. When we think of leadership, we often think of political science—the study of systems of governance at local, state, and national levels in countries around the world. But leadership is also evident in other fields of study.

Consider how leadership might be constructed in your major. What paradigm might professionals in your field assume as a shared view? What are the expectations of leaders? How do people relate in your discipline?

Anthropologists might study indigenous groups and try to discover how their leaders are selected and the qualities that the members of their culture believe are most important. Sociologists might study grassroots movements of people who embrace certain causes and how leadership develops in such groups. Psychologists might study the characteristics of leaders and followers and try to further the understanding of why they act in certain ways. Speech and speech communications majors often study how the messages leaders convey influence or inspire others to act. Organizational communicators are often concerned with how communication works in large, complex organizations and how various interpersonal communications can help or hinder such leadership processes. Education majors study leaders and leadership at all levels—from leadership in the classroom to being a district superintendent to running a college or university. Business majors study leadership in many different forms, including leading work teams, practicing entrepreneurship, and providing a vision for large businesses. Fine arts majors often learn the challenges of leadership experientially through being a first chair in an orchestra or directing a school play, and science majors experience leadership in research teams and various application projects. And the list goes on.

Each field of study may emphasize different elements of leadership, yet each field has an interest in how people can work more effectively together toward some outcome. "Leadership is like beauty: it's hard to define, but you know it when you see it" (Bennis, 1989, p. 1). Every academic major can benefit from a better understanding of the nature of leadership and every major has critical leadership issues for you to address in your career field. Think about your own major. How can knowing more about leadership make you more successful in your future career or other endeavors?

> Leadership Requires Openness to Learning

A story is told of philosopher-author Gertrude Stein lying on her deathbed. Her longtime partner, Alice B. Toklas, leaned over in despair at the impending passing of her companion and asked, "Gertrude, what is the answer?" Gertrude thoughtfully looked

up at Alice and replied, "What is the question?" Leaders and
participants ask questions, inviting others into the dialogue,
and are open to diverse ideas. The question mark becomes a tool
of leadership because participants need to ask questions, listen,
and learn. In his classic *Rules for Radicals*, Saul Alinsky (1989)
writes, "The question mark is an inverted plow, breaking up the
hard soil of old belief and preparing for the new growth" (p. 11).
Asking questions invites the group to examine its purpose and
practices instead of thoughtlessly continuing old practices.

> Conventional leaders, who may think they have all the answers and
> that their passive followers should merely obey, are the dinosaurs of
> rapidly changing times. These times call for leaders who know how to
> let go of the past in the face of uncertainty because they have done
> it before and have succeeded. It is a paradox. Effective leaders will
> be the ones whose experience has shown them that they cannot rely
> on their experience ... they will use the expertise they have gained
> through experience to tap the experience and creative energies of
> others. (Potter & Fiedler, 1993, p. 68)

Leadership today shows that there is great wisdom and
energy in the group. All members of the group have a great
deal to learn from each other. Certainly, learning occurs inside
the classroom, but it is very real in the world of experience.
Involvement on and off campus provides the laboratory for
enriching this learning.

Watkins and Marsick (1993) present a useful model that
applies to learning (see Figure 1.2). The model also applies to the
learning that occurs in teams and groups. This model presents

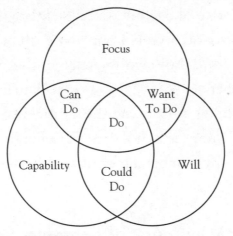

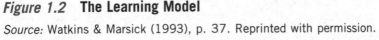

Figure 1.2 **The Learning Model**
Source: Watkins & Marsick (1993), p. 37. Reprinted with permission.

three components to learning: focus, or knowing about the learning opportunities; capability, including the resources and skills to learn; and will, or the motivation to engage in learning. You begin your exploration of yourself in the leadership equation when you examine your own goals, roles, and capabilities. Stop for a minute and think about something you are trying to accomplish. What is your focus? What do you need to accomplish this goal? What is your motivation or will to persist? On an even more complex level, we believe that the most effective organizations and communities are learning environments in which learning is ongoing, constant, pervasive, and valued.

Rapidly changing times and exploding information indicate we must all be lifelong learners. Over 20 years ago, scholar Peter Vaill (1991) commented that we must all be comfortable being beginners again all the time. "It is not an exaggeration to suggest that everyone's state of beginnerhood is only going to deepen and intensify so that ten years from now each of us will be even more profoundly and thoroughly settled in the state of being a perpetual beginner" (p. 81). This means admitting when we do not know something, yet having the confidence that together among a diverse group working together on a shared problem we can figure it out. Remember, all of us are smarter than one of us.

Personal Responsibility for Learning

The conventional view of leadership assumes that leaders do the planning and motivating and that they carry a major share of responsibility for accomplishing anything with their group. We do not believe this is true. All of us are responsible for ourselves and for helping others. The whole group of participants, including positional leaders, needs to make sure the environment is open to learning, making mistakes, and sharing knowledge. Any behaviors or circumstances that block learning in organizations are likely to block empowerment and inclusion as well.

Self-development, with the goal of students becoming more effective leaders and participants, is a primary goal of most colleges and universities. Leadership skills are life skills that can be applied to personal relationships as well as to work and organizational responsibilities. By redirecting your own life in the context of family, values, and dreams, you can become a productive colleague with others. As we said in the preface, we believe in this approach to leadership because all of us can learn about ourselves, about others, and about change. Through learning, we stay vital and renewed.

STUDENT ESSAY

As an early childhood education student, I discovered not only my passion for learning but also my interest in motivating others to become empowered leaders. These realizations encouraged me to become a Transition and Advising Program (TAP) Leader wherein I provided assistance to first generation students. Being the first in their immediate family to attend post-secondary education, the students shared the anxieties and frustrations brought about by college life. However, they also came in to our one-hour weekly sessions with the willingness to ask for help and the enthusiasm to grow as a student and an individual. My co-leader and I planned and implemented workshops based on their needs with topics such as presentation skills, handling group conflicts, stress management, and even ways to approach faculty members. It was remarkable to see how, throughout the course of the program, the students eventually realized their strengths and their potentials to be successful. In some occasions, they even helped their peers to have more confidence in their newfound abilities. Witnessing how their self-esteem strengthened, I understood the difference that I made as an effective leader. This further inspired me to lead, to empower, and to create brighter paths for my fellow students.

Issa Marie Mendoza is a graduate of Humber College Institute of Technology and Advanced Learning (Toronto) where she majored in early childhood education with honors. She served as a Transition and Advising Program leader, worked as a volunteer at the ECE Resource Centre, and actively participated in projects promoting children's welfare.

Experiential Learning

Understanding how you learn and develop leadership will be important to exploring yourself in the context of this book. David Kolb (1981; Kolb & Kolb, 2005) built on the work of such scholars as social psychologist Kurt Lewin and educator John Dewey to explore how learning occurs. Kolb suggests that we come to new information in one of two ways: by doing something (concrete experience) or by thinking about something (abstract conceptualization). We then process that information either by reflecting on the experience or the thought (reflective observation) or by applying that information (active experimentation). This process is best understood as a cycle. Figure 1.3 illustrates this process.

Much of how leadership is learned is in the real, concrete experiences of being in groups that are trying to accomplish something. Imagine you have just had an experience. To learn from that experience, you would want to reflect on it and make meaning from it. Why did that happen like it did, what does it mean? Next, you would form some hypotheses about it, and in thinking about it you would wonder if this is true for others—if it would work in other situations—and you would look for connections to other information you possess. Then you would want to apply this new theory or learning in a real situation. If I try this out will it work like I think it should? And

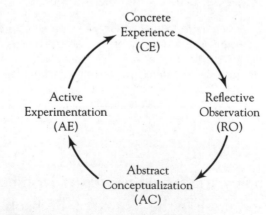

Figure 1.3 **Kolb's Experiential Learning Model**
Source: Adapted from Kolb (1981), p. 235. Used with permission.

the cycle continues. This may be best understood as "What?" "So What?" and "Now What?"

Kolb reminds us that what happens to us does not become experience without reflection. Without it, events are just things that happened. Many things happen from which we learn nothing because we do not reflect on those experiences to seek their deeper meaning.

> Relational Leadership

This book explores the evolution of leadership thinking and some of the many theories that help make meaning out of the varied and complex approaches to leadership. Yet studying leadership does not magically make you a better leader or participant. Studying leadership can expand your ability if you practice Kolb's cycle and try to apply what you have learned in your life and reflect on those applications.

As learners about leadership in the context of today's challenges and opportunities, we propose that you focus on core, basic principles of leadership that can guide your effectiveness. To reiterate: *we define leadership as a relational and ethical process of people together attempting to accomplish positive change.*

There is not one right way to lead. Leadership should not be studied as a recipe or a checklist. It is more important to develop a philosophy of leadership to guide your actions. This philosophy would value being ethical and inclusive. It would acknowledge the diverse talents of group members and trust the process to bring good thinking to the socially responsible changes group members agree they want to work toward.

Relationships are the key to leadership effectiveness. Because leadership is inherently relational, it is perhaps redundant to use the term *relational leadership*. There is, however, strength in the affirmation of repetition. Allen and Cherrey (2000), in their book *Systemic Leadership*, observed that "relationships are the connective tissue of organizations . . . , relationships built on integrity are the glue that holds organizations together" (p. 31). As leaders and participants in all our communities, we should be and expect others to be

- Purposeful
- Inclusive
- Empowering
- Ethical
- Process-oriented

How we relate and work together in all of our communities (families, classes, organizations, work sites, and neighborhoods) matters. You need to examine your role as a member of these communities, whether they are made up of five people in your family or fifty people on your residence hall floor.

> The Real World

Does this approach to leadership seem ideal and unrealistic or real and possible? Why don't we see these leadership practices widely embraced and used by all around us? This confusion between a preferred and an actual state is called cognitive dissonance (Festinger, 1962). When the president of your university speaks eloquently at the opening convocation about the campus being an ethical, learning environment open to change, yet your experience is that campus administrators resist trying anything new and even seem fearful of change, you likely feel dissonance. When the president of a student organization says, "We want to have all your feedback on this plan before we decide" and then proceeds to represent the plan so defensively that all comments are quickly silenced and you would not dare raise a question, there is dissonance.

Conversely, think of the times you have been treated with serious purpose, included, and aware that your contributions matter—perhaps in your study group, your favorite class, your office, or your committee planning a project such as a clothing drive for a homeless shelter. These are the places where you matter because you find congruence in the principles you value and in the values the group practices.

Even when things are not what they ought to be, each of us can practice a personal philosophy of being the kind of person, leader, or participant we value. This brings a sense of personal congruence and authenticity. Educators have been challenged to see that

> it is not nearly enough to teach students how the world is. We must also encourage them to think about how it ought to be. Without some hope for a better world, it is all too easy to think only of oneself and all too easy to leave the responsibilities of citizenship to others. (Harriger & Ford, 1989, p. 27)

Clearly, community is not someone else's responsibility. It is a commitment from each participant. Likewise, leadership is not someone else's responsibility. It is a shared responsibility among participants. In short, as a participant, leadership is your responsibility.

STUDENT ESSAY

My first lesson in leadership was on a softball field. I was a catcher, in position of authority and leadership. My job was to call the pitches and direct the plays on the field. Defensively, the team relied on me for my plan of action on each play. I was in charge of making orders without feedback. As a student, a professor at Florida Atlantic University immediately saw something in me that I thought I had lost since my days on the softball field. Professor Young saw leadership in me and opened a door for me to learn how to further develop as a student leader. The transition was difficult at first, I realized I couldn't bark orders like I did in softball; student leadership is about enabling others to act. I had to start delegating, I needed to educate, equip, and empower people. This was a huge turning point during my experience. I have since learned to stop thinking that my way is the only correct way and that our way is the right way. Since then I have been less stressed out about things, I have calmed down and learned to accept ideas.

Patricia A. Trueblood is a graduate of Florida Atlantic University where she majored in accounting and minored in business law. She was president of the Broward Accounting Students Association, Broward speaker pro-tempore, and active in the Davie Student Union Advisory Board.

> Chapter Summary

In this chapter, we have asked you to explore aspects of your unique characteristics and experiences that you bring to leadership. Rapidly changing, complex times indicate a need to work together in ways different from those promoted by conventional or industrial approaches to leadership. This chapter introduced the value that leadership must be for socially responsible purposes, and it presented an overview of leadership with an emphasis on followers as active participants in the leadership process. This relational approach to leadership is committed to positive change; it is inclusive, empowering, ethical, and process-oriented. Relational leadership is best practiced in learning organizations.

› About This Book

This book explores several critical themes in understanding relational leadership for complex times. Again, we refer you to the preface for more detail on how each chapter will evolve. There is also a student workbook you may find useful to guide you into meaningful experiences and further reflections on each concept. Being effective at relational leadership will be enhanced by engaging with the importance of these themes in the book:

- Understand yourself, others, and how you work together in communities
- Understand the importance of integrity, moral purpose, and positive change
- Understand how change occurs and why people resist or promote change
- Understand the importance of enhancing and applying individual and team strengths, developing greater levels of well-being for you and in others, and thriving together as individuals and organization.

> What's Next?

The next chapter presents an overview of how leadership has been understood over time. It discusses how the complexity of today's times demands a more relational way of solving shared problems.

> Chapter Activities

1. Which of the six foundational principles used to develop this book do you most closely agree with and why? Which is most difficult to endorse and why? Which is the most difficult to practice and why? Which is the easiest to practice and why?
2. Create words that could substitute for the term *follower* that would have an empowering connotation to others. How do you, or would you, react to being called a follower?
3. In response to the question "What is the purpose of leadership?" reflect and answer that question for yourself. What is your leadership purpose?
4. What community are you associated with or do you know about that is the most involving, ethical, empowering, and inclusive? How do people in this group empower others, make decisions, elicit feedback, and share power and authority? How does this community introduce and implement change?
5. How can knowing more about leadership make you more successful in your future career or other endeavors?
6. Using the Learning Model, stop for a minute and think about something you are trying to accomplish. What is your focus? How are you able to accomplish this goal? What is your motivation or will to persist?

7. What experiences have you had that you reflected on and from which you drew a leadership lesson? Using Kolb's model, describe that process.

ADDITIONAL READINGS

Lussier, R. N., & Achua, C. F. (2004). *Leadership: Theory, application, skill development* (2nd ed). Eagan, MN: Thomson-West.

Riggio, R. E., Chaleff, I., & Lipman-Blumen, J. (Eds.). (2008). *The art of followership: How great followers create great leaders and organizations.* San Francisco, CA: Jossey-Bass.

Chapter 2

The Changing Nature of Leadership

Leadership often is perceived as a prized, coveted phenomenon in our society. It is mentioned daily in newspapers, classrooms, student organization meetings, news broadcasts, and dinner conversations. Leaders who are revered by some people are admonished by others. To fully understand good leadership, it is equally important to understand bad leadership (Kellerman, 2004).

> Chapter Overview

In this chapter, we explore how the definitions and theories of leadership have changed over the years; we introduce some myths and truths about leadership, along with various metaphors of leadership. We also present some new perspectives about leadership that are now emerging out of recent scientific advances with more focus on leadership processes compared to traditional studies of leaders' behaviors and traits.

41

> The Complexities of Leadership

For decades, hundreds of leadership scholars have attempted to define the term, postulate theories, conduct research, and write about the topic; others believe that all you need is common sense to understand and practice leadership. As noted in Chapter One, the social construction of leadership makes it difficult to arrive at a single definition of the term *leadership* because "leadership means different things to different people" (Yukl, 1994, p. 2).

The meaning of leadership varies from one country to another. Leadership in a collectivistic society like Japan's looks different from leadership in an individualistic country such as Germany because of cultural norms, cultural values, and the use of power (Hofstede, 2003).

In a comprehensive study of culture and leadership entitled, The GLOBE project, a research team led by Robert House identified regional dimensions of culture (Northouse, 2013). Their study included 950 organizations in 62 world cultures. The most interesting finding from this longitudinal study is the universally desired leadership attributes from these 62 cultures. Some of those universal leadership attributes include positive, win-win problem solver, just, honest, communicative, encouraging, and team builder. They also discovered universally undesirable leadership attributes, which include irritable, asocial, dictatorial, noncooperative, and egocentric (Northouse, 2013). These universal traits are useful in understanding the commonly held beliefs about what others view as good and bad leadership from around the world. Many of these attributes are associated with the contemporary models of leadership identified in this book, including the Relational Leadership Model.

These cultural influences further illustrate the complexities of the study and practice of leadership. Scholars have remarked that "there are almost as many definitions of leadership as there are people who have attempted to describe the concept" (Stogdill, 1974, p. 259). Still others believe that "leadership is not a mysterious activity" (Gardner, 1990, p. xv) and that the tasks of leadership can be identified. What is your understanding of leadership?

STUDENT ESSAY

The global leadership opportunities presented to WPI students are greater than those of many other students throughout the world. While working abroad on their Interactive Qualifying Projects (IQPs), for example, WPI students are challenged to further develop their leadership skills by addressing complex societal problems as a team. In addition to this work, they must balance healthy living environments/habits and social aspects such as weekend travel.

As two WPI juniors that completed this project in Melbourne, Australia, we were fortunate enough to do all of this and learn a priceless leadership lesson in the process. On one of our many weekend excursions, we traveled to Tasmania where we learned an important group leadership lesson. With a total 3-hour hike, the group of 11 IQP students soon dissipated into smaller groups of 3–4 and, in this case, 2. As those who were capable of doing so charged ahead, there was one individual who needed to take the hike at a slower pace. Although it was neither convenient nor exciting to stay with this person, the other in this group knew it was the right thing to do.

Imagine yourself in this individual's shoes. Imagine knowing that everyone else had raced ahead and that you were the only one who could not quite keep pace . . . In this moment you need to take

(continued)

a step back and think about what is truly important—following the crowd because you are capable of charging ahead as well or staying with the person who is falling behind?

As a leader listening to this story, the correct answer should come to you quickly and simply—stay with the person who is falling behind. Out of the 10 other people hiking that day, only 1 of them stayed behind for the person who could not keep pace with the others. This may or may not surprise you—either way—this story represents perfectly two of the 7 Cs from the Social Change Model of Leadership—character and consciousness of self. Character: It's often described as "who you are when no one else is watching." Displayed through your words, but even more so through your actions, your character is what you make of it. In today's world, perception is reality. Being aware of your character has the potential to open many doors or close others—it's your decision.

The particular person that stayed behind to wait for the slower person demonstrated true character throughout this hike. As a leader, he made a conscious choice to stay behind and wait for the slower person, knowing that it was simply the right thing to do. His actions represent an honorable character. Consciousness of self: Throughout life, it is crucial to always be aware of your own beliefs, values, attitudes, and emotions that motivate you to take action in situations. Consciousness of self is the key to developing consciousness of others. As a leader, it is imperative to be conscious of not only your own emotions but also the emotions of those who surround you. As the words and actions of others have positive and negative impacts on you, your own words and actions can have positive and negative effects on others. During the hike, the person who stayed behind was clearly conscious of the slower person and that person's needs as an individual whereas those who sprinted ahead did not exhibit consciousness of others in the least regard.

As students having completed a global IQP, the concept of global leadership was reinstated in our minds throughout this hiking experience. Unlike other forms of leadership, it does not concern itself with being first. Rather, it requires a strength found within one's character to be actively conscious of the needs of others over oneself. On this global IQP, it was the actions that one takes on behalf of the group—in this case of the person who stayed behind for the other—that truly distinguished one's character and consciousness of others from others. In your own team settings and preparations to travel globally, remember the words of the person who stayed behind for the other . . . To the entire group: "We need to wait . . . we are only as fast as our slowest team member."

Stephen Berselli and Brooke Czapkowski are 2013 graduates of Worcester Polytechnic Institute (WPI). Stephen graduated with a B.Sc. in management information systems and a minor in international studies. Stephen was the founding president of Omicron Delta Kappa (ODK), an executive within Phi Kappa Theta, a member of WPI's National Residence Hall Honorary Chapter, and a campus tour guide. Brooke Czapkowski graduated with a B.Sc. in biochemistry. She was a founding member and director within Alpha Phi Women's Fraternity, acting vice president of ODK, Senior Class Board social chairperson, and Order of Omega National Greek Leadership Honor Society member. Both were active members of WPI's Leadership Development Committee.

Aside from the struggles and difficulties of studying leadership, society is crying out for capable and willing leaders to step up and make a difference in our communities and in our world. John W. Gardner (1993), former presidential cabinet member and founder and former chair of Common Cause, wrote an essay (first published in 1965) entitled "The Antileadership Vaccine" in which he made the point that people are less willing to take on the challenges of leadership because of the growing distrust society has shown toward leaders. Leading, whether through a formal position or without a formal title, can be a rewarding and self-fulfilling experience. It can also be a frustrating, exhausting, and difficult process.

Despite the sharp criticisms of leadership studies, many advancements have been made in the field to increase our knowledge of and appreciation for the complexities of leadership (Northouse, 2013; Hughes, Ginnett, & Curphy, 2012). We know more about leadership today than our ancestors did at the turn of the last century. Through research and analysis, many myths of leadership have been dispelled. Colleges and universities continue developing academic majors, centers, and schools devoted to the study and practice of leadership. Our understanding of leadership is sharpened by recent research on the interactions between leaders and followers, the concept of change, self-leading teams, individual expressions of leadership, and shared leadership. Distinctions have been made between studying specific leaders such as Malcolm X, former President Ronald Reagan, British Prime Minister Margaret Thatcher, former President of Ireland Mary Robinson, former and first female prime minister of Canada Kim Campbell, and Martin Luther King Jr.

An extremely important consideration in our understanding of leadership is the context in which it is practiced. Leadership for what purpose? This is a central question in our effort to dissect and understand leadership processes. The kind of leadership necessary to move social movements forward is very different from the type of leadership required in a military setting, especially on the battlefield. A more sharpened focus on leadership processes versus individual leader traits and behaviors deepens our understanding of the complexities and interactive nature of leadership.

› Myths About Leadership

The myths about leadership date back to the turn of the 20th century when leadership was first formally studied by psychologists and sociologists. In ancient Greece, only men with potbellies were thought to be great leaders. In Celtic lands, birds were thought to confer leadership powers. Historically, some believe that only people with charismatic personalities make powerful leaders. The myths of leadership include

- Leaders are born, not made.
- Leadership is hierarchical, and you need to hold a formal position (have status and power) to be considered a leader.
- You have to have charisma to be an effective leader.
- There is one standard way of leading.
- It is impossible to be a manager and a leader at the same time.
- You only need to have common sense to be an effective leader.

› Truths About Leadership

The truths about leadership we propose are based on our collective research and years of study and teaching, and on our own experiences as leaders. We propose the following:

1. *Leaders are made, not born.* Many people have the capacity to lead an organization, community, family, profession, and, most important, themselves. Some individuals will not describe themselves as leaders based on traditional notions of formal leadership when, in fact, they do make a difference in

their organization through their commitment, values, and action toward change. Leaders are not born with innate characteristics or skills predisposing them to be leaders (Gardner, 1990). A person's environment can influence the development of leadership skills and interests (Hughes, Ginnett, & Curphy, 1993; Komives, Owen, Longerbeam, Mainella, & Osteen, 2005).

2. *In today's fluid organizations, leadership occurs at all levels.* Progressive organizations are striving to flatten their hierarchies to empower people throughout the organization and to participate in the leadership process. Manz and Sims's (1989) self-managing teams concept is an example of people at the "worker-level" being responsible for high-level decision making and behavioral control over an organization's process and outcomes. People find meaning in their organizational life and work through shared experiences and a feeling of being empowered to make a contribution or difference.

3. *Having a charismatic personality is not a prerequisite for leadership.* A charismatic leader is one who has "profound and unusual effects on followers" (Yukl, 1994, p. 318). Charismatic leaders are often described as visionaries who have a strong desire for power; leaders have been called impression managers who have a keen ability to motivate others and set an example for others to follow (Yukl, 1994). However, many effective and accomplished leaders are not described as charismatic. For every positive example of a charismatic leader, we can find a negative charismatic. For example, Martin Luther King Jr. is described positively as a charismatic leader who organized a nation to fight for civil rights for all its citizens, whereas Adolph Hitler is viewed negatively as an example of a charismatic leader who influenced

a nation to senselessly and unmercifully kill millions of people because of their race, religion, sexual orientation, or disability.

4. *There is not one identifiable right way to lead an organization or group.* On an individual level, a person's leadership approach or style might be influenced by his or her sex, cultural identity, or personal value system. On an organizational level, the context of the setting might determine the type of leadership required to be effective. Leading volunteer civilian organizations calls for a very different leadership approach than does leading a for-profit organization.

5. *Some leaders and scholars believe it is important to make a distinction between the processes of management and leadership* (Bennis & Nanus, 1985; Gardner, 1990, Zaleznik, 1977). Gardner goes to great lengths to describe the differences between the functions of managers and leaders. He defines a manager as "the individual so labeled [who] holds a directive post in an organization, presiding over the processes by which the organization functions, allocating resources prudently, and making the best possible use of people" (p. 3). The manager is closely bound to an organization or institution, whereas a leader may not have an organization at all. Florence Nightingale is an example of such a leader. Yet others find the exercise of determining the differences between leadership and management to have little utility and use the terms interchangeably (Yukl, 1994).

Another proposition is that managers are preoccupied with doing things the right way, whereas leaders are focused on doing the right thing (Zaleznik, 1977). There are distinctions between management and leadership, and there is also overlap in the functions associated with both processes (Gardner, 1990). It behooves leaders who also perform managerial tasks such

as resource allocation and organizing systems to be effective
managers and to perform those functions well. It is possible, and
in some cases desirable, for a person to be an effective leader
while being an effective manager. The functions of both leadership and management, if they can be distinguished, are necessary
in organizations. Most importantly is the ability to discern when
and how to facilitate management and administrative functions
in the leadership process and who has the best strengths to
executive those tasks.

6. *Leadership is a discipline that is teachable* (Gardner, 1990;
Parks, 2005). Any participant with a desire to lead or to assume
leadership responsibilities can be taught certain skills and
processes. Leadership is not just common sense. Catherine the
Great, John F. Kennedy, Sitting Bull, and Harriet Tubman did
not rise to greatness serendipitously. They had a mission or
purpose and they all experienced life events that shaped their
values and sharpened their skills. Learning about leadership and
developing as a leader is a lifelong process involving preparation,
experience, trial-and-error, self-examination, and a willingness
to learn from mistakes and successes. Your own leadership
development might have started early in elementary school
as the lead in your sixth-grade play, or it may begin later in
your career when you become an elected official or community
activist at the age of fifty.

> Definitions of Leadership

The study of leadership has produced hundreds of definitions of
the term spanning several decades and dating back to the early
1900s (Rost, 1991). Although the term leader can be traced in

the English language to about 1300, the word *leadership* emerged
in the 1800s and was used in the context of political influence
(Greenwood, 1993; Stogdill, 1974). Less than a dozen formal definitions of leadership existed from 1900 to 1929. In the 1980s,
we witnessed a keen interest in the task of defining leadership,
with 110 definitions of leadership by scholars from a wide range
of academic fields (Rost, 1991).

An early definition offered by Mumford (1906–1907) defined
leadership as "the preeminence of one or a few individuals in a
group in the process of control of societal phenomena" (in Bass,
1981, p. 7). Mumford's definition portrays the leader as controller
of events and infers control over people. Early definitions such as
Mumford's typically describe leadership as one person controlling
others or inducing them to follow his or her command.

Contemporary definitions describe leadership as a relational
process based on mutual goals toward some action or change.
Another common aspect of most current definitions is that there
is a level of interaction between leaders and followers who are
working together to accomplish a goal or some type of action,
and the interaction often is based on some type of influence.
For example, Gardner (1990) defines leadership as "the process
of persuasion or example by which an individual (or leadership
team) induces a group to pursue objectives held by the leader or
shared by the leader and his or her followers" (p. 1). Rost (1993)
defines leadership as "an influence relationship among leaders
and their collaborators who intend real changes that reflect
their mutual purposes" (p. 99). Leadership scholar and author
of *Finding Your Voice: Learning to Lead . . . Anywhere You Want
to Make a Difference*, Larraine Matusak (1996) states that the
leadership process entails "initiating and guiding and working
with a group to accomplish change" (p. 5).

We want to emphasize that leadership, as defined in the Relational Leadership Model (to be discussed in the next chapter), is *a relational and ethical process of people together attempting to accomplish positive change.* The interactions between leadership and members provide the greatest insights into the complexities of the leadership process.

What does all of this mean, and why does it matter? Our understanding of how leadership works in contemporary organizations is influenced by an integrated framework of leadership definitions and theories that have emerged over time. Various academic fields such as anthropology, psychology, history, management, sociology, the arts, and philosophy add to the rich interdisciplinary nature of how leadership is studied and practiced. We know more about leadership now than we knew at the turn of the nineteenth century when only one scholarly definition of leadership could be found. Today, we know there is not one correct definition of leadership. This causes us to return to the question, What is the purpose of leadership? in deciding which definition best fits a given context or situation.

> Metaphorical Definitions of Leadership

Leadership also has been defined in interesting ways with the use of metaphors, that is, as "figure[s] of speech in which a word or phrase literally denoting one kind of object or idea is used in place of another to suggest a likeness or analogy between them: figurative language . . . " (*Webster's Ninth New Collegiate Dictionary*, 1986, p. 532). Cohen and March (1974) and Weick (1979) provide comprehensive examples of how leadership and organizations can be described and understood through metaphors. In their classic writing, Cohen and March (1974) use eight metaphors to describe how one might perceive university governance and the functions of presidential leadership: the competitive market metaphor, administrative metaphor, collective bargaining metaphor, democratic metaphor, consensus metaphor, anarchy metaphor, independent judiciary metaphor, and the plebiscitary autocracy metaphor. Metaphorical examples provide us with a clearer or more visual understanding of a concept, process, or phenomena.

A common contemporary metaphor likens leadership to an orchestra or symphony. Think for a moment of the role and tasks of a symphony conductor and the musicians. The conductor is responsible for bringing out the artistic talents and gifts of each symphony member, while the musicians work together to blend and harmonize the music. Integral to the success of a jazz band or symphony is how well the musicians harmonize together. The same is true in the leadership process.

Peter Vaill (1991) uses the metaphor of a performing art to describe artistry associated with management and leadership. Vaill encourages leaders to look at "action as a performing art" (p. 117), which allows examination of both the parts and the whole, as well as the interrelationships between the two. Form matters in art. Vaill illustrates how form or the quality process (p. 118) is inherent in management and leadership, using the example of whether the ends justify the means in weighing the importance of process and outcome.

Max De Pree (1989) also illustrates leadership as an art and parallels the leadership process, not as a science or a set list of tasks, but rather as a "belief, a condition of the heart"

(p. 148). De Pree's use of the art metaphor describes leadership as something intangible, a set of values, convictions, intimacy with one's work and passion. He goes on to say, "the visible signs of artful leadership are expressed, ultimately, in its practice" (p. 148). De Pree (1992) also uses the metaphor of a jazz musician to illustrate the leadership process:

Jazz-band leaders must choose the music, find the right musicians, and perform—in public. But the effect of the performance depends on so many things—the environment, the volunteers playing in the band, the need for everybody to perform as individuals and as a group, the absolute dependence of the leader on the members of the band, the need of the leader for the followers to play well. What a summary of an organization! (De Pree, 1992, pp. 8–9)

De Pree's (1992) leadership jazz metaphor is powerful in illustrating inclusiveness, valuing individuality, showing the importance of the public good, and empowering people to realize their gifts and talents. The leadership jazz metaphor describes the emerging new model of leadership in today's organizations and communities.

Rost (1993) uses the metaphor of leadership as an episodic affair. "Any time people do leadership, they are involved in a process that is bounded by time, subject matter, specific leaders and collaborators engaged in the process, place, and context... it is an episode in people's lives" (p. 103). Leadership then is time-specific, place-specific, and context-specific; individuals experience leadership in episodic moments. For example, leadership does not occur routinely in people's lives during every moment they are working or volunteering in the community.

People "do leadership episodically—ten minutes here, a half hour there, fifteen minutes now, and two hours later" (p. 103).

We even have a metaphor—the "Fosbury Flop"—to describe the paradigm shift in leadership (McFarland, Senn, & Childress, 1993):

> In high jumping years ago, from high school track meets to the Olympics, the men and women who won always used the traditional scissors kick. Then Dick Fosbury showed up and invented a whole new way to jump over the bar, which came to be called the "Fosbury Flop." Very soon, if you couldn't convert your old belief in the scissors kick to a new belief in this more effective "Fosbury Flop," then you could no longer compete in the event. (p. 184)

And so it is with leadership in an ever-changing world in which we live. Our technology is changing, our demographics are changing, the concept of a neighborhood has changed, our religions are changing, how we learn is changing, and how we relate to each other through social media has changed the formation of relationships. Maybe the first test of leading a dynamic and contemporary organization should be whether or not we can do the Fosbury Leadership Flop. The creators of Facebook and inventors of electronic tablets understood this shift extremely well.

> Generations of Leadership Theories

Next, we will explore the evolution of leadership theories and provide you with a glimpse of several major theories. This will give you a conceptual understanding of leadership theory. There is a wealth of information on leadership theories—so much that this chapter could be the basis of a book on leadership theory. At the chapter's end, you will find a list of sources that will give you a more in-depth description and analysis of leadership theories.

It cannot be overstated that leadership is a complex and elusive phenomenon. It is bewildering to wade through the swampy waters of incomplete leadership theories and often inconclusive research. The multidisciplinary nature of leadership adds to its contextual richness and reinforces the metaphor of leadership as an art form.

A metaphor can also be used to describe the state of leadership theory and research: leadership as an atom (Van Fleet & Yukl, 1989, p. 65). In earlier studies of the atom, it was proposed that the atom was "thought to be the simplest, single indivisible particle of matter" (Van Fleet & Yukl, 1989, p. 65). Just like the earlier scientific assumptions about the atom, leadership nearly a century ago was viewed as a simple, predictable, and uncomplicated construct. When leadership was placed under the microscope of social and behavioral scientists, it was discovered, as was the case with the atom, that leadership has many properties and many forms (Van Fleet & Yukl, 1989). "Where we once thought of leadership as a relatively simple construct, we now recognize that it is among the more complex social phenomena" (Van Fleet & Yukl, 1989, p. 66). Despite its criticisms and noted shortcomings, the field of leadership studies has been characterized as having a "robust (and respectable) intellectual history" (Heilbrunn, 1994, p. 66).

There are many ways to categorize the generations of leadership theories that have evolved over time. For the purposes of this chapter, leadership theory will be summarized using the following classification schema: great man approaches, trait approaches, behavior approaches, situational contingency, influence, chaos theories, and reciprocal leadership approaches. We will describe key leadership theories that have influenced scholars' and practitioners' understanding of leadership. These generations of leadership theories are presented in Table 2.1.

Great Man Approaches

Great man theories preceded trait approaches. Darwinistic thinking dominated the first theories in the eighteenth century, under the assumption that leadership is based on hereditary properties (Bass, 1981). The great man folklore is based on brothers of reigning kings who were ascribed to have abilities of power and influence. It was believed that the intermarriage of the fittest would produce an aristocratic class superior to the lower class (Bass). Great women such as Joan of Arc and Catherine the Great were ignored as examples of leaders who were born with innate or natural gifts.

Trait Approach

In the early 1920s, great man theories gave way to trait theories of leadership. Trait approaches marked the emergence of the second generation of leadership theories. If it was not who the leader was, then perhaps leadership could be understand by characteristics about those seen as leaders. It was assumed that leaders had particular traits or characteristics such as intelligence, height, and self-confidence that differentiated them from non-leaders and thus made them successful (Bass, 1981; Bass, 1990; Yukl, 1994).

Table 2.1 **Leadership Theories**

Approach	Time Period	Major Assumptions	Major Criticisms
Great Man	Mid-1800s to early 1900s	Leadership development is based on Darwinistic principles Leaders are born, not made Leaders have natural abilities of power and influence	Scientific research has not proved that leadership is based on hereditary factors Leadership was believed to exist only in a few individuals
Trait	1904 to 1947	A leader has superior or endowed qualities Certain individuals possess a natural ability to lead Leaders have traits that differentiate them from followers	The situation is not considered in this approach Many traits are too obscure or abstract to measure and observe Studies have not adequately linked traits with leadership effectiveness Most trait studies omit leadership behaviors and followers' motivation as mediating variables

Behavioral	1950s to early 1980s	There is one best way to lead Leaders who express high concern for both people and production or consideration and structure will be effective	Situational variables and group processes are ignored; studies failed to identify the situations in which specific types of leadership behaviors are relevant
Situational Contingency	1950s to 1960s	Leaders act differently, depending on the situation The situation determines who will emerge as a leader Different leadership behaviors are required for different situations	Most contingency theories are ambiguous, making it difficult to formulate specific, testable propositions Theories lack accurate measures
Influence	Mid-1920s to 1977	Leadership is an influence or social exchange process	More research is needed on the effect charisma has on the leader-follower interaction

(continued)

Table 2.1 **Leadership Theories (*continued*)**

Approach	Time Period	Major Assumptions	Major Criticisms
Reciprocal	1978 to present	Leadership is a relational process Leadership is a shared process Emphasis is on followership Leadership is an outcome of participants' and/or leaders' interactions on a common agenda or change initiative Outcome of leadership is social change	Lack of clarity and difficult to measure overall Further clarification is needed on similarities and differences between charismatic and transforming leadership Processes of collaboration, change, and empowerment are difficult to achieve and measure Lack of evidence showing actual transformation in organizations
Chaos or Systems	1990 to present	Attempts to describe leadership within a context of a complex, rapidly changing worldLeadership is a relational process Control is not possible, so leadership is described as an influence relationship The importance of systems is emphasized	Research is lacking Some concepts are difficult to define and understand Holistic approach makes it difficult to achieve and measure Difficult to measure change processing in dynamic, fluid environments and settings

Authentic Leadership Approaches	1990 to present	Leadership is genuine and transparent	Too complex to accurately measure and define constructs
		Authenticity emerges between and among leaders and participants interactions	Models and theories still in formative stages
		Develops over time	Unclear evidence in supporting outcomes of this approach
		Grounded in positive psychological behaviors and traits	Lacks research on application of strategies
		Leadership is values and purpose driven with an explicit moral dimensions	

Trait studies produced varying lists of personal traits that would guarantee leadership success to an individual who possessed these extraordinary qualities. The research questions based on trait theory were, What traits distinguish leaders from other people? and What is the extent of those differences? (Bass, 1990, p. 38). Ralph Stogdill provided evidence that disputed trait theories with the premise that "persons who are leaders in one situation may not necessarily be leaders in other situations" (Greenwood, 1993, p. 7). In summary, research failed to produce a list of traits to ensure which characteristics leaders must possess to be effective; this paved the way for the behavioral approach of leadership research (Rost, 1993). What a leader does became more interesting than what a leader is.

Behavioral Approaches

The "one best way" approach to leading is a phrase commonly used to describe behavioral leadership theories that promote the notion that there is one best way to lead (Greenwood, 1993; Phillips, 1995; Van Fleet & Yukl, 1989). If leadership could not be explained by leader traits and characteristics, then attention turned to the things leaders do—their behaviors, skills, and styles. The behavior approach includes the analysis of "what managers actually do on the job" (Yukl, 1994, p. 12), which is related to the content of managerial activities, roles, functions, and responsibilities. Effective and ineffective leaders also were compared in behavior studies to find out how the behaviors of effective leaders differed from those of ineffective leaders (Yukl). Historically, the field of psychology largely influenced studies on the behavior approach to further knowledge of leadership in the 1950s and 1960s (Hughes, Ginnett, & Curphy, 1993).

The Ohio State studies and the University of Michigan studies are known as the seminal research projects on behavioral leadership theories (Yukl, 1994). Results from the Ohio State studies produced two dimensions of managerial behavior toward subordinates: consideration and initiating structure. Consideration was described as "the degree to which a leader acts in a friendly and supportive manner, shows concern for subordinates, and looks out for their welfare" (Yukl, 1994, p. 54) and initiating structure as "the degree to which a leader defines and structures his or her own role and the roles of subordinates toward attainment of the group's formal goals" (p. 54). It is possible for an individual to be high on consideration and low on initiating structure because the two dimensions are independent of one another. An individual also could be high on both consideration and initiating structure. Blake and Mouton proposed a two-factor approach: concern for people and concern for production. They developed the Managerial Grid Model in 1964 (Greenwood, 1993; Yukl, 1994). Research using their model concluded that effective managers show high concern for people and production.

The Michigan studies on leadership behavior included the "identification of relationships among leader behavior, group processes, and measures of group performance" (Yukl, 1994, p. 59). Three types of behaviors were identified that provided a distinction between effective and ineffective managers: task-oriented behaviors, relationship-oriented behaviors, and participative leadership. These studies suggested that leaders focus on high performance standards. Like the Ohio State studies, the Michigan studies showed that effective leader behaviors vary with the situation. To date, there is little research on leader behaviors that shows which specific behaviors are appropriate for specific situations (Yukl, 1994). Criticisms of the behavior approach are that it offers simple explanations to complex questions (Yukl, 1994) and that certain leadership behaviors have not resulted in specific outcomes (Northouse, 2004). The majority of research on leader behaviors has ignored situational variables and group processes. The results have been inconclusive and inconsistent, which opened the doors for situational contingency approaches.

Situational Contingency Approaches

Situational contingency approaches propose that leaders should vary their approach or their behaviors based on the context or situation. The situation determines who will emerge as the leader—the leader being "the product of the situation" (Bass, 1990, p. 38). The major research question is, "How [do] the effects of leadership vary from situation to situation?" (Yukl, 1994, p. 285). Contingency theories incorporate situational moderator variables to explain leadership effectiveness (Yukl, 1994). Situational theories emphasize that leadership behavior cannot be explained in a vacuum; elements of the situation must be included (Bass, 1994).

The Least Preferred Co-Worker (LPC Model) and the Path Goal Theory are two major situational contingency theories. The LPC Model was developed by Fiedler in the mid-1960s and "describes how the situation moderates the relationship between leader traits and effectiveness" (Yukl, 1994). This contingency theory of leadership focuses on the importance of the situation in explaining leader effectiveness. The path-goal theory originated in 1957 by Georgopoulos and others but is well known for its later applications by Robert House in the early 1970s (Van Fleet & Yukl, 1989). Van Fleet and Yukl (1989) note:

> If a group member perceives high productivity to be an easy "path" to attain personal goals, then he or she will tend to be a high producer. On the other hand, if personal goals are obtainable in other ways, then the group member will not likely be a high producer. The task of the group leader is, then, to increase the personal rewards to subordinates for performance in order to make the paths to their goals clearer and easier. (p. 71)

Personal characteristics of group members and the work environment are the two contingency variables associated with path-goal theory. Skills, needs, and motives define personal characteristics of group members, whereas task structure, formal authority, system of organization, and the work group as a whole define the work environment (Van Fleet & Yukl, 1989). The effect of leader behavior is contingent on elements of the situation, which are task and subordinate characteristics (Yukl, 1994). These variables influence others' "preferences for a particular pattern of leadership behavior, thereby influencing the impact of the leader on subordinate satisfaction" (Yukl, 1994, p. 286). Concerns about this theory of leadership include a lack of supporting research and an unclear association between the commitment and competence of subordinates and their level of development (Northouse, 2004).

> Influence Theories

In 1924 and 1947, Max Weber used the term charisma in a managerial context "to describe a form of influence based not on traditional power or formal authority but rather on follower perceptions that the leader is endowed with exceptional qualities" (Yukl, 1994, p. 317). Interest in charismatic leadership initially grew out of political, social, and religious movements in situations where a leader would emerge out of a crisis or exhibit extraordinary vision to solve a problem (Bass, 1990; Yukl, 1994). It was not formalized until 1977 when Robert House proposed a formal theory of charismatic leadership that could be explained by a set of testable variables (Yukl, 1994).

Charisma is often attributed to leaders by their followers and is based on the perceptions of followers and the attributions of the leader, the context of the situation, and the needs of individuals and the group. There are several theories of charismatic leadership, including House's theory of charismatic leadership, attribution theory of charisma, a self-concept theory of charismatic leadership, and psychoanalytic and social contagion explanations of charisma (Yukl, 1994). These theories vary based on the variables associated with the influence processes and how charismatic leadership behavior is defined.

House's theory of charismatic leadership is used for its noted comprehensiveness and proposed set of testable propositions. House's theory "identifies how charismatic leaders behave, how they differ from other people, and the conditions in which they are most likely to flourish" (Yukl, 1994, p. 318).

Conditions that facilitate charismatic leadership include times of crisis and times when followers are willing to challenge the status quo (Hughes, Ginnett, & Curphy, 1993). Charismatic leadership has received mixed reviews as a standard of practice in leadership situations. Too much deference to an individual leader by followers can create a dangerous scenario whereby the leader misuses the power or delivers a vision with an empty dream (Yukl, 1994). As we noted earlier, just as there are positive charismatics, society has been blemished by negative charismatics who were powerful and influential enough to lead others to their deaths or lead organizations to their destruction. Kellerman (2004) inserts that there is much to learn from bad leadership or the dark side of leadership—leaders who created and sustained negative organizational cultures that resulted in the destructive of those organizations while also ruining people's lives. "We must come to grips with leadership as two contradictory things: good and bad" (Kellerman, 2004, p. 14).

❯ Reciprocal Leadership Theories

Since the late 1970s, a grouping of leadership theories emerged that focused on the relational and reciprocal nature of the leader-follower interaction. These theories emphasized the mutual goals and motivations of both followers and leaders, and elevated the importance and role of followers in the leadership process. In other words, leadership was not just something that a leader does to followers. Leadership is a process that meaningfully engages leaders and participants, values the contributions of participants, shares power and authority between leaders and participants, and views leadership as an inclusive activity among interdependent people. Participants are empowered to provide leadership and make significant contributions to achieving the vision of the organization. In some cases, the participants are transformed into leaders. The leadership process encompasses the essential role of all people, including participants. We call theories describing this process reciprocal leadership theories.

Profound examples of these theories in application can be found in civil rights movements, the women's movement, the gay rights movement, pro life and pro choice movement, anti-war movements, sustainability movements, and the most recent Occupy Wall Street movement. The historical social rights movements used coalitions and networks of people around the world to leverage change that transformed policies, practices, institutions, and whole nations. Some of these movements have an unfinished agenda, but they thrive based on the evolution of networks of people advancing a common agenda and purpose. They were inclusive of a vast number of people and were collaborative in nature, bringing diverse interests and people together to create a vision and execute strategies to realize deep and long-term change.

STUDENT ESSAY

My interest in the Occupy Wall Street movement first began last fall when my ethics professor showed us videos of police brutality against protestors. Seeing our first amendment rights being so violently infringed upon by servants of the state led me to researching the Occupy movement more in-depth. The following quarter I researched Occupy Wall Street extensively and this quarter I became an active participant in Occupy Chicago. Occupy is known as a leaderless movement, not because it has no leaders, but because all of its members are leaders. I led in my own way by sharing the research I did with friends and family. I truly believe change can happen if we act on the democratic rights given to us by our great country.

Mishal Qureshi is a junior majoring in international studies at DePaul University. She is an Arthur J. Schmitt Scholar, member of the Student Leadership Institute, organizer with the nonprofit Chicago Votes, and an active supporter and participant in social movements around Chicago.

Several theories could be included in the reciprocal leadership theory category. We focus on what we consider to be the major theories in this chapter because they most closely relate to the Relational Leadership Model, which will be presented in the next chapter. The major theories are servant leadership, transforming leadership, complexity leadership theory, shared leadership, and followership.

Servant-Leadership

Servant-leadership theory begins by viewing the leader first as a servant—a person who first wants to serve others. The servant, through focusing on the primary needs of others and the organization, then transforms himself or herself into a leader (Greenleaf, 1977). A servant-leader is someone who joins a club, a community, or a social movement with the sole goal of serving others to make a difference. The individual does not engage in these activities in order to lead the group or enhance a résumé. Mother Teresa was commonly characterized as a servant-leader (Rogers, 1996). There are many examples of servant-leaders in local communities—people who dedicate themselves to building communities so they become better places for others. These servant-leaders can be residents, local business people, community activists, and politicians.

Servant-leaders view institutions "in which CEOs, staffs, directors, and trustees all play significant roles in holding their institutions in trust for the greater good of society" (Spears, 1995, pp. 6–7), which is the reciprocal nature of this leadership process. Peter Block (1993) refers to this concept as stewardship. In the servant-leadership process, both leaders and participants are stewards of the organization who dedicate themselves to taking care of the needs of others and the organization's needs and to uplifting the mission and values of the enterprise.

The biggest difference between a servant-leader and a person who wants to lead an organization is the servant-leader's motive of putting the needs of others before his or her own needs. A person who joins the student government association because she wants to provide better academic services and advising based on the desires of the student community is an example of a servant-leader. Someone who gets involved with student government because she wants to run for office and maybe someday even be president is simply an example of someone with leadership aspirations. The end goal of servant-leadership is for those who are served to grow, to become more knowledgeable and empowered, to gain interdependence or independence, and to become servant-leaders themselves.

Servant-leadership has been critiqued heavily by researchers for its pejorative label and the lack of a measurable theoretical model (Northouse, 2013). Further, others view this model as having an emphasis on leaders as the primary initiators of the leadership process with followers in a more traditional, passive role.

Transforming Leadership Theory

A major reciprocal leadership theory—transforming leadership—was formulated by James MacGregor Burns in 1978. Burns (1978) defines transforming leadership as "a process where leaders and followers raise one another to higher levels of morality and motivation" (p. 20). Transforming leadership can result "in a relationship of mutual stimulation and elevation that converts followers into leaders and may convert leaders into moral agents" (p. 4). Leaders appeal to followers' "higher ideals and moral values such as liberty, justice, equality, peace, and humanitarianism, not to lesser emotions such as fear, greed, jealousy, or hatred" (Yukl, 1994, p. 351).

Transforming leadership is based on the assumption that leadership is "inseparable from followers' needs and goals" (Burns, 1978, p. 19) and the "essence of the leader-follower relation is the interaction of persons with different levels of motivations and of power potential, including skill, in pursuit of a common or at least joint purpose" (p. 19). Power is used to realize common goals and purposes and not for purposes of exploitation or manipulation. A unique aspect of transforming leadership theory is its moral component.

The end goal of transforming leadership is that both leaders and followers raise each other to higher ethical aspirations and conduct. Burns believed that transforming leadership could be practiced at all levels of an organization and by both leaders and followers. Examples of frequently mentioned transformational leaders include Gandhi, John F. Kennedy, Mother Teresa, Martin Luther King Jr., Abraham Lincoln, and Franklin D. Roosevelt (Bass, 1990; Burns, 1978). It is transforming leaders whom most people identify when they think about positive examples of leaders or role models (Bass, 1990).

Transforming leadership was contrasted with transactional leadership by Burns (1978) to demonstrate that the leader-follower interaction has two dimensions: transforming leadership and transactional leadership. Burns defines transactional leadership as the process whereby "one person takes the initiative in making contact with others for the purpose of an exchange of valued things" (p. 19). It is possible for a leader to engage in both transforming and transactional leadership. Transactional leadership appeals to the self-interests of followers, whereas transforming leadership appeals to higher ideals and moral values of both leaders and followers (Burns, 1978; Yukl, 1994).

For example, Gandhi, as a transforming leader, "elevated the hopes and demands of millions of Indians whose life and personality were enhanced in the process" (Burns, 1978, p. 20). Transactional leadership is exercised when a political candidate asks for votes in exchange for a promise to build more schools. Table 2.2 lists the fundamental values associated with transforming and transactional leadership (Burns, 1978; Yukl, 1994).

Critics of this theory focus on its overall lack of clarity and specificity, making this leadership theory difficult to measure (Northouse, 2013), although it is widely researched. It is also challenging to prove the degree that transforming leaders actually transform individuals and organizations. While the properties of transforming leader include ethical and moral dimensions, the focus on the elite leader in this theory has drawn criticism as being leader-centric (Northouse, 2013).

Table 2.2   Transforming and Transactional Leadership

Transforming Leadership	Transactional Leadership
(Based on higher or end values)	(Based on exchange or modal values)
Order	Honesty
Equality	Fairness
Liberty	Responsibility
Freedom	Due process
Justice	Courage

Complexity Leadership Theory

The reciprocal leadership theories have a sharp focus on informal leaders, leading without a formal position, and inclusivity in creating the vision and making that vision a reality. Complexity leadership theory mirrors the realities of a networked world, communities, universities and colleges, and organizations. We live in a nonlinear world that requires individuals and human systems to adapt to the complexities of change, chaos, and unforeseeable events. In the Knowledge Era in which we live, understanding these complexities is essential in advancing the study and practice of leadership. "Much of leadership thinking has failed to recognize that leadership is not merely the influential act of an individual or individuals, but rather is embedded in a complex interplay of numerous interacting forces" (Uhl-Bien, Marion, & McKelvey, 2007, p. 302). Lichtenstein, Uhl-Bien, Marion, Seers, Orton, and Schreiber (2006) define leadership as,

> . . . a dynamic process that emerges in the interactive "spaces between" people and ideas. That is, leadership is a dynamic that transcends the capabilities of individuals alone; it is the product of interaction, tension, and exchange rules governing changes in perceptions and understanding. (p. 2)

These scholars propose that the focus move from individual leaders to understanding a leadership event defined as "a perceived segment of action whose meaning is created by the interactions of actors involved in producing it . . ." (p. 2).

Complexity leadership theory puts the emphasis on the interactions of all involved in the leadership process and views leadership as an episodic event that may or maybe not include formal leadership. The conditions of change might be enabled by leaders, but the direct source of change is attributed to the interactive dynamics of all involved in the leadership process. The premise of this theory is that organizations are complex and nonlinear and that leadership itself is an outcome of relational interactions among members and co-creators (Lichtenstein et al., 2006). In complexity leadership theory, the emphasis shifts from individual leader impact and behaviors to the interactions among participants as a collective. Uhl-Bien, et al. (2007) emphasize the interdependent nature of people and their environment by observing that "agents must be interdependently related, meaning that the productive well being of one agent or aggregate is dependent on the productive well being of others" (p. 303).

The Occupy Wall Street movement is an example of complexity leadership theory in practice. There is not one single leader who is attributed with this movement; the movement evolved from a complex set of interactions of people who used systems thinking to organize and elevate a common agenda. Leadership emerged from the interactive space between the Occupy Wall Street activists and their ideas using network-based problem solving. In summary, complexity leadership theory enables creativity, learning, and adaptive responses through the interplay and interactions of people at all levels of the organization.

Adaptive Leadership

A corresponding theory of complexity leadership theory is adaptive leadership defined as, "an interactive event in which knowledge, action preferences, and behaviors change, thereby provoking an organization to become more adaptive... Adaptive leadership does not mean getting followers to follow the leader's wishes; rather, leadership occurs when interacting agents generate adaptive outcomes" (Lichtenstein et al., 2006, p. 4). Adaptive leadership calls upon participants at all levels of the organization to leverage their strengths and talents to effect change or address complex problems. Like complexity leadership theory, it is through the interactions of people in the organization that generate meaning and purpose, and ultimately leadership.

Tension also influences the leadership process in this model that can lead to adaptive change (Lichtenstein, et al., 2006). Tension is used as a way to realize innovation and generate new knowledge or new perspectives. The postindustrial paradigm of leadership placed formal leaders in the role of resolving tension for the group. Adaptive leadership calls for participants to see the value of tension as a way to generate new ideas and facilitate positive leadership outcomes. "Adaptive challenges are not amenable to authoritative fiat or standard operating procedures, but rather require exploration, new discoveries, and adjustments" (Uhl-Bien, Mario, & McKelvey, 2007, p. 300). In adaptive challenges, members and leaders together learn new ways to solve problems in real time (Heifetz & Linsky, 2002). "They contribute ideas and opinions, they play devil's advocate, and they address the 'elephants on the table' that others try to ignore" (Uhl-Bien et al., 2007, p. 311). Heifetz and Linsky (2002) assert that "when people look to authorities for easy answers to adaptive challenges, they end up with dysfunction" (p. 14). There is no rulebook or standard operating manual for many of the complex adaptive challenges organizations and communities face today.

Unlike transforming leadership theory where leaders elevate others to higher levels of morality and leadership, complexity leadership theory calls on all members to own the leadership process and to have responsibility trickle down and through the organization. Members take on leadership identities and take ownership of initiating change and sparking innovation. They no longer rely upon formal leaders to give them direction, authorization, or affirmation. In complexity leadership processes, formal leaders might take on more strategic and external roles for the organization. The learning capacity and the emotional and social intelligence of human capital are essential assets in the leadership process in a Knowledge Era (Uhl-Bien etal., 2007).

Shared Leadership

The shared leadership model is similar to complexity leadership theory and adaptive leadership theory with its emphasis on the leadership process. Shared leadership goes beyond including others in the leadership process. Pearce and Conger (2003) define shared leadership

> as a dynamic, interactive influence process among individuals in groups for which the objective is to lead one another to the achievement of the group or organizational goals or both . . . Leadership is broadly distributed among a set of individuals instead of centralized in hands of a single individual who acts in the role of a superior. (p. 1)

In the shared leadership model, leadership is owned by the whole system as opposed to individuals or the formal leader; the effectiveness of leadership is determined by the interactions and connections of the participants (Avolio, Walumbwa, & Weber, 2009).

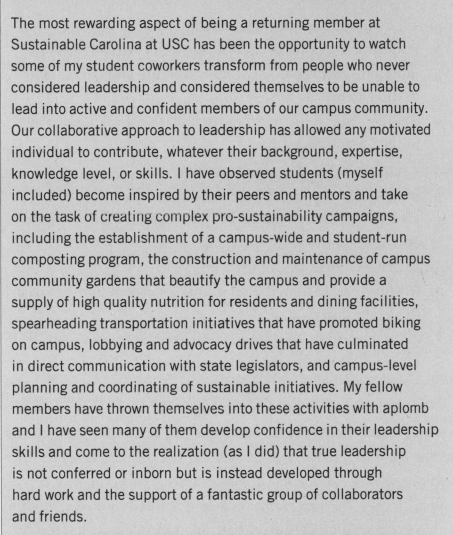

STUDENT ESSAY

The most rewarding aspect of being a returning member at Sustainable Carolina at USC has been the opportunity to watch some of my student coworkers transform from people who never considered leadership and considered themselves to be unable to lead into active and confident members of our campus community. Our collaborative approach to leadership has allowed any motivated individual to contribute, whatever their background, expertise, knowledge level, or skills. I have observed students (myself included) become inspired by their peers and mentors and take on the task of creating complex pro-sustainability campaigns, including the establishment of a campus-wide and student-run composting program, the construction and maintenance of campus community gardens that beautify the campus and provide a supply of high quality nutrition for residents and dining facilities, spearheading transportation initiatives that have promoted biking on campus, lobbying and advocacy drives that have culminated in direct communication with state legislators, and campus-level planning and coordinating of sustainable initiatives. My fellow members have thrown themselves into these activities with aplomb and I have seen many of them develop confidence in their leadership skills and come to the realization (as I did) that true leadership is not conferred or inborn but is instead developed through hard work and the support of a fantastic group of collaborators and friends.

Sam Johnson is a graduate of the University of South Carolina Honors College where he majored in biological science and minored in political science and is currently pursuing a masters degree in earth and environmental resource management. He has worked for the USC Sustainable Carolina program as well as the Columbia, South Carolina, nonprofit Sustainable Midlands and was a founding member of the USC-based Carolina Science Outreach.

Fletcher and Kaufer (2003) identify three shifts inherent in shared leadership:

Shift 1: Distributed and Interdependent
- leadership, responsibility, and authority are shifted from individual leader to shared responsibility and collective achievement
- interdependent interactions and relationships define the leadership process

Shift 2: Embedded in Social Interaction
- leadership occurs in and through relationships
- leadership occurs from the bottom up with followers influencing and initiating leadership

Shift 3: Leadership as Learning
- learning occurs from the relational aspects of individuals in the leadership process
- mutual learning, heightened understanding, and positive action comprise shared leadership (pp. 22–23)

Shared leadership goes beyond empowering others by the leader. It reenvisions the *who* and *where* of leadership by focusing on the need to distribute the tasks and responsibilities of leadership up, down, and across the hierarchy . . . and the *how* of leadership by focusing on the skills and ability required to create conditions in which collective learning can occur. (Fletcher & Kaufer, 2003, p. 24)

Followership   Followers in many ways have been viewed in the leadership literature as sheep in need of a leader to tell them what to do, how to do it, and when to do it. Important thinking about followership has been provided by Robert E. Kelley, a professor in the Graduate School of Industrial Administration at Carnegie Mellon University. Kelley (1992) redefines followership and leadership. He does not subscribe to the industrial model of leaders, in which leaders are superior to followers, but defines the roles of leaders and followers as having equally important but different activities. Followership is a role people assume in the leadership process.

Kelley (1988) outlines five followership patterns along the dimensions of independent, critical thinking and dependent, uncritical thinking, alienated followers, sheep, yes people, survivors, and effective followers. Effective followers share these qualities. They

- Manage themselves well
- Are committed to the organization and to a purpose, principle, or person outside themselves
- Build their competence and focus their efforts for maximum impact
- Are courageous, honest, and credible. (p. 144)

The reciprocal nature of leadership and followership is that followers see themselves as "coadventurers" (Kelley, 1988) with leaders. Organizational successes are due to both effective followership and effective leadership. Effective followers need to be empowered, honored for their contributions, and valued for the satisfaction and pride that they take in their roles of helping the organization achieve its goals and vision.

Two examples of followership in action come from opposite ends of the organizational continuum. New members of an organization can have an incredible impact by demonstrating their commitment through the aspects of followership just mentioned. This is also true of past officers of an organization. If they are able to stay connected to the organization, their positive impact can be extremely helpful to the current leaders.

Emerging Leadership Paradigms   Rost (1991) describes the leadership theories in the twentieth century using the Industrial Paradigm Model. Leadership theory in the twentieth century mirrored the industrial era in that the theories were "structural-functionalist, management-oriented, personalistic in focusing only on the leader, goal-achievement dominated, self-interested and individualistic in outlook, male-oriented, utilitarian and materialistic in ethical perspective, and rationalistic, technocratic, linear, quantitative, and scientific in language and methodology" (p. 27).

In summary, the theories that emerged from the early 1900s to the early 1970s are grounded in the industrial paradigm. For this reason, Rost (1993) calls for a "total transformation of our concept of leadership" (p. 98). The reciprocal leadership theories allowed us to experience a paradigm shift from the industrial paradigm to the postindustrial paradigm of leadership. We believe that a more integrated understanding of contemporary leadership theory is necessary—one that relies on new ways of thinking about leadership. We also acknowledge that many groups of people, for example women, often did lead in a reciprocal or shared manner so no paradigm shift occurred but their approaches were valued and adopted in conventional practices (Komives, 2011; Komives & Dugan, 2010). In the following sections, we will examine various aspects of this new, postindustrial paradigm.

> Leadership Maps for a Rapidly Changing World

As Luthans and Slocum (2004) note in their introduction to a special issue of *Organizational Dynamics*, "Faced with an unprecedented economic, technological, socio-political, and moral/ethical tumultuous sea of change, there is a need for new theories, new applications and just plain new thinking about leadership" (p. 227).

It is clear that the world is a lot messier than it once was believed to be. This may be an orderly world but the order is often obscured. It is a world in which control is not possible, especially if other people are involved—a world filled with chaos but one in which chaos is viewed as something to be embraced rather than feared. To successfully navigate in this world, new maps are needed—maps describing the leadership that is needed in an era of rapid change. As Stacey (1992) notes, "An old map is useless when the terrain is new" (p. 4), and the world is certainly a different place than it was 50, 40, 30, or even 20 years ago. Table 2.3 highlights some of the differences between the conventional and current perspectives of how the world operates.

Another way of conceptualizing this new world is to ask two questions. First ask, How is my life (or organization) like a machine? The words you might use to describe your life (or organization) using a machine metaphor apply to the rational, orderly

Table 2.3 **Moving from the Conventional to the Current**

Conventional Perspectives	Current Perspectives
Stability	Change/Risk
Certainty	Uncertainty
Controlled	Chaotic
Talk	Listen
Local or Global	Local and Global
Hierarchy	Web
Money and Bottom Line	Values and Vision
Driving by Dollars	Sailing with Soul
Divisions of the University	Communities of Learning
Teaching	Learning
Learning in the Classroom	Learning Everywhere
Explaining	Exploring
Weakness Fixing	Strengths Development
What's Wrong with Individuals	What's Right with Individuals
Receiving	Reflecting
Protecting	Connecting
Competing	Collaborating
Set Limits	Set Expectations
Critical Analysis	Critical Thinking
Time Management/Balance	Mindfulness
Set Course of Action	Nimbleness

Adapted from Kochner in McMahon, T., Kochner, C., Clemetsen, B., & Bolger, A. (1995). Reprinted with permission.

side of life. For example, as with machines, certain operating procedures must be followed to make organizations work in a bureaucracy. When using organizational or institutional funds or reserving meeting rooms, certain procedures must be followed. These procedures are predictable and do not vary from month to month. Not following these procedures will cause problems for the organization. You need tools to function and may refer to your skills as your "tool box."

Now ask, How is my life (or organization) like a weather system? The non-rational, unpredictable, uncontrollable side of life will be included in the words you will use. For example, like the weather, organizational crises are usually unexpected. They can occur without warning, and their emergence cannot be predicted precisely. Yet the organization must be prepared to deal with these storms. Both of these qualities are in operation at all times in the universe. To embrace only one perspective is to deny the other part of life. A former student government leader described the differences between these two perspectives in this manner: "The (rational/controllable) world is how I wish things were. The other (unpredictable/uncontrollable) world is how I know things are." Allen and Cherrey (2000, p. 20) summarize these "competing expectations and realities" in Table 2.4.

Table 2.4 **Competing Expectations and Realities**

The Way Things Ought to Be	The Way Things Actually Are
Perfection is expected the first time.	Informed experimentation is necessary.
Goals are predictable with complete certainty.	Additional and new goals will always appear.
Control is expected.	Absolute control is rare and cannot be maintained over the long term.
Efficiency is the standard of competence.	Redundancy and detours fuel creativity and innovation.
Predictability is assumed.	Probabilities are the norm.

Source: Allen & Cherrey (2000), p. 20. Used with permission.

Chaos, as we are using the term, has been defined as "order without predictability" (Cartwright, 1991, p. 44). As Stacey (1992) notes, "Chaotic behavior has two important characteristics . . . it is inherently unpredictable, while at another level it displays a 'hidden' pattern" (p. 62). This view of a world as turbulent, ever-changing, risky, and always challenging is echoed and expanded in some recent work describing the quantum or chaotic world. When you hear the word chaos, what do you imagine? Do words like unorganized, untidy, wild, scary, anarchy, messy, and unproductive come to mind? If you can let go of your need to have the world be completely rational and orderly, you may recognize this list of adjectives as a set of descriptors for how the world really operates. This notion of the world as yin and yang, rational and nonrational, orderly and messy is at the heart of how this real world is described. Using chaos and related concepts to describe leadership and life has been the focus of a number of different authors (Allen, 1990; Briggs & Peat, 1999; Eoyang, 1997; Holland, 1998; Lewin & Regine, 2000; Pascale, Millemann, & Goija, 2000; and Wheatley, 1999).

The chaotic world is a quantum world—a world of wholes, not parts. It is a world in which living things invariably organize themselves based largely on the feedback they gather from the environment around them. Finally, it is a world that cannot be controlled (Wheatley, 1999). This chaotic world has much to offer as we think about the changing nature of leadership. This section will explore the key elements to framing the world as more chaotic or more like a weather system than a machine.

> Relationships, Connections, and "Anding"

Relationships and connections are so important that Margaret Wheatley (1992) wrote, "None of us exists independent of our relationships with others" (p. 34). Another way to realize the importance of connections is to consider the concept of "andness." Andness occurs when you make a connection with something or someone—you are literally "anding" with it or them. Unless you "and" with something or someone, no exchange occurs, nothing is produced, no new energy is created. Think about it this way. We all know that $1 + 1 = 2$. But think about this in human terms. Think about your very best friend or co-worker. When you two get together, you accomplish amazing things, much more than any two people you know. In this case, a synergy exists and $1 + 1 = 5$ or 10 or even 100. Now consider working on a project with someone with whom you cannot "and" or connect. In this case, the two of you are like two skewed lines in space, never to intersect, $1 + 1 = 0$ (Meadows, 1982). If you can successfully "and" with the concepts of chaos theory, you will see countless examples of it in action every day. It is also important to note a need to shift our thinking. As Allen and Cherrey note (2000), "Systemic leadership is 'both-and' not either-or" (p. 21). Something might not be right or wrong, it might be right and wrong.

We believe that leadership must be purposeful, inclusive, empowering, ethical, and process-oriented. Helping the group create and continually incorporate such a compelling vision into its organizational life is a challenge for any leader. Most newly elected officers want to begin doing things immediately. The very idea of taking some time to thoughtfully reflect on why the organization exists and to determine what values and ideals it needs to reflect can seem like a complete waste of time. Being able to approach problems and dilemmas with an "andness" mentality might yield a better and more informed decision or action.

> Authentic Leadership

A profound development in leadership is a review of many reciprocal leadership models and post-industrial research leading some scholars to see an underlying theme in all these approaches which they have called "authentic leadership". As May, Hodges, Chan, and Avolio (2003) note, "Starting from a very basic point of view, authentic people are at the center of authentic leadership, and authentic leadership is at the base of all positive, socially constructive forms of leadership" (p. 249).

Luthans and Avolio (2003) describe authentic leadership as the confluence of positive psychology, transformational leadership, and moral/ethical leadership and the authentic leader as someone who is "confident, hopeful, optimistic, resilient, transparent, moral/ethical, future-oriented, and gives priority to developing associates to be leaders" (p. 243). In a similar vein, Avolio, Gardner, Walumbwa, Luthans, and May (2004) describe authentic leaders as "persons who have achieved high levels of authenticity in that they know who they are, what they believe and value, and they act upon those values and beliefs while transparently interacting with others" (p. 802).

The concept of authentic leadership adds much to our understanding of leadership. Avolio, et al. (2004) describe authentic leadership as a "root construct"—"at the very base or core of what constitutes profoundly positive leadership in whatever form it exists" (p. 818). As such, it recognizes the need to understand the powerful impact of hope, trust, and positive emotions and the need to understand the attitudes and behaviors of followers (Avolio, et al.). Followers are especially important to authentic leadership. Shamir and Eilam (2005) note, "authentic leadership includes authentic followership as well, namely followers who follow the leaders for authentic reasons and have an authentic relationship with the leader" (pp. 400–401). Gardner, Avolio, Luthans, May, and Walumbwa (2005) describe the relationship between authentic leader and follower as "characterized by: a) transparency, openness, and trust, b) guidance toward worthy objectives, and c) an emphasis on follower development" (p. 345).

Avolio, et al. (2004) note that "authentic leadership theory stresses the idea of leading by example (i.e., role modeling) through setting high moral standards, honesty, and integrity" (p. 807). May, Hodges, Chan, and Avolio (2003) offer the following "tasks" of authentic leadership: build followers' self-efficacy; create hope; raise optimism; and strengthen resilience (pp. 274–278). Shamir and Eilam (2005) describe authentic leaders in the following way:

1. Authentic leaders do not fake their leadership.
2. Relatedly, authentic leaders do not take on a leadership role or engage in leadership activities for status, honor, or other personal rewards.

3. Authentic leaders are originals, not copies.

4. Authentic leaders are leaders whose actions are based on their values and convictions. (pp. 396–397)

It is important to remember that authentic leaders can be directive or participative, and could even be authoritarian. The behavioral style per se is not what necessarily differentiates the authentic from inauthentic leader. Authentic leaders act in accordance with deep personal values and convictions, to build credibility and win the respect and trust of followers by encouraging diverse viewpoints and building networks of collaborative relationships with followers, and thereby lead in a manner that followers recognize as authentic (Avolio, et al., 2004, p. 806).

Although similar in some ways, it is important to note how authentic leadership differs from similar conceptualizations of leadership, particularly transformational leadership. Shamir and Eilam (2005) state that transformational leadership can be authentic or inauthentic. "Transformational leaders can be authentic or inauthentic and non-transformational leaders can be authentic" (p. 398). Relatedly, Avolio, et al. (2004) offer that "authentic leadership theory does not necessarily delve into the essence of transforming leadership articulated by Burns, which was to transform followers into leaders" (p. 807). While there are certainly similarities with other descriptions of leadership, authentic leadership, with its emphasis on core/root construct and positive emotions, offers a unique view of leadership available to all people.

› Chapter Summary

The studies on leadership theory are often described with what we call the "but" phenomenon. There are numerous theories on leadership, "but" we still know very little about if and how leaders make a difference and their effectiveness on the organization; leadership has been studied as a scientific discipline for several decades, "but" we still have made little progress; there are numerous research studies on leadership, "but" the results are often inconclusive and ambiguous.

Scholars, practitioners, and students of leadership are making considerable progress in reformulating their ideas and research questions to fit the changing nature of our organizations and our world. Leaders and leadership researchers are working collaboratively to forge new knowledge and discoveries about leadership processes in contemporary organizations. Scholars and researchers cannot work in isolation of individuals who practice leadership "out in the field" at all levels of an organization or in a community. As we continue to search for answers and knowledge about leadership, we see the glass as half full rather than half empty.

In this section, we also explored complexity leadership and adaptive leadership theories and noted how they are different from the linear, rational world that has been traditionally used as a model for how the world works. Leadership in this new world requires embracing rapid change, reframing identities and roles of leadership and participants, and continuous learning by all members of the organization and community. We have advanced our understanding of leadership as a byproduct of the interactions and processes of people together facilitating change and working from a common purpose. These are exciting, challenging, turbulent times in which to be alive. They call for new and different ways of conceptualizing and leading in organizations and the world.

Finally, we introduced the emergence of authentic leadership. With its focus on leadership as a core aspect of our very being; hope, trust, and positive emotions; and concern for understanding the attitudes and behaviors of followers, authentic leadership offers a new way for us to look at leadership.

❯ What's Next?

The next chapter presents a leadership model that emphasizes the role of relationships. This Relational Leadership Model highlights the importance of being inclusive, empowering, purposeful, ethical, and process-oriented.

❯ Chapter Activities

1. Describe your personal best leadership experience—an experience in which you were most effective. What theory or metaphor best describes your leadership approach and why?
2. What motivates you to take on leadership responsibilities or roles and why? Why do you lead?

3. For each of the leadership theory categories (trait, behavioral, and so on), provide examples of specific leaders and participants whose leadership can be described based upon that approach. Give examples of people who practice these theories.

4. Using Rost's postindustrial leadership definition and paradigm, describe how an organization, office, or community in which you belong would look like if this type of leadership was practiced. What would be the same? What would be different?

5. Think of a real example (one you experienced or observed or from current events) that is an example of complexity leadership theory in application. Describe the relationship of the participants and leaders. How is this example different from industrial models of leadership?

6. Identify an organization or community you are involved in. What would that organization look like if it was based on a shared leadership model. How might your own role be different?

7. Consider how Luthans and Avolio (2003) describe authentic leaders. Describe your own sense of hope and optimism. Similarly, consider the sense of hope and optimism within an organization with which you are familiar. How can you nurture the sense of hope and optimism in followers? How might a leader enhance the sense of hope and optimism within this organization?

8. Return to the definition of leadership complexity theory in this chapter. Identify an example of when you experienced or observed this theory in practice—in a real setting. How did this differ from traditional views of leadership?

ADDITIONAL READINGS

Avolio, B. J., & Gardner, W. L. (2005). Authentic leadership development: Getting to the root of positive forms of leadership. *Leadership Quarterly, 16,* 315–338.

Luthans, F., & Avolio, B. (2003). Authentic leadership development. In K. S. Cameron, J. E. Dutton, & R. E. Quinn (Eds.), *Positive organizational scholarship: Foundations for a new discipline* (pp. 241–258). San Francisco, CA: Berrett-Koehler.

Northouse, P. G. (2013). *Leadership: Theory and practice* (6th ed). Thousand Oaks, CA: Sage.

Pearce, C. L., & Conger, J. A. (2003). *Shared leadership: Reframing the hows and whys of leadership.* Thousand Oaks, CA: Sage.

Senge, P. M. (1990). *The fifth discipline: The art and practice of the learning organization.* New York, NY: Currency/Doubleday.

Wheatley, M. J. (2006). *Leadership and the new science: Discovering order in a chaotic world* (3rd ed). San Francisco, CA: Berrett-Koehler.

Chapter 3

∨

The Relational Leadership Model

◇

In the previous chapter, we reviewed how views of leadership have changed, from the belief that leaders are simply born to the idea that the best way to learn about leadership is to study the behaviors or practices of people who are viewed as leaders. Theorizing has evolved even further into an understanding of leadership as a complex process. Indeed, leadership is a transforming process that raises all participants to levels at which they can become effective leaders.

Leadership may best be understood as philosophy. At its core, understanding philosophy means understanding values. "Affect, motives, attitudes, beliefs, values, ethics, morals, will, commitment, preferences, norms, expectations, responsibilities—such are the concerns of leadership philosophy proper. Their study is paramount because the very nature of leadership is that of practical philosophy, philosophy-in-action" (Hodgkinson, 1983, p. 202). Exploring a philosophy of leadership identifies the fundamental essence of leadership. Those who study historical leaders are often analyzing the values and ethics that characterized their leadership.

> [P]hilosophical analysis . . . goes more like this: we live in a common world; we all have needs and hopes, feelings and ideals. We ask, What kind of people does it take to achieve these goals? and, more important, What kind of people does it take to help others achieve them, to create environments and societies—durable ones, sustainable ones—that will facilitate these goals? (Koestenbaum, 2002, p. xiii)

It is critical that we each develop our own personal philosophy— one we hope will include the elements of the model presented in this chapter.

> Chapter Overview

In this chapter we present a relational model of leadership to consider in building your own personal philosophy. We present each of the elements of the model in detail to give you more information about each component.

> Relational Leadership

Leadership has to do with relationships, the role of which cannot be overstated. Leadership is inherently a relational, communal process. "Leadership is always dependent on the context, but the context is established by the relationships we value" (Wheatley, 1992, p. 144). Although a person could exert leadership of ideas through persuasive writings or making speeches, most leadership happens in an interactive context between individuals and among group members. We emphasize once again: we view leadership as *a relational and ethical process of people together attempting to accomplish positive change.*

Chapter Two presented an overview of how leadership theories and models have changed over time. These changing frameworks are reflected in the descriptive terms that have been affixed to the word leadership. Examples of these leadership theories and concepts include situational, transforming, servant-leadership, authentic leadership, and principle-centered leadership. We have used the term *relational leadership* as a reminder that relationships are the focal point of the leadership process.

Relational leadership involves a focus on five primary components. This approach to leadership is purposeful and builds commitment toward positive purposes that are inclusive of people and diverse points of view, empowers those involved, is ethical, and recognizes that all four of these elements are accomplished by being process-oriented.

The model provides a frame of reference or an approach to leadership in teams and groups, as well as in contemporary organizations. With these foundational philosophies and commitments, an individual can make a meaningful contribution in any organization. This model is not a leadership theory in itself, and it does not address the change outcomes for which leadership is intended. The Relational Leadership Model does not seek to describe the way leadership is currently practiced in all groups or organizations; rather it is an aspirational model

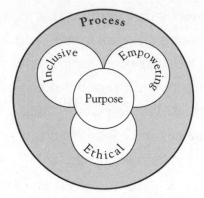

Figure 3.1 **Relational Leadership Model**

that we propose in developing and supporting a healthy, ethical,
effective group. It is a framework connecting five key elements
that can serve as a responsive approach to leadership. Figure 3.1
offers a visual image of the elements of the model.

The components of relational leadership are complex
concepts. Think about your own level of comfort or knowledge
about each component as you read the related dimensions
of each element. The model reflects how the organization's
or community's purpose influences the components of being
inclusive, empowering, and ethical. Purpose is the center of
the model, since it provides the context and focus of leadership
actions of individuals in a group. For example, the purpose of the
Habitat for Humanity Club on campus is to engage its members
to assist in providing houses for those who cannot afford them
on their own. The purpose includes others, empowers them
to use their leadership and talents to make a difference, and
is ethical in that it benefits others and improves the quality
of life in a community. How that purpose is achieved (the
process) is just as important as the outcome. How the goals are

accomplished and how others are involved in the process matters in the leadership process. The purpose is vision-driven and not position-driven. Leaders and members promote the organization's purpose through a shared vision and not for self-gain, such as achieving a higher leadership position or fame.

Table 3.1 identifies some important knowledge, attitudes, and skills that are embedded in each element. These reflect the knowledge, attitudes, and skills that would be helpful in understanding relational leadership. Brief applications of the core elements to the knowing-being-doing model conclude each section. For example, in order to practice being inclusive, you must

- Know yourself and others; engage yourself in learning new information as you develop the competencies required in your role (knowledge)
- Be open to difference and value other perspectives (attitudes)
- Practice listening skills, coalition building, interpersonal skills, and effective civil discourse (skills)

> Knowing-Being-Doing

Individuals involved in the leadership process (leaders, participants, co-creators, and so on) need to know themselves well before they can effectively work with others to influence change or achieve common purpose. It is not enough to simply drive an agenda or accomplish small or big wins. The leadership process calls for those engaged in it to be knowledgeable (knowing), to be aware of self and others (being), and to act (doing). The knowing-being-doing model represents a holistic approach

Table 3.1   **Relational Leadership Model Compared to Knowing-Being-Doing**

Leadership Component	Knowing (Knowledge and Understanding)	Being (Attitudes)	Doing (Skills)
Purposeful	How change occurs Core elements of change Role of mission or vision Shared values Common purpose	Hopeful Committed "Can do" attitude Likes improvement Commitment to social responsibility	Identifying goals Envisioning Meaning-making Creative thinking Involving others in vision-building process
Inclusive	Self and others Citizenship Frames and multiple realities	Open to difference Values equity Web-like thinking Believes everyone can make a difference	Talent development Listening skills Building coalitions Framing and reframing Civil discourse
Empowering	Power How policies or procedures block or promote empowerment Personal mastery Control is not possible	Believes each has something to offer Self-esteem Concern for others' growth Values others' contributions Willing to share power	Gate-keeping skills Sharing information Individual and team learning Encouraging or affirming others Capacity building Promoting self-leadership Practicing renewal

Table 3.1 **Relational Leadership Model Compared to Knowing-Being-Doing (*continued*)**

Leadership Component	Knowing (Knowledge and Understanding)	Being (Attitudes)	Doing (Skills)
Ethical	How values develop How systems influence justice and care Self and others' values Ethical decision-making models	Commitment to socially responsible behavior Confronting behavior Values integrity Trustworthy Authentic Establishes sense of personal character Responsible Expects high standards Puts benefit to others over self-gain	Being congruent Being trusting Being reliable Having courage Using moral imagination
Process-oriented	Community Group process Relational aspect of leadership Process is as important as outcomes	Values process as well as outcomes Quality effort Develops systems perspective	Collaboration Reflection Meaning making Challenge Civil confrontation Learning Giving and receiving feedback

to the leadership development of yourself and others. These three components are interrelated—the knowledge you possess can influence your ways of thinking, which can influence your actions. And it is also true that your beliefs and way of existing in this world (being) will influence your actions, which will influence your behaviors. This pattern of influence is circular and not on a straight path.

Other ways to view this holistic approach is by using the framework of knowledge, skills, and attitudes or head, heart, and practice. Palmer (1998) uses the phrase "head, heart, and practice" to describe the paradoxes in teaching and what happens when we keep the head (knowing and intellect) separated from the heart (being) and even further separated from practice (doing). Palmer argues that we need a synthesis of all three components in the teaching process. The same applies in the leadership process.

The Army coined the phrase "know, be, do" (Center for Army Leadership, 2004). People will collaborate with those who are credible (both leaders and members)—those who are knowing. Leaders need to demonstrate competence and maintain a certain amount of knowledge. Hesselbein and Shinseki (2004) offer four levels of skills essential to leadership: interpersonal skills, conceptual skills (ability to think creatively), technical skills (expertise required for position), and tactical skills (negotiation, human relations, and other skills necessary to achieve objectives) (p. 12). Knowing is an ongoing process that allows leaders to continue to develop, learn, and grow.

In the Army, the "be" means knowing what values and attributes define you as a leader (Hesselbein & Shinseki, 2004). "Your character helps you know what is right; more than that, it links that knowledge to action. Character gives you the courage to do what is right regardless of the circumstances or consequences" (p. 11). The Army's acronym of leadership is LDRSHIP: Loyalty, Duty, Respect, Selfless service, Honor, Integrity, Personal courage (p. 11). That is the essence of the "be" of leadership. The Lao Tzu quotations throughout this book are another example of being. This Eastern reflection of having a sense of self and being centered in self-awareness is important to relating well with others.

The "doing" of knowing and being means acting. Character and knowledge are not enough in facilitating change in the leadership process. Doing attempts to produce results, accomplishes the vision, creates change, and influences others to act. Sometimes leaders will fail to act because of indecision or due to a fixation on perfection. "Competent, confident leaders tolerate honest mistakes that are not the result of negligence. A leader who sets a standard of 'zero defects, no mistakes' is also saying, 'Don't take any chances' " (Hesselbein & Shinseki, 2004, p. 15). Being congruent is doing or acting in concert with your values and attitudes.

Learning is an outcome of the knowing-being-doing developmental model or feedback system. Be attuned to how new learning is changing your attitudes and behaviors or is changing you in general. It is important to reflect upon how and what you are learning as you go through those cycles. "Leaders promote learning in at least three ways: through their own learning on a personal level, by helping others in their units [organizations] learn, and by shaping and contributing to an organizational culture that promotes learning" (Hesselbein & Shinseki, 2004, p. 133).

As you continue reading this and the following chapters, consider how this model is adding to your knowledge. How can you take this information and incorporate it into your beliefs surrounding leadership? What actions can you take with this new knowledge? Consciously examining your thoughts, feelings, and actions allows you to continue to learn and grow as a leader and as a human being.

> Relational Leadership Is Purposeful

Being purposeful means having a commitment to a goal or activity. It is also the ability to collaborate and to find common ground with others to facilitate positive change. Creating positive change can mean working hard toward resolving differences among participants, finding a common direction, and building a shared vision to improve the organization or enhance others in some way. Even if a participant does not have a vision, that person knows enough to ask others, "Remind me what we are working toward. What do we all hope will happen?" Trusting the process, several in the group will chime in with their ideas, and someone will have the talent to express those words in terms of the vision and purpose that will bring nods of agreement from nearly every person present. It is important that all group members be able to articulate that purpose and use it as a driving force for collective action. That is an essential element in relational leadership.

The conventional paradigm of leadership often asserts that the positional leader must have a clear vision. Research, however, has shown two primary types of vision activity: personalized vision and socialized vision (Howell, 1988). Personalized vision refers to a person, usually the person with legitimate authority, announcing a dream or plan and imposing it on others. Participants seem to have little choice and must adopt this vision, which results in varying degrees of personal ownership or commitment. Imagine the board of trustees of a community college hiring a new president whose vision is to convert the community college to a four year college granting degrees in technology and allied health fields. That vision will drive all the president's actions, whether faculty, staff, or students agree.

Socialized vision is building a vision from among group members, recognizing that people support what they help create. Sharing vision does not mean that each person must possess a vision, but that each person must be involved in the process of building a vision with others. Such a vision is a picture of "a realistic, credible, attractive future" for yourself or your organization (Nanus, 1992, p. 8). Imagine that the same board of trustees empowers the new president with the challenge to take advantage of growth in the area and current market demand for college graduate and work with college personnel to identify this new future. An inclusive process and assessment of options might identify the same vision to be a four year college granting degrees in technology and allied health fields; or it may result in continuing to be a two year college but with an expanded online offering and new emphasis in STEM field supports. "Effective leaders don't just impose their vision on others, they recruit others to a shared vision. Especially in our digital age, when power tends to coalesce around ideas, not position, leadership is a partnership, not a sinecure" (Bennis & Thomas, 2002, p. 137). Think about your personality preferences. Do you have ideas about your future and a vision of how things might be? Do you think creatively and see possibilities in everything, or are you shaking your head right now, thinking "No way! This is hard for me."

After hearing a presentation on empowering leadership and the importance of shared vision, one of our colleagues approached us. She said, "I just am not creative and cannot articulate a vision. I am practical and realistic. I feel capable but am more of a maintainer than a builder. I can keep things going more than I am able to think them up in the first place." The first piece of advice that organization consultant Burt Nanus (1992) shares with those trying to avoid failures in organizational vision is, "Don't do it alone" (p. 167).

Being purposeful with a group vision that includes a positive change effort helps you set priorities and make decisions congruent with that dream. "Vision animates, inspirits, and transforms purpose into action" (Bennis & Goldsmith, 1994, p. 101). This action component to vision is described well by the engraving in an eighteenth-century church in Sussex, England:

> A vision without a task is but a dream,
> a task without a vision is drudgery,
> a vision and a task
> is the hope of the world.
>
> (*From* Transcultural Leadership, *p. 106, by* G. F. Simons, C. Vázquez, *& P. R. Harris. Copyright © 1993, with permission from Elsevier*)

"To be motivating, a vision must be a source of self-esteem and common purpose . . . The core of the vision is the organization's mission statement, which describes the general purpose of the organization" (Yukl, 1989, p. 336). One approach that is used by executives to develop shared visions is an exercise involving magazine articles. Organizational members are asked to identify their favorite magazine or a magazine closely related to the organization's purpose and write a feature story that will describe the organization in the future (four or five years from the present) using headlines (Yukl). This powerful activity allows everyone to dream together and to begin the visioning process using creativity, imagination, and passion.

Your individual, purposeful commitment to the shared vision of a group project means you will do your part, share resources, and support your teammates because you expect the same of them. Vision guides action. "It's not what a vision is, it's what a vision does" (Kazuo Inamori, as cited in Senge, 1990, p. 207). A vision of a homecoming weekend reaching the broadest possible group of alumni will guide all the committee's choices about how to diversify that event.

A vision inspires energy and purpose. The late General Norman Schwarzkopf observed, "I have found that in order to be a leader, you are almost serving a cause" (Wren, 1994, p. 4). Purposeful participants have emotionally identified with a purpose and a dream. "There is no more powerful engine driving an organization toward excellence and long-range success than an attractive, worthwhile, and achievable vision of the future, widely shared" (Nanus, 1992, p. 3).

> Working for Positive Change

One common purpose that pulls people together is working toward change. Change processes can have various motives associated with them. The Relational Leadership Model supports positive change—that is, change that improves the human condition and that does not intentionally harm others. The antithesis of this is facilitating change that is destructive, like the attacks on the World Trade Center in New York City.

In his classic *Leadership for the Twenty-first Century*, Rost (1991) proposed that leadership happens when the group *intends* to accomplish change, not just when they *do* accomplish change. Having the intention of improving a situation, accomplishing a task, or implementing a common purpose is part of the change process. Change may not happen for many reasons, but the core fact that the group intended to make a difference is central. John Parr (1994), president of the National Civic League, writes, "Positive change can occur when people with different perspectives are organized into groups in which everyone is regarded as a peer. There must be a high level of involvement, a clear purpose, adequate resources, and the power to decide and implement" (p. xiii).

Some situations are profoundly hard to change. It is hard to move away from the status quo—the way things are. Change theory proposes that change often begins when something unfreezes a situation. The cycle is often presented as unfreezing → changing → refreezing. This "unfreezing" may be caused by a trigger event, such as a carjacking in a remote campus parking lot, a campus riot following a sporting event, a hate crime, or a disappointingly small attendance at a group's expensive activity. People pay attention to the problem with a focus they did not have prior to the incident. Unfreezing may also occur when external policies change—when a new law is enacted, for example. Unfreezing makes it possible to address an issue or policy that has not commanded the attention of those who need to address it. The change process is then engaged and the issue is addressed.

Even after a change is implemented, it would be an error in these times even to consider any issue "refrozen." Instead, it is best to consider the outcome to be "slush," so that the solution is seen not as final but as permeable and open to be readdressed easily. It may be best to consider solutions as automatically open for review, regularly evaluated, and flexible. The classic change model (Lewin, 1958), describing the change process as moving from the present state through a transition state to a desired state, still works, but we encourage caution that the desired state should now be viewed as less rigid.

Change can be thought of as moving some situation away from the status quo to a different place and positive change would mean to a better place. To understand why that movement is hard, examine the driving forces pushing for change and the resisting forces striving to keep change from happening to preserve the status quo. Clearly, not all change is appropriate or supportable. When it is, the driving forces working toward change should be enhanced and the restraining forces minimized. This "force-field analysis" is a classic and useful method for identifying aspects of the situation that could enhance change (Lippitt, 1969, p. 157).

Kotter and Cohen (2002) refer to the concept of "removing barriers in the mind" as another reason that people are resistant to change or to changing. "After years of stability, incremental change, or failed attempts at change, people can internalize a deep belief that they are not capable of achieving a leap. They may not say out loud 'I can't do it,' but at some level they feel it, even when it is not true" (p. 112). It is important to understand that the mind can both disempower and empower individuals toward change.

We are constantly faced with the dynamic tension of how things are and how we think they ought to be. This "is-ought" dichotomy asks us to face reality but work toward true transformative change, real change—to move toward the more hopeful vision. This "creative tension" brings energy to the change effort (Senge, 1990, p. 150). Connecting personal hopes and commitments to a group vision is a creative process. This process can be time-consuming. As we describe more fully in Chapter Eight, when a group is newly formed, the process of building a group vision can be energetic and hopeful if the group quickly comes to agreement and commitment, or it can be anxious and cautious if the group shows little agreement. When joining an ongoing group in which a vision has already been established, new participants have to determine whether they can connect to that vision or feel they can help shape the continued evolution of the group's vision over time.

> Relational Leadership Is Inclusive

Being inclusive means understanding, valuing, and actively engaging diversity in views, approaches, styles, and aspects of individuality, such as gender or culture, that add multiple perspectives to a group's activity. As a foundation for valuing inclusion, you will have a chance to explore your own attitudes and attributes in Chapter Four and examine those of others in Chapter Five. Table 3.1 highlights aspects of being inclusive to illustrate how you might explore this component. It means understanding how different groups or individuals

STUDENT ESSAY ◆

Elected president of the ISACA Chapter at Miami University for the spring of 2011, I had immediate concerns for our chapter's welfare. We were experiencing declining membership, dwindling participation, and decreased professional event opportunities. These trends necessitated revitalizing our chapter before it became nonexistent, so I called the executive team to action with a sense of purpose.

I explained the chapter's dire situation during our first executive meeting, emphasizing the importance that we take immediate action to stem the negative downturn we were experiencing before we ceased to exist. Suggesting that the executive team silently contemplate the potential fate of our chapter, I followed by seeking resounding team commitment to revitalization. Rallying to the call, our whole team agreed to put forth the intense effort required.

The team's new sense of purpose provided tremendous motivation and focus; nearly doubling our chapter's membership, greatly increasing membership participation, and providing significant professional event opportunities. The purpose instilled in our executive team to ensure our chapter's successful future produced the best year in our chapter's recent history. Leading with purpose assures our ISACA Chapter will remain both available and influential at Miami University for many years to come.

Jonathan Tudor is a 2012 honors and business honors graduate of Miami University where he majored in management Information systems and minored in game studies. He was president of the Information Systems Auditing and Control Association (ISACA) Miami Chapter, CIO of Miami Business Consulting, cofounder of the Miami University Video Game Design Club, and a member of Beta Gamma Sigma and Phi Kappa Phi.

might approach issues from different perspectives or frames, maintaining the attitudes that respect differences, building on each others' strengths, and valuing equity and involvement. It means thinking of networks and webs of connection instead of seeing issues and problems as isolated and discrete. Who else on campus—what people, offices—care about an issue that also concerns your group? Being inclusive embraces having the skills to develop the talent of members so they can be readily involved. Listening with empathy and communicating with civility are communication skills that facilitate the inclusion of others. Inclusiveness breeds new leadership and creates a positive cycle that sustains the quality of an organization over time.

You saw in the last chapter that although many things seem unpredictable and even unconnected, there is unity in nature; seemingly unrelated parts influence each other as well as the whole. By applying these concepts to the leadership world, we learn to understand that the group or organization represents unity or wholeness built from and influenced greatly by the smallest subunits of that system. "As we move away from viewing the organization as a complex of parts and deal with it as a unity, then problems met in leadership can make more sense and solutions become obvious" (Fairholm, 1994, p. 59).

Individuals are important because they concurrently represent and influence the whole. The purpose, vision, and values of the whole come to life as each individual member describes and applies them. The goal is not to overcome the variations and differences among participants—indeed, those variations bring creativity and energy—but to build shared purpose. Being inclusive means developing the strengths and talent of group members so they can contribute to the group's goals.

"Leading others to lead themselves is the key to tapping the intelligence, the spirit, the creativity, the commitment, and most of all, the tremendous, unique potential of each individual" (Manz & Sims, 1989, p. 225).

> Leaders enhance the learning of others, helping them to develop their own initiative, strengthening them in the use of their own judgment, and enabling them to grow and to become better contributors to the organization. These leaders, by virtue of their learning, then become leaders and mentors to others. (McGill & Slocum, 1993, p. 11)

It is not sufficient just to be a participative leader involving group members in the work of the organization. Organizations have to go further and recognize that in many cases the organizational culture has to change to involve effectively people who have different backgrounds and different views and who may not embrace the dominant cultural norms. In addition to its practice, the language of inclusivity is exceptionally important. How we talk about people in the organization, how we refer to them (colleagues versus subordinates or participants versus followers), and how the organization is structured are indicators of inclusive environments (Hesselbein, 2002). Think about the message being sent by using the word *we* instead of the word *I*. You might engage in a conversation with someone and hear an excessive use of the word *I* from that person. What impression did that individual make on you? Did you feel engaged in the conversation? Hesselbein (2002) describes the model of inclusion best by stating, from her own experiences,

> Building the inclusive, cohesive, vibrant institution does indeed require the biggest basket in town—for it has to have room for all of

us. Not just the favored few, those who look alike and think alike, but all who are part of the community of the future. When equal access prevails, the synergy of inclusion propels us far beyond the old gated enclaves of the past into the richness of opportunities that lie beyond the walls. (p. 20)

Groups would benefit by examining practices that might block inclusivity. A group might be so accustomed to voting on every decision that it has alienated members who find this process uncomfortable. Those members might like to use a consensus model of decision making to ensure that the views of all are included in each significant decision. For example, the extreme use of Robert's Rules of Order has the potential to cut off discussion when issues are unresolved and the direction is unclear. Another illustration is when a student union program committee traditionally provides music or movies of interest to only one segment of the campus. The committee would need to examine that practice and involve others with different interests in order to diversify programming. Organizational practices, such as always meeting at 9 p.m., might exclude the involvement of people such as adult learners and those who cannot be on campus at that time because of family or work obligations, or because commuting is a problem. When the group realizes, for example, that no commuter students, or students of color, or men are involved in their activities, that should be a signal that something is wrong. Other ways of communicating and consulting with people should be found, as should other ways of including diverse interests in group decision making.

STUDENT ESSAY

One of the most significant concepts I have been introduced to through my work in WE LEAD is public dialogue. In November of 2011, a group of students, a faculty advisor, and I planned and moderated a public dialogue forum concerning prescription drug abuse in West Virginia. I had never participated in that type of event, and I had no idea that it would be such a transforming experience. The atmosphere felt in that room full of law enforcement offers, local politicians, businessmen, community members, and students was one of empowerment, awareness, and unity. Each participant voiced opinions, and some shared their personal stories on the subject. For some it was a moment of enlightenment on the subject, and for others it was a moment during which they realized they were not alone. I had no idea that simply gathering people to talk about an issue could be so productive. One of the greatest aspects of WE LEAD is that it introduces students to various different types of leadership and problem-solving strategies that are often overlooked.

Justin Frye is a graduate of West Virginia Wesleyan College where he majored in exercise science. He was an active member and coordinator of the WE LEAD (Wesleyan Engaging Leaders through Education, Awareness & Development) Health & Wellness Issue Team, executive member of Student Senate, and a representative of the student ambassador program.

> Involving Those External to the Group

Being inclusive also means identifying the shareholders and stakeholders external to the group who have some responsibility (a share) or interest (a stake) in the change that is being planned. It would be exclusive, not inclusive, for a group to assume that they should or could accomplish a major change alone. For example, an organization like the Latino Student Union might seek to change a campus practice about how scholarship programs are advertised to new Latino students. Being inclusive means the Latino Student Union should also consider which other campus groups or offices might be stakeholders in resolving this issue because they have a shared interest or could be affected by the consequences of any action (Bryson & Crosby, 1992). The Latino Student Union might then reach out to form coalitions or some involvement with such groups as the Council of Black Fraternity and Sorority Chapters, the Black Student Union, the Multicultural Affairs Committee of the Student Government Association, and other related student organizations such as the Honors Program. In addition, the Latino Student Union should identify the shareholders in resolving the issue—the Financial Aid Office, the Dean of Students Office, and the Office of Minority Affairs. Staff in each of these offices would want to get the word out to students about their programs and need not be thought of as negative or antagonistic to the changes. They might in fact appreciate help in resolving problems they too experience in the current process.

Stakeholders may not all hold the same view of a problem, and they may not all seek the same solutions. Bryson and Crosby (1992) clarify how a stakeholder's position on an issue (ranging from high support to high opposition) is influenced by the importance with which they view the issue (ranging from least important to most important). This makes stakeholders' responses more understandable (see Figure 3.2). As they work

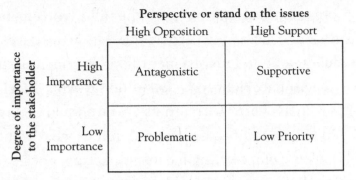

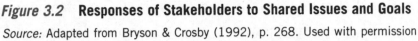

Figure 3.2 **Responses of Stakeholders to Shared Issues and Goals**

Source: Adapted from Bryson & Crosby (1992), p. 268. Used with permission

toward being more inclusive, relational leaders will want to assess possible stakeholder reactions in determining their approaches.

Even if stakeholders disagree on an issue, they should be involved. Involvement helps stakeholders gain new views on issues and may build support among various stakeholders toward an intended change. They also bring in an outside viewpoint, which contributes to the overall knowledge of the group. Stakeholders might see dimensions of an issue that the group is blind to. Building support and forming coalitions are related skills for relational leaders.

❯ Relational Leadership Is Empowering

"Thriving on change demands the empowerment of every person in the organization—no ifs, ands, or buts" (Peters, 1989, p. xiv). Empowerment has two dimensions: (1) a sense of self that claims ownership, claims a place in the process, and expects to be involved, and (2) a set of environmental conditions (in the group or organization) that promote the full involvement of participants by reducing the barriers that block the development of individual talent and involvement. Empowerment is claimed ("I have a legitimate right to be here and say what I feel and think") as well as shared with others ("You should be involved in this; you have a right to be here too; tell us what you think and feel"). Being empowering means mitigating aspects of the organizational climate that can block meaningful involvement for others. Empowering environments are learning climates in which people expect successes yet know they can learn from failures or mistakes. It is important to establish organizational environments that empower others to do and to be their best.

The root word in the concept of empowerment is power. Understanding power dynamics is essential in moving toward a philosophical commitment to empowerment. Where possible, positional leaders must be willing to share their power or authority, and participants must be willing to assume more responsibility for group outcomes. Power has traditionally been viewed on a zero-sum basis. Conventional approaches assumed that if one person in an organization is very powerful, then some-one else has less power. In truth, different types of power exist concurrently among people in any kind of relationship. Power dynamics range from power "over" (autocratic approaches) to power "with" (collaborative approaches) or power "alongside" (collegial approaches). Some approaches to leadership would go further and describe power "from," referring to the authority and power afforded to a leader from a group of participants. Effective positional leaders know that their power and ability to be effective comes from the members of their group—their participants (Kouzes & Posner, 1987).

Sources of Power

How a person uses power and reacts to the power of others must be examined in relational leadership. In their classic work, French and Raven (1959) identify five primary sources of power that individuals bring to their relationships with others. These bases of social power are expert power, referent power, legitimate power, coercive power, and reward power. As noted in Table 3.2, they later added informational power to this taxonomy (Raven & Kruglanski, 1975).

Expert power is the power of skills or competences. Expertise may come through professional development and formal education (such as that received by engineers or medical doctors) or from extended experience (such as being the mother of three

Table 3.2 **French and Raven's Bases of Power**

Type	Definition
Reward	The person can deliver positive consequences or remove negative consequences.
Coercive	The person can deliver negative consequences or remove positive consequences.
Legitimate	Group members believe the person ought to have power because of his or her position or responsibilities.
Reference	Group members do what the person wants out of respect, liking, and wanting to be liked.
Expert	Group members believe the person has a special knowledge or skill and is trustworthy.
Informational	Group members believe the person has useful knowledge not available elsewhere.

Adapted from Johnson & Johnson (2006), p. 237.

children or being a seasoned baseball player). We trust experts and give them power over us based on their assumed higher level of knowledge or experience.

Referent power refers to the nature and strength of a relationship between two or more people. Think of the wise senior who is so highly regarded that her words carry great weight in the group discussion.

Legitimate power is due to the formal role a person holds, usually because he or she has the responsibility and authority to exert some degree of power. For instance, the president of a student organization has power to make certain decisions due to the nature of his or her role. The instructor can decide to make a grade change when a student asks for a review of a grade on a paper. However, those in authority generally know that their legitimate power is fragile.

Coercive power influences individuals or groups through imposing or threatening punitive sanctions or removing rewards or benefits. Coercion accomplishes behavior change but usually at great cost to the relationships among those involved. Because leadership is an influence relationship, it is essential that this influence be "noncoercive" (Rost, 1993, p. 105).

Conversely, reward power influences behavior through the ability to deliver positive outcomes and desired resources. Rewards may be extrinsic, like raises, plaques, or special privileges. They may also be intrinsic—intangibles like praise or support.

Informational power is attributed a person who has information needed by the group and not available anywhere else. This source of power may be evidenced in highly effective verbal or written communication, including "rational argument, actual data, and logic" (Johnson & Johnson, 2006, p. 237). Although it may be similar to expert power, a person with informational power may not be an expert in a field but has a source of information needed by the group.

You may intentionally use some source of power. For example, you might download the student handbook on your laptop so you can read the university's rule on a topic to the group when needed. Conversely, others may attribute some source of power to you without your knowing what is happening, as, for example, when someone fears your disapproval because you have referent power or that person perceives you to have coercive power. To empower ourselves and others, it is essential to understand power.

Understanding Power

In many cases, we give power away. We do it when we do not trust our own opinion if it contradicts that of an expert. We assume the expert knows more. Yet when the doctor too readily concludes that you just need bed rest and you know it's something more serious, you should insist that your doctor explore other alternatives. When the person with legitimate power announces a plan or an approach, we give power away if we do not say, "We would like to talk about that approach first because we might have some additional ideas that would be helpful." We may also have power attributed to us that is undeserved. When the group assumes that because you are an English major you would be best at writing the group's report, they may be in error.

Power is not finite and indeed can be shared and amplified. Some think that power should be framed differently and seen in a similar frame as love: the more you give away, the more you get. If the leadership paradigm of your colleagues is very conventional, they may see the sharing of power as indecisiveness or an avoidance of responsibility. Others may abuse the power shared with them, but those in legitimate authority roles who share their power usually find that they build stronger groups.

For the society to get its work done, leaders and the systems over which they preside must be granted some measure of power. It is a common experience for leaders today to have far less power than they need to accomplish the tasks that we hand them. They must have the power to get results (Gardner, 2003, p. 201).

Gardner (2003) goes on to say that those who hold power must be held accountable. Leaders are in a greater position of power when they hold themselves accountable first before waiting for others to implement a system of checks and balances.

Hoarding power in leadership risks negative responses from others, such as sabotage, withdrawal, resistance, anger, and other behaviors that would contradict the positive goals and objectives of the group. "The key gift that leaders can offer is power" (Bolman & Deal, 2003, p. 341). When people can use and hear their voices in the life of an organization or community, they will feel a sense of justice and a belief that they matter.

Self-Empowerment

Empowerment is claiming the power you should have from any position in the organization. Self-empowerment then is the recognition that you have a legitimate right to be heard and the self-confidence to be part of a solution or the change process. "The E-word by itself, is a non sequitur unless it's used with self-discovery . . . it provides a means of empowering yourself as you explore your natural, educational, and professional attributes in sizing up your leadership prospects" (Haas & Tamarkin, 1992, p. 35). Murrell (1985, pp. 36–37) presents six methods through which you might become empowered:

1. Educating (discovering/sharing information and knowledge)
2. Leading (inspiring, rewarding, directing)
3. Structuring (creating structural factors such as arranging your day, bringing people to the table, changing policies or processes so that the change lives beyond the people who created it)
4. Providing (making sure others have resources to get their job done)
5. Mentoring (having close personal relationships)
6. Actualizing (taking it on—being empowered—claiming it)

Valuing the empowerment of all members creates a larger group of participants or citizens who generally take more ownership of group tasks and processes and who feel committed to the outcomes of the change. Practicing empowerment creates leader-full organizations instead of merely leader-led organizations.

Mattering and Marginality

Empowerment places you at the center of what is happening rather than at the edges, where you might feel inconsequential. This may be understood best by examining the concepts of mattering and marginality. Schlossberg (1989b) has extended and

STUDENT ESSAY

The best leaders do their work from the ground up. They are among their constituents, not above them, demonstrating the very ideals and actions that they ask from them. These leaders empower the members of their group to take ownership and to invest in the cause. Empowerment is one of the most impactful tools a leader can have, and it requires communication of purpose, articulation of goals, infusement of spirit, and a true understanding of the people and the environment you engage. A great example of student empowerment is through Pillars for Carolina, an extended orientation at the University of South Carolina. Through this week-long event, underclassmen are empowered to serve as staff and mentors to incoming freshmen, teaching them traditions of the campus, how to get involved once the semester starts, and important resources they will need to thrive in the collegiate atmosphere. Not only are these leaders investing in their school and its future leaders, but they are also empowering the first-year students to take ownership of their new adventure in the college realm. Only in its second year, Pillars has already seen a great deal of success, with both the mentors and former participants serving in other vital leadership roles on campus. Together these students are equipping each other to be great leaders, and they are in the process of empowering the whole campus to grow and progress.

Nick Riley is a recent graduate of the University of South Carolina where he majored in chemistry and psychology. Now pursuing a Ph.D. in analytical chemistry at the University of Wisconsin, he frequently calls on the leadership skills he gained through involvement with a wide array of student organizations, investment in community service, and his time playing club sports.

applied the work of sociologist Morris Rosenberg on mattering to her own work in studying adults in transition. "Mattering is a motive: the feeling that others depend on us, are interested in us, are concerned with our fate . . . [which] exercises a powerful influence on our actions" (Rosenberg & McCullough, as cited in Schlossberg, 1989b, p. 8). In new situations, in new roles, or with new people, we may feel marginal, as if we do not matter unless the group welcomes us and seeks our meaningful involvement. In contrast, mattering is the feeling that we are significant to others and to the process. Think of the anxiety and perhaps marginalization of potential new members coming to their first meeting of the Campus Environmental Coalition—or any group. They could be scarcely noticed, become isolated, and perhaps be ignored, or they could be welcomed, involved, and engaged, and know that they matter. Think about the positive feelings imparted to a first-year student when an upper-class veteran of an organization requests his or her opinion on an issue.

Empowering Environments

Groups, organizations, or environments can promote mattering or can keep people on the periphery—in the margins. We need environments that promote the development of the human spirit on a local scale, thus creating a "fundamental shift of mind, in which individuals come to see themselves as capable of creating the world they truly want rather than merely reacting to circumstances beyond their control" (Kiefer & Senge, 1984, p. 68).

Empowerment is likely to happen in organizational environments where people recognize that things can always be better than they are now. Empowering organizations seek to eliminate fear or humiliation and operate on trust and inclusivity. If you do not feel empowered in a particular group, you might assess the dynamics in the organization to see if they are encouraging or controlling. There may be an in-group and an out-group, and those in the out-group are excluded from access to information and opportunities to shape decisions (Kohn, 1992). Hazing is an unfortunate practice of those in the in-group abusing those in the out-group with the misguided logic of testing their fitness or commitment. When this is physically or mentally harmful, it has no place in truly empowering environments. If the organizational dynamics are basically supportive, however, perhaps you need to enhance your self-empowerment by building competencies, networks, or attributes to let you make a meaningful contribution.

Empowerment and delegation are not the same thing. A leader cannot give tasks to participants to do, no matter how important those assignments may be, and simply assume that participants will subsequently feel empowered. Indeed, if the leader retains a great deal of power or control when delegating, participants may feel manipulated, unprepared, resentful, or victimized. Conversely, if a positional leader has clearly acted congruently in sharing authority and responsibility with the group and has its trust, then sharing tasks can be empowering and can enhance community. Empowerment is achieved by enabling the involvement of group members and conveying faith in them.

> Relational Leadership Is Ethical

A seven-year-old goes into the grocery store with his father. Upon arriving home, the father discovers that little Johnny has a pocketful of candy that was not a part of the purchase. Horrified at Johnny's stealing, the father demands that Johnny return the candy to the store, confess to the store manager, apologize for his behavior, and promise never to steal from any store again. For some of us, an incident like this was our first real lesson in what is good and what is bad, what is virtuous and what is immoral. Early in our lives, in lessons such as this one, we were taught to value honesty over dishonesty, kindness over cruelty, and doing the right thing over breaking the law.

Ethical and Moral Leadership

The Relational Leadership Model emphasizes ethical and moral leadership, meaning leadership that is driven by values and standards and leadership that is good—moral—in nature. The language we use to examine ethical, moral leadership is of utmost importance. Some have a tendency to use the terms *ethics* and *morals* interchangeably (Henderson, 1992; Walton, 1988). Others differentiate between them, yet draw a strong relationship between ethics and morals (Shea, 1988). Shaw and Barry (1989) define ethics as "the social rules that govern and limit our conduct, especially the ultimate rules concerning right and wrong" (pp. 2–3).

The derivation of ethics is from *ethos*, from the Greek word for "character" and "sentiment of the community" (Toffler, 1986, p. 10). Other definitions of ethics include "the principles of conduct governing an individual or a profession" and "standards of behavior" (Shea, 1988, p. 17). Being ethical means "conforming to the standards of a given profession or group. Any group can set its own ethical standards and then live by them or not" (Toffler, 1986, p. 10). Ethical standards, whether they are established by an individual or an organization, help guide a person's decisions and actions. For the purposes of this model, ethics will be defined as "rules or standards that govern behaviors" (Toffler, 1986, p. 10).

Bill George, author of *True North* (2007), used the metaphor of true north as a leader's internal compass to illustrate the importance of staying true to one's values and principles, even in the face of adversity or when you might be tempted to deviate from your core values. George (2007) asserts that your values are the foundation of your true north and your leadership principles "are values translated into action " (p. 86).

Professions often establish codes of ethics or standards that serve as normative expectations for people in a particular profession. Lawyers must adhere to the American Bar Association's code of ethics for attorneys, and the American Medical Association promotes a code of ethics for physicians. Every McDonald's restaurant prominently displays a code of standards that pledges excellence in its food and service. Upon closer examination, these organizations are promoting standards by which they expect professionals and employees to live.

Moral means "relating to principles of right and wrong" (Toffler, 1986, p. 10) or "arising from one's conscience or a sense of good and evil; pertaining to the discernment of good and evil; instructive of what is good or evil (bad)" (Shea, 1988, p. 17). Morals are commonly thought to be influenced by religion or personal beliefs. Moral leadership is concerned with "good" leadership; that is, leadership with good means and good ends.

Our philosophy of leadership is values-driven. Again, our definition underscores this: leadership is a relational and ethical process of people together attempting to accomplish positive change. Using this philosophy, leaders and participants act out of a sense of shared values—the desire to cause real change and a commitment to mutual purposes. The actions of leaders and participants emanate from a set of values, which we hope are congruent and shared. Values are "freely chosen personal beliefs" (Lewis, 1990, p. 9) or the "guiding principles in our lives with respect to the personal and social ends we desire" (Kouzes & Posner, 1993, p. 60). Simply stated, values are our personal beliefs.

Although there is much disagreement in the leadership literature over definitions and theory, and about whether leadership is values-neutral or values-driven, it is safe to say that most people expect leaders to do the right thing. A 2003 Gallup Poll on Governance found that only 53% of those surveyed had "a great deal" or "a fair amount" of trust in the government of their state (Jones, 2003, p. 1). Trust in state governments has declined since the events of September 11, 2001. Securing and keeping the trust of your constituencies is central to leadership. A Gallup Youth Survey conducted in 2003 revealed that 67% of youth between the ages of 13 and 17 reported "a great deal" to "a fair amount" of cheating in their schools, with half of them indicating that they also cheated (Kidder, 2005, p. 267).

The Harris Poll showed a sharp decline of the percentage of American people polled stating they have high levels of confidence in Congress from the highest levels of confidence at 43% in 1966 dropping sharply to about 7% in 2011 (Hurley, 2012). A similar trend was found in the Harris Poll when identifying what percentage of people had great levels of confidence in business. In 1966, 55% of people polled reported having high levels of confidence in business in the United States while only 13% reported that same level of confidence in 2011 (Hurley, 2012).

A major factor in the loss of confidence in these sectors was the lack of trust in these leaders.

College students, however, want to be part of the solution. An Association of American Colleges and Universities 2007 study (Dey & Associates, 2008 cited in O'Neill, 2012) of education for personal and social responsibility, found that "more than 90 percent of twenty-four thousand students surveyed at twenty-three institutions agreed that education for personal and social responsibility—which encompasses outcomes such as striving for excellence, contributing to a larger community, and taking seriously the perspectives of others—*should be* a major focus of college" (p. 7). The study reported that of that large number in agreement, "more than 50 percent of students *strongly* agreed that this kind of education should be a major focus on campus" (p. 7). This study also included responses from over 9,000 college administrators and educators, including faculty, student affairs professionals, and senior academic administrators, "more than 90 percent agreed that personal and social responsibility outcomes should be a major focus of the institution, and more than seven in ten strongly agreed" (O'Neill, 2012, p. 7). There appears to be a gap in what students and educators expect of college and what happens in reality.

> Nearly one-half of students overall strongly agreed that they came to college aware of the importance of contributing to the greater good, but only one-third strongly agreed that the campus had helped them to expand their awareness, to learn the skills necessary to change society for the better, or to deepen their commitment to change society for the better. (O'Neill, 2012, p. 20)

Your study of ethical leadership in college is a critical experience for your future roles.

As leaders and citizens, our challenge today is to close the gap between our expectations of ethical leadership and the reality of frequent breaches of ethical conduct by those in leadership roles. We need bold, courageous leadership—leadership that is by word and deed ethical and moral. It is encouraging that a growing number of people express their abhorrence of the breaches of ethical conduct by national and local leaders and that a vast majority of the populace believe that ethics play a critical role in leadership. It is particularly encouraging that recent studies of college students (O'Neill, 2012) affirm that students value this as part of their college experience.

Former Secretary of Health, Education, and Welfare and President of Common Cause John Gardner (1990) thoughtfully makes the connection between shared values and a moral commitment to do the right thing:

> In any functioning society everything—leadership and everything else—takes place within a set of shared beliefs concerning the standards of acceptable behavior that must govern individual members. One of the tasks of leadership—at all levels—is to revitalize those shared beliefs and values, and to draw on them as sources of motivation for the exertions required of the group. Leaders can help to keep the values fresh. They can combat the hypocrisy that proclaims values at the same time that it violates them. They can help us understand our history and our present dilemmas. They have a role in creating the state of mind that is the society. Leaders must conceive and articulate goals in ways that lift people out of their petty preoccupations and unite them toward higher ends. (p. 191)

Gardner implies that leadership "toward higher ends" is ethical in nature and includes positive, constructive ends rather than results or outcomes that are destructive, harmful, or immoral.

To underscore the importance of the relationship between leadership and ethics, we join with those scholars who propose that ethics is the central core of leadership. Without a commitment to doing the right thing or a sound code of ethical standards, leadership cannot emerge. Although some argue that the phrase "ethical leadership" is redundant because leadership cannot be experienced without an element of ethics, we feel that leadership that lacks ethical behavior and actions is anything but leadership. Consider the example of Adolf Hitler. Indeed, right now you may be thinking that Hitler was a leader but you are averse to what he was leading, and some leadership theorists would agree with you. We share the views of other scholars, however, that Hitler's actions were not aligned with our notions of leadership. They were acts of dictatorship (Burns, 1978).

Burns (1978) elevates the importance of values and ethics in the leadership process through his theory of transforming leadership. He notes that

> the ultimate test of moral leadership is its capacity to transcend the claims of multiplicity of everyday wants and needs and expectations, to respond to the higher levels of moral development, and to relate leadership behavior—its roles, choices, style, commitments—to a set of reasoned, relatively explicit, conscious values. (p. 46)

Aligned with Burns's bold thinking to cast leadership in a moral foundation is the 1990s shift in societal views, from leadership as values-neutral to leadership as values-driven (Beck & Murphy, 1994; Bok, 1982, 1990; Gandossy & Effron, 2004; Kouzes & Posner, 2002; Northouse, 2004; Piper, Gentile, & Parks, 1993). Moral or ethical leadership is driven by knowing what is virtuous and what is good.

Leading by Example

As an exercise, a leader and a participant must ponder soul-searching questions such as, What do I stand for? How far am I willing to go to advance the common good or to do the right thing? Based on their research on leaders, Kouzes and Posner (2008) propose five practices of exemplary leadership. One of these practices is "Modeling the Way" or practicing what one preaches. Their findings show how important it is that leaders live the values they espouse. Being congruent with one's values helps one be perceived as an authentic leader (Avolio & Gardner, 2005).

Leading by example is a powerful way to influence the values and ethics of an organization. This means aligning your own values with the worthy values of the organization. Exemplary leadership includes a congruency between values and actions. The aphorism attributed to Ralph Waldo Emerson—"What you do speaks so loudly that I cannot hear what you say"—implies an even greater emphasis on the importance of values being congruent with actions. Nobel Peace Prize recipient Jimmy Carter is the first contemporary president said to have pursued higher goals after the presidency. Indeed, his work in diplomacy and in community service such as Habitat for Humanity attests to the congruence between his values and his actions. It is one thing to profess values and quite another to act on them.

The task of leading by example is not an easy one. Most, if not all, leaders begin with the goal of wanting to do the right thing. Some leaders get derailed by peer pressure or the temptation to trade leading for the common good with leading for personal gain or the uncommon good. What sustains ethical and moral leadership is a stubborn commitment to high standards, which include honesty and trustworthiness, authenticity, organizational values, and doing the right thing. It takes courage and chutzpah to stand among your peers and advocate a decision that is right yet unpopular. Imagine the tremendous courage of a student who steps in and stops his peers from flipping over a car during a campus riot. Or the fraternity chapter member, band member, or ROTC junior officer who says, "No, I do not think we should make our pledges drink until they pass out and then drop them off naked in the woods. It is not only dangerous but it is not how I want to bring them into our brotherhood. I won't be a part of it, and I hope you will not either. I will help plan activities that are fun and more worthwhile, but we cannot do this."

Although it appears that we are stating the obvious by stressing the importance of leading by example and with integrity, there are, regrettably, numerous accounts of local and national leaders who have been caught embezzling, putting humans at risk for the sake of profit, and hiding the truth. Richard M. Nixon began his presidency with good intentions and then succumbed to political corruption. Leading with integrity is not a neat and tidy process, yet it probably is the driving force that allows leaders to continue in their capacities. We will return to the topic of ethical leadership in Chapter Six with a closer examination of ethical decision making, ethical theories, and creating and sustaining ethical environments in groups and organizations.

> Relational Leadership Is About Process

Process refers to how the group goes about being a group, remaining a group, and accomplishing a group's purposes. It refers to the recruitment and involvement of members, how the group makes decisions, and how the group handles the tasks related to its mission and vision. Every group has a process, and every process can be described. Processes must be intentional and not accidental. The process component of the Relational Leadership Model means that individuals interact with others and that leaders and other participants work together to accomplish change. The process creates energy, synergy, and momentum.

When asked how her view of the universe as orderly in its chaotic state has influenced her work with organizations, Wheatley (1992) observed, "The time I formerly spent on detailed planning and analysis I now use to look at the structures that might facilitate relationships. I have come to expect that something useful occurs if I link up people, units, or tasks, even though I cannot determine precise outcomes" (pp. 43–44). When groups design and implement ethical, inclusive, empowering processes that further a shared purpose, they can trust the processes to take them through difficult times, resolve ambiguous tasks, and be assured that together they will be better than they might be individually.

Too often, processes devalue the people involved by being highly controlled, valuing winning at all costs, excluding or shutting out those who have an interest in change, or expecting everyone to think and act alike. Attending to the process means being thoughtful and conscious of how the group is going about its business, so participants might say, "Wait a minute. If we do it this way, we'll be ignoring the needs of an important group of students and that is not our intent." Wheatley (2003) believes that we live in a process world. She states that

> we would do better to attend more carefully to the process by which
> we create our plans and intentions. We need to see these plans,

standards, organization charts not as objects that we complete, but as processes that enable a group to keep clarifying its intent and strengthening its connections to new people and new information. (p. 516)

Several key processes are essential to relational leadership. These processes include collaboration, reflection, feedback, civil confrontation, community building, and a level of profound understanding called meaning making. We will discuss several of these here and in subsequent chapters. Being process-oriented means that participants and the group as a whole are conscious of their process. They are reflective, challenging, collaborative, and caring. Being process-oriented means being aware of the dynamics among people in groups. Many groups jump right into the task or goal and lose a focus on the process. When participants focus on the process of group life or community life, they are forced to ask, Why do we do things this way? How could we be more effective? Participants ensure that the groups keeps working and learning together.

Cooperation and Collaboration

Competition seems embedded in many of our American structures. The adversarial legal system, sports teams, the game of poker, and the competitive free market economy all illustrate the way competition permeates our shared life. It is hard to imagine a different paradigm. Even while avoiding trying to beat others and not needing to always be number one, many people feel a strong need to compete with themselves. Perhaps they need to better that last exam grade or beat their last computer gaming score.

It is well established that "cooperation is superior to competition in promoting achievement and productivity" (Johnson, Maruyama, Johnson, Nelson, & Skon, 1981, p. 56). In the early 1980s, researchers at the University of Minnesota reviewed 122 studies conducted over a 50-year period on the role of competitive, cooperative, or individual goal orientations in achievement. They further distinguished the strong benefits of cooperation (not competition) in the internal functioning of the group from the incentives when competing with other external groups (Johnson et al., 1981).

Studies consistently show that members of various kinds of groups prefer positional leaders and colleagues who establish cooperative or collaborative relationships with them instead of competitive relationships (Kanter, 1989; Spence, 1983; Tjosvold & Tjosvold, 1991). Even a group member who enjoys competition in athletics is not likely to enjoy working in a setting such as a committee, study group, or job site in which others are competitive and try to beat each other or use competitive practices like withholding information or degrading others' contributions. Indeed, "the simplest way to understand why competition generally does not promote excellence is to realize that trying to do well and trying to beat others are two different things" (Kohn, 1992, p. 55). A person's best work is done under conditions of support and cooperation, not under fear, anxiety, or coercion.

The concepts of cooperation and collaboration are different.

Collaboration is more than simply sharing knowledge and information (communication) and more than a relationship that helps each party achieve its own goals (cooperation and coordination). The purpose

of collaboration is to create a shared vision and joint strategies to
address concerns that go beyond the purview of any particular party.
(Chrislip & Larson, 1994, p. 5)

Wood and Gray (1991) assert that "collaboration occurs
when a group of autonomous stakeholders of a problem engage in
an interactive process, using shared rules, norms, and structures,
to act or decide on issues related to that domain" (p. 146). For
example, Microsoft and Intel collaborated on developing wireless
applications for PDAs and smart phones. These companies had
a shared vision that was achieved by working together rather
than in competition with each other. Former presidents George
H. W. Bush and Bill Clinton, who were once in fierce political
competition with one another, worked collaboratively on natural
disaster relief projects in the face of the Southeast Asian tsunami
in 2004, Hurricane Katrina in 2005, and the earthquake in Haiti
in 2010.

Both cooperation and collaboration are helpful processes:
cooperation helps the other person or group achieve their own
goals, whereas collaboration joins with another person or group
in setting and accomplishing mutual, shared goals. The "collaborative premise" is a belief that "if you bring the appropriate
people together in constructive ways with good information,
they will create authentic visions and strategies for addressing
the shared concerns of the organization or community" (Chrislip
& Larson, p. 14). It would be cooperation for the Habitat for
Humanity group to send their membership recruitment flyer out
with the Food Cooperative flyer to save postage or for them to
attend another group's event. It would be collaboration for those
two groups and several others with a common environmental
purpose to design a new flyer to attract new members to these

shared causes or to work collaboratively together to plan a larger event.

Chapter Two described how music provides a good metaphor for this kind of teamwork. Musicians must be individually skilled and committed, yet know that they are part of a collective—a team. Further, imagine a performance of jazz music with improvisational dance. Both dancers and musicians find wonderful rhythms and sounds, simultaneously interpreted, shaping each other's work. The collaboration, respect, and commitment to their common purposes as dancers and musicians are obvious. Yet those artists did not just walk into a studio and create movement. The dancers knew their bodies and the musicians knew their instruments. They knew how and why and when to react. For the group to be effective, all members must be prepared to do their part. Their self-awareness of their own strengths, limits, talents, and abilities created the collaboration in their joint effort. In a parallel manner, think of a terrific class project in which individuals volunteer their knowledge and skills ("I can do the Prezi presentation" or "I can call those businesses for donations"), and the division of labor starts to shape a strong project. Knowing yourself well and seeking to know the members of the group creates a group atmosphere conducive to collaboration.

Meaning Making

Leadership requires a process of true understanding (that is, making meaning) throughout the shared experience of the group. Processing the process makes it transparent and keeps it open to critique and change. Meaning has both cognitive (ideas and thoughts) and emotional (feelings) components, which "allows a person to know (in the sense of understand) some world version (a representation of the way things are and the way they ought to be) and that places the person in relation to this world view" (Drath & Palus, 1994, p. 4). Part of this meaning making involves the recognition that in our rapidly changing world, we are continually challenged to see that data become information, information becomes translated into knowledge, knowledge influences understanding, understanding translates into wisdom, and wisdom becomes meaningful thought and action. Imagine this flow (Komives, 2000) as

Data → Information → Knowledge → Understanding → Wisdom → Thought and Action

Meaning making is "the process of arranging our understanding of experience so that we can know what has happened and what is happening, and so that we can predict what will happen; it is constructing knowledge of ourselves and the world" (Drath & Palus, 1994, p. 2). Drath and Palus make it clear that two understandings of the word *meaning* guide our thinking about meaning and leadership. One use is when symbols, like words, stand for something. This process of naming and interpreting helps clarify meaning and is essential for the perspectives needed in reframing and seeing multiple realities. For example, one person might call a particular action lawlessness, and another might call it civil disobedience. What one person might call destructive partying, another might see as group bonding and celebration. Coming to agreement on the interpretations of symbolic words and events helps a group to make meaning. Senge (1990) refers to these as "mental models."

The second use of the word *meaning* involves "people's values and relationships and commitments" (Drath & Palus,

1994, p. 7). People want to matter and lead lives of meaning. When something is of value, one can make a commitment, find personal purpose, and risk personal involvement—it matters, it has meaning. In contrast, if something is meaningless or of no value, then it does not engage emotion and build commitment. However, we should be careful not to judge too quickly. Sometimes, important matters may seem to have no value. For example, a group of students expressing concern about getting safely to their cars in remote parking lots after late-night classes deserves a careful hearing. Those listening may be student government officers who live in nearby residence halls or campus administrators who have parking spaces near their buildings and never thought about this as an issue. The relational empathy skill of trying to see things from the perspective of another will validate that meaning. (Refer to Chapter Five for more on relational empathy.)

Understanding how we make meaning helps a group frame and reframe the issues and problems they are seeking to resolve. The framing process involves naming the problem and identifying the nature of interventions or solutions that might be helpful. If a problem is framed as, "The administration won't provide money for additional safety lighting," it leads to a set of discussions and strategies focused on changing the administration. Reframing means finding a new interpretation of the problem that might create a new view that helps a group be more productive (Bryson & Crosby, 1992). Reframing this same problem might bring a new awareness of coalitions, shareholders, and stakeholders if it were readdressed as, "How can we unite the talent of our campus to address the problem of a dramatic rise in crimes against women?"

Reflection and Contemplation

During the rapid pace of change, the need to make meaning from ambiguous material requires individuals and groups to practice reflection. Reflection is the process of pausing, stepping back from the action, and asking, What is happening? Why is this happening? What does this mean? What does this mean for me? What can I learn from this? Lao Tzu (Heider, 1985) encourages time for reflection:

> Endless drama in a group clouds consciousness. Too much noise overwhelms the senses. Continual input obscures genuine insight. Do not substitute sensationalism for learning. Allow regular time for silent reflection. Turn inward and digest what has happened. Let the senses rest and grow still. Teach people to let go of their superficial mental chatter and obsessions. Teach people to pay attention to the whole body's reaction to a situation. When group members have time to reflect, they can see more clearly what is essential in themselves and others. (p. 23)

Smith, MacGregor, Matthews, and Gabelnick (2004) believe that "reflective thinking should be metacognitive" (p. 125). Metacognition is "thinking about one's thinking—now considered essential for effective learning and problem solving" (p. 126). Reflection can be accomplished when a group intentionally discusses its process. If groups discuss their process at all, they usually reflect only on their failures. They try to find out what went wrong and how to avoid those errors again. To be true learning organizations, groups also need to reflect on their successes and bring to every participant's awareness a common understanding of answers to such questions as, Why did this go so well? What did we do together that made this happen? How can we make sure to work this well together again? Horwood (1989) observes that "Reflection is hard mental work. The word itself means 'bending back.' . . . The mental work of reflection includes deliberation . . . rumination . . . pondering . . . and musing" (p. 5). Reflection is a key process in becoming a learning community. You will remember from Chapter One that it is a key part of how experiences become information in Kolb's learning cycle.

In a study of successful leaders, Bennis (1989) observed that these effective leaders encouraged "reflective backtalk" (p. 194). They knew the importance of truth telling and encouraged their colleagues to reflect honestly what they think they saw or heard. "Reflection is vital—at every level, in every organization . . . all [leaders] should practice the new three Rs: retreat, renewal, and return" (p. 186). One form of group reflection is when the group discusses (or processes) a shared experience. As a difficult meeting winds down, any participant (or perhaps the group's adviser) might say, "Let's take time now at the end of this meeting to process what we liked about how we handled the big decision tonight and what we think we should do differently next time." Reflection is also useful for keeping a group on track. A group might intentionally review its goals and mission in the middle of the year and discuss how their activities are supporting that mission or whether they should be redirected. Reflection is an essential component of a process to keep individuals and the whole group focused and intentional.

Contemplation is a form of reflection that allows us to think deeply about the events around us, our feelings, and our emotions. Chickering, Dalton, and Stamm (2006) describe contemplation as "the cerebral metabolic process for meaning

making. The food that we chew and swallow, that then enters
our stomach, only nourishes us, only becomes part of our
bloodstream, muscles, nerves, and body chemistry when it is
metabolized" (p. 143). The experiences of life operate in a
similar way. In the absence of reflection and contemplation,
the knowledge that we acquire and the experiences that we
go through can "end up like the residue from food we don't
metabolize" (p. 143). Reflective practices allow us to think about
what is occurring around us and to us and then to make meaning
from those experiences.

> What Would This Look Like?

You will acquire many leadership skills over time. It is easy to
confuse some management tools—like running meetings or
planning agendas—with real leadership. However, using the
principles of relational leadership, you can reframe typical skills
like agenda planning so that they are more effective. The goals of
the agenda for your group meeting will not be just to get through
the topics to be presented or decided in the quickest time but
will involve the most people, empower voices that might have
been excluded before, make sure no one is railroaded and that
fair decisions are made, involve others in building an agenda,
and use collaborative practices.

Remember the times you have been to a meeting whose
leader made all the announcements. A small group of two or
three in-group members seemed to run the whole show, and you
never said a word. We have all had that experience. You felt
marginalized and might have wondered why you even bothered

to attend. Think of a meeting in which people disagreed hotly and then someone quickly moved to vote on an issue. A vote was taken with the resulting majority winning and a dissatisfied minority losing or feeling railroaded.

Imagine the differences in a meeting whose positional leader or convener says, "It is our custom to make sure everyone is involved and heard before we try to resolve issues. The executive committee has asked three of you to present the key issues on the first agenda item; we will then break into small groups for fifteen minutes to see what questions and issues emerge before we proceed and see what we want to do at that point. In your discussion, try to identify the principles that will be important for us to consider in the decision we eventually make." Even if you do not agree with this approach, you would feel more comfortable suggesting a different model because the tone of the meeting is one of involvement and participation.

> Chapter Summary

Conditions in our rapidly changing world require that each of us become effective members of our groups and communities in order to work with others toward needed change and for common purpose. The way we relate to each other matters and is symbolic of our social responsibility. Taking the time needed to build a sense of community in a group acknowledges that relationships are central to effective leadership. Relational leadership is purposeful, inclusive, empowering, ethical, and about process. Attention to those practices builds a strong organization with committed participants who know they matter.

> What's Next?

After understanding the various ways leadership has been viewed
and the current need for new models of leadership that value
relational approaches, it is essential to understand people as
participants in those relationships. Perhaps the most important
person to understand is you. The next chapter, which begins
Part Two, encourages you to explore aspects about yourself
that are important in leadership; following that is a chapter
exploring aspects of others and how they may be different from
yours. The final chapter in Part Two addresses the importance of
ethics and integrity in the leadership process and in establishing
relationships with others.

> Chapter Activities

1. Think of a leader whom you would consider to be a role
    model, someone who practices what he or she preaches and
    lives by high standards. Think of local, national, or histori-
    cal exemplars. What is it about the role model you identified
    that qualifies that person as an exemplary leader? What val-
    ues does he or she profess, and what practices does he or she
    consistently live by?
2. Describe your leadership philosophy using all three compo-
    nents of the knowing-being-doing model.
3. Describe your leadership compass. What principles or ethics
    guide your personal life and your leadership?
4. Identify a situation in which you successfully used one
    or more of French and Raven's sources of power. What

contributed to your effective use of each of those sources of power? Think of an example of a leader who abused one of these sources of power. What were the consequences of that person's leadership?

5. As you review the five elements of this Relational Leadership Model, which are most comfortable for you and why? Which involve knowledge, skills, or attitudes that you have not yet learned or developed?

6. In their simplicity, models often omit concepts that could have been included. What concepts would you add to any of the five elements of this model, or what new elements do you think should be included?

ADDITIONAL READINGS

Chrislip, D. D., & Larson, C. E. (1994). *Collaborative leadership: How citizens and civic leaders can make a difference.* San Francisco, CA: Jossey-Bass.

Gandossy, R., & Effron, M. (2004). *Leading the way: Three truths from the top companies for leaders.* Hoboken, NJ: Wiley.

George, B. (2007). *True north: Discover your authentic leadership.* San Francisco, CA: Jossey-Bass.

Hurley, R. F. (2012). *The decision to trust: How leaders create high-trust organizations.* San Francisco, CA: Jossey-Bass.

Komives, S. R., Wagner, W., & Associates. (2009). *Leadership for a better world: Understanding the social change model of leadership development.* San Francisco, CA: Jossey-Bass.

Kouzes, J. M., & Posner, B. Z. (2008). *The student leadership challenge: Five practices for exemplary leaders.* San Francisco, CA: Jossey-Bass.

Exploring Your Potential for Leadership

The relational leadership model (RLM) emphasizes the importance of relationships among participants in the process of purposeful change. Developing and maintaining healthy and honest relationships starts with a knowledge of self and an openness to appreciate and respect others.

This section contains three chapters to enrich your self-awareness. These chapters help you explore yourself in relation to others as foundational components of developing a personal leadership philosophy. Chapter Four features an assessment developed by The Gallup Organization, the Clifton StrengthsQuest, with instructions on how to take this online assessment by using a code in this book to access the assessment. Upon completing the StrengthsQuest, you will receive a profile report describing your top five strengths—this assessment underscores the importance of knowing yourself well and what you are best at doing (your strengths). Also highlighted in this chapter is the VIA assessment, which is a free online assessment indicating your character strengths.

The last chapter of this section explores the importance of the ethical dimension of the RLM and of being a person of character, living a life of integrity. This chapter asserts that in all settings, relational leadership must be grounded in ethical processes, create ethical climates, and produce moral actions and outcomes. Creating an ethical climate in all contexts is an important dimension of the RLM.

Lao Tzu (Heider, 1985) noted:

The wise leader's ability does not rest on techniques or gimmicks or set exercises. The method of awareness-of-process applies to all people and all situations.

The leader's personal state of consciousness creates a climate of openness. Center and ground give the leader stability, flexibility, and endurance.

Because the leader sees clearly, the leader can shed light on others. (p. 53)

In the relational leadership model presented in the previous chapter, we encouraged you to be purposeful, inclusive, empowering, ethical, and process-oriented. Think again about what you need to know or be or do to participate effectively in relational leadership. You might return to Table 3.1 to assess yourself and these concepts again.

Ask yourself some thoughtful questions to explore your self-awareness, awareness of others, leadership, and this model:

Purposeful: Do you have clear goals and an awareness of commitments that are important to you? Do you have to get your own way, or are you able to find common purpose with others? Do you know how change occurs?

Inclusive: How comfortable and effective are you including others? Do you understand your own motivations when you agree or disagree with others? When you interact with people different from you, are there differences you find easy to accommodate or difficult to understand?

Empowering: Do you know how to build on your own strengths and on the strengths of others? Do you find it easy or difficult to share authority and responsibility?

Ethical: Do you find it easy to act with integrity and authenticity? Can you identify the values and principles that guide your actions? Are you trusting or distrustful of others?

Process-Oriented: Do you know what approaches you prefer for facilitating change and accomplishing goals? Do you prefer collaboration
or competition? How effective are you at civil discussions, even
when you strongly disagree with someone?

The most productive thing you could do to become more effective as a leader and as an active participant is to learn to see yourself
clearly. This section will help you explore what you value, how you
are developing character, how you learn best, what your strengths are,
and how aspects of yourself (like your gender, culture, and communication pattern) have been shaped. In learning to see these aspects of
yourself, we hope you can see these same things in others.

Chapter 4

Understanding Yourself

Imagine the times you have been sitting in class or a meeting and had thoughts like these:

- The president of our organization is an excellent public speaker. Why can't I be just like her?
- When my classmate came to me for advice, I was able to listen and help him feel better about himself and his situation.
- Why in the world do I always pick away at all the details of an idea and end up sounding so negative?
- I am so proud that I didn't hesitate a minute to disagree when she made such a hurtful comment.
- My sense of humor really helped the group get through a tense moment tonight and keep things in perspective.

Seeing your own strengths and nonstrengths and those of others so clearly requires focused reflection. Being aware of how you prefer to think, to relate, to learn, and to find personal meaning is an important self-awareness skill. Being able to articulate what you believe and what you value helps you understand your own motivations and behaviors. Knowing your strengths and understanding how to manage your nonstrengths helps you grow and relate to others with authenticity and credibility.

Because leadership happens in the context of interpersonal relationships, self-understanding is essential to authenticity in those relationships. Perhaps the most basic life traits that translate to leadership effectiveness are honesty, authentic self-awareness, and the openness to grow, learn, and change.

> Chapter Overview

In this chapter we challenge you to think of the things about yourself that shape your personal identity and fuel your motivations. We explain the role of self-awareness in leadership, including aspects of self-concept and self-esteem. We also explore how you form your values and the role of values in developing character. Understanding your signature and character strengths and how to apply them in your life, knowing your dimensions of emotional intelligence and the impact of those on others, and assessing your own well-being maximize your performance and the performances of others. Understanding yourself is a prerequisite to participating in leadership processes. This chapter includes two self-assessment instruments, the Clifton StrengthsQuest and VIA, designed to provide heightened awareness around your strengths and character strengths.

› Understanding Yourself

What makes you the way you are? How much of your perception, values, temperament, personality, and motives come from the way you were raised, the influence of your surroundings, and your contextual environment? How much of the way you are is inborn or genetic?

Debates have raged for years over whether to attribute human behavior to nurture (socialization) or nature (heredity). Becoming aware of the influence of either nurture or nature in your own development is essential to understanding yourself. For example, you may be tall and may have learned that some people find you imposing; they assume you will be outgoing and aggressive, even though you are quiet and shy. Or you may be small but have learned that people react eventually to the quality of what you have to say. Some might even say, "You seem bigger than your height." You may have learned to be relational or thoughtful or funny or anxious.

Regardless of how you came to be the way you are, you can intentionally choose to develop desired traits or skills. You cannot change your height or some other genetic attribute, but you can address many of the things you have learned by bringing them into your awareness. Although you cannot always change the way others view you because they bring their own biases and attributions, you can at least be authentic as you try to be the person you would like to be in life.

Discussing your self-awareness is a form of the psychological study of individuality. If you feel uncomfortable with the concept of individuality, it could be because describing human perception or behavior in categories or types makes you feel boxed in or stereotyped. You may feel constrained or categorized. You may also feel uncomfortable because focusing on your own needs or on yourself is considered selfish or inappropriate in your family or culture. Instead, we hope you welcome the opportunity for personal insight by reviewing the ways scholars understand the range of human behavior.

By knowing how others respond, you can assess how their response is like or unlike your own. For example, if you have

STUDENT ESSAY

To understand yourself as a leader you have to understand who you are first. You have to understand how you handle situations. You have to know what it is you want to do. This cannot all be done in one day but over time it can be achieved. This past year I have been an office manager and in the beginning I doubted myself and because of this my coworker's doubted me as well. Seeing this, I decided to improve myself. So, one day at a time, bit-by-bit I was improving my personality, my character, and myself in general. I was organizing my life, finding out who I am now and what I am doing. Since I have started doing this I have seen great improvement in myself, especially my confidence and my coworkers' confidence in me. It's not easy to understand yourself but taking it day by day you grow and with growing comes the understanding to who you are. I understand myself to be an organizer and that works best for me. I understand myself to be who I am and that is what counts. It is also about expressing your individuality.

Penelope Shapansky, is a junior at Ripon college with majors in English and a self-designed major in journalism. She is a member of the Black Student Union, a leader of the Ripon College Days paper, a resident assistant, and an office manager.

had a death in your family or the loss of someone you love, you may find comfort in knowing that there are predictable stages in the grief process for many people (i.e., denial, anger, bargaining, depression, and acceptance) and that your personal reactions are very normal (Kübler-Ross, 1970). Because you are unique, however, you may find your grief reaction to be more pronounced or less severe than Kübler-Ross's (1970) model suggests, based on such factors as how close you were to the person who died, the comfort you receive from your family, your religious practices, or your capacity to respond to grief from a state of equanimity. Whatever the phenomena being presented in various theories about human behavior, you can then connect with what is most like you or least like you to better understand yourself and to see how others might be similar to or different from you.

> Self-Leadership Development

The classic Star Wars movies were filled with deeper meaning behind their adventuresome entertainment. In *The Return of the Jedi*, young Luke Skywalker seeks to learn the secrets of the famous Jedi Master, Yoda. Luke is initially incredulous that this small, green creature is The Master, and he is further disappointed not to be given or taught Yoda's secrets. Yoda instead takes Luke on a journey into himself, teaching him to focus and trust his own internal power to literally move mountains. This inward journey provides the self-awareness of identifying abilities, strengths, and weaknesses for Luke and each of us. The journey develops a sense of trust in yourself to be congruent and to truly know the basis of your effectiveness.

The common observation of many acknowledged leaders is that no one can teach you about yourself except you (Bennis, 1989). And a common human temptation is to try to be like someone else, but that is like trying to live someone else's life. Counselors, advisers, friends, or family can help with this process, but awareness ultimately requires you to be introspective about yourself and to be who you authentically are in this world. Bennis (1989) observes four lessons from which to develop self-knowledge:

- You are your own best teacher.
- Accept responsibility. Blame no one.
- You can learn anything you want to learn.
- True understanding comes from reflection on your experience. (p. 56)

"Leadership means self-discovery, getting a better yield out of your attributes" (Haas & Tamarkin, 1992, p. 6). In your life so far, you have probably learned to set goals, motivate yourself to meet them, and feel personally responsible if you do not. It is hard for some people to translate the life skills of self-control and internal motivation into guides of action as members of a group. If you often sit in a meeting and think, "It's not my responsibility; I will just let the leaders do it. After all, it's their job," then you need to develop more self-leadership skills.

Your decision to be a person who can make a difference (evidenced by reading this book) is a statement about self-leadership. You know you cannot credit or blame external factors such as teachers, supervisors, parents, or positional leaders for your behaviors. Sadly, there may be acts of discrimination or oppression that have held you back, but you are now looking ahead and asking, What can I do to matter and to make a difference in the things that are important to me?

› Esteem and Confidence

John W. Gardner (1990) tells a story of sitting beside Martin Luther King Jr. at a seminar on education. The first presentation was a speech entitled, "First, Teach Them to Read." After observing this title, King whispered to Gardner, "First, teach them to believe in themselves" (p. 10).

How you think and feel about yourself is the energy that fuels your motivation. Self-concept is how we objectively describe ourselves; usually, it is based on our roles and attributes. You might say, "I am a mother of a two-year-old and like to go with the flow, keeping all my options open" or "I am an older-than-typical student with above-average intelligence and high motivation" or "I am a creative person with musical abilities." Self-esteem is the subjective element of how you feel about yourself. For example, you might say, "I am a creative person with musical abilities but am unskilled socially and uncomfortable around those in authority. I feel proud of my musical and creative skills and feel disappointed in myself for not being more socially skilled." Self-awareness would lead to having an accurate self-concept. Honoring your strengths and addressing your weaknesses are essential first steps toward higher self-esteem.

Esteem is enhanced if you can identify your strengths and weaknesses and know that you are growing and progressing in the areas you want to improve. High self-esteem is a result of valuing your self-concept. Low self-esteem may mean you expect something better or different than you feel. You may have a 3.3 grade point average as a biology major, have a group of supportive friends, and have just been elected vice president of your campus chapter of Amnesty International. You may feel proud and have high regard for those accomplishments. If, however, you are working for a 3.9 because you want to go to medical school, you might feel badly about your grades and have low esteem about your academic ability.

Self-confidence is the ability to know that you can rely on your strengths, competencies, and skills in the many contexts in which you find yourself. Some people consistently do well in whatever they do, but they are never sure they can do well and therefore have low self-confidence. Perhaps self-confident people have better memories and know that they have done well before and can do so again.

Accepting ourselves is perhaps one of the hardest life tasks. Realizing that you cannot change some things about yourself is a step toward higher self-esteem. For example, you will not become 6′2″ if you are now 5′6″; you will not become another race, change your siblings, or get rid of your freckles. You can, however, learn new skills and add to your knowledge base. You can increase your confidence by maximizing your strengths and managing your weaknesses.

If some aspects of yourself are negative influences on your self-esteem, you must differentiate between those you can actually do something about from those you just need to think about differently, which can lead to a higher level of self-acceptance. Perceiving things differently is called cognitive

STUDENT ESSAY ◆

How can someone be expected to lead a group of individuals, when she or he is unaware of who he is himself? Well, the answer is quite simple: she or he can't. When I was a leader in my Residential Learning Community made up of future educators, it was first extremely important to understand myself, and my role as their leader. First, I had to decide just what I wanted to do with the organization and how I wanted to run it. Most important was how I wanted to lead this organization. Did I want to take a professional approach or more of a casual approach? I always struggled with this, and felt that I was not the most capable leader of this organization. Since then, I have really learned to focus on myself and what leadership style I can consistently take on in order to always be an effective leader. I did this by asking myself what mattered to me, how I can portray that to others, and what is expected of me by the individuals I am leading. Once these questions are answered, a leader truly understands him or herself, and is ready to be an effective leader.

Justin Tarbell is a James Madison University Duke who is studying Spanish, secondary education, and human resources development. Justin is involved in many leadership positions on campus such as student government, student ambassadors, and proudly served as an orientation leader.

reframing—a different way of thinking. You may have felt bad when thinking of your personality as shy and quiet, but you might feel empowered to frame those same characteristics as being thoughtful and reflective. Reflecting on her own youth, singer-actress Bette Midler said, "I didn't belong as a kid, and that always bothered me. If only I'd known that one day my differentness would be an asset, then my early life would have

been much easier" (cited in *The Quotable Woman*, 1991, p. 39).
Human differences are not problems to solve, but rather assets to
accentuate.

> Finding Your Ideal Self Through Mindfulness

Committing to your own leadership development is an important
key to growth, renewal, learning, and personal transformation. Leadership development is a lifelong journey leading to
greater discoveries and higher impact. Boyatzis and McKee
(2005) describe great leaders as "awake, aware, and attuned to
themselves, to others, and to the world around them . . . Great
leaders are emotionally intelligent and they are mindful: they
seek to live in full consciousness of self, others, nature, and
society" (p. 3). Mindfulness means a holistic way of living and
being in tune with yourself and what is happening around you.
"Mindfulness is the capacity to be fully aware of all that one
experiences inside the self—body, mind, heart, spirit—and to
pay full attention to what is happening around us—people, the
natural world, our surroundings, and events" (Boyatzis & McKee,
2005, p. 113).

Rooted as an ancient concept, psychologists, neuroscientists,
and Buddhist philosophers provide scientific evidence that
inform mindfulness practices and demonstrate their effects on
self-awareness, increased creativity, and flexibility in thinking
patterns. This ability and habit to be acutely aware of all
the clues available to you around your emotions, thoughts,
interactions, and physical sensations leads to greater congruency
with your values and your actions. It means listening to your

body, listening to your heart, and listening to your inner voice of intuition. "Mindfulness starts with self-awareness: knowing yourself enables you to make choices about how you respond to people and situations" (Boyatzis & McKee, 2005, p. 120).

Research on the effects of mindfulness practices such as meditation have shown positive effects on mental functions, including stress reduction, physical health (boost to immune system), and greater resilience (bouncing back from adverse experiences) (Davidson & Begley, 2012). New patterns of responding to threatening situations or negative emotions such as fear and insecurity are made possible through retraining your brain to respond with a greater capacity to redirect your thoughts and feelings. "Mindfulness retrains these habits of mind by tapping into the plasticity of the brain's connections, creating new ones, strengthening some old ones, and weakening others" (p. 205). You might even reach a state of equanimity that Hanson (2009) describes as allowing your brain to transform bad moments into good ones. "With equanimity, your initial reactions to things—reach for this carrot, push away that stick—are left in a mental mud-room so that the interior of your mind remains clear and clean and peaceful" (p. 109). Being in a state of equanimity allows you to respond more openly, with greater steadiness of emotion, intention, clarity, understanding, and tranquility (Hanson, 2009). "The spaciousness of equanimity is a great support for compassion, kindness, and joy at the happiness of others" (p. 117).

Quieting your brain to reach levels of mindfulness requires practice and a commitment to turn those practices into habits. There are many scientifically validated mindfulness practices, including meditation, yoga, listening to enjoyable music, reflective writing, and walking as a few examples. The key is to select practices that work for you and allow you to soften the noise in your brain and pay attention to what is happening inside you and around you.

Mindfulness has two key benefits connected to leadership development: it allows you to reflect more deeply about who you are and connect those beliefs with your actions. Mindfulness also results in gaining greater insights about others and situations around you, resulting in greater clarity, deeper insights, and authentic connections with others. It provides you with an expression of your leadership grounded in your values and character congruent with your actions. Engaging in mindfulness practices allows you to become more grounded, demonstrate greater leadership presence (congruency), and makes it possible to be more agile in your leadership expressions (capacity to roll with the punches or respond when under attack).

> Emotional Intelligence

Traditional notions of effective leadership often included traits such as intelligence, toughness, and vision, along with the possessing a high level of technical skills. Studies of what makes leaders effective today have transcended these qualities to include self-awareness, self-regulation, motivation, empathy, and social skill. These qualities are defined as emotional intelligence (Bar-On, 2007; Goleman, 1998; Shankman & Allen, 2008). Emotional intelligence is defined as "the capacity for recognizing our own feelings and those of others, for motivating ourselves, and for managing emotions well in ourselves and in our relationships" (Goleman, 1998, p. 317). In his study of analyzing which personal capabilities resulted in extraordinary performance by leaders, Daniel Goleman (2004) found that the competencies associated with emotional intelligence, such as self-awareness, empathy, and self-regulation, were more highly linked to excellent performance than were technical and cognitive skills. In fact, Goleman found that the highest ranking leaders who were star performers had greater levels of emotional intelligence compared to average performers among senior leadership ranks. The five components of Goleman's emotional intelligence model are self-awareness, self-regulation, motivation, empathy, and social skill.

You might be wondering whether skills associated with these five areas of emotional intelligence can be learned. These skills can be learned and developed over time through feedback from others and from greater awareness of your impact on others. For example, listening is a core skill associated with empathy and is an essential skill for all leaders. Empathy in leadership means being able to understand and respond to others' feelings and to take those feelings into account when making decisions (Goleman, 2004). Having the ability to work with others and manage relationships in the leadership process encompasses the component of social skills. Defined in this manner, social skills are learned behaviors and are at the foundation of the Relational Leadership Model—engaging with others around a common purpose or agenda.

In summary, the emotional intelligence of leadership goes beyond technical and cognitive skills. Emotional intelligence, as a learned set of behaviors, provides building blocks in establishing relationships and deepening relationships with others. Developing and enhancing your emotional intelligence takes time and starts with a genuine desire and commitment to learn about yourself and your impact on others.

> Developing Your Talents and Strengths

One of our greatest assets as human beings is our talents (Buckingham & Clifton, 2001). Everyone has talent. The most sustainable resources on this planet are human talents. Knowing yourself well includes knowing your talents—what you are naturally good at doing. *Talent* is "any recurring pattern of thought, feeling, or behavior that can be productively applied" (p. 48). A *strength* is "consistent near perfect performance in any activity" (p. 25). Unfortunately, we often work from the deficit model—focusing on, and maybe even obsessing about, our weaknesses. Trying to fix our weaknesses takes away from our ability to lead and work from our talents and strengths. We do not have enough time in our life span to fix our weaknesses or to try to transform our weaknesses into strengths while also trying to work from our natural talents. What you pay attention to is what grows.

Effective leaders know what they do best and apply their strengths in all aspects of their lives. This does not mean that you should ignore your weaknesses. Instead, you should be aware of those things that you do not do well and find ways to manage them so that you can be more productive and be more fulfilled. One strategy of managing your weaknesses is to surround yourself with others who have talents that are different from yours and are needed to successfully achieve results or accomplish change. If you manage your weaknesses rather than trying to fix them, you will have more time to focus on your strengths.

When you play to your strengths, you are working from the philosophy of talent. Buckingham and Clifton (2001) propose two assumptions that can guide you in your leadership:

1. Each person's talents are enduring and unique.
2. Each person's greatest room for growth is in the areas of his or her greatest strength (p. 8).

Too often, we believe that our best strategy to grow and develop is to improve our weaknesses. The Gallup Organization conducted more than two million interviews over ten years asking high-performing individuals to describe what they did that made them excel (Buckingham & Clifton). They discovered 34 patterns or prevalent themes of human talent (see Table 4.1). Their research shows that these 34 themes of talent (behaviors) can explain a broad range of excellent performance. Buckingham and Clifton observe, "the real tragedy of life is not that each of us doesn't have enough strengths, it's that we fail to use the ones that we have" (p. 12).

Table 4.1 **The 34 Themes of the StrengthsFinder**

Achiever	Activator	Adaptability	Analytical
Arranger	Belief	Command	Communication
Competition	Connectedness	Context	Deliberative
Developer	Discipline	Empathy	Fairness
Focus	Futuristic	Harmony	Ideation
Inclusiveness	Individualization	Input	Intellection
Learner	Maximizer	Positivity	Relator
Responsibility	Restorative	Self-Assurance	Significance
Strategic	Woo		

Adapted from Buckingham & Clifton (2001).

In various aspects of your life, including your memberships and in leadership, there is pressure to be all things to all people. Combined with this is the misunderstood premise of being a well-rounded individual, which often results in mediocrity and not excelling at what you are naturally best at doing. The strengths approach in leadership development means maximizing what you already have in you versus trying to transform your weaknesses into strengths or trying to be all things to all people.

STUDENT ESSAY

Before engaging in any type of leadership, you must understand your own strengths and weaknesses. By assessing your personal pattern of strengths and weaknesses, you can better anticipate obstacles you may encounter and surround yourself with individuals whose assets best fit the needs of the group. Personal reflection can lead to a better understanding of not only yourself, but also your role as a leader. As a leader, you must acknowledge what you hope to give to the group and anticipate any shortcomings that you may have. In addition, gaining a deeper understanding of yourself as a leader can help you to become more aware of how to use your strengths for the progress of the group and compensate for your weaknesses.

Jessica Erwin is a graduate student at the University of Texas at Arlington earning a master of education degree in educational leadership and policy studies. She was a staff advisor for the Fall Leadership Retreat and graduate intern for New Maverick Orientation.

Leading from a philosophy of talents and strengths is an outgrowth of an emerging field called "positive psychology." Positive psychology has moved away from the clinical diagnostic approach of looking at what is wrong with an individual to paying attention to what is right within each person. It is the scientific study of positive emotions and positive behaviors. Language is key in positive psychology with a focus on describing what is right about people and organizations. Using this approach, weaknesses would be referred to as nonstrengths. Research emanating from positive psychology reveals that humans remember four negative memories to every positive one (Roberts et al., 2005). However, individuals *respond* to praise and positive affirmation. In your leadership development, your confidence and your motivation to grow increase when your strengths and talents are affirmed. Leading from this framework will energize you and others in an inspirational way, open up new and more possibilities, and allow you and others to maximize and apply your strengths.

Each person brings a different mix of strengths and weaknesses to any situation. The irony is that some of your strengths, if overemphasized, become your weaknesses, and things you consider weaknesses may actually be seen as strengths by others. You may be a strong critical thinker who can readily find flaws in logic. That can be a valuable strength in helping your group prepare and present its position on a topic; or it can be seen as negative and blocking if someone is presenting an idea to you and you just naturally begin to be critical instead of trying to connect and listen. The converse can be true as well: to be humble and quiet may mean your opinion is never heard and your voice is left out of decision making. But it can also mean you are a keen listener who is very tuned in to others' thoughts. Leadership self-awareness grows when you can identify your personal strengths and weaknesses while also understanding the shadow sides of your strengths.

Identifying Your Passions and Strengths

Clifton and Nelson (1992) suggest that you pay attention to the things you see others doing and to your inner mind saying, "Oh, I would love to try that." Sometimes it is hard to identify strengths. Listen for the times you say, "I feel I've accomplished something great when I do that." Clifton and Nelson recommend that you find your strengths by trying these strategies.

1. Listen to yourself when you have done something well, even if no one else noticed.
2. Identify the satisfaction you feel when you know something you did was terrific and gives you a feeling of well-being.
3. Know what things you find easy to learn quickly: organizing your lab report, talking to strangers, mastering a new computer technology, reading patiently to a small child.
4. Study your successes for clues of excellence, for "glimpses" (Clifton & Nelson, 1992, p. 50) of what can be excellent—for what things you do very well. Whether giving a speech or helping someone feel very special, by examining whatever your success has been, you will discover what you can do well.
5. Think about your patterns of excellence—when you are able to sing every word of a song you like, when you are able to grasp the deeper meaning in a complicated class presentation, when you practice a skill (whether cooking, playing basketball, or public speaking) and you feel it improve each time you do it. Clues to your strengths are all around you. Identifying and labeling them can affirm your confidence and esteem by acknowledging that you do bring reliable talents to situations and can contribute to the leadership process.

Consider this simple yet powerful metaphor to guide your daily actions and interactions called, "Don's Theory of the Dipper and the Bucket" (Rath & Clifton, 2004). Everyone has something like an invisible bucket that can get filled or emptied on a regular basis by an invisible dipper. When your bucket gets emptied, you feel negative and let down. When your bucket is full, you feel positive. The "dipper" is a powerful tool in leadership that allows us to fill another's bucket by saying positive things and focusing on what he or she is good at. You can also use the dipper to dip from someone's bucket, making that person feel diminished. Our own sense of esteem is enhanced when we use the dipper to fill someone's bucket. When we fill our own buckets and others', we are affirming our own and others' strengths and talents.

Think about what you do best and then think about how you felt when you received recognition for a job well done. You were probably motivated to continue doing what you did because you were good at it and you enjoyed doing it. When someone filled your bucket, it probably made you feel good about yourself. Organizational research has shown that when you have opportunities to do what you are best at doing and when you are recognized for that, you will experience more meaning and satisfaction in what you are doing and your productivity will increase as a result (Buckingham & Clifton, 2001). Leading from your talents and strengths will keep your bucket filled.

Managing Your Nonstrengths

All of us can learn to manage our nonstrengths. Some think that weaknesses "can be removed but they cannot be transformed into strengths. The goal, therefore, is to manage weaknesses so the strengths can be freed to develop and become so powerful they make the weaknesses irrelevant" (Clifton & Nelson, 1992, p. 73). A person can either manage weaknesses so that they do not repress other strengths or overcome them and turn them into strengths.

So what do Tom Cruise, Orlando Bloom, Keanu Reeves, Whoopi Goldberg, Leonardo da Vinci, Pablo Picasso, Thomas Edison, Albert Einstein, and John Lennon have in common? Each of them has or had dyslexia (http://www.dyslexia.com/qafame.htm). They may never be quick readers or accurate spellers, but they manage those limitations and have found ways to prevent them from blocking their strengths. Tom Cruise said, "I had to train myself to focus my attention. I became very visual and learned how to create mental images in order to comprehend what I read" (http://www.dys-add.com/backiss.html#famous). Helen Keller could not see, hear, or speak, but she learned to communicate remarkably well. Olympic athlete Jackie Joyner Kersey deals daily with asthma. Their limitations vary, but these gifted people have learned to manage them so that their strengths prevail.

We encourage you to focus on your strengths and develop your talents. Some weaknesses, however, may be problematic because they cause you to function poorly. These need to be tackled directly. For example, you may not speak well in front of a group. You can, however, manage this by learning ways to make a presentation more comfortable for you, like using a power point presentation, using handouts, or encouraging group interaction. The actor James Earl Jones had a debilitating childhood stutter, which he overcame so successfully that he became a remarkable orator. One of our students observed that she thought herself to be a terrible speaker, but she enjoyed class discussions and had fun arguing her points. She clearly had a talent that could help her manage a nonstrength. One of her classmates pointed out the connections among those skills. What she perceived as a weakness was viewed differently by others.

A powerful strategy is to maximize your impact by partnering with others who have complementary strengths. If you are excellent at arranging and organizing tasks, but not good at developing strategies to take your project to the next level, you might partner with others who are strategic and can think futuristically. Buckingham and Clifton (2001) refer to this as complementary partnerships (p. 155).

Identifying Your Signature Strengths

In this edition of *Exploring Leadership* you have an opportunity to identify your top five signature strengths with Clifton StrengthsQuest from the Gallup Organization. By completing this assessment, you will gain insights about your most dominant strengths. This assessment is based on the behaviors you are best at doing—it is not a personality assessment such as the Myers-Briggs Type Indicator. If you purchased a new copy of this book, you will find a unique code to use to take the Clifton StrengthsQuest in the back of your book. Go to The Gallup Organization website http://www.strengths.gallup.com where you can enter your code and access your assessment (see page vi for more information). You will want to remember your code and password if you intend to return to this website to review your top five strengths profile.

It will take you about 25 minutes to complete the Clifton StrengthsQuest. Respond to each pair of statements with top-of-mind choices—try not to overthink these statements. There are no right or wrong choices or choices that are better than others. All 34 signature themes are valuable and needed in groups and in leadership processes. After you complete the assessment, you will receive your profile by email describing your top five strengths. Carefully read your report and notice what resonates most with you and reflect on how you might maximize those strengths in all aspects of your life. Your strengths profile provides one piece of evidence about what you do best.

As you reflect on your top five strengths from your strengths profile report, remember that the strategy is to maximize what you already have and manage your weaknesses so that they become virtually irrelevant. You might be tempted to spend more time fixing your weaknesses, which means that your strengths will not get full play in your leadership. The following parable entitled, A *Silly Story*, illustrates the importance of accentuating yours and others' strengths in the leadership process:

A Silly Story

Once upon a time, the animals decided they must do something heroic to meet the problems of a "new world," so they organized a school. They adopted an activity curriculum consisting of running, climbing, swimming, and flying. To make it easier to administer, all animals took all the subjects.

The duck was excellent in swimming—in fact, better than his instructor—but he made only passing grades in flying and was very poor in running. Since he was slow in running, he had to stay after school and also drop swimming in order to practice running. This was kept up until his web feet were badly worn, so then he was only average in swimming. But average was acceptable in school, so no one worried about that except the duck.

The rabbit started at the top of the class in running, but he had a nervous breakdown because of so much make-up work in swimming.

The squirrel was excellent in climbing until he developed frustration in the flying class, where the teacher made him start from the ground up instead of from the tree-top down. He also developed "charley-horses" from over exertion and then got a C in climbing and a D in running.

The eagle was a problem child and was severely disciplined. In the climbing class, he beat all others to the top of the tree, but he insisted on using his own way to get there.

At the end of the year, an abnormal eel that could swim exceedingly well and could also run, climb, and fly a little had the highest average and was the valedictorian.

Character Strengths and Virtues

Another useful tool in understanding the strengths of your character through positive traits was developed by Peterson and Seligman (2004) and called VIA. The VIA classification includes three conceptual levels: virtues, character strengths, and situational themes. Virtues are universal core characteristics and include wisdom, courage, humanity, justice, temperance, and transcendence. Peterson and Seligman believe that "these virtues must be present at above-threshold values for an individual to be deemed of good character" (p. 13). They say that character strengths are "the psychological ingredients—processes or mechanisms—that define the virtues" (p. 13).

Character strengths allow you to develop perspective and include strengths such as creativity, curiosity, and open-mindedness. "Situational themes are specific habits that lead people to manifest given character strengths in given situations" (p. 14). For example, school themes might be different from work themes or family themes. You might be competitive at school but not in social situations with your friends. Situational themes are used to achieve strengths in a given context, and individuals can achieve similar results using different situational themes. The StrengthsFinder measures talents and strengths while the VIA measures character strengths using a strengths-based approach to measuring character. The VIA classification scheme is organized around six virtues (Peterson & Seligman, 2004):

1. Courage: "doing what is right, even when one has much to lose" (p. 36)
2. Justice: fairness; citizenship; equity
3. Wisdom and knowledge: "intelligence hard fought for, and then used for good . . . noble intelligence—in the presence of which no one is resentful and everyone is appreciative" (p. 39)
4. Humanity: showing generosity and being altruistic; exhibiting prosocial behaviors such as kindness and benevolence
5. Temperance: the ability to monitor and manage emotions; showing self-control
6. Transcendence: having a connection to someone higher than oneself that inspires hope, awe, and gratitude; achieving meaning and purpose beyond self-interest

The VIA classification includes 24 character strengths that are organized around these six virtues: See Table 4.2.

Table 4.2 **VIA Classification**

Wisdom and Knowledge	Courage	Humanity
Creativity	Bravery	Love
Curiosity	Perseverance	Kindness
Judgment	Honesty	Social Intelligence
Love of Learning	Zest	
Perspective		

Justice	Temperance	Transcendence
Teamwork	Forgiveness	Appreciation of Beauty and Excellence
Fairness	Humility	Gratitude
Leadership	Prudence	Hope
	Self-Regulation	Humor
		Spirituality

Adapted from Peterson & Seligman (2004).

Peterson and Seligman developed the VIA Survey assessment to measure these 24 character strengths. The VIA Survey is scientifically validated and is available free at the following website: www.viacharacter.org. Simply click on "Take the free VIA inventory of strengths" link and follow the instructions. The online survey will take approximately 25 minutes to complete. A comprehensive VIA report will be sent to you by email shortly after you finish the assessment. Your report will identify your top character strengths, giving you greater insights into what makes you who you are.

> Factors That Shape Your Leadership Identity

Several central, salient characteristics have probably made you the person you are and the person you will become as you age. Consider how your ethnic, racial, or cultural background has made a difference and shaped the way you are. How do you believe or behave differently because you are a man or a woman? How has your sexual orientation influenced your attitudes and behaviors? How does your age influence your interests and views? Do you have specific abilities or disabilities that shape your perceptions or skills? How has your birth-order position in your family influenced your development? What significant roles do you have that bring responsibilities that shape your decisions—being a son or daughter, a volunteer, a parent, an office manager, a Sunday School teacher, or an athlete? How has your sense of spirituality shaped your worldview? How important is religion in guiding your thinking? How has your family's socioeconomic status influenced your development and your views of leadership? Individuals may do things differently because they are male or female, old or young, Irish Catholic, Jewish, or Muslim. Mapping your personal context must include many elements that contribute to your sense of identity.

No matter what your sexual, racial, ethnic, or religious identity, a global mindset is also critical "because the very abilities required to deal with a diverse, multicultural world can also be helpful in effectively working with one another" (Cabrera & Unruh, 2012, p. 21). Cabrera and Unruh (2012) describe the importance of having a global leadership identity—not just acting globally but *being* global. They define global leaders as "understanding the cultural, social, or political differences that keep contributors apart and find ways to build, cultivate, and connect them despite, and sometimes because of, those differences" (p. 12). Global leadership is a mindset and a part of an individual's leadership identity. We live in an interconnected world that calls upon leaders to *be* global. Having a global mindset means being able to suspend judgment about others who are different from you while also having the ability to analyze situations from multiple and competing perspectives. Using listening skills to understand different cultural backgrounds and committing to learning about cultures that are different from your own are part of what it means to have a global mindset as a leader.

Cabrera and Unruh (2012) argue that global leadership identity is like a muscle that can be strengthened over time with focus and practice. Engaging with others from different cultures and gaining new knowledge and experiences about various places from around the world is a start to cultivating your global leadership mindset. You might consider joining a group that will stretch your knowledge about other cultures and identities. Instead of sitting in the dining hall with others who are just like you, share a meal with individuals from other cultures.

We believe the capacity for leadership is within each of you. As we noted in Chapter Two, many observers of leadership agree that leaders are made, not born and that everyone has a "leader within" (Haas & Tamarkin, 1992). Meaningful interaction and effective leadership processes can result if individuals are aware of their own motivations and where others are coming from. The leader-within-you may be willing to assume positional leadership roles or may be more comfortable with active participant roles. Either way, within you is the capacity to make a difference.

> Values, Beliefs, Ethics, and Character

As difficult as it may be to determine how characteristics like your gender, ethnicity, or religion influence the way you think and act, it is even more complicated and important to identify the values and beliefs that lead to your ethical behaviors and build your character.

Values and Beliefs

Among the hardest things to articulate are the values that guide actions. If your actions and thoughts are a mystery to you, you may not have adequately examined your own value system. Beliefs shape values, which influence thoughts and actions. If you can articulate your values, then you are likely to be aware of the principles and beliefs that serve as your guides.

Contrasts in value systems are rarely as clear as when Star Trek's Mr. Spock dispassionately says to Bones, a surgeon on the U.S.S. Enterprise, "You are too emotional, Doctor. That is not logical." Bones always explodes and shouts back, "Mr. Spock, how can you be half human and not have one ounce of feeling in you?" Each of us has preferences in how we construct our own value systems. You may prefer to be logical and scientific or you may be emotional; you may prefer to be concrete or you may just come to know what is important by using your intuition. Knowing that you have preferences in how you construct your value system should help you understand yourself and others better. No one process is preferred over others; your process reflects how you have come to construct meaning from your experience.

The discussion of values should always raise the crucial question, Whose values and for what purpose? Some values, such as promise keeping and nonviolence, are so fundamental that they have been found to be norms in most civilized societies (Bok, 1990). In a study of diverse men and women committed to meaningful change, researchers asked each person, "If you could help create a global code of ethics, what would it include? What moral values, in other words, would you bring to the table from your own culture and background?" (Kidder, 1995, p. 17).

STUDENT ESSAY ◆

In order for me to truly understand myself as a leader I first had to understand why I became a leader in the first place. In my case, I mainly became a leader to support a friend who was trying to rebuild a club. Before she asked for my help, I had no interest in becoming a leader. I felt this way mainly because I did not think I had the qualities of a leader. Once I was in the position, I had to figure out why I wanted to continue as a leader and why people were actually paying attention to what I had to say. I realized that the core values that make up my personality are fundamental values that many other people share. Those core values include dependability, determination, fairness, open-mindedness, and encouragement. By incorporating the opinions and ideas from the members and leaders of our club, without compromising my values, I realized that other people respect me for that. That in itself is what makes other people believe in me and want to listen to what I have to say. Through this process of thought, I realized that I had the qualities of a leader all along; I simply did not realize it.

Cheryl Kintz is a undergraduate student of Florida Atlantic University where she is majoring in psychology and minoring in biological science and sociology. She is vice president of the Broward Psychological Association, is an active member of Omicron Delta Kappa, and is involved in various community service projects.

Their findings led to eight moral values likely to be exceptionally important in our shared global future: love, truthfulness, fairness, freedom, unity, tolerance, responsibility, and respect for life (pp. 18–19).

Values such as these are integral to the development of character. Understanding values becomes a central component to understanding others and to achieving a common purpose. Imagine this scene:

Shaking his head, Scott approaches his two friends, Khalil and Michael. "I just cannot believe it!" Scott laments. "I just heard that James vetoed the activity fee allocations to the student Hillel Association. I think he is biased and power hungry and I'm quitting student government. I just won't have anything to do with student government anymore, not with a president who does stuff like that!"

"Hey, just wait a minute, Scott," Michael implores. "I've always known James to be fair and reasonable, and I trust him. Something else must be going on that we just don't understand. He must have a reason if he did this, and knowing him like we do, I bet it is a good reason. There's probably more behind his decision than we can see right now."

"Yeah, I agree completely. I know him pretty well and he's OK. Let's go talk to him," Khalil adds.

James's character and reputation for integrity among those who know him are solid and defensible. When a person is known for a solid value system grounded in integrity and authenticity, others may disagree with a decision but cannot find fault with the character of the decision maker. Concurrently, Scott did not know James well enough to form the opinion Michael and Khalil shared but he did have the strength of his convictions that he would quit an organization over such actions. That is also a measure of someone's integrity and is also a possible reaction to an intolerable ethical dilemma or values conflict. Values were behind these students' reactions.

Character and Ethical Behavior

Integrity in relationships is central to the value systems needed among people working together toward change. Authenticity is rooted in action that is "both true and real in ourselves and in the world" (Terry, 1993, pp. 111–112). Whether framed as integrity, authenticity, or credibility, the very core of your character is central to sincerely linking with others in the spirit of community to work toward change.

A person of character promotes ethical decision making and expects ethical behavior from others. The Josephson Institute of Ethics proposes six pillars of character that are "enduring and indispensable" to ethical leadership practices (Jones & Lucas, 1994, p. 4). These pillars are trustworthiness, respect, responsibility, fairness, caring, and citizenship.

Trustworthiness is far more than telling the truth. Being worthy of trust means being honest, demonstrating integrity, keeping promises, and being loyal. It means being known for standing up for your own convictions. Respect means that you treat others considerately, not that you admire or agree with all their views or behaviors. Being respectful is a commitment to treating others in ways that do not demean or take advantage of them. Responsibility means accepting accountability for your own actions and being conscious of the moral and ethical implications of deciding not to act. Being responsible means being accountable, pursuing excellence, and exercising self-restraint.

Fairness is working toward an equitable outcome. Being fair means being open-minded, willing to listen, and confronting your own biases that might influence your decisions. Caring means your awareness of being concerned for each person's well-being and your attention to not being hurtful. Care requires empathy and kindness. Citizenship is the civic virtue of knowing that as a member of a community, you have responsibilities to do your part to contribute to the well-being of the group. Citizenship means you are willing to abide by laws and societal obligations.

A Person of Character

- Is trustworthy (is honest, has integrity, keeps promises, is loyal)
- Treats people with respect (is courteous, nonviolent, nonprejudiced, accepting)
- Is responsible (is accountable, pursues excellence, shows self-restraint)
- Is fair (just, equitable, open, reasonable, unbiased)
- Is caring (kind, compassionate, empathetic, unselfish)
- Is a good citizen (is law-abiding, does his or her share, performs community service, protects the environment)

After a concert on campus one Friday night, two students were counting the ticket sales receipts. The money in the cash drawer was $120 short for the number of tickets sold. Baffled at the difference, the students turned in the accounts the next day and presented the problem to the Student Activities Office. That afternoon, a third student came into the office carrying an envelope containing $120. The money had apparently come in during a ticket sales rush and was set aside instead of being locked in the cash drawer.

The office accountant clerk asked her, "Why didn't you just keep the money? No one would have known."

The student's quick, indignant reply was, "But I would have known, and I don't do things like that!"

That student's consciousness of her own value system and commitment to integrity was so embedded that she could not imagine behaving any differently. The trust and respect she earned in her relationships led to an assessment of her character that was above reproach. Another example in the news was when a student volunteer, who was helping with the clean-up after Hurricane Katrina in 2005, found $30,000 in cash in a vacated house and turned the money in to the authorities. "Leadership . . . requires a special kind of dedication, a special kind of belief. I think that you must have defined for yourself a set of moral and ethical values in which you chose to make your decisions in life as you move along. Then you must be true to yourself" (Schwarzkopf, as cited in Wren, 1994, p. 5).

› Chapter Summary

This chapter discussed some important aspects of self-awareness that become key to understanding yourself as a participant and as a leader. The chapter explored ways to examine your strengths and weaknesses, with a goal of developing your talent and having a realistic self-concept with healthy self-esteem and self-confidence. We then reviewed basic values that are essential in a person of character. The StrengthsFinder and VIA self-assessments were offered as tools for greater self-awareness and application in your leadership.

› What's Next?

Understanding yourself and building your capacity for self-leadership is a foundational asset for effectively relating to others. Chapter Five will encourage you to explore yourself in the context of others. The chapter will further present how interpersonal relations can be enhanced by understanding differences and commonalties with others. This understanding is helpful in communicating and building empowering relationships with other participants.

> Chapter Activities

1. Think about your gender, ethnicity, sexual orientation, special abilities or disabilities, age, socioeconomic status, religion, birth order, and any other possible influences that come to mind. How have these factors influenced your personality and learning preferences?

2. Write your own personal mission statement. What is your purpose in life? What values are important to you? What do you want to be? What attributes and capabilities are important to you?

3. Review Bennis's lessons for developing self-knowledge and provide examples from your own life. When were you your own best teacher? When did you accept responsibility for something that did not go well? When did you learn something you really wanted to learn? When did you learn something through the process of reflection?

4. Looking at your top five strengths from the StrengthsFinder assessment report, how can you apply these in your leadership? Identify an example of how you applied each of these five strengths within the last week. How do you apply these talents in your leadership? How can these strengths be integrated in your leadership?

5. Think about all the behaviors you do currently in your leadership or membership role. Which ones are you doing that

are in your top five strengths? Which ones are not? How can you bring your strengths into better alignment with your leadership?

6. Many people use positive affirmations to enhance their self-esteem. While they will not make up for a lack of skill or ability, they can help you develop your confidence. An example might be, "I am going to do a good job speaking in front of this group." Saying this phrase over and over to yourself, up to 20 times throughout the day, can help you believe in yourself. Develop two or three affirmations that you can use to strengthen your self-confidence.

7. Another technique is creative visualization. Although this will not make up for a lack of skill or ability, it can help you develop your confidence. Identify something you have to do in the next couple of days that is causing you to worry. Now visualize yourself accomplishing this activity successfully. Repeat this visualization whenever you begin to worry about the upcoming event. After the event is over, consider whether or not using visualization helped you.

8. Using the dipper and bucket metaphor, go to The Gallup Organization Web site at http://www.bucketbook.com/drops/electronic/thanks.aspx and send someone an electronic drop to fill his or her bucket.

9. As a simple mindfulness practice, think about a current feeling you are experiencing. Where does it reside within your body? Where do you feel the impact most? What specifically can you to do attend to this feeling?

10. Think of a good act or gesture you did within the last 24 hours. Think of three additional good deeds. Reflect on what you did that enriched someone's life, whether it was a small or large gesture. Now think of someone who has helped

you in your lifetime. Appreciate that person's kindness and impact on you—what are you most grateful for? Think of a challenging moment or encounter you have experienced recently. Can you picture yourself transcending the problem? Are you able to experience equanimity? (Salzburg, 2011).

11. After reviewing your VIA profile, what stood out the most to you and why?

12. From your VIA report, identify three to four of your top character strengths. Within the last week, how have you applied those in your life? In your leadership?

ADDITIONAL READINGS

Boyatzis, R., & McKee, A. (2005). *Resonant leadership: Renewing yourself and connecting with others through mindfulness, hope, and compassion.* Boston, MA: Harvard Business School Press.

Cabrera, A., & Unruh, G. (2012). *Being global: How to think, act, and lead in a transformed world.* Boston, MA: Harvard Business Review Press.

Davidson, R. J., & Begley, S. (2012). *The emotional life of your brain: How its unique patterns affect the way you think, feel, and live—and how you can change them.* New York, NY: Hudson Street Press.

Goleman, D. (2004, January). What makes a leader? *Harvard Business Review,* pp. 1–11.

Hanson, R. (2009). *Buddha's brain: The practical neuroscience of happiness, love, and wisdom.* Oakland, CA: New Harbinger.

Rath, T., & Clifton, D. O. (2004). *How full is your bucket: Positive strengths for work and life.* New York, NY: Gallup Press.

Salzburg, S. (2011). *Real happiness: The power of meditation.* New York, NY: Workman.

Chapter 5

Understanding Others

Consider this situation:

Place yourself in a typical meeting of an organization in which you are a member. Have you ever found yourself wondering . . .

Laurie wonders why the men in the organization seem to dominate the discussions. Martina wonders why some of the group's members never say anything.

James wonders why some of his peers enjoy controversy so much. They seem to enjoy the disagreement and heated debate.

Patrick wonders what it's like to be one of the few students of color in the room. Julianna wonders if the students in the organization who are gay feel safe.

Angela wonders if those students who are very religious are offended by any of the conversations going on during the meeting.

Remi and Bolorma wonder why this and other student organizations are not interested in recruiting international students such as themselves.

What do you wonder about the motives and behavior of others when you're sitting in a typical organization meeting?

A central goal of understanding yourself is to develop a sense of awareness that can result in true community and common purpose with others. There are three central questions (Komives, 1994) to ask yourself in any setting:

- How am I like no one else here?
- How am I like some others here?
- How am I like everyone here? (p. 219)

Each of us brings uniqueness and individuality to any situation. As we explored in Chapter Four, your strengths, skills, background, and preferences create a unique person—you. But you are not alone. To be truly inclusive and empowering, you must also understand others. The importance of this cannot be overstated. As the nation becomes more diverse and the world becomes smaller and more connected through technology, it becomes "flatter" (Friedman, 2005). Understanding others is a necessity for all leaders. It is also one of the most sought after skills in college graduates. "Learning from people who are different from you—and recognizing your commonalities—is an important part of your education and essential preparation for the world you will join" (Michigan State University, p. 2)

> Chapter Overview

In this chapter we briefly explore some characteristics of
gender, ethnicity, and culture that illustrate how differences
need to be understood as you work toward leadership that is
inclusive and empowering. We also explore various leadership
processes—including communication, conflict resolution, and
decision making—that are influenced by diverse approaches.
We conclude with a discussion of communication skills, such as
empathy and assertiveness that are useful in working effectively
with others in leadership.

> Individuality and Commonality

In Chapter Four you explored yourself. Others might be similar
to you or very different from you. Even if others look the
same, they may have different strengths, values, preferences, or
approaches to learning. Some of these differences in ourselves
and others come from aspects of our identity—including gender,
sexual identity, ethnicity, age, religion, socioeconomic status,
ability—some come from our environments.

   In the grand scheme of living human species, we are more
alike than we are different. Research into the human genome
has certainly confirmed this. Finding common human purpose
is the focus on which to center our perceptions of difference.
The poet Maya Angelou (1994) has remarkable insight into the
commonalties of being human. In her poem "Human Family,"

she describes all of our uniqueness as people that set us apart, but concludes, "We are more alike, my friends, than we are unalike" (pp. 224–225). And yet, whenever we are in group situations we need to do our best to keep in mind how members of the group are similar and how they are different. To consider one but not the other is incomplete and does a disservice to the people with whom you are working.

In any group setting, you can look around and see others who look like you. You will see men or women, people with visible racial or ethnic characteristics, or people of different ages. Also, you might see people wearing symbolic attire like your own: a wedding ring, a sorority pin, a pink triangle, a Star of David, or carrying a skateboard. You might also identify with others when they express ideas you agree with, share experiences you have had, or have goals you also hold, regardless of visible characteristics that might have initially made them seem unlike you. You may begin to find similarities of interests: being in the same major, living close together, thinking alike about current politics, working out daily, being parents, or being affiliated with the same religion. Finding some people like you creates a feeling of association called social identity and leads to the identification of subcommunities.

On a transcendent level, something binds you to everyone around you, no matter how different they may seem: you all want to learn the subject in a particular course; you all value the goals of the organization meeting you have attended, be it the residence hall association, the aikido club, or a Bible study class; or you all want to work toward a common purpose like changing the university's policy on weekend library hours. The challenge of leadership is coming to common purpose from the vast differences that individuals bring to a situation. Finding the purpose, vision, and common commitments that create a "we" from a group of individuals is the challenge of community.

The English language may well be the only one that values the individual to such a degree that the word for the first person singular—I—is capitalized. This emphasis on the individual is grounded in a predominantly Western tradition. Those with non-Western roots may find it easier to envision *we* because those cultural traditions emphasize the collective, the family, or group. To truly establish a sense of we, the individual needs to let go of self enough to see the connections to others.

Buber (1958) encouraged an exploration of "I-Thou"; leadership educators have encouraged "I→you→we" (National Invitational Leadership Symposium, 1991). This might best be expressed symbolically by showing that the focus on the individual (I) needs to be deemphasized (i) to truly listen and engage with another (you) as equals, so that all can move forward to become a community (we) (see Figure 5.1).

One challenge, then, is to understand yourself well enough to know how others see you and to modify your own behaviors and attitudes to encourage a spirit of openness and connection with others. The second challenge is to engage in the hard work of understanding others so that together you can form meaningful community and engage in coalitions for group change.

$$\begin{array}{ccc} \text{"I"} & \Rightarrow & \text{"i"} \\ \Uparrow & \Rightarrow & \text{"we"} \\ \text{"you"} & & \end{array}$$

Figure 5.1 **I, You, and We**

Groups are made up of great diversity. Even if members are all of one sex or one race or one major, there are great differences in personality, strengths, learning preferences, and experiences. The pluralism of a group refers to the plethora of differences that need to be understood in order to accomplish shared purposes. Pluralistic leadership results when heterogeneous groups of people work together to accomplish change. Pluralistic leadership is enhanced when a person understands, develops an appreciation for, and possesses the skills needed to communicate across these borders and come to common understandings.

> Understanding Gender Diversity

Let's begin by having you ask yourself, "How does my gender influence my attitudes and behaviors? How does my experience as a man or woman shape my worldview and how might it shape the worldview of others?" Characteristics of gender differences are too numerous to develop fully, but it is important to realize that we all deal with both sex roles and gender roles. The two terms are often used interchangeably, but sex roles are those expectations resulting from biology, like pregnancy or muscle mass, whereas gender roles are socially constructed expectations that get labeled masculine or feminine.

Gender roles are often limiting and inaccurate when assigned to individual men and women. For example, although only women can bear children, women are not the only sex to be nurturing of children. While it is certainly evolving, historically men's involvement in the development of children has been limited because that role has been considered feminine and nurturing. Likewise, women may be athletic, but it has been hard for women to engage in sports that require high physical contact, like football, because those sports are considered masculine. Women who are not nurturing or men who are not athletic may suffer from gender role discrimination by acting or being different from conventional paradigms. Likewise, those who hold a conventional leadership expectation that leaders should be decisive, in charge, competitive, and self-reliant may be holding a traditional masculine paradigm that excludes many women, as well as many men who are very capable but who do not lead from that perspective.

From the beginnings of our lives, our gender role perceptions are shaped by the many messages we receive from the environment. Even those parents who make sure the storybooks their children read do not promote gender role or sex role stereotypes and who give dolls to their sons and trucks to their daughters soon realize that other socialization agents (like peers, toys, television, and conversations on the bus going to school every morning) reinforce traditional gender messages. Many boys learn to be tough, objective, unemotional, and competitive, and many girls learn to be polite, caring, emotional, and supportive.

To understand how men and women have come to be as they are, we can learn from children's development. The way we play in childhood establishes patterns of how we work and communicate as adults. Boys often play outside in rough-and-tumble games, and extraverted leaders shout commands in competitive settings. Winning or losing becomes very important. Most games are played by teams. Even inside games like video or computer games often have elaborate hierarchical systems with complex rules and procedures that involve dominating or annihilating enemies and are frequently preferred by boys. Girls, however, often play inside in calm settings with one another or with a small group of friends. Their play stresses intimacy and values social relationships. Many of their preferred games have no winners or losers but every person gets a turn—consider such games as jumping rope, hopscotch, or playing house (Tannen, 1990). The social learning that happens with play and many other experiences often leads females to seek and value intimacy and relationships, whereas males often seek and value independence.

Intimacy is key in a world of connection in which individuals negotiate complex networks of friendship, minimize differences, try to reach consensus, and value the appearance of superiority that would highlight differences. In a world of status, independence is key, because a primary means of establishing status is to tell others what to do, and taking orders is a marker of low status (Tannen, 1990, p. 26).

Only recently in entertainment do we find people who play roles that are different from conventional gender roles. Can you think of a television show or movie in which a woman played a role traditionally viewed as being for a man? Or in which a man played a role traditionally reserved for a woman? It is perhaps more likely to find a woman chief of detectives or member of the military than it is to find a man as a kindergarten teacher or nurse.

Men and women tend to hold different attributions for their successes and failures. Many women tend to credit their successes to external factors like luck and being in the right place at the right time. They might say, "Oh, I don't deserve the credit.

So many people helped." They credit their failures to internal factors like not being prepared or not having the right skills or not having enough time. Many men, in contrast, tend to credit successes to internal factors like being prepared and capable and attribute their failures to external factors like fate, others not doing their part, or bad luck.

However in the last thirty years, "psychological and physiological data on sex-linked traits suggest that the degree of overlap between the sexes is as important, or more important, than the average differences between them" (Lipman-Blumen, 1984, p. 4). Both men and women are capable of making good decisions, leading effectively, being responsible group members, and communicating with clarity, but they may go about doing those things differently than the other sex would (Eagley, Karau, & Makhijani, 1995). The fact that we persist in observing differences speaks to the power relationships that continue to exist in which men's ways, views, and artifacts have had higher status. Because men have traditionally held many visible leadership positions, the conventional paradigm of leadership was often socially constructed as having these same male characteristics. It's interesting that in recent years the gender conversation has shifted. Now, for many, boys and men are not achieving all that they should or could (Kimmel, 2008).

Expectations that limit people's range of roles and suppress their individuality are likely to inhibit their effectiveness in their communities. Sex or gender, however, is only one identity perspective we bring to a situation. We all have other salient social identities that are based on attributes such as our culture, ethnicity, age, or sexual orientation.

> Understanding Cultural Diversity

Culture encompasses everything about how a group of people thinks, feels, and behaves. It is their pattern of knowledge. It is a "body of common understandings" (Brown, 1963, p. 3). Culture is

> An integrated pattern of human behavior that includes thoughts, communications, languages, practices, beliefs, values, customs, courtesies, rituals, manners of interacting and roles, relationships and expected behaviors of a racial, ethnic, religious or social group; and the ability to transmit the above to succeeding generations. (National Center for Cultural Competence of Georgetown University—http://www.ncccurricula.info/glossary.html)

We may be so embedded in our culture that it is hard to see it clearly.

Culture is, therefore, a broad term that could be applied to an office or a campus, to aging, or to a group of people who share a common race or ethnicity. Many cultures coexist simultaneously in any group. Effective leaders need to develop an appreciation for multiculturalism to build inclusiveness, collaboration, and common purposes. A prerequisite to developing a greater sense of multiculturalism is the conscious awareness of culturally informed assumptions (Helms, 1992; Pedersen, 1988).

Culture has often been described in terms of race and ethnicity. We encourage you to be cautious about the construct of race. We have long known that race is a "somewhat suspect concept used to identify large groups of the human species who share a more or less distinctive combination of hereditary physical characteristics" (Hoopes & Pusch, 1979, p. 3). The California Newsreel entitled *Race—The Power of an Illusion* explores this concept in detail in a three-hour video series and presents evidence that the very concept of race has no biological foundation. According to their website,

> The division of the world's peoples into distinct groups—"red," "black," "white," or "yellow" peoples—has became so deeply imbedded in our psyches, so widely accepted, many would promptly dismiss as crazy any suggestion of its falsity. Yet, that's exactly what this provocative three-hour series by California Newsreel claims. *Race—The Power of an Illusion* questions the very idea of race as biology, suggesting that a belief in race is no more sound than believing that the sun revolves around the earth. Yet race still matters. Just because race doesn't exist in biology doesn't mean it isn't very real, helping shape life chances and opportunities. (http://www.newsreel.org/nav/title.asp?tc=CN0149)

As noted educator Derald Wing Sue (2003) states, "Many difficulties exist, however, in using race as a descriptor" (p. 34).

Nevertheless, historically, race has been a very powerful aspect of life in the United States and continues to impact every campus today. It has been used to marginalize whole groups of people, and students on campuses experience racism every day. The Relational Leadership Model, with its emphasis on inclusion and empowerment, embraces the belief that the group, team, organization, community, nation, and world will be made better when all participants are heard, made visible, and valued for their contributions.

Historically, the dominant culture—the culture in the powerful majority—has not had to examine its beliefs and

practices because it is not disadvantaged by them. The majority
norms often became the standards used to judge others who
are not in the majority. America's attention to racial and
ethnic diversity has led to new awareness of what it means to be
White and of European origin in the American culture. Peggy
McIntosh (1989) coined the phrase the "invisible knapsack"
to describe the concept of "White privilege." This weightless
knapsack is filled with provisions that help White people travel
through life more easily. Even well-meaning people in the
majority culture often take for granted the benefits of White
privilege, which include shopping without being followed,
being able to buy or rent housing of their choice, and easily
finding toys and pictures that look like themselves (Talbot,
1996). In a general sense, it is useful to think of the privileges
afforded any of us by virtue of personal characteristics that
place us in a powerful "majority" (for example, being male,
heterosexual, able-bodied, educated, financially comfortable)
and examine closely how unconsciously affirming the privileges
associated with those characteristics may actually cause or
influence the oppression of others, even though oppression
is unintended. Cris Cullinan (1999) describes privilege in a
slightly different way. She notes that people with privilege are
presumed to be innocent, worthy, and competent. We must
examine how the characteristics of these forms of privilege
may be attached to our expectations of what it means to be
a leader or to not be a leader, and we must learn to value,
or at least recognize, that leadership may take on different
characteristics.

STUDENT ESSAY

I have assisted in the progression of diversity awareness and related factors at St. Norbert College. Many women of color on campus were experiencing issues of discrimination, loneliness, self-esteem issues, or just wanted a place to comfortably express their feelings in a safe place. The campus has also struggled with the retention of students of color. My solution was to create a program that would create an inspiring atmosphere for women of color on-campus. I started the first women of color, monthly dinner series as a Friday night activity. Each dinner had a different theme, activities, food, and guest speakers. The group will continue after I graduate, adding volunteer projects to their activities as well as mentoring high school girls and inspiring them to pursue higher education. Not only did I develop profound leadership qualities at St. Norbert College, but I was able to mentor and assist other women of color to become engaged in leadership activities on campus by giving them the support they initially needed to succeed to their highest ability.

Montriesia Gourrier is a graduate of St. Norbert College receiving her degree in sociology and minoring in leadership studies. She was a Diversity Scholarship recipient, a dean's list student, and peer mentor. She actively engaged in social activism studies as well as promoted diversity awareness initiatives on the campus and the surrounding community.

> Understanding International Diversity

Understanding how to work with persons from other countries is even more complex but can be an exciting and rewarding experience. At times, it can also be very challenging. One of the

great opportunities afforded to college students is the chance
to get to know and work with students from other nations and,
perhaps even to study abroad. As Javidan and House (2001)
noted in describing global leaders, "To be successful in dealing
with people from other cultures, managers need knowledge about
cultural differences and similarities among countries. They also
need to understand the implications of the differences and the
skills required to act and decide appropriately and in a culturally
sensitive way" (p. 292). Kets de Vries and Florent-Treacy (2002)
note that global leadership development means increasing one's
adaptability, cultural empathy, acceptance of ambiguity, lack of
xenophobia, cultural relativity, awareness of one's own roots and
cultural biases, and "as if" quality (p. 307). They go on to note,
"An outlook of cultural relativity, excellent relational skills,
curiosity, and emotional intelligence distinguish successful global
leaders" (p. 304).

Project GLOBE (Global Leadership and Organizational
Behavior Effectiveness), an extensive international study of
thousands of middle managers, defined culture as "a set of
shared values and beliefs" in which the values are "people's
aspirations about the way things should be done" and the
beliefs are "people's perceptions of how things are done in their
countries" (Javidan & House, 2001, p. 293). This study identified nine dimensions of culture that differed from country to
country: assertiveness, future orientation, gender differentiation,
uncertainty avoidance, power distance (power expected to be
shared unequally within the culture), institutional emphasis on
collectivism versus individualism, in-group collectivism (membership in small groups and families), performance orientation,
and humane orientation (fairness, generosity, caring) (Javidan &

House, 2001). Some countries seem to be higher than others in different dimensions. For example, people in the United States are thought to be more male-dominated than people in England but less than people in Germany. (See House, Hanges, Javidan, Dorfman, & Gupta, 2004, for the complete report.) As with any attempt to generalize large groups, information in reports such as this should be viewed and used with great caution. That being said, when working with others from different nations, realizing they may differ from you in the dimensions mentioned in this report can help you understand them better and work with them more effectively.

Knowledge about other countries becomes increasingly important as the world becomes more connected or "flat" (Friedman, 2005). It is also an area in which U.S. students could improve. Rebekah Nathan (2005) is the pen name of an anthropologist who went "undercover" and lived in a residence hall posing as a freshman. As she discovered,

> The single biggest complaint international students lodged against U.S. students was, to put it bluntly, our ignorance. As informants described it, by "ignorance" they meant the misinformation and lack of information that Americans have both about other countries and about themselves. (p. 84)

> Your Cultural Heritage

We encourage you to read about your cultural heritage to see how you may have acquired the values and beliefs of your culture or ethnicity and determine in what ways you have diverged from them. Read also about a group that is different from your own. You might study the White or European American cultures,

African American or Black culture, Asian American cultures, Latino or Hispanic or Chicano cultures, Native American traditions, and international students who come from other countries. Learn more about aging and adult development, deaf culture, religious diversity, and regional differences. In any case, it will be useful to be aware of the assumptions that a person coming into a group might have that would influence that person's behavior. It may be most useful to start with you.

Cultural Competence

One term that has recently come into use to describe the awareness, knowledge, and skills needed to operate effectively in this global, multicultural world is "cultural competency." Milton Bennett (2011), a noted international education specialist, describes a similar term in this manner—"Intercultural Competence: a set of cognitive, affective, and behavioral skills and characteristics that support effective and appropriate interaction in a variety of cultural contexts" (p. 3). Exhibit 5.1 describes both some things we know about the concept and ways to become more competent in this area.

Building Multicultural Appreciation

Being an effective leader or participant in a diverse organization or being a leader who brings diversity to the organization requires that we know more about developing an openness and appreciation of various cultures and aspects of how others may differ. Paul Pedersen (1988) supports this idea by noting that individuals need to develop their awareness, knowledge, and skills to be able to work effectively in a multicultural environment. Bennett (2004, 2011) provides us with a useful framework from which to examine our own growth in this area with the

Exhibit 5.1: Intercultural Competence

A Few Things We Know About Intercultural Competence
Cultural knowledge does not necessarily lead to competence.
Cultural contact does not necessarily lead to competence.
Cultural contact may lead to reduction of stereotypes.
Language learning may not be sufficient for culture learning.

What Does Lead to Intercultural Competence?
Intentional and developmentally sequenced program design.
Balancing challenge and support; anxiety reduction.
Facilitating learning before, during, and after intercultural
    experiences.
Depth of intercultural experiences, language immersion.
Intercultural competence training.
Cultivating curiosity and cognitive flexibility.
(Bennett, 2011, p. 5)

Developmental Model of Intercultural Sensitivity (Table 5.1). In this six-stage model, people move from having minimal contact with others who are different through various stages to seeing difference as wrong to eventually reaching a state of having a strong sense of who they are as cultural beings and an appreciation of how cultures are similar and different.

Stage One—Denial of Difference. People with this predominant experience are "in denial" about cultural difference—they are unable to experience differences in other than extremely simple ways.

Stage Two—Defense against Difference. People with a predominant experience of Defense experience cultural difference in a polarized way—us and them.

Stage Three—Minimization of Difference. The predominant experience of Minimization is that of having "arrived" at intercultural sensitivity. The polarized experience of Defense has given way to a recognition of the common humanity of all people regardless of culture ("We are the world").

Stage Four—Acceptance of Difference. When Acceptance is the predominant experience, people experience cultural difference in context.

Stage Five—Adaptation to Difference. Adaptation is the application of Acceptance, and it is likely to become the predominant experience when there is a need to actually interact effectively with people of another culture.

Stage Six—Integration of Difference. The experience of Integration is of being a person who is not defined in terms of any one culture—typically a person who is bicultural or multicultural. (Bennett, rev. 2011, pp. 1–11)

Janet Bennett (2011) takes this framework and identifies specific aspects for the cognitive, affective, and behavioral areas. The cognitive area involves cultural self-awareness, culture-general knowledge, culture-specific knowledge, and interaction analysis. The affective area includes curiosity, cognitive flexibility, motivation, and open-mindedness. Finally, the area of behavioral skills involves relationship building skills, behavioral skills (listening, problem solving, empathy), and information gathering skills.

The goal of this process is multiculturalism, which is not a final state but an ongoing process of comfort in learning about and appreciating one's own and other cultures. This is a lifelong learning task. This openness to new experiences enriches a

Table 5.1 **Developmental Model of Intercultural Sensitivity**

Stage	At This Stage, Learners Say...
I. DENIAL OF DIFFERENCE People with this predominant experience are "in denial" about cultural difference—they are unable to experience differences in other than extremely simple ways. They may be perplexed when asked about their own culture, because they have not considered how culture impacts their own or others' lives. They might ask well-meant but naive questions about other cultures ("do they have television in Japan?") and make superficial statements of tolerance ("live and let live"). In some cases, people with this orientation may dehumanize others, assuming that different behavior is a deficiency in intelligence or personality.	"Live and let live, that's what I say." "All big cities are the same—lots of buildings, too many cars, McDonalds." "As long as we all speak the same language, there's no problem." "The main concerns I have involve knowing how to get around and ordering in restaurants." "With my experience, I can be successful in any culture without any special effort—I never experience culture shock." "All I need to know about is politics and history—I can figure out the rest of it as I go along."

(continued)

Table 5.1 **Developmental Model of Intercultural Sensitivity (*continued*)**

Stage	At This Stage, Learners Say . . .
II. DEFENSE AGAINST DIFFERENCE People with a predominant experience of Defense experience cultural difference in a polarized way—us and them. They feel "under siege" by people that they stereotype in simplistic and negative ways, protecting themselves with a hardened boundary between themselves and the "others." Typically, one's own culture is exalted, and other cultures are denigrated with negative stereotypes. This hierarchical view of culture may lead people to assume a kind of social Darwinism wherein they place their own culture at the acme of development and civilization.	"Why don't these people speak my language?" "When I go to other cultures, I realize how much better my own culture is." "My culture should be a model for the rest of the world." "These people don't value life the way we do." "Boy, could we teach these people a lot of stuff." "What a sexist society!"
A common variation is a Reversal of the two poles, so that one's own culture is denigrated and other cultures are uncritically lauded. While Reversal may superficially seem to be more culturally sensitive, it is nevertheless still dualistic and overly simplistic.	"These people are so urbane and sophisticated, not like the superficial people back home." "I am embarrassed by my compatriots, so I spend all my time with the host country nationals." "I wish I could give up my own cultural background and really be one of these people."

Table 5.1 **Developmental Model of Intercultural Sensitivity (*continued*)**

Stage	At This Stage, Learners Say...
III. MINIMIZATION OF DIFFERENCE The predominant experience of Minimization is that of having "arrived" at intercultural sensitivity. The polarized experience of Defense has given way to a recognition of the common humanity of all people regardless of culture ("We are the world"). The familiar cultural worldview is protected by believing that deep down we are all alike, either physically/ psychologically or spiritually/philosophically. This assumption of similarity is then invoked to avoid recognizing one's own cultural patterns, understanding others, and eventually making necessary adaptations. The assumed commonality with others is typically defined in ethnocentric terms: since everyone is essentially like us, it is sufficient in cross-cultural situations to "just be yourself."	"The key to getting along in any culture is to just be yourself—authentic and honest!" "Customs differ, of course, but when you really get to know them they're pretty much like us." "I have this intuitive sense of other people, no matter what their culture." "Technology is bringing cultural uniformity to the developed world" "While the context may be different, the basic need to communicate remains the same around the world." "No matter what their culture, people are pretty much motivated by the same things." "If people are really honest, they'll recognize that some values are universal." "It's a small world, after all!"

(*continued*)

Table 5.1 **Developmental Model of Intercultural Sensitivity (*continued*)**

Stage	At This Stage, Learners Say . . .
IV. ACCEPTANCE OF DIFFERENCE When Acceptance is the predominant experience, people experience cultural difference in context. They accept that all behaviors and values, including their own, exist in distinctive cultural contexts and that patterns of behaviors and values can be discerned within each context. They see cultures as offering alternative viable solutions to the organization of human existence, and they are curious about what the alternatives to their own culture are. Acceptance does not mean agreement or preference for alternative values, but rather acceptance of the distinctive reality of each culture's worldview.	"The more difference the better—it's boring if everyone is the same" "People in other cultures are different in ways I hadn't thought of before" "I always try to study about a new culture before I go there." "The more cultures you know about, the better comparisons you can make." "Sometimes it's confusing, knowing that values are different in various cultures and wanting to be respectful, but still wanting to maintain my own core values." "When studying abroad, every student needs to be aware of relevant cultural differences." "My home-stay family and I have had very different life experiences, and we're learning from each other" "Where can I learn more about Mexican culture to be effective in my communication?"

Table 5.1 **Developmental Model of Intercultural Sensitivity (*continued*)**

Stage	At This Stage, Learners Say ...
V. ADAPTATION TO DIFFERENCE The experience of Adaptation is one of consciously shifting perspective and intentionally altering behavior. Adaptation is the application of Acceptance, and it is likely to become the predominant experience when there is a need to actually interact effectively with people of another culture. With the acceptance of another culture's organization of reality, Adaptation can proceed by allowing one to reorganize experience in a way more like that of the other culture. This is intercultural empathy. The ability to empathize with another worldview in turn allows modified behavior to flow naturally from that experience. It is this natural flow of behavior that keeps code-shifting from being fake or inauthentic.	"To solve this dispute, I'm going to have to change my approach." "I know they're really trying hard to adapt to my style, so it's fair that I try to meet them halfway." "I greet people from my culture and people from the host culture somewhat differently to account for cultural differences in the way respect is communicated." "I can maintain my values and also behave in culturally appropriate ways." "In a study abroad program, every student should be able to adapt to at least some cultural differences." "To solve this dispute, I need to change my behavior to account for the difference in status between me and my counterpart from the other culture." "I'm beginning to feel like a member of this culture." "The more I understand this culture, the better I get at the language."

(*continued*)

Table 5.1 **Developmental Model of Intercultural Sensitivity (*continued*)**

Stage	At This Stage, Learners Say...
VI. INTEGRATION OF DIFFERENCE The experience of Integration is of being a person who is not defined in terms of any one culture—typically a person who is bicultural or multicultural. The experience of Integration may occur when individuals intentionally make a significant, sustained effort to become fully competent in new cultures. It may become the predominant experience for nondominant group members who have adapted (not assimilated) to a dominant or colonial culture, or it may characterize persons who grew up or lived for extended periods in other cultures. A marginal cultural identity allows for lively participation in a variety of cultures, but also for an occasional sense of never really being "at home." People with this orientation experience themselves as "in process," and they generally have a wide repertoire of cultural perspectives and behavior to draw on.	"While sometimes I feel marginal in groups, I am able to move in and out of them with relative ease." "Everywhere is home, if you know enough about how things work there." "I feel most comfortable when I'm bridging differences between the cultures I know." "Whatever the situation, I can usually look at it from a variety of cultural points of view." "In an intercultural world, everyone needs to have a intercultural mindset." "I truly enjoy participating fully in both of my cultures." "My decision-making skills are enhanced by having multiple frames of reference."

Adapted from Bennett, Milton J. (rev. 2011). A developmental model of Intercultural Sensitivity. Retrieved from IDRInstitute website http://www.idrinstitute.org (pdf). Used with permission.

person's own life and makes it possible to share aspects of a person's own culture that may be of value to others.

Imagine this model (see Table 5.1) helping the aging culture to be more open to youth culture or the Black Student Union and the Jewish Student Union coming to an appreciation of each other's perspectives. Think of the lessons many could learn from Native Americans. A benefit of multiculturalism is to grow beyond seeing the world only in our own terms to seeing the legitimate views of others. This appreciation does not mean we will agree or even find decision making easy, but it should mean that we will understand other views.

STUDENT ESSAY

This past Spring Break, Student Coordinators Henna Pithia and Nicola Freeman and Program Coordinator Jennifer Gamble took a group of 13 students to Costa Rica for a global sustainability and cultural immersion program. Throughout the duration of the one week stay in Costa Rica, students lived on an eco-friendly farm, which functioned as a learning center, and also immersed themselves in the Costa Rican culture by participating in home stay programs, teaching at local schools, and participating in other community events. The purpose of this alternative spring break program dealt with leading in groups and teams to create change and empower students to learn in new and creative ways.

As student coordinators, Nicola and Henna helped implement the Costa Rica program by helping to present proposals to possible sponsors, leading discussions in Costa Rica about cultural immersion and personal growth, and helping to organize post-departure learning opportunities such as the Costa Rica Program Symposium and a Costa Rican themed night in the dining facilities.

(continued)

Nicola and Henna also helped lead the team by facilitating the cultural immersion process for various students on the trip. Henna and Nicola served as resources for students who were feeling challenged by various aspects of the new environment and also served as facilitators in creating conversations that encouraged cultural understanding and competence. Having these student coordinators in addition to the program coordinator was extremely beneficial in terms of helping students deal with culture shock, acclimatizing them, and thus allowing them to experience a new environment, learn from it, and let it change them.

Henna Pithia is a graduate of the University of California, Irvine where she double majored in international studies and political science. She was team manager for the green campus program and a resident advisor for two years, as well as a peer educator for the course, HIV/AIDS, and a fellow for an undergraduate research opportunity program. She is now attending law school at the University of Southern California and hopes to pursue a career in international human rights law.

> Attitudes Toward Differences

How we view others who are different from ourselves is complex. There is some evidence that this is a developmental or sequential process during which we move from complete unawareness as a child to some degree of acceptance or appreciation as a mature adult. Through the years, we begin to learn through positive and negative experiences. As a result of these experiences, some people learn to dislike and fear differences. In extreme cases, fears can lead to racism, homophobia, or sexism. Other experiences lead us to be appreciative and to embrace many differences.

In the previous section, we illustrated the progression from ethnocentrism to multiculturalism. One model that applies to attitudes toward many differences is the Riddle Scale (cited in Leppo & Lustgraaf, 1987). As depicted in Table 5.2, the first four

Table 5.2 **The Riddle Scale: Attitudes Toward Differences**

Negative Levels of Attitudes

Repulsion	Views people who are different as strange, sick, crazy, and aversive. Views anything that will change them to be more "normal" or part of the mainstream as justifiable.
Pity	Views people who are different as somehow born that way and feels that that is pitiful. Sees being different as definitely immature and less preferred, so to help those poor individuals one should reinforce normal behaviors.
Tolerance	Sees being different as just a phase of development that most people "grow out" of. Thus one should protect and tolerate those who are different as one does a child who is still learning.
Acceptance	Implies that one needs to make accommodations for another's differences; does not acknowledge that the other's identity may be of the same value as one's own.

Positive Levels of Attitudes

Support	Works to safeguard the rights of those who are different. One may be uncomfortable oneself but one is aware of the climate and the irrational unfairness in our society.
Admiration	Acknowledges that being different in our society takes strength. One is willing to truly look at oneself and work on one's own personal biases.
Appreciation	Values the diversity of people and is willing to confront insensitive attitudes.
Nurturance	Assumes the differences in people are indispensable in society. Views differences with genuine affection and delight and is willing to be an advocate of those differences.

Source: Adapted from Leppo and Lustgraaf (1987). Copyright by John Leppo. Adapted with permission from Dorothy Riddle, "Scale for Homophobia," unpublished document.

stages of the scale (repulsion, pity, tolerance, and acceptance) are negative attitudes because they come from a belief that the person who is different is somehow of less value than oneself. The second four stages of the scale (support, admiration, appreciation, and nurturance) are positive levels of the scale because the other person is of value just as oneself is. Dorothy Riddle developed this model originally as a Scale for Homophobia to understand attitudes toward gay and lesbian people, but our students have found it helpful as a conceptual model for understanding other differences, as well as attitudes toward people with physical disabilities or different religious practices.

> Microaggressions

Microaggressions, a term recently popularized by psychologist Derald Wing Sue (2010), are "brief, everyday exchanges that send denigrating messages to certain individuals because of their group membership" (p. xvi). They tend to focus on a person's race, gender, or sexual orientation. For this example we focus on racial micoaggressions—"commonplace verbal, behavioral, or environmental indignities, whether intentional or unintentional, that communicate hostile, derogatory, or negative racial slights and insults to people of color" (p. 29). They come in three forms:

Microinsults (often unconscious). "Communications that convey rudeness and insensitivity and demean a person's racial heritage"

STUDENT ESSAY   ◆

Mike wore bold accessories, loved to get glamorous in drag on the weekends, and always shared his hilarious stories with me just before class started.

During a class lecture on the professor's research on gay men, a classmate snickered about how gay people "grossed him out." Mike and I, hearing the comment, just rolled our eyes.

"He's stupid," I mouthed.

Comment after comment, I watched Mike freeze with every insult, like if he didn't move, maybe the comments wouldn't hurt—but they did.

Finally, after three weeks of regretting my silence, I turned around and asked if I could speak to this classmate outside during one of our class breaks. I did not want to publicly embarrass him; that wouldn't work. With my heart racing, I explained to him that his "gay" comments were insensitive and hurtful ... to me.

"I sit *right there*, and I can hear you. So I'm asking you to stop." And he did.

After class, I spoke to Mike and burst into tears from the pressure of confronting a virtual stranger. But Mike just hugged me and smiled saying, "I know what you did was for me, so thank you."

Trina Tan received her bachelor of arts in English from California State University, Fullerton, where she served as administrative chair for the Association for Intercultural Awareness. She was a NASPA Undergraduates Fellow and now works for Organizing for America, a community organizing project of the Democratic National Committee.

Microassaults (often conscious). "Explicit racial derogations characterized primarily by a violent verbal, nonverbal, or environmental attack meant to hurt the intended victim through name-calling, avoidant behavior, or purposeful discriminatory actions"

Microinvalidation (often unconscious). "Communications that exclude, negate, or nullify the psychological thoughts, feelings, or experiential reality of a person of color" (p. 29)

Microaggressions are important to understand because they help explain what many people from marginalized groups go through on a daily basis. Have you ever had the experience of hearing of a negative situation involving a friend of yours who is a person of color and thinking to yourself, "I wonder what the fuss is all about . . . this didn't seem like a big deal to me." What was left out was the fact that this experience may have been one of ten, twenty, or a hundred that your friend experienced in one day. It became literally "the straw that broke the camel's back." Developing a strong sense of relational empathy can help you appreciate what is truly happening when other students share with you their stories of life on and off campus.

> Communication

You may observe a range of communication behaviors in a group. Some people may be highly verbal, with strong oral traditions; others may be verbally reserved, preferring thoughtful writing. Some may be outgoing, expressive, and emotional, whereas the cultural assumptions of others lead them to be thoughtful, objective, and analytical. Depending on the mix of individuals, some will be open and revealing, whereas others will be closed and guarded. Some cultural assumptions lead people to be direct and factual; others have learned to be symbolic and metaphorical. Some have been taught to value direct, bold eye contact; others find respect in indirect body language.

Some have learned to be timely and to value promptness; other cultures value casual approaches. Understanding the mix of preferred communication patterns in any group helps the group be more informed in its interaction. Instead of judging another to be wrong or disrespectful, it is useful to ask yourself, Within that person's context, how do I understand this action or practice? And how would they want to be treated?

One aspect of communication we have found to be useful is the idea of speech communities. "A speech community exists when people share norms about how to use talk and what purposes it serves" (Wood, 2004, p. 115; citing Labov, 1972). This can be important to keep in mind, because persons from different speech communities may misunderstand each other (Wood, 2004). Speech communities can be determined by gender, ethnicity, workplace, interests, or other groupings that share a common core of patterns about language and how it is used. "Recognizing and respecting different speech communities increases our ability to participate competently in a diverse culture" (p. 119). For example, students who are devoted players of a particular game like Halo have a language all their own that people who do not play this game probably would not know. Experienced members of a student government organization can develop their own language, using acronyms and inside jokes, that can be less than inclusive when used around newly elected representatives.

Finally, it is important to remember the key role that nonverbal communication plays. As Wood (2004) notes, "Like verbal communication, nonverbal patterns reflect the values, perspectives, norms, and heritage of specific cultures" (p. 134). We communicate with our physical appearance, personal space, facial expressions, gestures, touching, eye contact, the expression of emotions, and orientation toward time—all of which have cultural components (Andersen, 2003; Wood, 2004). This is one of those areas in which we can find ourselves saying, "I don't know what the big deal was; this wouldn't have bothered me." When we are trying to connect with others, it is imperative to remember that "different is just different; different is not wrong."

> Conflict Resolution and Decision Making

You might observe individuals with a range of behaviors from the confrontational to the very subtle. Some may encourage taking responsibility and being accountable; others will tend to blame; still others will seek harmony and face-saving. Some believe their way is right and are closed to other options, whereas others seek connections among options. Some resolve conflict by being deferential to authority, whereas others have learned to be confrontational to authority figures. Finally, some people will link resolution to values like harmony with nature. Conflict resolution is a critical aspect of relational leadership. Almost any change effort will involve some degree of conflict. Remaining focused on the purpose of the change while maintaining positive relationships is necessary. At the same time, it is also important to remain ethical and inclusive. This is certainly challenging, but even more necessary in times of conflict when the tendency can be to try to go it alone or to try to just make it all "go away."

The way in which decisions are made reflects either those who value the power of majority rule and prefer voting or those who seek inclusion of the minority opinion and value consensus.

In some groups, if the will of the group does not emerge as apparent, an issue may be dropped completely and brought up at a later time. Some believe that the hierarchy and authorities should decide, whereas others think that the experts or those involved should decide.

Relational leadership requires communication skills that help each person seek to understand others, not just persuade them. All communicators should constantly ask themselves—How do my perspectives and preferences shade my view? In what ways could I be understood more correctly and understand with greater insight?

> Leadership and Communication

Just about everything done in life is enhanced by being a more effective communicator. Communication skills involve far more than persuasive talking or skillful writing. As one student leader told us, "God gave me two ears and one mouth; I figure that's a message to listen more than I talk." The Chinese language, like many Asian languages, includes symbols that depict related concepts to create new meaning. The Chinese pictogram for listening is made up of the symbols for ears, eyes, and heart (see Figure 5.2).

For most of us, hearing is a natural and almost automatic process. Listening, however, is more difficult and is a "purposive activity" requiring one to be intentionally "mindful" (Gudykunst, 1991, p. 38). True listening is far from a passive activity.

Listening and communicating in a pluralistic context requires one to listen with empathy. Listening with empathy

Listening is when you use . . .

Ears  Eyes

Heart

To give undivided attention.

Figure 5.2 **Listening**

Source: From Simons, Vázquez, & Harris (1993), p. 37. Copyright 1993 with permission, from Elsevier.

is an "intellectual and emotional participation in another person's experience" (Bennett, 1979, p. 418). Empathy means you are using another person's standards and reference points to understand that person's experience. In contrast, sympathy is putting yourself in the other person's place but retaining your own perspective and still using your own standard of judgment. In other words, "sympathy is about feeling sorry for or sad about" the other person (Cormier & Hackney, 2005).

You are using empathy if you are able to see yourself understanding the experiences of others from their point of view, imagining how they feel, and connecting with the emotions others are experiencing when they communicate. This means trying to see others as they would want you to see them and becoming able to understand what others are feeling without being told directly (Gudykunst, 1991, p. 122). Imagine a friend with low self-confidence who confides, "I made a comment in our meeting today and it was awful! People laughed at me." Showing sympathy and remembering times you have said things like that when you just needed a morale boost, you might say, "Oh, I am sure it wasn't that bad, and what you said was just

Student Essay

In the Arizona Blue Chip Program, I served as a team leader for ten first year students. I had a pretty talkative group, which usually led to great discussion, but one student was consistently quiet. I tried every trick in the book to get this student to open up, but was unsuccessful for the most part. When decorating T-shirts for an event, the rest of the group was busy talking about how to cut the shirts and just socializing in general, but the quiet student tucked herself in a corner I was worried she was not interested in the decorating process at all. Many of the other students invited her to sit with them and decorate with them, but the student stayed in her corner. About 30 minutes later, she showed us an amazingly elaborate design she had been working on to unify us as a team. That night I learned that just because someone does not show their engagement in the most typical fashion, it does not mean they are not gaining anything from the process. Being inclusive as a leader is so incredibly important because people have different strengths and assets that could go unnoticed if a leader ignores them and does not provide tailored opportunities for them to engage.

Michelle Faas is a senior at the University of Arizona studying accounting. She is currently an assistant theme coordinator for the Arizona Blue Chip Program, an administrative assistant for the Graduate Program in Neuroscience, and an active member in the Alpha Kappa Psi Professional Business Fraternity.

humorous; probably no one even remembers." Responding with empathy, however, you might say, "I know how hard it is to speak up in that meeting. You don't talk much in that setting and it must have been very scary." The second response leads to more genuine dialogue than the first, which denied your friend's emotion and the apparent pain of the experience.

Renowned psychologist Carl Rogers would often require someone to restate what was said by a previous speaker before making their comment, to build a listening skill and an awareness of empathy. You learn to listen for empathy if you try to find a point of agreement or genuine understanding with a previous speaker and build on it instead of immediately criticizing, rejecting, or denying the point. "Seek first to understand, then to be understood" (Covey, 1991, p. 123). This requires one to pause, think, restate for understanding, then build on that point. Criticism that comes too quickly leaves the first speaker thinking he or she was not heard.

Empathic communication is difficult. Think of the complexity of processes in typical conversation. The content of what we say and how we say it influence the receiver in forming meaning from what we shared. Communication involves both verbal and nonverbal components. Think of the complexity in this verbal process:

What I meant to say
What I actually said
What you heard me say
What you think I mean
What you mean to say
What you actually say
What I hear you say
What I think you mean

Each element in that process is influenced by our cultural and gender lenses. For example, who would you say talks more, men or women? Common stereotypical perception is that women talk more, yet in almost any coeducational class or setting, men are likely to be the first to speak, and they will speak more often for longer periods (Hart & Dalke, 1983). What men and women include in their speech varies as well. Deborah Tannen (1990) notes a difference in public speaking and private speaking. Another way of stating that is that males prefer report-talking and females engage in rapport-talking (p. 77). Men's speech promotes their independence and is often used to share information or opinions, to tell jokes, or to relate stories. Women's speech, even in public settings like meetings or classes, seeks to find connections with others and build relationships. Often, women will add a tag line to the beginning or end of an opinion to provide bridges for others in the conversation. They do not want to stand out or apart. For example, a woman might say, "It's just my opinion, but . . ." or "I know there are many different views, but . . ." or "I think . . . Do you agree or disagree with that?"

> Assertive Communication

Socialization has clearly played an important role in how we have learned to converse with each other. Some women feel silenced, or have silenced themselves, by assuming their opinions are of less value than others or by being socialized to avoid conflict. They have learned to be harmonizers or peacemakers. Some men feel it is more manly to be aggressive, assuming that their opinions are of more value and that others should acquiesce.

In every communication, each person has a right to be heard and a responsibility to listen. Each has a right to make a request or ask a question, and the recipient has the right to make his or her own decision without apology. Imagine an assertiveness contin-uum with three positions: a person might be unassertive, assertive,

Table 5.3 Illustrations of Unassertive, Assertive, and Aggressive Communication

The Question: "Could you substitute for me at the event tonight? I have had something come up and cannot go after all."	
Unassertive response: Even though you have several plans, you reply almost meekly. You deny your own rights and are intimidated into compliance. You may feel trapped or afraid to say no. You are fairly passive.	"OK, sure. I guess I can."
Assertive response: This response acknowledges that the other person had every right to ask, and you have a right to make your own decision. Being assertive means you can say no without feeling guilty or without apologizing.	"No, I have other plans and cannot do it." Depending on your style, you might say, "I am sorry I cannot substitute. You might ask me again sometime when I would have a little more time to change my plans, but thanks for thinking of me."
Aggressive Response: This response denies the other person had any right even to ask for your help and is rarely appropriate.	"How dare you ask me to do this? You always slack off on your responsibilities, and I won't stand for it."

or aggressive (Alberti & Emmons, 1974). If you are unassertive, you passively give up your rights to others and let them take advantage of you. After an encounter, you may often wish you had said or done something different. Table 5.3 illustrates this continuum.

Being assertive does not mean that you get your own way but that you did what you could to be understood. In a similar way, practicing relational leadership does not mean that the group will go along with what you think should happen in the group; it means that you have done your best to respect their involvement, listen for true understanding, and be a productive community member.

> Difficult Dialogues

Learning to talk about sociocultural issues like politics or religion can be challenging, yet it is critical for anyone in a leadership position. Developing skill in these kinds of discussion was the number one way suggested to enrich campus leadership programs: "Discuss sociocultural issues everywhere. Engaging conversations across difference was the single-strongest environmental predictor of leadership outcomes" (Dugan & Komives, 2007, p. 17). Janet Bennett offers a number of ways to encourage you to maintain your "intercultural curiosity" (Exhibit 5.2). This is necessary when you find yourself engaged in a difficult sociocultural dialogue.

Exhibit 5.2: Principles for Enhancing Intercultural Curiosity

1. Suspending our assumptions and value judgments
2. Practicing cultural humility
3. Enhancing our perception skills
4. Developing multiple perspectives
5. Increase our tolerance of ambiguity
6. Asking questions as culturally appropriate
7. Becoming participant observers as appropriate
8. Becoming analytically inquisitive
9. Assessing the credibility of our intercultural sources

Source: Bennett, 2011, p. 10. Used by permission.

However, there are things that well-intentioned people may say that can derail sociocultural conversations. Diversity consultant Maura Cullen (2008) lists and describes many of these in her book *35 Dumb Things Well-Intentioned People Say*. For example:

"Some of my best friends are . . . "
"I know exactly how you feel!"
"I don't think of you as . . . "
"It was only a joke! Don't take things so seriously!"

Most important is the concept of "intent versus impact." It has been our experience that people will say things with an "intent" of not meaning to hurt anyone yet the "impact" turns out to be very harmful. While some may give you a pass for not knowing any better, others will expect you to be knowledgeable when it comes to issues of diversity. As a leader it will serve you well to learn as much as you can about these issues and practice them in a variety of settings.

> Relational Empathy

Working effectively together requires "relational empathy" (Broome, 1993, p. 97). Relational empathy goes beyond merely understanding another "in which the emphasis is upon the re-creation in the listener of the meaning originally created by the speaker" (p. 98) and seeks shared meaning. Relational empathy recognizes the importance of context. It may mean creating a new "third culture" (p. 103) that synthesizes the positions from the two individual perspectives, culture, and context and builds a new culture, an environment of empathy and insight. "As sharing of contexts takes place, organizations of diverse people start weaving a new context" (Simons, Vázquez, & Harris, 1993, p. 39).

This third culture, or common context, develops its "own jargon, definitions, visions, and understandings" through which members from different contexts can come together (Simons et al. 1993, p. 39). In these organizations, the culture says

- People are good, honest, and trustworthy
- People are purposeful
- Each individual has a unique contribution to make
- Complex problems require local solutions
- Me and you versus me or you (Kiefer & Senge, 1984, pp. 75–78)

These beliefs about the goodness of people guide how we approach others. "Self-fulfilling prophecy" demonstrates that people may indeed become as you see them (Argyris, as cited in Yukl, 1994, p. 176). If you think no one will get along in the group, conflict is bound to occur and be harmful. If you believe people will avoid responsibility, then you may shape your own behavior to be controlling and negative, and you may act discouraged. Those with whom you are engaged are likely to become as you anticipate. Conversely, if you think people will try to get along, want to face their sources of conflict, be helpful, and take responsibility, then you approach your behaviors in hopeful ways that make that prophecy come true.

Imagine going to your first group project meeting thinking that people will just goof off, that you will end up doing all the work, and that no one really cares. You then look for evidence of those assumptions, and at the smallest indication you think, Aha!—I knew it! Imagine instead going to your first project committee meeting thinking, We are all busy so we will have to be careful about what we take on, but people will want to do their part, and we can come up with something worthwhile.

There are very real differences in environments, and groups may be negative in one setting and welcoming in another. The biggest difference in how a setting is perceived is the internal assumptions that guide expectations—how one will be in that setting and how being that way brings out responses in others. Building this new third culture meets the challenge inherent in the opening question: How am I like everyone else here?

Using relational empathy you will have a better sense of what challenges are facing the other students in your team or organization. This social perspective taking requires you to go beyond your own experience to understand the lives of others. For example, older students in your group may be juggling multiple family and work responsibilities and may be caring for their parents. Religious beliefs can impact what days and times students are available to meet, as well as what kind of language they like to use and hope others will use. Socioeconomic status can impact where students live and what financial resources they are able to contribute to the group. Gender and sexual identity can impact feelings of safety when walking on campus after dark and feelings of belonging. Students with ability issues may have concerns about meeting in certain places. Ethnicity/race can impact how much of a sense of belonging students feel on the campus. We are not offering these as "excuses" for certain behaviors or nonbehaviors. We are offering them as a reminder that we all have issues that can impact our ability to bring our "best selves" to any assignment, meeting, or group. As a leader it is critical to have a good sense of how members of the group or organization are experiencing the campus and surrounding environment.

> Cultural Influences on Leadership Behavior

Awareness of how such aspects of diversity as sex, race, ethnicity, age, sexual identity, religion, ability, or socioeconomic status influence our own behavior and that of others in groups is a step toward being an effective relational leader. No group is totally homogeneous; we differ in personality preferences, attitudes, styles, value systems, beliefs, and opinions, based on our cultural influences. Relational leadership values effective leadership processes within heterogeneous groups. Many leadership practices could be described as participative because they value the empowerment of followers, but relational and pluralistic leadership seeks to change the very culture of the organization or group to see the diversity of the group as a true asset (Loden & Rosener, 1991).

It clearly would be inaccurate to describe people based on only one aspect of their identity. Behaviors grow from a complex interaction of many salient background factors; it is more useful to observe people's behaviors and seek to understand their attitudes than to presume differences among people that are based on stereotypes. It is useful to examine the range of human behaviors that are essential in leadership settings. Consider the cultural influences in such leadership processes as communications, conflict resolution, and decision making.

Diversity consultant R. Roosevelt Thomas Jr. (2006) offers the following thoughts:

> The diversity focus will shift from a concept centered around race and gender, the civil rights movement, and social justice to a craft for making quality decisions in the midst of differences, similarities, tensions, and complexities ... What must be kept in mind is that many if not most social justice issues can be conceptualized as challenges in making quality decisions in the midst of differences, similarities, and tensions. Adoption of a craft that facilitates such decision making would enhance the probability of achieving social justice goals. (p. 49)

Thomas also identifies specific ways in which he believes the diversity conversation will change in the future (see Exhibit 5.3). Read through Exhibit 5.3. Which of these changes are you already seeing? Do you agree with the consultant that our future diversity conversations will change in these ways?

Exhibit 5.3: Ten Expectations for the Future

One. Future leaders will differentiate between representation and diversity. Representation will refer to the presence of multiple races and both genders in the workplace, while diversity will refer to the behavioral differences, similarities, and tensions that can exist among people when representation has been achieved ...

Two. Future leaders will not think in terms of diversity, nor will they view it only as an extension of the civil rights movement. Leaders will concern themselves with diversity management and view it as a craft—one that can complement traditional civil rights initiatives that focus efforts solely on issues of race and gender ...

Three. Future leaders will define diversity management as "making quality decisions in the midst of differences, similarities, and tensions." This definition will allow them to deal with all kinds of discussions involving differences, similarities, and tensions and to see themselves as engaged in diversity management...

Four. Future leaders will not automatically assume that all racially inappropriate behavior is caused by racism. They will recognize that people can have difficulty making quality decisions in the midst of differences, similarities, and tensions for reasons other than bias...

Five. In contrast to today, future leaders will be more willing to admit having difficulty making decisions in the midst of diversity. They will also be more comfortable discussing specific ways in which they are challenged by particular types of diversity. In part, this will be because they can distinguish between diversity in the broader sense and the race and gender focus of the civil rights movement. As a result, difficulty with diversity is less likely to be seen as a moral offense and more likely to be seen as managerial uncertainty or ineffectiveness—particularly in those instances where the "isms" are not the undergirding factors...

Six. As these trends emerge, future leaders will grow in their understanding of diversity management as a craft...

Seven. Leaders armed with the diversity management craft will become more comfortable with tension and complexity. We all have witnessed the ineffectiveness of individuals who are uncomfortable with diversity tensions, and most of us have yet to say, "I just cannot get enough complexity." Instead, we struggle to "keep it simple" and indeed to avoid complexity. This may appear to reduce tensions, but it does so at the risk of distortion and ineffectiveness...

Eight. Given the universality of diversity management, leaders across the globe will make it a global craft as opposed to one

(*continued*)

confined to the United States. Leaders will use the craft both within and across borders as globalization becomes ever more the norm . . .

Nine. Future leaders will be more strategic in their approach to diversity and diversity management. Decisions as to where to focus attention and how to respond to issues will be guided by an organization's mission, vision, and strategy. Accordingly, what will be appropriate in one setting may not be appropriate in another if differences exist with respect to mission, vision, and strategy. Strategic context will be defining . . .

Ten. As future leaders master the application of the craft in their workplaces, inevitably and eventually they will turn their attention to diversity issues within their countries and communities. In the United States, for example, this will mean addressing the various divides we experience along at least the following lines: race, class, ethnicity, gender, politics, geography, and religion . . .

(Thomas, 2006)

Martin Davidson (2012) continues with this theme by noting that leaders must move from "managing diversity" to "leveraging difference." He continues:

> But actually working in a way that builds on difference is a huge challenge. It requires more than leading teams and organizations that are made up of people with varied social identities, backgrounds, and experiences. That's important, and typically it is what we talk about when we think about diversity. But that is not enough. Leaders who leverage difference adopt a mindset of leadership that emboldens them to revision everything they do. (p. 51)

Davidson (2012) says we do this by adopting a "leveraging difference mindset" always assume that difference matters, be curious, and connect with leaders from the margin.

> Chapter Summary

The ability to understand others, be understood by others, and together create an effective organizational or group environment is the challenge of relational leadership. Truly understanding the influences of our cultural heritage, gender, and other aspects of our difference helps us work together toward change. We usually find we are more alike than we are different. Expecting commonalties, good will, and shared purposes can become a self-fulfilling prophecy. This awareness helps us create a new third culture in any group.

> What's Next?

In the next chapter we offer an overview of leadership and ethics, underscoring the importance of leading with integrity. We review strategies for creating and sustaining ethical organizations and models of ethical decision making.

> Chapter Activities

1. How are your communication, conflict-resolution, and decision-making behaviors or tendencies influenced by your perceptions of the gender, race, ethnicity, family practices, or other characteristics of others in the group?
2. Referring to Milton Bennett's Developmental Model of Intercultural Sensitivity, think about where you are currently in

this model. What stage best describes you now? What experiences will help you expand your openness to others?

3. Ask a friend who is different from you to take you to an event or gathering at which the majority of others will be like your friend. What is easiest and hardest for you to understand about the practices in that group? Which of your own characteristics make it hardest for you to gain this understanding?

4. Refer to Table 5.3: Illustrations of Unassertive, Assertive, and Aggressive Communication. Think of a recent communication in which someone asked you to do something or asked for a favor. Based on this chart, what type of response did you give? Are you satisfied with that response? Why or why not? If not, how would you respond differently if you could do it over again?

ADDITIONAL READINGS

Cullen, M. (2008). *35 dumb things well-intentioned people say*. Garden City, NJ: Morgan James.

Johnson, A. G. (2006). *Privilege, power and difference* (2nd ed). Boston, MA: McGraw-Hill.

Kimmel, M. S., & Ferber, A. L. (Eds.). (2003). *Privilege: A reader*. Boulder, CO: Westview.

Kivel, P. (2011). *Uprooting racism: How White people can work for racial justice* (3rd ed). Gabriola Island, BC, Canada: New Society.

Wise, T. (2005). *White like me: Reflections on race from a privileged son*. Brooklyn, NY: Soft Skull. http://www.timwise.org

Yoshino, K. (2006). *Covering: The hidden assault on our civil rights*. New York, NY: Random House.

VIDEO RESOURCE

Adelman, L. (Executive Producer). (2003). *Race—The power of an illusion.* (Three-episode video). (Available from California Newsreel, Order Department, P.O. Box 2284, South Burlington, VT 05407.)

WEB RESOURCE

Chimamanda Adichie: The danger of a single story. http://www.ted.com /talks/chimamanda_adichie_the_danger_of_a_single_story.html

Chapter 6

Leading with Integrity

Imagine yourself in the following situations:

- You are a resident assistant and while making the rounds on your residence hall floor one evening, you are drawn to noise coming from one of the rooms. You knock on the door and discover a few of your resident students are in the room smoking marijuana. This is the same room in which you saw another resident assistant leave the room just before you knocked on the door. Given the odor and what you observed, it was clear to you that these activities had been going on for quite some time. What do you do about your peer resident assistant and the students in the room?
- You are collecting money for a major campus philanthropy to support cancer research. The daughter of your physics professor is also participating in this project as a member of the philanthropy. You notice that she takes some cash to buy a case of

beer at the end of a long day of soliciting donations. What do
you do?

- You just signed an honor code pledge agreeing to abide by academic honesty policies, including any witnessing of cheating incidents. Your best friend is in your accounting course and you observe him cheating during an in-class exam. What do you do?

Too often, we find ourselves in ethical dilemmas like these, and our tendency is to react quickly to resolve them or pretend we did not notice. However, avoidance leaves you troubled, and quick decisions preclude careful thought about all the aspects of the situation, which could raise questions of character and ethics if participants rush to decisions that are void of ethical considerations. Participants might get caught up in competition that causes them only to focus on the bottom line or on winning at all costs. They may feel the need to please others, without stopping to think about the implications of the decisions and their long-term effects. They may tend to shove problems under the rug to avoid tarnishing the organization's reputation or to avoid causing conflict in the group.

We need to learn to slow the process down and reflect on the ethical and moral aspects of actions and decisions. If you are used to resolving ethical dilemmas quickly, then it might be a challenge for you to stop, reflect on the situation, involve others in helping to address it, and weigh all possible alternatives of action. The key is to allow you and others some time to work through complex problems and engage in a process that includes reflection before action. Consider the inclusive, process, and empowering components of the Relational Leadership Model.

By including group members in resolving ethical dilemmas, they will feel empowered. The process of engaging them can lead to more informed decisions and solutions.

Our world news is full of examples of breaches of ethics and laws in all professions. Frequently, the focus of these stories is on leaders who are expected to lead with integrity given their unique responsibilities to the public and their stakeholders. These stories make the news because negative events sell newspapers and have more emotional appeal. There are just as many positive examples of leaders and leadership processes that advance principles and values while accomplishing goals. While we learn what not do to from the negative examples, we can learn just as much from the positive examples.

> Chapter Overview

In Chapter Three we introduced the ethical component of the Relational Leadership Model, emphasizing the importance of ethics in the leadership process. In Chapter Four we explored essential elements of personal values and character and in Chapter Five covered concepts related to leading with integrity, such as understanding others, conflict resolution, and the cultural influences of leadership. This chapter includes (1) a discussion of the process of creating and sustaining ethical organizational environments, (2) an analysis of the moral dimensions of transforming leadership theory, and (3) an examination of the ethical influences that participants have on their organizations through behavior modeling. Practical applications of ethics and leadership are highlighted using ethical decision-making models.

> Creating and Sustaining an Ethical Organizational Environment

Understanding and applying ethical theories and models that operate from organizational values or codes of conduct, as well as being aware of your own moral development and that of others in your organizations, helps create and sustain ethical organizational environments. Nash (1990) proposes four qualities that are necessary for participants to advance ethical standards in an organization.

1. Critical thinking skills to analyze and convey the ethical components of a problem or dilemma.
2. Possession of a high degree of integrity to stand up for your personal and professional ethics.
3. The ability to see situations from others' perspectives (showing concern for others).
4. Personal motivation to do the right thing. (pp. 43–47)

It is important when using these ethical decision-making models and principles that you are prepared to receive criticism, see members revolt, and perhaps experience a decline in membership. Not everyone in an organization is prepared or willing to do the right thing or has a moral orientation. Some would prefer to take the easy way out, do what is more economical, or take the path of least resistance. Nash's idea of having personal courage is of utmost importance when trying to make the right decision for the good of an organization in the face of opposition from the membership. Part of the leadership process is to fully explain to others the problem at hand and the basis for the action or decision.

These four qualities of leadership, when translated into behavior and action, help create an ethical organizational environment. When you identify a problem as having moral or ethical implications and involve others in the decision-making process, you provide another example of how an ethical environment is established. Several strategies and interventions can be used to create and maintain an ethical climate in a group or organizational setting. The process of doing so should be intentional and include all the elements of the Relational Leadership Model and the dimensions of knowing-being-doing.

All participants—positional leadership and members alike—should be equally empowered to set a tone in the organizational climate that will foster and support ethical and moral actions and sensitivities. The organization's mission or the group's common purpose should be the driving force for identifying its values. Participants should identify and operate from a shared set of core values that guide the organization's activities, actions, and decisions. These core values will enable individuals to work toward a common purpose and provide a common understanding of the organization's principles and standards. Members are empowered to hold each other accountable, participate in moral talk or dialogue, and work together to sustain an ethical environment. Appointing one person to be the group's ethicist or standard bearer will not achieve the same degree of ethical climate as when all participants are concerned with doing what is right. In fact, it may be counterproductive when a leader handles ethical dilemmas alone or in isolation from other members of the organization.

While the news is filled with examples of breaches of ethics by leaders, entities such as the Ethisphere Institute, a nonprofit organization, promotes the most ethical companies around the world through a competitive selection process. In 2012, 5,000 organizations from 100 countries were nominated and 145 were selected for the Ethisphere ethics award (http://ethisphere.com/). These 145 winners were chosen based on an elaborate ethics selection system used by Ethisphere called the Ethics Quotient. Factors considered include ethics codes, ethics resources and employee training programs on ethics, whistle-blower protection, and internal communications by employees at all levels of the organization on matters related to ethics, policies, and laws. Ethisphere received a record number of applications in 2012, attributing the increase to a growing number of employees who want to work in organizations with values and standards in alignment with their own. An impressive number of organizations have received this recognition since 2006, when Ethisphere launched this award, including companies like Petco, General Electric, Kao Corporation (Japan), Patagonia, American Express, Target, Starbucks Coffee, and Standard Chartered Bank (UK).

Learning from Good and Bad Leadership

Craig Johnson (2012) uses the powerful metaphor of light and shadow to illustrate the differences between ethical and unethical leadership. Leaders who cast light facilitate ethical processes and uphold ethical principles in their actions and in how they treat others. Those who cast shadows abuse power, manipulate information, are deceitful, and act incongruently (p. 3). Behaviors and traits of leaders who cast light include humility, compassion, courage, optimism, and integrity.

Now consider Enron, a corporation in the early 2000s that had a detailed 64 page code of ethics document that was later sold on e-Bay with this one word description, "Unopened" (Kidder, 2005, p. 203). The Enron board waived many of its ethics policies, including allowing Andrew Fastow, its chief financial officer, to work for Enron and another entity that was clearly a conflict of interest for the company. After the collapse of Enron, the board noted that that exception should have been "a red flag the size of Alaska" (p. 203).

As the Enron case demonstrates, not all leadership is "good"—our learning about leadership can come from both positive and negative exemplars. Kellerman (2004) and Lipman-Blumen (2005) address the notion of bad or toxic leaders and their resulting negative consequences. Kellerman divides bad leadership into two categories: "bad as in ineffective and bad as in unethical" (p. 32). Her definition of ineffective leadership includes the failure of achieving a desired change whereas "unethical leadership fails to distinguish between right and wrong" (p. 34). Someone can be an ineffective leader but be considered an ethical leader; while the goals were not accomplished, the person still led with integrity. Ideally, leaders and followers are effective *and* ethical as they work to achieve a shared vision or a common agenda.

Lipman-Blumen (2005) describes toxic leaders as those "who engage in numerous destructive behaviors and who exhibit certain dysfunctional personal characteristics. To count as toxic, these behaviors and qualities of character must inflict some reasonably serious and enduring harm on their followers and their organizations" (p.18). In some cases, followers can influence nontoxic leaders to the toxic realm of behaviors or, at a minimum, they support the actions of toxic leaders. Here are a few examples of behaviors and traits associated with toxic leaders:

- Leaving their followers worse off than they found them
- Violating the basic standards of human rights of their own supporters, as well as those of other individuals and groups they do not count among their followers
- Consciously feeding their followers illusions that enhance the leader's power and impair the followers' capacity to act independently (e.g., persuading followers that they are the only ones who can save them or the organization)
- Misleading followers through deliberate untruths and misdiagnoses of issues and problems
- Insatiable ambition that prompts leaders to put their own sustained power, glory, and fortunes above their followers' well-being
- Enormous egos that blind leaders to the shortcomings of their own character and thus limit their capacity for self-renewal
- Reckless disregard for the costs of their actions to others, as well as to themselves
- Cowardice that leads them to shrink from difficult choices (pp. 19–22)

What is rewarded and recognized often teaches others about what is acceptable and unacceptable behavior within an organization. Creating awards and recognition for members who help sustain an ethical environment by taking risks to do the right thing is a powerful way to publicly acknowledge and promote ethical behavior. Communicating about ethics and encouraging dialogue is a powerful way to deepen the organization's commitment to ethics. Bringing ethical considerations to members and raising ethical issues and questions publicly shows others the value and priority placed on ethics.

On the other side of the award continuum, unethical behavior should be addressed, but in a different manner. Public humiliation was a practice commonly used in the past to confront and punish violators of the law or ethical standards. Some cultures continue this practice today. Participants have the shared responsibility of confronting individuals who violate the organization's standards and practices. Although we do not condone public humiliation as a motivational method, members need to know that they will be held accountable for such breaches. Participants have an obligation under the principle of "doing no harm" to protect an individual's right to confidentiality when addressing a violation of rules or standards and ensuring that due process is provided and safeguarded.

Ethical Lapses

Some organizations lack a positive ethical environment because leaders and participants are not committed to a moral orientation. These types of organizations may, in fact, reward unethical behavior because it is seen as "improving" the organization. An example of this would be an organization that uses unethical practices during membership recruitment to increase its membership. This type of organizational environment would support shortcuts, poor-quality work, cover-ups, and a lack of personal responsibility for mistakes or problems.

Colleges and universities have their share of major ethical lapses. In 2011, a major scandal unfolded at Penn State University involving a former assistant football coach, Jerry Sandusky, who sexually abused young boys on university property and under the auspices of his nonprofit organization, The Second Mile, during the period of 1998–2010. The late Joe Paterno, then head coach of the football team, the athletic director, a vice president, and the university president were included in the indictment for failing to alert the appropriate authorities when observers of Sandusky's actions came forward with information.

One of those witnesses reported Sandusky's behavior to Coach Paterno. Joe Paterno was known as a coach who espoused values such as honesty, responsibility, community, and character among his players. Coach Paterno reported the initial incident, but failed to follow-up when he continued to observe Jerry Sandusky at official university events with children from his nonprofit organization. Then numerous victims came forward describing the violations committed by Jerry Sandusky. The university received serious sanctions from the NCCA, including the loss of student football scholarships, ineligibility to compete in bowl games, and a $60 million fine for failing to take action. Public outcry was polarized with people outraged over the cover-up of Jerry Sandusky's criminal acts on one side while others believed the sanctions were too harsh against Penn State by punishing innocent football players, former players, and students.

Numerous leadership lessons can be extracted from the Penn State incident. The most important leadership questions surrounding the Penn State incident include the following: How did this situation go unnoticed for nearly twelve years before it came to the public's attention? What responsibility did the leadership of Penn State have, including Coach Joe Paterno, to intervene when the first allegation about Jerry Sandusky was reported in 1998? What behaviors and traits from Lipmen-Bluman's toxic leaders foreshadow troubling dynamics in this situation? What responsibilities does a football coach or any leader have to ensuring a full investigation was conducted after initially reporting an incident such as this one? How could this be prevented at universities and colleges in the future? What are the leadership lessons from this case on power, accountability, transparency, congruency, decision making, and organizational culture?

A 2012 Gallup Values and Beliefs Poll on moral values in the United States showed that Americans are twice as likely to rate the country's state of moral values as "poor" compared to rating them as "excellent" or "good" (Gallup Poll Social Series, 2012). Only 19% polled believe the moral climate in this country is improving. These indicators point to the growing number of Americans who believe that the moral climate in the United States is going in the wrong direction. In a survey of Fortune 500 employees conducted by the Ethics Resource Center in 2012, 53% of workers observed unethical conduct in their workplace (2012 National Business Ethics Survey of Fortune 500 Employers). In this same survey, 59% of employees believed their companies had strong ethical cultures compared to 53% of U.S. workplaces. Another interesting finding tied management's commitment to ethics: 48% reported misconduct in companies where management demonstrated a strong commitment to ethics compared to 89% in Fortune 500 organizations where management's commitment to ethics was the weakest. These findings suggest that leadership plays a role in creating and sustaining ethical organizational climates.

We witness hundreds of examples of leaders who lack personal courage or a moral orientation in their dealings with people, money, laws, policies, and other matters. They set a climate in their organizations that rewards unscrupulous behavior. We read of their actions in the newspaper and say, "What were they thinking?!" These examples contribute to a deteriorating sense of moral values in society. A frequent outcome of these breaches is what Rushmore Kidder (1995) calls "CEMs"—Career-Ending Moves (p. 38). Engaging in morally questionable or unethical behavior often results in CEMs. Martha Stewart, CEO of Omni Living, brought down her company over the cover-up of an insider trading scheme and received a federal prison sentence; Ken Lay, CEO of Enron, duped shareholders and others, destroyed his company, and entered his trial facing a maximum sentence of 175 years in prison; former Senator John Ensign resigned from office for using funds to cover up an extramarital affair; and the President and Dean of the Business School at West Virginia University resigned under fire for showing preferential treatment of the state's governor's daughter by falsifying her transcript.

These examples of ethical lapses produced Career-Ending Moves for each of these leaders. Although Martha Stewart has made a come-back since her release from prison, her image and reputation have been tarnished.

Individuals committed to leading with integrity are faced with their own dilemma of what to do when their values and principles clash with the organization's standards. This is a very difficult situation and offers only three choices: (1) ignore or put up with the situation; (2) address the situation and work to change the organizational climate into one that is ethical in nature; or (3) leave the organization. This is a difficult situation and one with which leaders struggle every day. Kidder (2005) describes ethical fitness as "getting in shape to tackle the tough ethical dilemmas as they arise. That same fitness applies to our ability to express moral courage" (p. 157). Being ethically fit means being mentally engaged—thinking about the dilemma you are facing, reasoning through it, and grappling with the tough issues. All of this requires practice—thinking through potential ethical dilemmas so you are used to this process when faced with a real dilemma. This is one way to prepare for the ethical fitness test.

> Moral Purpose as an Act of Courage

It takes personal courage to do the right thing. Sherron Watkins, a former executive of Enron, displayed personal courage when she exposed breaches of conduct by her boss Ken Lay (Lucas & Koerwer, 2004). Watkins risked losing her high-level and high-paying job in doing so. She showed both personal courage and integrity in taking a stand against the unethical practices of Enron. In an interview, Watkins described her efforts as "symbolizing that individual actions matter and that you have to take ownership for your actions when you are in a position of leadership" (Lucas & Koerwer, 2004, p. 44). Gregg Levoy (2000), former reporter for the *Cincinnati Enquirer*, uses the metaphor of stone sculpting to illustrate integrity and personal courage:

> To tell if a stone is "true," you bang on it with a hammer. A dull tone indicates a fault; the stone will crack when you work on it. But

a clear ring, one that hangs in the air, means the stone is true. It has integrity. It will hold up under repeated blows. (p. 22)

More in-depth examination is needed of leaders and participants who are ethical in their dealings and who model good leadership—leadership that is moral, courageous, and responsible. Usually, we start searching for ethical leaders who were national or historical figures. But we know leaders like that in our everyday lives—local business leaders, faculty and administrators, religious leaders from the local community, committed citizens of a neighborhood organization, your peers, family members, and nonprofit leaders who often work quietly and with humility to serve others.

Kidder (2005) describes moral courage as "the quality of mind and spirit that enables one to face up to ethical challenges firmly and confidently, without flinching or retreating" (p. 72). Moral courage can be viewed as the intersection of three conceptual fields: principles, danger, and endurance (Kidder). It took moral courage for Nelson Mandela to be imprisoned for eighteen years in his opposition to apartheid in South Africa. Having an awareness of danger is key in possessing moral courage.

A willingness to endure some type of hardship such as risk losing friends or a job is a component of moral courage. The opposite would be doing or saying nothing or turning away when faced with ethical dilemmas. Upholding your principles and putting them into actions allows leaders to operate with moral courage. Tremendous scrutiny was leveraged against the leaders of British Petroleum (BP) for ignoring signs of faulty equipment that resulted in one of the biggest oil spills in history in the U.S. Gulf coast in 2010. The company's leaders failed to exhibit moral courage when they made cost-cutting decisions and valued their bottom line over safety.

STUDENT ESSAY

I feel that the many organizations and aspects of community service that I have participated in have strengthened my learning and leadership abilities. Within each leadership position, there is the opportunity to make decisions that are personally beneficial. I believe student leadership is about serving students and having the integrity to hold oneself to a higher standard, to make decisions that are fair and beneficial to all. I choose to represent my school and community in a manner that I am proud of and that I hope others will follow. Integrity makes a great leader, provides the foundation for an organization to be prosperous, and establishes the difference between a student and a student leader.

Jake Swanson is currently a junior at Iowa State University where he is majoring in global resource systems with emphases in emerging global diseases and business management. He was president of the Freshmen Council, serves as a senator on the Government of the Student Body, chairman of the WinterFest Committee, and is active in his fraternity, Beta Theta Pi.

> Assumptions about Ethical Leadership

There are many myths and misunderstandings about "good" leadership—leadership that is both ethical and effective (Ciulla, 1995). Lucas and Anello (1995) propose eight assumptions about ethical leadership, which are central themes in the study and practice of ethical leadership:

1. *Ethics is the heart of leadership.* It is the central issue in leadership (Ciulla, 1995). You cannot have a complete discussion about leadership without including the ethical components associated with leadership processes. "Good leadership" means leadership that is effective, in that goals were achieved, and that

follows a sound and ethical process. The means justify the ends when leading with integrity.

2. *All leadership is values-driven.* We need to reframe leadership so that it represents values that reflect good (ethical) leadership. Participants and leaders bring to the organization their own values and beliefs about how people should be treated, notions of what is right versus what is wrong, and ideas about what is just and fair. Organizations and communities are values-driven as opposed to values-neutral.

3. *Personal values intersect with organizational values.* The journey to ethical leadership begins with an examination of personal values, as well as ongoing reflection of personal core values and how these values are related to the values of an organization or community. Your personal moral compass will guide you in wrestling with ethical dilemmas and eventually will point you in the direction of making a decision based on ethical analysis, consideration of opposing viewpoints, your personal values, and the values of your organization.

4. *Ethical leadership can be learned.* Ethical learning is a process involving experience, reflection, conceptualization, and application. Trial-and-error experiences can sharpen your ethical analysis, as well as your reflection about notions of what is just and fair in a given situation. You can learn this before you must act or make a decision. The life experiences you gain over time will affect your development as an ethical leader.

5. *Ethical leadership involves a connection between ethical thought and action.* Linking moral reasoning with values and action is imperative in leadership. The point of this chapter is not to have you memorize dozens of ethical theories. The goal is

to engage you in ethical analysis and insights based on theories and concepts applied to real-life experiences.

6. *Character development is an essential ingredient of ethical leadership.* A leader's character is defined by his or her actions and behaviors, not simply by the values that are espoused. Leaders can be popular yet not be respected by the public because they lack congruency between their values and actions. In other words, they don't walk their talk.

7. *Ethical leadership is a shared process.* Members at all levels of an organization or community have the opportunity and responsibility to participate in the process of exercising ethical leadership. Ethical leadership is a shared process, not just the responsibility of a positional leader. Leaders and participants share the responsibility of advancing core organizational values and of doing the right thing. Members often are called upon to be courageous and to advocate for what is right, despite risks such as losing a job or alienating friends. Organizations that are empowering and inclusive involve members in wrestling with ethical dilemmas and seek their advice on how to resolve problems.

8. *Everything we do teaches.* Role modeling is a powerful way to influence the ethical climate in families, organizations, and communities. We learn by watching others, and we make judgments about what is acceptable and unacceptable behavior in organizations. If any member (including the positional leader) routinely discriminates against other students in a membership recruitment process, then others in the organization might believe it is acceptable to exclude students of color in extending invitations to join the group. Conversely, if a leader values diversity and decides to increase the number of minorities by

50% on her senior staff, then other managers of the company
will most likely follow her strategy.

Leading with moral purpose calls for an examination of your
assumptions about what is ethical and what is unethical, what is
good leadership versus bad leadership, what are toxic behaviors
versus nontoxic behaviors and traits, how far you are willing to
go to advance your core values and do the right thing, what are
you willing to risk to achieve the values of justice and fairness,
and how will you wrestle with an inconsistency between your
values and the values of your organization. The goal is not to discover easy answers or quick fixes to these issues but to engage in
an ethical analysis and to use your moral imagination in solving
problems and dilemmas.

> Cultural Assumptions

Ethics exist in a cultural context; they are culturally bound
or culture-specific. There is no universal agreement on what
behaviors or practices are considered appropriate, legal, ethical,
or moral across cultures (Henderson, 1992; Toffler, 1986).
For example, the intentional oppression of and discrimination
against women in Saudi Arabia is considered ethical, legal, and
moral in that country but is unethical, illegal, and immoral
in the United States. Ethics are also temporal in nature,
especially in light of changing laws and legal norms. What was
considered by many to be an ethical and legal standard practice
until the 1960s—having separate water fountains for Blacks
and Whites—is considered illegal, unethical, and immoral

today. Laws and regulations influence the changing nature of ethical practices and behaviors, especially in the business world.

Some might argue that there are universal moral values (Kidder, 2005). Kanungo and Mendonca (1996) assert that, "morally good acts are based on moral laws that are universal because they incorporate fundamental values such as truth, goodness, beauty, courage, and justice. These values are found in all cultures, although cultures may differ with regard to the application of these values" (p. 35). From interviews with 24 leaders from 16 different countries, Kidder (2005) identified seven common values among them: love, truthfulness, fairness, freedom, unity, tolerance, responsibility, and respect for life (pp. 43–44). Seligman (2002) identified six virtues common to more than 200 religious and philosophical traditions: wisdom and knowledge, courage, love and humanity, justice, temperance, and spirituality and transcendence (p. 133). Although different cultures might provide varying definitions of these virtues, the basic ideals of these virtues are similar from culture to culture.

Anthropological studies have documented the divergent moral views and practices interculturally and intraculturally (De George, 1986). Notions of right and wrong or justice and injustice are validated by the values and attitudes of a given culture (Donaldson, 1989). To place worth on moral concepts through intercultural comparison is futile. For example, many American women believe the veil worn by Moslem women constitutes sexist behavior and oppressive practices. What is socially practiced and acceptable in one culture is repudiated in another. This brings up the painful or perhaps sobering reality that there is no moral consensus in international affairs. Ethics and morals differ not only among various countries, but also among individuals in the same country.

Cultural tolerance implies that differences in practices are recognized, but not for the purpose of imposing or changing the practices to suit a particular cultural belief (Donaldson, 1989). Cultural relativism is germane to a specific culture, society, or community. The goal in comparing cultural practices is to understand them, not to judge them as good or bad. For example, leaders of multinational business organizations must follow the local laws, norms, mores, and practices associated with the country in which they are conducting business.

Corruption is a culturally constructed behavior, with varying degrees of tolerance and therefore varying frequencies of occurrence across countries. The Corruption Perceptions 2011 Index, published by the world's leading nongovernmental organizations fighting corruption, ranked 183 countries and territories from zero to ten, with ten being a clean score and zero indicating most corrupt. The index is a poll of polls, reflecting the perceptions of business people and country analysts. Out of the 183 countries, the majority received a score below five of ten. New Zealand, Denmark, and Finland were ranked the top three countries earning the designation as the most clean, while North Korea and Somalia were at the bottom ranked as the most corrupt. The United States was ranked 24 out of 183. Examples of corruption include parents bribing underpaid teachers to receive educational benefits for their children or large amounts of public funds wasted or stolen by public officials. Leaders in the countries who received the cleanest scores possessed a strong commitment to anti-corruption legislation and policies while also upholding human rights and freedoms.

Developing a global mindset and cultivating diversity are important components of ethical leadership. Johnson (2012) identifies 14 personal competencies for establishing crosscultural relationships. The following are a few of these competencies:

1. Be nonjudgmental
2. Be flexible
3. Listen attentively/observe carefully
4. Assume complexity
5. Manage personal biases
6. Show respect
7. Show empathy (pp. 374–375)

These cultural considerations illustrate the complexity of the cultural influences of leadership and ethics and show the connection between ethics and culture. The following section offers an overview of ethical theories and foundations in leadership.

> Ethical Theories and Moral Purposes

The study of human behavior as it relates to ethics and ethical development reaches back to the philosopher kings (Aristotle, Plato, Socrates), as well as to 18th- and 19th-century philosophers and scholars such as Immanuel Kant and John Stuart Mill. Ethical theories provide a glimpse into how human judgments are made and the thought processes individuals engage in to solve ethical dilemmas and other problems. In the next section, we describe transforming leadership theory as the foremost theory that incorporates a moral component as its foundation for leadership.

> Transforming Leadership Theory

A leadership theory that includes a strong component of ethics and morals is James MacGregor Burns's transforming leadership theory. As noted in Chapter Two, transforming leadership is a process in which "leaders and followers raise one another to higher levels of morality and motivation" (Burns, 1978, p. 20). Transforming leadership reaches moral dimensions when the leaders' and participants' behavior and ethical aspirations are elevated by mutual influences on one another (Burns, 1978). Transforming leadership involves persuasion, a desire to change something, and multidirectional influence relationships between leaders and participants (Rost, 1991). In any leadership situation, participants can, and often do, influence leaders to higher ethical ends.

Values or ideals such as peace, justice, fairness, liberty, equal opportunity, and people's general welfare are expressed by transformational leaders. Burns (1978) labeled these ideals as "end values" (p. 43). Leaders, superiors, participants, peers, followers, and others influence these values through specific behaviors. "The leader's fundamental act is to induce people to be aware or conscious of what they feel—to feel their true needs so strongly, to define their values so meaningfully, that they can move to purposeful action" (p. 44).

Transforming leadership theory is about the relationship and influence between leaders and followers. Burns (1978) describes this symbiotic relationship as an interaction of power and shared values. "It is the power of a person to become a leader, armed with principles and rising above self-interest narrowly conceived that invests that person with power and may ultimately transform both leaders and followers into persons who jointly adhere to modal values and end-values" (p. 457). The moral purposes of both leaders and participants are the key factors in the transforming leadership process. Change results from these shared moral purposes.

Of the seven characteristics Tichy and Devanna (1986) use to characterize transforming leaders, two relate to ethical and moral dimensions of leadership: courageous and value-driven. Transforming leaders have the courage to "confront reality even if it is painful" (p. 30) and have healthy egos to withstand peer pressure. Possessing positive self-esteem (not needing to please others to win their favor) is a necessary element of leading with moral purpose. This contrasts with leading to win a popularity contest (needing to be liked by others). For example, the president of the Senior Council decided to follow her school's alcohol policy and not permit members to take cases of beer on the spring break trip, despite the fact that the membership had unanimously voted to take alcohol on the trip. In this case, the president decided to do what was right despite popular sentiment and knowing that most people would be upset with her decision.

Transformational leaders also are value-driven. They have a core set of values that are consistent with their actions. There are several ways in which a leader can inspire others to higher levels of morality—through influence and through modeling behaviors that become the standards for others to follow.

> Modeling a Moral Purpose

If participants admire or identify with another member or leader, they will be more likely to imitate that person's behavior. Social learning theory provides a framework for understanding how individuals learn from others (Sims & Lorenzi, 1992). Bandura (1977), the pioneer of social learning theory, postulated that people can learn indirectly from observation or by vicarious learning (Bandura, 1977; Manz & Sims, 1981; Rosenthal & Zimmerman, 1978; Sims & Manz, 1981). Observational learning has its history in the practices of ancient Greeks, who referred to this concept as imitation or mimesis. Greek scholars selected the best models in Greco-Roman literature to teach their young students (Rosenthal & Zimmerman, 1978, p. 33). Behavioral modeling by leaders and participants offers a type of vicarious learning stimulus in organizational settings.

Models in organizations are capable of eliciting ethical or unethical behavior. Exemplars or models significantly influence the ethical decision making in organizations. For example, a student president of the Latino Student Union who wants everyone in the organization to feel empowered will practice sharing power and authority with leaders and members and will create opportunities for members to make meaningful contributions to the organization. Through observing the president, other organizational leaders empower committee chairs and members and involve them in the decision-making process.

Vicarious learning or behavioral modeling has important implications for the leadership process. Organizational and community members can learn ethical practices by observing those who model these practices in their leadership approaches. For example, members of the marching band who substituted a new activity for their traditional fundraiser—showing an X-rated movie—because such movies are degrading and offensive to women model social responsibility to other members of the campus community. They took a stand against that tradition and replaced it with another venue.

Another illustration of behavioral modeling by leaders occurs when a football coach benches the star player for violating a team rule, even though the coach needs that player to clinch the final playoff game. Organizational and team members learn that negative consequences result from such behavior by observing how a peer is treated. Sims and Lorenzi (1992) refer to this phenomenon as "outcome expectation" (p. 143). Participants also might infer that the leader possesses a high degree of integrity and is motivated to do the right thing. The behavior of the leader, or the coach in this example, then influences team members to act ethically because that is what is reinforced or because they want to avoid punishment for unethical behavior—or both.

Participants also model behavior that inspires leaders' ethical awareness (Chaleff, 1995). For example, the members of a student-owned food co-op influenced the student-manager to use empathy in deciding whether to dismiss an employee who missed work three days in a row to care for his ill, elderly grandmother. The members asked the manager to consider the fact that the employee was putting himself through school and that he was the only relative who could care for his grandmother. They suggested that the manager revise the work schedule to allow the employee time to help his grandmother and still maintain some hours at the co-op. In this example, the members were modeling how empathy could be used by putting themselves in the employee's situation and realizing what the impact of dismissal would be.

Modeling also can have external effects that extend beyond organizational boundaries. Ben Cohen and Jerry Greenfield, of

Ben & Jerry's Ice Cream, modeled a type of socially responsible behavior in the business world when they donated 7.5% of pretax profits to social programs. By doing this, Ben and Jerry attempted to model a moral standard for other business leaders to follow (Howell & Avolio, 1992). The Dell computer company is known as a leader in its industry for its recycling initiatives; Toms Shoes donates a pair of shoes to a disadvantaged child with each pair sold; and Newman's Own product line, founded by Hollywood actor Paul Newman, donates all of its profits to charitable organizations. We also witness examples of corporate irresponsibility from companies like Walmart that have a record of using discriminatory practices based on race and sex in hiring employees; and Nike operated sweat shops that employed child laborers in developing countries.

These examples, both positive and negative, illustrate that modeling by leaders and participants affects the ethical climate of organizations. Another form of modeling is when leaders or participants engage in discussions of ethical issues or bring up ethical dilemmas that can be resolved through an exchange of multiple perspectives.

❯ Moral Talk

How often have you found yourself in an organizational meeting or in a classroom where someone raises ethical or moral questions around a particular issue your group is working on? It is often hard to know how to approach a conversation about moral questions. Leaders and participants would benefit by engaging in conversations that allow people to explore

STUDENT ESSAY

Author Douglas Adams once said, "To give real service, you must add something which cannot be bought or measured with money, and that is sincerity and integrity." My name is Melissa Looby and I am a freshman at Rollins College in Winter Park, Florida. Before I arrived at school, I was presented with the opportunity to become a first year team member of a student-led service learning organization called Join Us in Making Progress, or J.U.M.P. I had always been interested in service throughout high school, partaking in many mission trips and facilitating many philanthropy projects in various clubs. I joined this first year team, later became the co-chair of the Hunger and Homelessness impact area, and went on to become the student coordinator. It is my passion for service that allows me to lead with such integrity. My biggest inspiration is the progress I know is being made as well as the pure joy and help service brings to others. Service is selfless, messy, and unpredictable, but it is my passion that inspires others to lead with integrity as well. My hopes were to not only be the best leader I can be, but also to empower and inspire others to feel a passion for service. Sincerity and integrity are what make real service impactful, but it takes integrity and service to make great leaders.

Melissa Looby is a music major at Rollins College. She is involved in Sigma Alpha Iota, the music fraternity for woman, the Delta Zeta sorority, and student coordinator for Join Us In Making Progress (JUMP), a service-learning organization.

the moral complexities and dimensions of problems or dilemmas. Bird and Waters (1989) provide an interesting notion of modeling or influencing ethical behavior through verbal exchanges or "moral talk" or "dialogic leadership" (Neilson, 1990, p. 765).

The dialogic leader initiates discussions with peers and members about what is ethical and what the material interests of individuals are. Dialogic leadership or moral talk can be used in student organizations as a way to model ethical approaches and to help create and sustain an ethical environment. For example, a student president of an honor society includes on the meeting agenda a discussion of the nature of the group's test files. A member speaks up at the meeting about her concern that a few of the exams in the files have been stolen. She then asks members if maintaining those files is the kind of activity the group should engage in, knowing that this is a violation of the college's honor code. A discussion ensues about whether or not the activity is counter to the organization's mission and the organization's values of academic excellence and integrity.

A real-life example of how a student government member used dialogic leadership to inspire leaders and members of the group to discuss values and ethics occurred when the student used the game of Scruples at a retreat. Although it appeared as if the members were just playing a game, in reality they were participating in conversations about how they would approach a series of dilemmas posed by questions on the cards. At the end of the game, the student government member asked others to reflect on what had just happened and how they, as a group of elected officials, should work together to confront complex issues back on campus.

Unfortunately, individuals often hesitate to participate in moral talk or discussions about ethical dilemmas (Bird & Waters, 1989). Although the topic of ethics is encountered often, little discourse about ethics takes place among group members. This lack of discussion about ethics is referred to as "moral muteness" (Bird & Waters, 1989). Reasons for this include avoidance of complex problems with moral overtones, protection of the positional leader's own managerial flexibility in solving problems, and avoidance of dealing with varying ideological or moralistic perspectives—all of which potentially inhibits the problem-solving process. Group members might also avoid discussion of ethics and morals due to their own ethical illiteracy. The potential harm caused by not modeling this through conversations or discussions is the neglect of moral abuses or an environment that is indifferent to moral considerations. It is the shared responsibility of members and leaders to initiate moral talk and to avoid moral muteness.

Moral expressions have the potential to arouse feelings of connection with moral action. The language in moral talk has to be connected with experiences and expectations of people involved in the organization for the modeling effect to occur. Moral talk can be used as a type of modeling influence when the dialogue is used to identify problems, consider issues, advocate and criticize policies, and justify and explain decisions (Bird & Waters, 1989; Pocock, 1989). Leaders and participants can use moral talk to influence others to carefully consider their perspectives and positions on issues.

Ask yourself this question: *Is it lonely or lovely at the top?* You might think that it is lonely at the top because leaders sometimes make decisions based on principles and ethics that also are unpopular choices. In those situations, leaders sometimes report feeling lonely at the top. Trevino, Weaver, and Brown (2007) raise another dimension of this question about leaders' perceptions that it is *lovely* at the top. In their study of senior managers' perceptions compared to those of lower level employees across three companies, they found that senior managers were more likely to have a positive perception of their respective organization's ethics (adherence to ethical standards by everyone in the company) compared to lower level employees who had more negative perceptions of their organizations' ethics in practice. In summary, their research showed that individuals with different organizational identities (senior managers compared to lower level employees) hold different perceptions of organizational ethics, with senior managers holding a more positive view.

To avoid the gap in these perceptions, leaders can seek out the pulse of their organization's ethics by asking members questions about how well the organization "walks its talk" in addressing ethical issues and dilemmas. Leaders also can communicate on a regular basis their commitment to values and ethics (Trevino et al., 2007) by making this a regular agenda item at meetings and participating in workshops on ethics with members.

> Ethical Decision-Making Models

The leadership process is filled with daily ethical dilemmas and problems that do not have readily identifiable solutions and that leaders and participants need to confront and resolve. It is not solely the responsibility of the leader to address these dilemmas or confront unethical behavior. The Relational Leadership Model, with its emphasis on inclusive and process-oriented leadership to achieve results for the common good, suggests that leaders and members both be included in addressing ethical dilemmas. Leaders and participants together need to be reflective, challenging, caring, purposeful, and consultative when working through ethical issues.

There are several approaches you can use to resolve ethical dilemmas. Some situations might call for using a professional code of conduct. For example, the professional conduct of lawyers and physicians is guided by standards upheld by their respective professional associations. Religious and counseling professionals are guided by a strict adherence to client confidentiality unless a client is a potential harm to self or others. Many campuses have sexual harassment and nondiscrimination policies that also guide behavior. Fraternities and sororities have rituals that serve as statements of organizational standards and values. Students may follow an honor code in classroom testing practices. Student governments are often bound to constitutions and bylaws that assist in decision-making processes related to funding and student organization recognition.

Like leadership, ethics is not a neat and tidy concept. Not all situations can be resolved by the application of professional codes or organizational standards (Beauchamp & Childress, 1979; Kitchener, 1984). It requires human judgment and analysis to even determine whether a situation represents an ethical dilemma or something else, such as a personality conflict between two members.

Although one of several models could be used to guide ethical decision making, the following section includes models that can be used as practical tools in resolving ethical dilemmas. All these models should be used by leaders and participants together to collaboratively work through problems. The models should be applied with careful analysis rather than with a rigid application of any particular model; reflection and a careful consideration of other factors are needed. These models call for the use of your moral imagination—visualizing new alternatives to old or unsolved problems. Otherwise, these frameworks cannot stand on their own.

> Practical Applications

Imagine this scenario. You attend a college that has a strict academic honor code calling for community members to turn in anyone who violates the code. You are also the president of the Interfraternity Council. During an exam, you notice a fraternity brother, who is also one of your best friends, cheating from another classmate. How do you go about confronting this situation? Do you follow the code and turn your fraternity brother in to the judicial office? Or do you try to influence him after the exam not to cheat in the future because you will have to turn him in and it would look bad for your fraternity? Or do you begin to initiate a decision-making process that will guide you from the stage of interpreting the situation—if I respond in a certain way, how will it affect others?—to the final stage of acting with your convictions and moral purpose in mind? Or do you do nothing, acting without moral purpose?

Ethical decision-making models encourage people to work through dilemmas with a moral purpose in mind and provide frameworks in which to guide decision making and analysis. Rather than react quickly to dilemmas, you should carefully consider various steps, including ethical analysis, toward making sound decisions.

Kidder (1995) defines tough choices as, "those that pit one 'right' value against another" (p. 16). "The really tough choices, then, do not center upon right versus wrong. They involve right versus right. They are genuine dilemmas precisely because each side of the problem is firmly rooted in one of our basic, core values" (p. 18). An ethical dilemma stands for right-versus-right situations in which two core moral values come into conflict, as distinct from dilemmas that stem from the right-versus-wrong issues that produce moral temptations. Kidder (2005) provides a framework for examining right-versus-right choices using a four dilemma paradigm model:

1. Justice versus mercy: fairness and equity conflict with compassion, empathy, and love
2. Short term versus long term: immediate needs run counter to future goals
3. Individual versus community: self versus others or small group versus larger group
4. Truth versus loyalty: honesty competes with commitment, responsibility, or promise-keeping (pp. 18–23)

These dilemma paradigms represent values that collide with each other. The death of Terry Schiavo, who was kept on a life support for nearly 15 years beginning in 1998 after collapsing in her home and never regaining consciousness, represented a legal case in which the values of justice versus mercy clashed. This dilemma raged into a public debate about the moral and legal rights of life and death.

A classic example of a truth versus loyalty dilemma occurred in April of 1996 when David Kaczynski turned his brother,

Theodore Kaczynski, in to the authorities because he suspected him of being the Unabomber—the man who plagued the country for more than two decades by sending bombs through the mail, killing or permanently harming several innocent victims. David Kacyznski is an example of a courageous individual who did what he believed was right and honest. He did so at the painful expense of knowing that his brother, if found guilty, would be given a serious criminal sentence, perhaps even the death penalty. David Kaczynski acted with emotional agony because he wanted to believe that his brother was not the Unabomber. This incident illuminates the difficult human struggle that occurs when the values of truth versus loyalty are in conflict or when the values of individual versus community collide. Under this circumstance or a similar one, ask yourself, Would you turn one of your siblings or your best friend in to the FBI if you thought he or she was the Unabomber? Or if your mother hit a pedestrian and fled the scene of an accident? Which value would you choose and act upon?

A more recent example of an honesty versus loyalty dilemma occurred in 2008 when Mark and Andrew Madoff, Bernard Madoff's sons, reported to authorities that their father was operating a major Ponzi scheme, which robbed billions of dollars from over 1,000 investors. Bernie Madoff was arrested the next day by the FBI and received a lifetime prison sentence, the legacy earned from running one of the largest financial fraud schemes in the world. Mark and Andrew Madoff faced multiple dilemmas in this case, including what to do with the wealth they accumulated through their father and through their employment in his company. Two years later, Mark Madoff committed suicide after struggling emotionally with the pressure from mounting lawsuits against the family and negative media attention.

STUDENT ESSAY ◆

It's Friday night and one of your first nights being on duty as a Resident Assistant; that alone makes you feel good because you were chosen out of a large crowd and are taught that you should always uphold the standards and rules of the college. Obliviously this is easier said than done.

Being just a second year in college and a new member of a Greek organization there is nothing more scary then going to your Greek organizations floor knowing that you are about to have a dilemma. On one hand you can leave your friends alone and ignore policy violations going on, and on the other hand you can document your friends and have them be furious at you and potentially not speak to you for a while.

But there is no choice, you know you need to knock on the door and document what is happening.

Hard decisions always have to be made, but doing the ethical thing is what is right even if that means making your friends angry or losing some in the process. Being given a leadership position is a privilege and should be treated as such.

Darcie First is a senior at Ripon College where she studies anthropology and business management. She was a member of the residence life staff for three years and president of the Ripon Anthropology Association.

❯ Kidder's Ethical Decision Making Model

Kidder (1995) provides three principles for ethical decision making (pp. 24–25):

1. *Ends-based thinking*: Philosophers refer to this as utilitarianism, best known by the maxim, *Do whatever produces the*

greatest good for the greatest number. Based on cost-benefit analysis, this maxim is based on determining who will be hurt and who will be helped. At the heart of this principle is an assessment of consequences, a forecasting of outcomes.

2. *Rule-based thinking*: Kant's "*categorical imperative*: follow only the principle that you want everyone else to follow. Ask yourself, "If everyone in the world followed this rule of action I am following, would that create the greatest good or the greatest worth of character?" Rule-based thinking is based firmly on duty—what we ought to do rather than what we think might work. This is deontological thinking, meaning "obligation" or "duty."

3. *Care-based thinking*: putting love for others first. The Golden Rule is an example of care-based thinking—*do to others what you would like them to do to you*. Care-based thinking puts the feature of "reversibility" into play: test your actions by putting yourself in another's shoes and imagining how it would feel if you were the recipient, rather than the perpetrator, of your actions.

These three principles can be applied in examining dilemmas as you begin to work through their complexities and then decide the right course of action. An effective approach is to use each of the three principles before making a decision or taking an action. Kidder further provides nine checkpoints to use when faced with an ethical dilemma.

Kidder's Nine Checkpoints for Dealing with Ethical Issues

1. Recognize that there is a moral issue
2. Determine the actor
3. Gather the relevant facts
4. Test for right versus wrong issues
5. Test for right versus right paradigms
6. Apply the resolution principles (ends-based, rules-based, care-based)
7. Investigate the "trilemma options": Is there a third way through this dilemma (middle ground sometimes will be the result of a compromise between two rights)?
8. Make the decision—this requires moral courage, an attribute essential to leadership
9. Revisit and reflect on the decision—go back over the decision-making process and seek its lessons; this feedback loop builds expertise and helps adjust the moral compass (pp. 180–186)

Consider the following situation. You are the president of the college's Young Democrats or Young Republicans Club. Your group has discovered that an unflattering article about the club will be printed in the next day's campus newspaper. Club members begin planning a scheme to steal all the newspapers before students get them in the morning. Using the examples of ethical decision-making models, how would you approach this situation? What are the moral dimensions of this situation? Is it a violation of a constitutional right to freedom of the press, or a violation of the school's honor code? Would you convince members not to execute their plan because they might get caught and the club might loose its charter? Or would you threaten to turn them in if they proceed? Or would you influence them not to do this because it is wrong to steal these papers and an obstruction of the constitutional right of freedom of the press? If the group proceeds to steal the newspapers, would reporting them to the campus judicial office result in their expulsion from school and possibly prevent them from ever having the chance to complete their college degrees? If you did nothing, would you be modeling behavior to others that condones an illegal act? What should you do? What are alternative courses of action? How will your decision affect the ethical environment of your organization? What would you do if members actually stole the papers?

> Ethical Principles and Standards

In the helping professions, several scholars have adapted Aristotle's ethical principles, which serve as the foundation for living an ethical life and as principles or standards to guide physicians, psychologists, and counselors in particular (Beauchamp & Childress, 1979; Kitchener, 1984). Beauchamp and Childress (1979) proposed five principles of biomedical ethics, which were later adapted by Karen Strohm Kitchener, a professor of education, for the counseling psychology field. These five ethical principles are (1) respecting autonomy, (2) doing no harm, (3) benefiting others, (4) being just, and (5) being faithful. As a leader or member, you can use these five principles illustrated in

Exhibit 6.1 as a critical evaluative approach to moral reasoning and ethical decision-making processes (Beauchamp & Childress, 1979). Using the critical evaluative approach allows leaders and members "to illuminate our ordinary moral judgment and to redefine the bases for our actions" (Kitchener, 1984, p. 45).

There are many applications of these five ethical principles in leadership and in organizational settings. Using these principles should help you determine the correct course of action and should have a bearing on how your decisions will affect others. Using the five principles, imagine that you are the chair of the homecoming committee and that the promotions subcommittee designed a homecoming T-shirt that you find to be offensive to ethnic groups. The committee spent $10,000 on the shirts, which are being sold by organizational members. The $10,000 must be replaced in the budget by the T-shirt sales. Which of the five principles would you use in working through this dilemma? Do any of the principles clash with one another, such as respecting the autonomy of the committee and doing no harm to others who might be hurt by the symbolism on the T-shirt?

Professional associations have codes of ethics that are standards used to guide professionals' decision making and actions. The Center for the Study of Ethics in the Professions has gathered over 850 codes of ethics for a wide range of professions including law, governments, engineering, the health care industry, sports, fraternal social organizations, and the media, to name a few (http://ethics.iit.edu/). There is a debate on the usefulness of professional codes of ethics, yet codes can protect professionals from pressures that could lead to questionable conduct. They are

Exhibit 6.1: Five Ethical Principles in Decision Making

◆

Respecting Autonomy: providing leaders and members with freedom of choice, allowing individuals to freely develop their values, and respecting the right of others to act independently. Autonomy, like constitutional rights and liberties, has conditions and does not imply unrestricted freedom. A major assumption of autonomy is that an individual possesses a certain level of competence to make rational and informed decisions.

Doing No Harm or Nonmaleficence: providing an environment that is free from harm to others, both psychological and physical. Leaders and members refrain from "engaging in actions which risk harming others" (Kitchener, 1984, p. 47).

Benefiting Others or Beneficence: promoting the interests of the organization above personal interests and self-gain. The notion of promoting what is good for the whole of the organization or community and promoting the growth of the group is upheld in the principle of beneficence.

Being Just or Justice: treating people fairly and equally. This principle is traced to Aristotle's work on ethics.

Being Faithful or Fidelity: keeping promises, being faithful, and being loyal to the group or organization. Being faithful is a principle premised on relationships and trust. If you as a leader or member violate the principle of fidelity, it is difficult or impossible for others to develop a trusting relationship.

a unifying document of the common values and ethics associated with any given profession. They can be used as a decision-making tool when confronted with professional dilemmas.

A quick and informal decision-making model, commonly referred to as the "newspaper test," can influence your actions and decisions. Consider this—before you act or decide, think about whether or not you would be comfortable with your actions or behaviors appearing in the newspaper. Will your decision pass the newspaper test?

These ethical decision-making models can help you reach a more informed and carefully analyzed decision before you take any action. Too often, we are tempted to quickly put out fires or react to pressing dilemmas without engaging in a process that would provide some assurance that the right decision was made. These models alone will not necessarily help you resolve every dilemma you encounter. They provide a framework to guide your decision making. They do not provide the moral imagination and creative thinking that are needed to address complex situations.

> Chapter Summary

Leading with integrity is a complex process that includes the moral development of an individual, the influence of role models, values-driven leadership, and the organizational environment. The process of developing into an ethical participant and creating ethical environments does not occur overnight. Groups and organizations are made up of humans who can and do make mistakes, which is part of the learning process. Raising questions around ethical issues is a fundamental component of leading with integrity. People who lead with moral purpose often have as many questions as answers. Leading from the Relational Leadership Model means leading with moral purpose: empowering others to lead by example, including other participants in resolving ethical dilemmas, acting ethically to positively affect the public good, and using a process to approach problems that do not offer clear solutions.

Our society is calling for leaders and participants alike who can be trusted and who are committed to doing the right thing. Despite the turbulent and fast-paced nature of our world, leading with a moral purpose is central to the leadership process. Imagine what an organization, community, or the world would look like if everyone would strive to create and sustain an ethical environment by rewarding ethical acts, engage in moral talk, and carefully work, as a group, toward resolving dilemmas by using decision-making models.

> What's Next?

The preceding chapters have shown how important the nature of relationships is in leadership and how complex it is to lead with moral purpose. In the following section, you will learn about the complexities of teams, groups, organizations, and communities. Understanding yourself and others is a key component of leading with integrity. We challenge you to integrate this knowledge with the interdependent nature of working with others in various types of settings to facilitate positive change.

> Chapter Activities

1. Think of a national, historical, or local person who you believe is an ethical leader. What skills, behaviors, attitudes, or characteristics does that person exhibit? Think of a national, historical, or local person who you believe is an

unethical leader—a person who practices bad or toxic leadership. What skills, behaviors, attitudes, or characteristics does that person exhibit? How have both leaders' behaviors influenced or impacted followers or others in the organization?

2. Think of a person who has served as a role model to you. Why did you choose that person? What skills, behaviors, attitudes, or characteristics does that person exhibit?

3. How can or do you serve as a role model to others in your group or community?

4. How would you approach someone in your group or community who is behaving unethically or violating the group's standards?

5. Think of an ethical dilemma you have faced or somehow were involved with. Work through that dilemma using one of the three ethical decision-making models. How would you initiate moral talk with others in your group?

6. Think of a time when you or someone else served as a transforming leader. What was that experience like? How did the leader and members inspire each other to higher levels of morality?

7. Think about an organization in which you are currently a member and answer the following questions. How would you describe the ethical climate in this organization? What does the organization do to encourage members to do what is right? What does the organization do that may encourage inappropriate behavior? What happens when someone violates the ethical standards of the organization? How could the organization become more supportive of ethical behavior? List the

ways you could reward ethical behavior in your organization. Develop an action plan to put these ideas into place.

8. List the ways you could reward ethical behavior in your organization, residence hall, place of employment, and so forth. Develop an action plan to put these ideas into place.

9. Identify an organization or institution you believe has a strong commitment to ethics. How would you describe that organization? How do the members and leaders of that organization create and sustain an ethical organizational environment? How do they model ethical behaviors? How is this organization different from others?

10. Using Johnson's metaphor of casting light and casting shadow, identify an example of a leader who casted light and a leader who casted a shadow. How did others respond to each of them? What leadership lessons can you learn from both?

11. Identify an ethical dilemma you faced in which there were two competing values such as honesty and loyalty. How did you work through that dilemma and what was the outcome? What, if anything, would you do differently if you could go back in time to that same situation?

ADDITIONAL READINGS

Johnson, C. E. (2012). *Meeting the ethical challenges of leadership: Casting light or shadow*. Thousand Oaks, CA: Sage.

Kellerman, B. (2004). *Bad leadership*. Cambridge, MA: Harvard Business School Press.

Kidder, R. M. (1995). *How good people make tough choices: Resolving the dilemmas of ethical living*. New York, NY: Fireside.

Kidder, R. M. (2005). *Moral courage: Taking action when your values are put to the test.* New York, NY: William Morrow.

Lipman-Blumen, J. (2005). *The allure of toxic leaders.* New York, NY: Oxford University Press.

Transparency International 2004 Annual Report (pp. 1–24). Retrieved February 8, 2006 from http://www.transparency.org/publications /annual_report

Trevino, L. K., Weaver, G. R., & Brown, M. E. (2007). It's lonely at the top: Hierarchical levels, identities, and perceptions of organizational ethics. *Business Ethics Quarterly, 18*(2), 233–252.

PART III

Context for the Practice of Leadership

Any leadership setting can be viewed as a community of people working together for shared purposes. Relational leadership is best practiced by thinking about any kind of group or organization as a community.

In the *Tao of Leadership*, Heider (1985) interprets,

> The leader who understands how process unfolds uses as little force as possible and runs the group without pressuring people.
>
> When force is used, conflict and argument follow. The group field degenerates. The climate is hostile, neither open nor nourishing.
>
> The wise leader runs the group without fighting to have things a certain way. The leader's touch is light. The leader neither defends nor attacks.
>
> Remember that consciousness, not selfishness, is both the means of teaching and the teaching itself. Group members will challenge the ego of one who leads egocentrically. But one who leads selflessly and harmoniously will grow and endure. (p. 59)

Groups and organizations are best understood as interdependent communities of people working together to accomplish their shared purposes.

This part explores how groups develop through stages, how they can be enhanced by attention to process, and how they can become building blocks for complex systems and organizations. Leadership in groups and committees is substantially different from the complexity of leadership in organizational systems (for example, a college, a company, a hospital, a church). The last chapter in this section describes organizations and the importance that they be self-renewing entities, able to stay adaptable, nimble, and developmental for their members.

Chapter 7

Being in Communities

Denise is at home not feeling well. She overslept and is sorry to have missed the commencement committee meeting this morning. The phone rings and Jason is on the line. He has Stacy and Carl in his room, and they are worried because Denise did not come to the meeting.

JASON: Denise, it's Jason and I'm here with Stacy and Carl. Our committee was really worried when you didn't show up this morning and no one heard from you. Dean Jacobs asked if anyone knew if you were OK, since you are always right there. You sound terrible! Are you OK?

DENISE: [*clearing her throat*] Thanks, Jason. It feels really good to know you all noticed. I have a killer cold. It hit me late last night. I slept right through the meeting, but sorry I didn't call so you wouldn't worry.

JASON: That's OK, Denise. Hope you feel better. Stacy says she'll drop some résumés of the possible commencement speakers by your house tonight because we are all supposed to be ready to vote on one of them as our recommendation to the senior class council for Friday—oh, Stacy says to ask, Do you need anything she can bring when she comes by?

This committee appears to be a healthy community. Denise's absence was noticed by committee members and by the adviser. They cared enough to check on her and to pick up copies of materials in her absence. Denise felt badly that she worried them. Denise knows from this encounter that she matters.

Community is a compelling feeling, whether on a smaller personal level or on a macro or national level. On a personal level think of how comfortable and affirmed you feel in healthy communities like your family, your residence hall floor, a wonderful seminar, or your office; conversely think of how anxious or uncomfortable you are in hostile or dysfunctional communities. Remember all the ways in which communities pull together in times of crises: Newtown, Connecticut, in 2012 after shootings at Sandy Hook Elementary School; Aurora, Colorado, following the massacre in 2012 at the opening of the Batman movie; the devastating tornado in Joplin Missouri in 2011; and the colleges that took in displaced students after Hurricane Katrina in 2005.

❯ Chapter Overview

Envisioning each group or organization you are in as a community provides a mental model that will respond to the relational needs of these rapidly changing times. Individuals function concurrently in many different kinds of community. Thinking of each of your formal and informal groups as a community provides a frame for the interdependence of relational leadership. This chapter discusses the nature of communities, principles of community development, and your role as an active member of your communities of practice.

> The Importance of Community

Knowing about community, philosophically believing in the worth of community, and being skilled at developing and sustaining community are essential aspects of relational leadership. To value community is to value our interdependence. Ideal, perfect communities do not exist in reality. We all live, work, and learn in imperfect communities, which, if they are striving to be better, become supportive environments for individual and group growth. Any group of people that come together for a purpose (such as a neighborhood, an office, a class, or a city experiencing a natural disaster) "continually participate in conversations about the questions 'Who are we?' and 'What matters?' " (Wheatley & Kellner-Rogers, 1996, p. 17). They ask "Who are we together?"

Gardner (1990) asserts that *"skill in the building and rebuilding of community is not just another of the innumerable requirements of contemporary leadership. It is one of the highest and most essential skills a leader can command"* (p. 118, emphasis in the original). Relational leadership calls for attending to community as a discipline. The term "discipline" in this case refers to a concept to be studied, learned, and practiced, as one would learn academic disciplines such as biology, English, or history (Gozdz, 1993).

It is not enough to understand self and others; understanding is essential to creating and nurturing the context in which the group or organization functions. Thinking of the relationships in that setting as a community focuses participants' attention on the responsibilities, the processes, and the spirit of working together.

Think of the most effective and meaningful classes, clubs, committees, or groups you have experienced. You probably felt a commitment to the whole and felt like you mattered and were meaningful to others in that setting. Not all groups feel that way. You can probably recall or imagine a group you had to be a part of but which held little value for you or in which you felt little in common with others or little commitment to the task in that setting. That group may have accomplished its goals, but few members would say they enjoyed working together; they probably would not want to work together again if given a choice. Relational leadership asks you to envision the context of the setting as a healthy community, which leads to a whole paradigm of expectations and norms for working together effectively as participants in shared leadership.

> Elements of Community

A community is most often described as "a social group that not only shares an identity and structured pattern of interaction, but also a common geographical territory" (Goodman, 1992, p. 48). However, community is not just a place where interaction occurs, but it is also an attitude of connection and commitment that sustains relationships and purpose. Sharing that community commitment is the essence of relational leadership. The phone call to Denise might not seem to illustrate leadership on the surface, but imagine a small committee or class whose members matter so much to each other and to the adviser or professor that someone's absence is not only noticed but becomes a matter of concern, and whose members look out for the person's needs. In that environment, each participant feels a sense of ownership and shared leadership.

Communities know they are a collection of individuals who accomplish their goals through trust and teamwork. Teamwork requires processes to make decisions, methods of communication, and a commitment to some level of participation by community members. Gardner (1990) extends the traditional definitions of community to refer to effective communities as those that practice these eight elements:

1. Wholeness incorporating diversity
2. A shared culture
3. Good internal communication
4. Caring, trust, and teamwork
5. Group maintenance and governance
6. Participation and shared leadership tasks
7. Development of young people [or new members]
8. Links with the outside world (pp. 116–118)

Through their work together, community members develop a shared culture that is concerned about new members. Effective communities realize they are not insular but are in a constant, dynamic interaction with their broader environment. Binding all of this together is the awareness that a group is a community—the shared culture may reflect that spirit of community. The spirit of community makes many other relational processes possible.

Many traditional views of community are changing. Conventional views present communities as homogeneous groupings of people who have much in common and may even resemble each other in ideology, race, or class. Those may indeed be communities, yet "cultural and ethnic diversity (and all other forms of diversity, as well) are necessary resources for building community. A true community cannot exist without diversity" (Gudykunst, 1991, p. 146). Diversity of ideas, diversity of skills, diversity of experiences, and diversity of worldviews bring to a group's shared goals the many talents of people gathered as a community. If all community members saw things the same way, had the same skills, and had the same life experiences, their ability to be resilient and face change would be limited. "Community is that place where the person you least want to live with always lives. And when that person moves away, someone else arises to take his or her place" (Palmer, 1981, p. 124).

Other traditional views have held that communities need face-to-face interaction, which is possible only through close geographic proximity. However, the term *community* also describes those with common identity and interaction but without geographic proximity. References to "the medical community," "the Deaf community," or "the spiritual community" reflect their common frame or perspective and not their physical daily interactions. Many members of these communities do find ways to meet and think together. Professional society meetings through associations and conventions or webinars provide a forum for the development of community connections.

Electronic networks have provided a creative way for communities of common interest to interact. Internet chat rooms, blogs, message boards, online discussion groups, and sites such as Facebook are linking people across the globe into selective communities in which minds meet. There are those who express concern that electronic communications like Facebook posts, email, text messaging, and chat rooms diminish community; indeed, it is possible to become isolated from face-to-face interaction when using the computer for most of your interactions. But the effective and responsible use of electronic communication can facilitate community. Think

STUDENT ESSAY

I've been fortunate to have access to leadership development opportunities in my area, but not everyone is so lucky—and how do those unlucky students find a community of leaders with which to connect? As technology becomes more advanced, for the first time these students have an alternative option: online communities. Working with the National Collegiate Leadership Association, I've been able to help create a virtual space for leaders across the country not only to connect to leadership resources, but to each other. Perhaps the most rewarding part of this experience has been when two students who would never have spoken to each other, or even known of the other's existence, make a connection. It's exciting that I'm able to become a leader in a time when creating new communities, and the ability to truly connect to them, is becoming more and more accessible every day.

Janae Phillips is a senior at the University of Arizona majoring in family studies and human development. She is an assistant theme coordinator for the Arizona Blue Chip Program, the student lead for the National Collegiate Leadership Association, and the president and cofounder of the University of Arizona Harry Potter Alliance chapter.

of how you feel closer to the community of your high school
friends when you can join a Facebook site with them wherever
they now live—like at other colleges, in the military, or at
work. Cyber communities have provided support connections
for gay and lesbian students and students with disabilities who
may otherwise feel isolated. Studies demonstrate that offline
and online relationships do not differ in depth or breadth and
may even be associated with social well-being (Bonebrake,
2002).

You can also find identity and feel a sense of community
with others without interacting. For example, if you are an avid
environmentalist, you feel a close connection to the struggles
of Greenpeace International or the Sierra Club when you read
about them in the news. If you participate in community service
concerned with abused children, you feel anguish over the latest
tragedies reported on the radio and can empathize with social
workers struggling to find solutions. If you are a father, you smile
to see other dads at the playground comforting a child with a
scrapped knee. If you are a member of a national organization
like a sorority, you may feel immediate kinship with a sister
from another chapter whom you met while you were both on
vacation. You might even seek out certain communities when
you move to a new town because you know you will be welcomed
as a new member.

As human beings, we all want meaningful connection
to others. Settings that are inclusive and empowering, in
which there is purposeful change being accomplished through
ethical and collaborative processes, are the epitome of effective
communities. Relational leadership flourishes in settings that
value the elements of community.

A Common Center

In his 1958 classic *I and Thou*, Martin Buber contends that in our life together, some form of community is what makes life worth living. He describes community as a group of people who have made a choice around a common center. A true community is not a collection of people who all think alike; it is a collection of people with differing minds and complementary natures.

We participated in a group of leadership educators who struggled with the role and importance of community in shared leadership. This group eventually defined community as the "binding together of diverse individuals committed to a just, common good through shared experiences in a spirit of caring and social responsibility" (National Invitational Leadership Symposium, 1991, p. 19). Developing communities like this depends on relational leadership that deeply values the inclusion of all members, empowered to work together toward common purposes.

In these communities, openness, transparency, and dialogue are central practices. True dialogue requires listening and being willing to give up the need for control, even when your ideas and thoughts are in conflict with those of another. Without the willingness to give up control, you engage in monologue that cannot promote community. Being in community requires the realization that a member's own needs will not always prevail. Buber (1958) reminds us that this does not mean accepting views of others just to create a false peace; rather, it means keeping in mind the commitment to greater values. "Communities speak to us in moral voices. They lay claims on their members. Indeed, they are the most important sustaining source of moral voices other than the inner self" (Etzioni, 1993, p. 31). Stop and think

of how authentic and genuine you are as a supporting member of
the communities that matter to you. How do you support the
community that is your family, your apartment-mates, your
office, or your major?

Communities are where we exhibit the values to which we
are committed. The difference between our espoused values and
actual behaviors becomes transparent in communities. Indeed,
"communities are the mirrors in which we see our true selves"
(Hesselbein, Goldsmith, Beckhard, & Schubert, 1998, p. xiii).

Communities of Practice

It is not sufficient to think of yourself as being a mere member
of multiple communities; membership may mean having only
a passive connection or being a name on a roster. You may be
highly involved and committed to the success of your fraternity,
the senior class council, an ethnic or religiously affiliated group
you are a part of, or the service organization you co-lead. However, because of limited time, disinterest, or shifting priorities,
you may become affiliated with only one of those communities
and not highly active in the others.

No one has enough time or energy to be highly involved
in every community with which they identify. Being a member
of a community of practice, however, implies an engagement
with others who are working toward some action. The people
in that community are doing something, and you are a part of
that in some meaningful way. "Each person belongs to many
communities of practice but with varying degrees of centrality. In
some communities of practice we are only peripherally involved;
in others we are centrally involved" (Drath & Palus, 1994,
p. 11). You may have intentionally decided that this is the time

to devote more time and energy to your family, to some special needs in your job, or to your senior thesis project, so you cannot do as much as you might like in your worship community or in your other organizations.

Just as there are residence hall floors where residents keep their doors shut and do not even talk on the elevators going down to classes in the morning, there are also floors where residents are in and out of each other's rooms, gather in the floor lounge to watch a favorite reality TV show, and cluster in the same section of the dining hall for dinner each evening. A person can lead an isolated life while surrounded by people in classes, in the snack bar, or at work—or a connected life when meaningfully involved in a community. Even within the larger environment, one can find what Harvard sociologist Herbert Gans calls "urban villages" (cited in Etzioni, 1993, p. 120). Urban villages are the many small communities within larger systems. The giant lecture class can become an urban environment of small villages through the use of such class structures as discussion groups and team projects.

The social networks we form in these communities of practice are critical to accomplishing shared goals as well as to our personal identification and satisfaction. A high level of people's involvement in their diverse communities characterizes the nature of American democracy. Twenty years ago, Robert Putnam (1995) focused attention on this aspect of American life when he studied the involvement of people in civic life and saw declines in indicators like labor unions, church attendance, and PTA meetings. These symptoms are captured in his observation that "between 1980 and 1993 the total number of bowlers in America increased by 10%, while league bowling decreased by 40%" (p. 70)—so he concluded that Americans were now "bowling alone." New kinds of organizations and issues have grown to capture Americans' attention, such as environmental groups like the Sierra Club, book clubs, and hobby clubs—and support groups have grown to the point that 40% of all Americans claimed to be part of a group that cares for and supports members (Wuthnow, as reported in Putnam). Most Americans have replaced socializing with neighbors with socializing with friends and colleagues from the workplace (Putnam). This shift from being involved in groups that work for civic outcomes to groups that promote more personal outcomes deserves attention. Noting the importance of social networks, Putnam describes the value of social capital, "by analogy with notions of physical capital and human capital—tools and training that enhance individual productivity—'social capital' refers to features of social organization such as networks, norms, and social trust that facilitate coordination and cooperation for mutual benefit" (p. 67).

Focusing on communities of practice also raises the question, How can those communities best function to fully engage community members? The policies, behaviors, expectations, norms, and other structures may promote or may prohibit your meaningful involvement in that community. Assume that you are very committed to the community of practice that is the office of your part-time job. An office culture that includes you in decision making, supervision that promotes your personal development, reward systems that show your work is valued, coworkers who support and trust each other, and office celebrations of team successes all create an environment that bonds people to this community. Assess the environment of any of your communities of practice to determine how their structures and processes may be blocking meaningful identity and involvement with that culture. Addressing that information can help it become a more effective environment.

Being "in community" requires an awareness of reciprocal processes. An individual has to decide to be part of the larger community, and the community has to involve and welcome individuals. Harvard sociologist Charles Willie (1992) asserts that in any community (that is, work group, classroom, neighborhood, or volunteer organization) there are concurrent obligations of contributive justice and distributive justice. Each individual in the community must practice contributive justice. Individuals contribute to the group's belief that it is fair and reasonable for each to do his or her part in the greater whole, uphold obligations, and feel a commitment to shared purposes. Conversely, the community must practice the distributive justice of caring for all community members and ensuring that each is included, is heard, and is not hurt or disadvantaged through community membership. Some people in communities do not uphold their responsibilities or share the transcendent values that bind a community together. Communities sometimes act to remove members who are not willing to uphold shared values. The student who persistently pulls false fire alarms may not be an appropriate member of a residence hall community, nor is the member of a lab team who sabotages other teams' experiments appropriate for that community.

Communities thrive on "serial reciprocity" (Ulrich, 1998, p. 161). This means that on his residence hall floor, Chris will help Mary move her refrigerator, and Mary repays that kindness, not necessarily by helping Chris back, but when she helps floor-mate Dianne put up flyers in the hall; Dianne likewise pays Mary back when she picks up the trash that has spilled out of the trash can at the end of the hall (Ulrich, 1998). The responsibility each floor resident feels toward the others in the community of the floor creates the civic culture of the floor to generate and regenerate its sense of community.

Responsibilities and rights go hand-and-hand in communities. Arun Gandhi (1998) shares many lessons he learned as a small boy from his grandfather, Mohandas Gandhi. Among those lessons were his grandfather's reflections on what caused violence in human life:

- Wealth without work
- Pleasure without conscience
- Knowledge without character
- Commerce without morality
- Science without humanity
- Worship without sacrifice
- Politics without principle
- Rights without responsibilities (p. 90)

Learning to feel responsible for others in our communities of practice is critical for our human connection.

> The Development of Community

On the first day that you and 30 other residents move into your new residence hall floor, or 50 students come to a first class, or a committee of 12 convenes its first meeting, community does not magically happen. The development of a spirit of community must happen intentionally.

STUDENT ESSAY

My story starts in a tiny chair, the ones for two-year-olds. I started volunteering at the child center on campus. Over the course of three years I've watched the children learn to walk, talk, and write. I've helped them grow but they've also helped me grow as a person and leader. They taught me to share, be patient, and just to appreciate the little things in life. I've been able to apply these simple life lessons to my current leadership role, in particular my role as a resident assistant. I think one of my most memorable experiences here at the University of California, Merced has been my time working as an RA in the first year residence halls. I learned that being a leader is not just when you are presenting or leading a group. Leadership includes taking initiative and having the patience to work for hours with a student that just needs to be heard. It's when you are woken up in the middle of the night to help someone through a traumatic life experience. The opportunity to work with people at their best or worst challenges me as a leader and has made me who I am today. To build a safe, inclusive learning community for my residents and to guide these 60 students through their first year in college is a honor and experience that makes me appreciate and continue to give back to my communities.

Heidi Chan is a fourth year at University of California, Merced where she is pursuing a major in sociology and minor in public health. She has been a volunteer at the UC Merced childhood education center for four years, worked as an orientation leader for two summers, and is a second-year resident assistant.

Scott Peck (1987) has identified four stages of developing true authentic community. The first stage is *pseudocommunity*. In this stage a group may feel like things are just fine, people seem to be getting along, relationships are courteous, but it is in reality a superficial, underdeveloped level of community. For example, "pseudocommunity is conflict-avoiding; true community is conflict-resolving" (p. 88).

The second stage of community building is *chaos*. During this stage there is a noisy din of different views. Different people or factions are asserting their perspectives from which to set the community's agenda or determine important processes. Committee members may promote individual agendas; cliques form on the residence hall floor. This stage can be dangerous because some give up and retreat instead of working through this stage. It is important to find meaning in the idea that even "fighting is better than pretending you are not divided" (Peck, 1987, p. 94). This stage is similar to the storming stage of group development presented next in Chapter Eight.

Peck (1987) observes that groups take one of two paths out of chaos: organization or emptiness. Organization leaves the source of fighting untouched, by establishing structures, rules, and systems to manage and handle the differences of opinion. For example, the residence hall floor group makes a new policy to rein in those who are misusing the floor lounge; or a committee, frustrated with long debates, decides to vote on decisions and let the majority rule. The structures may solve the immediate problem, but the source of tension and disagreement may fester. Although it is counterintuitive to think of the term *emptiness* as signifying something good, emptiness is Peck's term for the process of community members emptying themselves of their barriers to true communication like assumptions about others or preformed perspectives on how things should be; thus becomes the third stage in community building.

This third stage is the realization that many personal feelings, assumptions, ideas, stereotypes, or motives become barriers to truly listening and understanding (and being understood). Again, emptiness refers to emptying oneself of the assumptions and preconceived notions that may block one from truly listening. It may mean someone saying, "Wait a minute. This argument is beginning to sound like the freshmen think all the seniors are money-hungry, selfish egoists, and the seniors think the freshmen are unrealistic, naive idealists. We need to let go of those assumptions and look at the good thoughts each group is raising."

In the fourth stage, *true, authentic community*, conflict still arises, but there are ways to be heard, and the community members usually know they cannot reach consensus or any level of agreement without dissensus or disagreements to create truly better decisions. Building community is creating a feel of "we" out of lots of "I's." Many groups never get past pseudocommunity and find ways to courteously interact and get their work done. That may be sufficient for their purposes, but ongoing groups that are doing difficult work would benefit from recognizing Peck's stages and working toward authentic community.

Communities that engage in this developmental process and reach a stage of authentically functioning as a community often err by not recognizing that being a community is a process, not an end state. Communities are not static—they constantly change. New members join the group, external crises cause new levels or types of conflict, and key members, who had been instrumental to nurturing community, leave. Communities must recognize when they need to attend to the cycle of rebuilding a genuine community.

Participants who want to be highly engaged in the work of any community need to assess the ways in which they can become effective community members. Gudykunst (1991) proposes that individual participants practice these seven community building principles:

1. *Be Committed*: Commitment to others is prerequisite for community to exist.
2. *Be Mindful*: Think about what we do and say. Focus on the process, not the outcome . . . be contemplative in examining our own behavior.
3. *Be Unconditionally Accepting*: Accept others as they are; do not try to change or control them . . . minimize expectations, prejudices, suspicion, and mistrust.
4. *Be Concerned for Both Yourself and Others*: Engage in dialogue whenever possible . . . consult others on issues that affect them and be open to their ideas . . . fight gracefully.
5. *Be Understanding*: Strive to understand others as completely as possible.
6. *Be Ethical*: Engage in behavior that is not a means to an end, but behavior that is morally right in and of itself.
7. *Be Peaceful*: Do not be violent [or] deceitful, breach value promises, or be secretive . . . strive for internal harmony . . . and harmony in relations with others. (pp. 147–148)

If each participant has the mental model of their organization as a community and practices community-building skills, the group will be enriched. Participants will listen more keenly, respect each other even when there are disagreements on specific issues, seek resolution of differences, and learn more in the process. Etzioni (1993) challenges us to "lay claims on others to be similarly involved in, and dedicated to, community" (p. 142).

Table 7.1 **Connecting Relational Leadership to Elements of Community**

Relational Leadership (See Chapter Three)	Elements of Community (Gardner, 1990; Gudykunst, 1991)
Inclusive	Wholeness incorporating diversity; links with the outside world; Be Committed; Be Unconditionally Accepting
Empowering	A shared culture; group maintenance and governance; development of young people [or new members]; Be Understanding; Be Concerned for Both Yourself and Others
Ethical	Caring, trust, and teamwork; Be Ethical
Purposeful	Participation and shared leadership tasks
Process-Oriented	Good internal communication; Be Mindful; Be Peaceful

Modeling and practicing this kind of participation is essential to being a contributing community member. Relational leadership is directly linked with building community. Table 7.1 illustrates the connections among the elements of relational leadership, with the understandings of the elements of community from Gardner (1990) and the advice on community-building principles from Gudykunst (1991).

College Communities

For hundreds of years, college campuses have been described as communities of scholars or as learning communities. Yet in reality, a sense of true community is not always a shared experience. Hate crimes happen on campus, incivility can be found in senate meetings, some organizations devalue the purposes of other

organizations, and not all people know or care about each other.
The Carnegie Foundation for the Advancement of Teaching
(1990) conducted a major study of what students, faculty, and
staff would like to change about their campuses. All groups
agreed that they need a renewed sense of community—not a
return to an older, homogeneous model, but a kaleidoscopic
community that embraces differences and finds common purpose.
The Foundation promoted the concept that healthy college
communities would be purposeful, open, just, disciplined, caring,
and celebrative. Campuses can take purposeful steps to valuing
being together in community.

As a microcosm of the society, the entire college campus
is a community and includes multiple communities. There
are communities within the various positions on campus (for
example, students, faculty, administrators, staff, alumni). Within
those groups are smaller community clusters (for example,
seniors, the Asian Student Association, graduate students); each
cluster has unique needs and shares community issues. There are
communities by departments and by the programs of functional
units (for example, the history department, the engineering
college, the student activities office, the intercollegiate athletics
program, the women's center). All of these communities are
bound together by the common goals of being a community
of people committed to learning and to advancing their own
education and the education of others.

Different organizations have different purposes and focus.
Higher education communities emphasize such elements as collegiality, learning, scholarship, academic freedom, and student
development. A social organization might emphasize friendship,

fun, and enriching experiences. A sports team stresses competence, teamwork, and fitness. Regardless of the special mission and focus of those groups and organizations, the people in them will experience healthy communities if they intentionally practice the discipline of community.

"The global community of the future will be, at best, a series of communities that are interdependent and diverse, embracing differences, releasing energy, and building cohesion" (Hesselbein, Goldsmith, Beckhard, & Schubert, 1998, p. xi). Our smaller communities become a fractal of developing global communities. "Identifying our common interests and broadening our relationships will be the defining elements of twenty-first century communities" (Morse, 1998, p. 230). "The broader global community will be enhanced by the health of the many smaller communities that constitute the whole. Those living within each community define all community" (Hesselbein, et al., 1998, p. xi).

Committing to promote and develop community in the places you function on campus is a key way of building and supporting the larger campus community.

> Chapter Summary

Framing any group or organization as a community of people working together for shared purposes enhances relational leadership. Thinking of that group as a community connects participants to a shared paradigm of expectations and obligations. To flourish, communities require relational leadership. Relational leadership practices value community as the context in which meaningful change can occur.

> What's Next?

The smallest relational communities are groups or teams. Whether informal or formal, understanding how these units are formed and thrive follows in Chapter Eight.

> Chapter Activities

1. Think about a particular community of which you are or have been a member. Which of Gardner's eight elements of community were especially visible in this community? Which were missing and why?
2. Describe a community of which you were an active member. Try to relate this community to the four stages of community development as outlined by Peck. Did you experience each stage? If not, why not? What was each one like? How were they similar? How were they different?
3. To what degree is some kind of community awareness essential for the Relational Leadership Model? Can the model still be a helpful frame to guide your leadership role (as a participant or as a positional leader), even if a sense of community does not exist in your groups or organizations?
4. Think about a healthy community that you are or were associated with and identify its characteristics. Now think about a community you know of that is unhealthy or is in the early stages of community development. What has contributed to the status of this community? How would you go about strengthening this community?

5. Communities sometimes are strengthened during times of crisis. Provide an example not already mentioned in this chapter of a community in crisis that became stronger as a result.

ADDITIONAL READINGS

Chinn, P. L. (2007). *Peace and power: Creative leadership for building community* (7th ed). Boston, MA: Jones and Bartlett.

Pearce, C. (2009). *Communities of play: Emergent cultures in multiplayer games and virtual worlds*. Boston, MA: Massachusetts Institute of Technology Press.

Peck, M. S. (1987). *The different drum: Community-making and peace*. New York, NY: Simon & Schuster.

Schmitz, P. (2012). *Everyone leads: Building leadership from the community up*. San Francisco, CA: Jossey-Bass.

Chapter 8

∨

Interacting in Teams and Groups

———◇———

Your university is celebrating its 100th anniversary and your student organization, Students in STEM, was asked to sponsor an activity or program as part of the celebration. Your group decided to put a planning team together with ten members. Juan volunteered to be the team leader and began calling meetings. When the team met for the first few times, members brainstormed ideas like conducting a fundraiser to buy a bench to place at the entrance of the science building quadrangle or putting on a concert open to the campus and local community. With the anniversary celebration two months away, the group decided to put on a concert.

At the following meeting, Juan told the team members that their organization did not have the funds to do this. Members were disappointed and confused about their role in planning this event. A few questioned the purpose of hosting this anniversary activity when their mission was to sponsor educational outreach and peer tutoring to science majors. Juan tried to facilitate another brainstorming activity, but the group members got frustrated and started to leave. At the following meeting, now six weeks before the celebration, only three members showed up, and there was great concern about not having an event identified and not knowing what resources they had to carry out their task.

What are some of the reasons this group failed?

> Chapter Overview

This chapter explores the characteristics of groups, the way groups develop, and the dynamics among group members in order to emphasize how leadership in groups is process oriented. The chapter identifies teams as a distinct type of group and presents concepts of teamwork and collaboration in group work with applications of the Relational Leadership Model. Further, the chapter explores how to work with member strengths in group and team settings. Also included in this chapter is an application of The Gallup Organization's strengths-based leadership model in team and group settings.

> Understanding Groups

In an average week, you experience many types of groups. Some of these are highly structured, with clear roles and processes. Examples are a class or a student government senate meeting. Other groups are loosely structured and informal, like a discussion at a dining hall table or a pick-up softball game.

However, the kind of group that is pertinent to this discussion of leadership is not just any gathering of people. For our purposes, a group is considered to be three or more people "interacting and communicating interpersonally over time in order to reach a goal" (Cathcart, Samovar, & Henman, 1996, p. 1).

There are many different dimensions to how groups are structured, and each has implications for the leadership dynamics in that group. Three key dimensions that help us understand different types of groups are purposes, structure, and time.

1. *Purposes:* Groups exist for very different purposes but they all have a reason for their existence; they range from informal friendship support groups to highly focused task groups to groups like a staff that delivers a service or a product over time. The architectural maxim that "form follows function" applies to groups as well. The purpose of a group should lead to the structures and processes needed to help the people in the group accomplish its purposes. Highly structured groups may be organizations (e.g., clubs).

2. *Structure:* Structure relates to the mechanisms for how the people in the group relate to each other. Some groups are highly structured, with hierarchical roles or positions; others are undefined and evolve. Leadership roles in groups range from leaderless groups, in which a group of people get together to do something but no one is the formal leader, to highly structured groups with a person in a position as the formal leader—the president, chairperson, or director. In the informal setting, participants share needed roles, and leadership emerges or is all around in the group. In the formal, structured setting, the positional leader may be accountable but may use

diverse styles ranging from highly autocratic (making all the decisions and directing or controlling the followers) to engaging group members and empowering them through the relational leadership elements presented in this book. Even in hierarchical organizations, there are informal leaders who influence the group or decision-making processes because of their seniority, their past stature in the organization, or their personalities. In campus student organizations, seniors who have been in the group for three or four years might exhibit this type of influence without holding a formal position.

3. *Time:* Groups exist over varying time periods. The group may be time-limited (meeting once to discuss a specific issue or completing a task in three meetings) or it may meet for a specified amount of extended time. Members may have a specified term of appointment, as would a representative from your major to the student senate for a year or being in a class for a semester. The group may be an ongoing group (like staff members at work, your family, or a fraternity). Time-limited groups are often called a task force or ad hoc committee. Ongoing groups use such names as committee, board, or council. The duration of the group raises different challenges. Time-limited groups with a short time frame must quickly establish rapport and common purposes and engage members to be active and focused on their role. Ongoing groups must deal with member motivation over time, establish processes to welcome and bring new members into the group, and keep the group focused on its purposes.

Think for a minute about the groups you are involved with. What are the purposes for which the groups were created? What structures help them accomplish those purposes? What roles do group members assume? How do these groups vary in time commitment? How does the length of time change the dynamics of the relationships? Those groups clearly develop differently. One challenge to leadership is to attend to the process of group development in order to facilitate the most involvement of the most members in the most effective way to make the best decisions.

> Group Development

Robert is visiting his friend Sean before spring break and attends a meeting of Sean's Business Entrepreneurs Club (BEC). Sean is a cofounder of this group. Robert is puzzled at what he sees. The group argues for most of the meeting about whether they should (1) engage in designing a logo for boxer shorts to sell and use the profits for a BEC party or (2) design a T-shirt to raise money as a service for a local youth recreation league. There are two loud factions, with several people competing for attention and trying to be seen as leaders. Robert is puzzled by this and realizes that the group has some problems.

It would help Robert to realize that most groups, whether formal or informal, go through fairly predictable stages of development as a group. One classic model labels these group development stages *forming, storming, norming,* and *performing* (Tuckman, 1965). If the group can handle the important issues at each stage, it can accomplish its purposes and stay vibrant and healthy. If the group is struggling, it can revisit a stage to intentionally relearn together how to be effective. Sean's group is struggling with the storming process, which is characterized by differing opinions and goals, and may need to revisit the purposes of the group usually addressed in the first stage of forming.

Forming

Forming is the group's initial stage of coming together, which includes such tasks as member recruitment and affiliation. How will I fit with this group? What information do members need? When will the group meet? How will the group communicate? What will the type of commitment mean? What are the purposes and mission of the group? What agreements are needed to make this group functional? The forming stage of development is when team building initially occurs and trust is established. Successful strategies of this forming stage include understanding the purpose of the group, getting to know each other, and building open, trusting relationships that value inclusion.

Storming

Storming is the stage in which the group starts to get in gear and differences of opinion begin to emerge. If the group is not clear about its purposes and goals, or if the group cannot agree on shared goals, then it may collapse at this stage. Members of Sean's Business Entrepreneurs Club have vastly different expectations of what the group should do: service or profit or both. They need to revisit some of the processes of the forming stage and resolve that issue so they can deal with the decisions of what projects to select. In this stage, individuals engage in self-assertion to get their needs recognized and addressed.

Storming can be a short process, in which the group comes to pretty clear direction, or it can be destructive. Some groups establish such trust in each other and in their process that the storming process is resolved quickly. Indeed, some members who feel like storming may never raise their issues because they are strongly connected to shared purpose and know their assertions would not be useful. Some groups exist in this storming phase and develop adversarial models of operating. They may depend on it so much that it becomes the way of getting their work done. The two-party political system and the check-and-balance processes of government are examples. Other groups have become accustomed to adversarial processes but would do better to develop more effective ways of relating. Examples include the constant conflict on some campuses among faculty and administrators or between the Greek-affiliated and independent leaders in the student senate.

Norming

Norming follows storming. Once the group resolves key differences, it establishes patterns of how it gets work done. The group sets up formal or informal procedures for which things come to the whole group, which reports are needed, who is involved in what, and how people interact. At this stage, individuals in the group deal with both intimacy and identity. Members of the group begin to understand the group's culture. For example, do meetings always start ten minutes late so people can visit with each other for a few minutes first? Do members understand whether they should volunteer for new projects or wait to be invited? The group practices that evolve in the norming stage are often more obvious to outsiders than to those in the group. These practices and characteristics might also describe the personality of the group.

Performing

Performing is the fourth stage of group development. Built on the strong foundation of the previous three stages, the group now cycles into a mature "stage of equilibrium"—getting its work done (Lippitt, 1973, p. 229). Time-limited groups may need to get quickly to the performing stage to get their work done in a timely way. They need to intentionally and effectively work through the previous stages and not skip right to performing without the foundational processes. Time-limited groups still need the team-building steps so essential in the forming stage; in the storming stage they need to encourage diversity of opinion and wrestle with common purpose, and in the norming stage they must clearly establish group processes to effectively perform their task. Ongoing groups with a longtime duration will have to stay renewed (see Chapter Nine) and continually recycle to be effective. Otherwise, they risk becoming dysfunctional or even terminating. Even the most successful groups have to revisit this cycle when new members join (forming), when new issues challenge the group's purposes (storming), or when new processes are needed because old ones no longer work (norming). Table 8.1 illustrates the aspects of the Relational Leadership Model that might help the group successfully deal with each stage of its development (Tuckman & Jensen, 1977).

Adjourning

The fifth stage, adjourning, is the final stage of group development for many groups. Tuckman and Jensen (1977) amended their stage model to accommodate the closure stages that groups experience. Groups exist over different time frames. All short-term groups, like task forces or ad hoc committees, need to plan on their eventual termination. This is a difficult stage for groups to enter because it marks a period of closure and finality (Smith, 2005). Some members experience a sense of loss at

Table 8.1 **Relational Leadership and Stages of Group Development**

When the Group Is...	Relational Leadership Philosophy Would Encourage Participants to...
Forming	Be inclusive and empowering. Make sure all the shareholders and stakeholders are involved. Seek diverse members to bring talent to the group. Model the processes of inclusion and shared leadership. Identify common purposes and targets of change.
Storming	Create a climate in which each person matters and build commitment to the group as a community of practice. Be ethical and open. Be patient, to give divergent views a full hearing. Be aware when you may be biased or blocking the full participation of another. Handle conflict directly and openly, encouraging participants to identify their biases. Revisit the purposes of the group and targets of change.
Norming	Be fair with processes. Practice collaboration. Keep new members welcomed, informed, and involved. Clarify the individual's responsibility to and expectations of the group and the group's responsibilities to and expectations of individuals.
Performing	Celebrate accomplishments and find renewal in relationships. Empower members to learn new skills and share roles in new ways to stay fresh. Revisit purposes and rebuild commitment.

this stage. The adjourning stage should include a celebration and recognition of the group's accomplishments, as well as a reflection on the lessons learned about what was effective and what was ineffective. Groups that have experienced longevity also can face the adjourning stage if their mission or purpose becomes irrelevant. In this case, the sense of loss is heightened, and some might experience anger about the organization's closure. Even so, it is important for the group to go through the adjourning stage as a learning experience and as a time to acknowledge the members' contributions.

Groups that do not engage in a continual revisiting of the cycle to stay active and vital may find themselves moving toward this final stage of group development. If a group does not maintain new members or keep up with current issues and needs, it may find itself unable to perform and may need to dissolve. It may be necessary for a new group to be formed, with new purposes and new members. Groups that intend to exist for a long time, often with no planned end in sight, need to stay vibrant and healthy if they are to continue effectively.

We visited a campus where the former Black Student Union (BSU) took the bold step of voting itself out of existence. Its programs had developed into social events with dwindling attendance. Most members felt that they could do social events through other avenues and that this group needed a broader scope. The circumstances on campus led many of the African American student leaders to think they needed a group with a more active educational and campus advocacy role. The key members decided to involve other non-Black student leaders in a planning session and formed a new group named Umoja—a Swahili word for unity. They sought a more diverse membership around their new purposes and were widely credited on that campus for strong programs and events that attracted a wide range of participants and benefited the whole campus. Although it would have been perfectly fine for this BSU to evolve into a social organization, it was not the intent of the leaders or members that the focus be social, so they boldly reorganized to accomplish social action and campus change around racial and ethnic unity with a new name and new structures. This was indeed a strong and courageous action; few groups would vote themselves out of existence or go through such a transformation, yet many groups need to do so.

STUDENT ESSAY

BioBlitz is a 24 hour species assessment that is conducted by scientists and citizens working together in a natural area. This is the flagship event of SEEDS, the FAU ecology club. Occurring in early April each year, BioBlitz is a mammoth event attracting over 300 FAU students. For the last couple of years I have coordinated BioBlitz. In early January my team and I meet to discuss preparations. Each year we start off very excited. The initial planning is flawless, the contributing thoughts from executive officers constructive, and our momentum seems unstoppable. Toward the end of February things begin to look different. Certain tasks were never started, others were not executed, and several members are lost in a sea of exams and homework. Nevertheless I push my team on. We can do it. By March our momentum has seemingly vanished. We are pushing desperately to make progress on purchase orders and advertising. As April arrives the imminent presence of BioBlitz lights our fires once again. We scurry around like chipmunks preparing for winter and manage to plan and execute another successful BioBlitz. Our final thoughts settle on the delusion that next year we will be more consistent in our planning.

Josh Scholl is an undergraduate biology major at Florida Atlantic University pursuing a focus in ecology. He is the former president of the student organization SEEDS (Strategies for Ecology Education, Diversity, and Sustainability) and the director of the Council of Student Organizations.

Active participants need to continually assess their group's development. We have a colleague who encourages group members always to ask, "*Should we, could we, are we?*" "Should we?" leads a group to clarify their purposes and direction. "Could we?" asks the group to anticipate the storming and norming stages to see if they are up to the task. "Are we?" is the constant formative evaluation cycle in the performing stage to see if the group is truly doing what it sets out to do. Evaluation is both formative and summative. Formative evaluation—Are we?—is asked at various times for the purpose of reshaping plans and directions. Summative evaluation might ask, Did we? at the end of a task or event to see if it met original plans. When the cook tastes the soup, it is formative evaluation. But when the customer tastes the soup, it is a summative evaluation.

> Dynamics in Groups

Groups engage in various processes that are often called group dynamics. Group dynamics is the study of the group's life (Johnson & Johnson, 2006). Group dynamics include such processes as how the group makes decisions, how the group handles its conflict, and how the group meets its leadership needs.

Group Roles

One of the foundations for understanding group dynamics is to recognize that in any interactive setting, individuals engage in communication patterns that may signal roles they are adopting in the group. Groups depend on two kinds of roles:

group-building roles and task roles. Participants engaging in both kinds of roles are absolutely essential to effective group dynamics. Group-building roles are actions that focus on the group as people, including the relationships among members. Group-building roles attend to the process of the group. These have also been called group maintenance roles. Task roles focus on accomplishing the purposes of the group, including giving information and opinions and moving the group along on tasks by summarizing and by using various decision-making strategies. Task roles are focused on the content of the group discussion.

On occasion, group members may demonstrate some individual dysfunctional roles that actually hamper the group's progress. Someone may doggedly push his or her point like a broken record, even if the group is ready to move on. A person like this is called a *special interest pleader* and may have a secret reason for saying things—a hidden agenda. A member may resist or block any group action by being negative and disagreeable about everything. A person like that is called a *blocker*. We should stress that dysfunctional roles are those that truly hamper a group's goals or progress; participants who express negative opinions because they are truly concerned about a course of action are helpful to the group and should not be confused with someone who is a blocker. Someone who effectively uses humor (no matter how goofy) to relieve tension or create harmony should not be confused with someone who acts like a *clown* and never takes the group seriously or diverts the group from its focus—the latter may be exhibiting a dysfunctional role. Someone who is quiet at meetings but is actively engaged in listening and thinking and who is willing to support the group's decisions is an *active member* (who might typically be called a follower), whereas someone who sits in the back reading a newspaper and not even listening is a *nonparticipant*.

Examples of common roles that help us understand group dynamics are presented in Table 8.2. These roles have evolved from the early group dynamics research in the 1940s and 1950s (Benne & Sheats, 1948; Knowles & Knowles, 1959) and remain useful today. Think of examples you use or see others using. Describe the various roles you have played in different groups. Are there any similarities between groups? Do you find yourself playing the same role no matter what the group? Or do your roles vary? Do the roles you play give you any insights into how you act as a member of a group?

Each of us has a preferred set of practices we are most comfortable with in a group. This might be called our *role set*. You may find it more comfortable or easier in a group to seek opinions from others, make sure people have a chance to share their ideas, or summarize what was discussed before a vote. Someone else might like to share an opinion or give information. Your role set likely builds on your strengths. To perform effectively, the group needs participants to practice both task and group-building roles. You may prefer to do mostly group-building functions or mostly task functions.

Although any individual participant or positional leader may not perform in all roles comfortably, it is useful to know which roles the group needs and to ask someone to engage in them. For example, you may be terrible at summarizing discussions because they all seem a jumble to you, but if you know that a summary is needed before the group makes its final decision, you can intervene. In this case, you might say, "It would help me if someone

Table 8.2 **Examples of Common Roles in Groups**

Roles	Role Description	Example of Role in Use
Task Roles		
Information seeker	Aware that the group needs more facts or data before proceeding.	"We cannot vote on this yet; we need more information first, so let's ask Sharon to brief us at the next meeting."
Opinion seeker	Aware that the group needs more insight, ideas, or opinions before proceeding.	"What do you think, Roger? You have had a lot of experience with this topic."
Opinion giver	Sharing one's views, feelings, or ideas so the group has the benefit of one's thinking.	"I strongly think we must increase the budget for this project if we intend to serve more students."
Summarizer	Condensing the nature of the opinions or discussion in a capsule format for clarity.	"Before we go further, is it accurate to say that while some of us think we should not spend much money, we all agree we should do this project?"
Clarifier	Elaborating or explaining ideas in new words to add meaning.	Showing how something might work if adopted. "Jim, did you mean we need more involvement, meaning quantity, or better involvement, like quality?"

(continued)

Table 8.2 **Examples of Common Roles in Groups (*continued*)**

Roles	Role Description	Example of Role in Use
Group-Building Roles		
Gatekeeper	Inviting those who have not yet spoken or who have been trying to say something into the conversation.	"Tanya has been trying to say something on this for a while—I'd like to hear what that is."
Encourager	Welcoming all individuals and diverse ideas. Responding warmly to promote the inclusion and empowerment of others.	"What the sophomores just said about this issue was really enlightening. I am really glad you took some risks to tell us that. Thanks."
Mediator	Harmonizing conflict and seeking to straighten out opposing points of view in a clear way.	"You two don't seem as far apart on this issue as it might seem. You both value the same thing and have many points of agreement."
Follower	An active listener who willingly supports the group's actions and decisions.	"I haven't said much, but this has been a great discussion and I feel really informed. I am comfortable with the decision."

Note: For other descriptions of roles in groups, see Benne & Sheats (1948) and Knowles & Knowles (1959).

would summarize the key points on both sides of this issue so I can fully understand before I vote." Someone who is comfortable with that role will provide that needed process. It is empowering for participants to be asked to contribute their preferred roles or bring their strengths to the group process.

Group Norms

Imagine attending your first meeting of an ongoing group. You walk into the room and begin observing other group members for a clue to what is acceptable or expected. Does the group stay focused on its agenda or wander into other discussions? Do members seem friendly and social or distant and isolated? Do people sit formally and wait to be called on by the chair or is there a more open discussion? All of these kinds of practices are the norms or rules of conduct that lead to consistent practices in a group.

Some norms are explicit and clearly seen by all participants. When you play cards you expect to follow suit; when you play baseball, you expect to bat in order. When your group uses Robert's Rules of Order, you know you must make motions, seek a second to the motion, speak in turn, and plan to vote on the motion eventually. Other norms may have evolved through the cultural practices of the group—arranging the chairs in a circle, starting each meeting with introductions of new members and guests, congratulating group members on their accomplishments, or celebrating birthdays. It may be a group norm to ask the advisor for any comments or observations at the end of the meeting.

Group norms contribute to the concept of group climate. Climate is like the group's personality. Just as individuals have personality, so do groups. Perhaps one group you are in is open, flexible, and supportive, uses humor often, and views each person as important, whereas another is formal, guarded, distrusting, impersonal, and stuffy. If you want your group to have a distinct personality, it is useful to consider what group norms will lead to those desired outcomes. Group norms are developed by the processes the group uses. The Relational Leadership Model is designed to create a group in which members feel highly engaged.

Creative Conflict

The storming stage of group development can paralyze a group's progress. Unresolved conflict at any stage can create a group climate that is tense and hostile, but it can also be an effective method for improving the group's outcomes.

What words or emotions come to mind when you think of the term conflict? For most people, the idea of conflict is uncomfortable and creates a knot in the stomach; most of us would prefer harmony. In many earlier leadership books, the term conflict does not even appear in the index or the topic is handled in a power dynamics model or in a section on how to win your own way.

Conflict can result from such issues as clashes in personalities, differing expectations of roles (role conflict), or disagreement over ideas. Personality conflicts can often be understood by returning to personality preferences and strengths (presented in Chapters Four and Five) and being more focused on listening to and understanding others. Role conflicts are best handled by thinking of what assumptions you may be bringing to the conflict about your own role or your expectations of others that clash with their assumptions. Conflict in ideas is often called controversy, and a full airing of differences of opinions and ideas is essential for a group to make the best decisions. Such controversies need to be handled with civility and open dialogue (Higher Education Research Institute, 1996).

It is not uncommon for people to want to avoid conflict, so they often ignore it or pretend it does not exist. Some say it is like having an elephant in the room. Everyone is aware of the tension that a huge conflict creates—like an elephant standing in the corner—but no one talks about it. Still others diffuse conflict by acting as if it is unimportant or can be handled at another time. True communities resolve conflicts rather than avoid them. When conflict is confronted, it is usually best to employ negotiation and mediation strategies instead of power strategies.

The resulting different conflict resolution outcomes have been described as win-win, win-lose, and lose-lose. In win-win outcomes, both sides are heard and are satisfied with the resolution of their differences. The group often emerges as stronger for the discussion, and the decisions made may be significantly better than they would have been without the dialogue. In win-lose outcomes, one side uses power strategies to win by out-talking, putting down, or rushing to a premature vote. But in the process, a loser is created. The participants who lost (and their potential allies) feel marginalized, angry, and even resentful. The group's harmony is jeopardized and participants are not empowered or included. In lose-lose outcomes, both sides use power strategies and get so entrenched, rigid, or hurtful that no effective resolution is reached, even in compromise.

Reciprocal and relational models of leadership know that some conflict is natural and inevitable. The Relational Leadership Model encourages processes to handle conflict that will promote inclusivity and empowerment. By anticipating that when great people get together they will have differences of ideas and approaches, the group can set some ground rules (that is, group norms) to guide the openness and honesty with which they will raise issues of possible conflict. These ground rules can "create an environment 'safe' for differences" (Lappé & Du Bois, 1994, p. 251). Such ground rules might include agreeing that everyone will have a chance to be heard who wants to speak and that the group will look for points of agreement as well as disagreements. Handling all these disagreements with civility is essential (Komives & Wagner, 2009). Each person should commit to making "no permanent enemies" in the group (Lappé & Du Bois, 1994, p. 255) in order to be inclusive of all members' opinions.

Conflicts are useful when they raise perspectives that need attention before the group moves to resolution. The more homogeneous a group is, the more essential it is to think through an issue from multiple perspectives. Even if there is little diversity in the group, someone might say, "If there were transfer students here, how would they see this policy, and should we reconsider any parts of it?" or "If international students were here, would they see any issues we have not yet addressed?" In this way, at least decisions are informed by the broadest possible thinking, even if no person is physically present who holds a divergent view.

Group Decision Making

Traditional views of leadership often assume that a group or organization has a formal leader with the authority and responsibility for making final decisions. Indeed, on many occasions the positional leader has to make a decision on behalf of the group. Some possible reasons for this are that there may be no time to hold a group meeting or consult with group members, or the leader may be representing the group in another meeting and need to speak for the group, or the leader may judge that the decision is not a major one and not worth group time and energy. Whenever a positional leader is faced with making an individual decision, the Relational Leadership Model will be useful in guiding the decision process. The leader should ask herself these questions:

- Does this decision support our vision and mission? (purposeful)
- What opinions do my group members have about this issue? (inclusive)
- Will this decision heighten our involvement or limit involvement? (empowering)
- Is this the right thing to do? Is it principled? (ethical)
- Should I slow down making this decision so that others can get involved? (process-oriented)

    In formal, hierarchical organizations with positional leaders, participative leadership is often thought to involve "the use of decision procedures intended to *allow* other people some influence over the leader's decisions" (Yukl, 1989, p. 83 [emphasis added]). The values in participative leadership acknowledge that a better decision is made and receives greater acceptance when those involved are part of that decision process. Group members may be empowered, learn more effective leadership skills, and sustain a higher commitment to the process when others are involved. You will see a profound philosophical difference when you examine the word *allow* in the definition of participative leadership. *Allow* correctly identifies who—the positional leader—has responsibility and who can involve or not involve others, as that leader chooses. In most work settings and in volunteer organizations, for the leader to presume that she should make the decision or "allow" the involvement of others is a conventional way of looking at the situation. A more useful perception would be to assume instead that the unit (the organization, the work unit, the group) must be involved with key decisions—has the right to be and should be. Now the question becomes how they should best be involved, not whether they should be. Clearly, there is tension in formal settings about the authority and role of participants in the decision-making process. We sense a shift in people's expectations—that they want, indeed often demand, a role in decision making. Examples include student evaluation of course instruction, parent involvement in school-based management, and employee involvement in selecting benefits packages.

Yukl (1989) identified a continuum of four possible decision-making procedures: autocratic → consultation → joint decision → delegation or participation. They range, in the amount of influence others have on the decision, from no influence (in which an autocratic decision is made) to high influence of others in the process (in which complete delegation has occurred).

Johnson and Johnson (2006) describe seven methods of decision making: (1) decision by authority without discussion, (2) expert member, (3) average members' opinions, (4) decision by authority after discussion, (5) minority control, (6) majority control, and (7) consensus. Each of the decision-making methods may have its own purpose, but relational leadership would promote consensus models whenever possible. When a trusting group climate exists, groups may select other models and be comfortable using minority control or majority control.

In our view, some decisions are best made by an authority or expert. However, most groups would benefit by shifting important decisions that affect the entire community to a discussion and consensus model. More and more participants in groups expect to be involved in decision making, and, indeed, involvement is essential to a relational, empowering approach. Positional leaders who make important decisions in an autocratic manner find that they alienate workers and group members, even when they, as leaders, have the authority to make those decisions.

Consensus does not mean that every single decision is made by the entire group, nor does it mean that a majority vote equals reaching consensus. An important task of teams is to make decisions, and most teams prefer to reach consensus on critical issues. Rayner (1996) provides the following definition of consensus: "Consensus does not mean that everyone on the team thinks the best possible decision has been reached. It does mean that no one is professionally violated by the decision

and that all team members will support its implementation"
(p. 74). Achieving consensus is not always easy and can be
a time-intensive process, taking much longer than making a
decision by voting or giving feedback and asking the leader to
make the decision. Rayner offers the following guidelines for
reaching consensus within a team:

1. Clearly define the issue facing the team
2. Focus on similarities between positions
3. Ensure that there is adequate time for discussion
4. Avoid conflict-reducing tendencies (e.g., voting) (p. 76)

Not all decisions warrant the attention of the entire group.
It would be absurd to waste group members' time or resources by
meeting on everything. It is useful to think of two dimensions
of decisions: the need for quality in the decision and the need
for acceptance of the decision. Quality of the decision refers to
its importance and accuracy. The art festival committee may
decide to hold a film festival, but the particular films selected
may not matter. A committee or individual can decide following
some guidelines from the group. Any decision that needs high
acceptance by those involved usually has to be handled in an
open and inclusive manner. The art festival committee might
need help staffing the event, but to assign committee members to
time slots could be a mistake. The approach to staffing requires
high acceptance; these members may need to be involved in the
scheduling.

Consensus brings the highest commitment among participants, is the most informed by the diverse knowledge bases

in the group, and takes the most time. Consensus requires
that the group become comfortable with handling conflict and
be informed by the rising controversies that can lead to a good
decision. Groups that are uncomfortable with controversy or
who do not handle it in a civil manner may move prematurely
to vote just to get the group to move on. Consensus requires
that the group be willing to use strategies like active listening,
compromising, and working in a collaborative manner. Encouraging divergent points of view, listening for understanding, and
allowing people to disagree with each other with civility are
important hallmarks of consensus-building processes.

When teams fail to reach consensus, it is often because they
do not allow enough time for members to discuss perspectives
and opinions to discover common ground or because conflict is
mismanaged or reaches a level that erodes trust among individuals. Mutual respect and trust among group members is a critical
component to successfully achieving a decision by consensus.

Teams and Teamwork

Many look to the sports metaphor of a team to illustrate how
individuals need to work together toward a common purpose.

> We can no longer afford the luxury of even a few individualists work-
> ing in isolation from the rest of the organization ... Strength is not
> in the individuals, but in the team. Put a group of superstars together
> on any team, whether baseball, hockey, football or soccer, and they
> will still lose if they operate as individual superstars. But once they
> start operating as a team, they become unbeatable. (Taylor, 1989,
> pp. 124–125)

Many organizations have adopted that metaphor and reconceptualized the work unit as a team. Hospitals have a team for each patient, with a primary care nurse as team coordinator, and businesses have cross-functional teams that bring together staff from shipping, marketing, and manufacturing to do product advancement. This metaphor has implications for morale, motivation, support, common purpose, diverse roles, and inclusion. Previously, we have used the metaphor of jazz and referred to participants as an ensemble. For the purposes of this book we also use community as a metaphor for groups of participants.

Whatever the metaphor, participants in the same group should share the goal of working toward being an effective team. Strong ensemble casts on popular TV shows often show the reciprocity of collaborators working together for shared purposes. Think of the appreciation of differences among the television characters of Glee or of Harry Potter and his buddies at Hogwarts.

Teams and Groups

Just as collections of people do not automatically constitute groups, all groups are not teams. Kotter and Cohen (2002) observe that a powerful group has two characteristics—it is made up of the right people and it demonstrates teamwork. Teams are, however, one kind of group. Teams are more than just a group of people working together. Hughes, Ginnett, and Curphy (1993) distinguish between groups and teams, noting that although both have the characteristics of mutual interaction and reciprocal influence, teams have a stronger sense of identity and common goals or tasks; in addition, task interdependence is higher within a team than in a group, and team members usually have more distinctive roles than group members.

Types of teams range from those that function like working groups, in which individual accountability is high (such as a golf team), to true teams that could not accomplish their goals individually (such as a football team or the homecoming committee). Table 8.3 shows the distinction between working groups and teams.

Quinn (1996) defines a team as "an enthusiastic set of competent people who have clearly defined roles, associated in a common activity, working cohesively in trusting relationships, and exercising personal discipline and making individual sacrifices for the good of the team" (p. 161). Much has been written about when teams unravel or fail at accomplishing their goals, but here is a visualization of what it is like when teams achieve synergy and reach their potential. Dee Hock, the former CEO of Visa International makes the following observation about teams:

> In the field of group endeavor, you will see incredible events in which the group performs far beyond the sum of its individual talents. It happens in the symphony, in the ballet, in the theater, in sports, and equally in business. It is easy to recognize and impossible to define. It is a mystique. It cannot be achieved without immense effort, training, and cooperation, but effort, training, and cooperation alone rarely create it. Some groups reach it consistently. Few can sustain it. (Quinn, 1996, p. 162)

Parker (2003) defined a team as "a group of people with a high degree of interdependence, geared toward the achievement of a goal or the completion of a task" (p. 2). Three common

Table 8.3 **Working Groups Versus Teams**

Working Groups	Teams
A strong, clearly focused leader is appointed.	Shared leadership responsibilities exist among members.
The general organizational mission is the group's purpose.	A specific, well-defined purpose that is unique to the team.
Individual work provides the only products.	Team and individual work develop products.
Effectiveness is measured indirectly by group's influence on others (e.g., financial performance of business, student scores on standardized examinations).	Effectiveness is measured directly by assessing team work products.
Individual accountability only is evident.	Both team and individual accountability are evident.
Individual accomplishments are recognized and rewarded.	Team celebration. Individual efforts that contribute to the team's success are also recognized and celebrated.
Meetings are efficiently run and last for short periods of time.	Meetings have open-ended discussion and include active problem solving.
In meetings members discuss, decide, and delegate.	In meetings members discuss, decide, and do real work together.

Source: From Johnson & Johnson (1994), p. 504. Published by Allyn and Bacon, Boston MA. Copyright © 1994 by Pearson Education. Reprinted by permission of the publisher.

types of team are functional, self-directed, and cross-functional (Parker). Functional teams tend to resemble hierarchical organizations, in which power and authority are contained at the top. The self-directed team is typically a group whose members possess all the technical knowledge and skills to accomplish a task or goal, with a certain degree of power delegated to it from a leader or manager. Cross-functional teams usually are composed of individuals from a variety of skill sets, departments, or areas that combine skill sets that no one person possesses. For example, a company like Apple Computer or Facebook might form a cross-functional team that consists of a software engineer, marketing and sales specialist, project manager, and applications designer to invent a new product.

Teams must have clear goals to achieve success. Often, teams either do not take the time to formulate goals or set goals that are unclear and unattainable. The SMART rubric provides a framework for teams to use as they establish their goals (Parker, 2003, p. 94):

1. Specific—the goal must be clear to everyone
2. Measurable—it is quantifiable
3. Attainable—the goal must be realistic and possible to achieve
4. Relevant—the goal is in alignment with the direction of the organization and its overall strategy
5. Time-bound—there is a set time frame by which the goal will be achieved (e.g., within a semester or within a year)

STUDENT ESSAY

Being a leader cannot be defined. It is something that is felt and shared. It is not something you are born with. Through Blue Chip I have learned it is something you develop. I came into Blue Chip with a desire to become a great leader. All I could think about was that I wanted to improve my speaking skills and confidence. But leadership is not about the leader; it is about your team and the people you lead. On February 19, I learned what this meant. The University of Arizona hosts the National Collegiate Leadership Conference, an annual student-run leadership conference with over 650 participants. This year I had the privilege of being part of that planning committee. I did not know what to expect but I knew that I had poured my heart into planning and was ready for anything. Unfortunately, you cannot plan for everything and unforeseen events occurred. And that is how our team became a family. Through encouraging smiles, reassuring hugs, trust and shared passion for our event; we helped each other when we were at our lowest point and shared genuine gratitude at our highest. Our advisors stepped back with trust in their eyes, empowering us to grow as leaders.

Laura Soto is a junior at University of Arizona with an early childhood education major and a minor in sociology. She's been a team leader for the Arizona Blue Chip Program, excursions chair for the National Collegiate Leadership Conference, camp director and auction director for Camp Wildcat, is a part of the University Medical Center volunteer staff, and has traveled internationally with the Lions Club.

An example of a SMART goal is responding to all emails that the team receives about its upcoming event within 24 hours.

Teams are more than a combination of skill sets or functional roles carried out by individual members. Teams are a blending of people with diverse backgrounds, histories, styles, talents, and personalities.

The following are some factors that are critical for a team's success (Parker, 2003, p. 260):

- Disregard organizational boundaries in an effort to arrive at the best solution
- Be sensitive and responsive to the concerns and considerations of other team members in the design of projects
- Understand that common goals and targets are mandatory of all team members
- Provide open and frequent (risk free) communications
- All team members pull their own weight and share a common objective
- Capitalize on team members' strengths
- Develop a sense of trust among all team members
- Be willing to accept and try ideas that are different from the norm, even if it means modifying the established process
- Use a bit of humor when discussions get tense and the pressure to complete a task is high

Team Learning

Individual learning is the conventional norm for a college student. Only you can read that book, write that computer program, or take that test. However, learning occurs in many other ways—through group projects, in experiential settings, and in study groups. Whenever a team has a shared responsibility, it has to find a way to learn together, not just learn separately. "The learning unit[s] of organizations are 'teams,' groups of people who need one another to act" (Senge, 1993, p. 134). Approaches to team learning include accumulating the learning preference of the majority of members (for example, a scientific research group in which everyone prefers facts and details or a friendship group in which most are flexible and casual). However, intentional team learning requires intentional practices.

Team learning happens in dialogue with each other and through reflection on shared experiences. Dialogue is a "sustained collective inquiry into everyday experience and what we take for granted" (Senge, Kleiner, Roberts, Ross, & Smith, 1994, p. 353). Dialogue is far more than the mere words used to share meaning. It includes the tone of voice, laughter, pauses, difficulty in finding the right words, and amount of discussion needed to come to some meaning. When a team is in dialogue, participants are aware of the process of their communication as well as its content. For true understanding to result, it is important that both teams and groups establish ground rules or norms to handle their inevitable controversies with civility (Higher Education Research Institute [HERI], 1996; Komives & Wagner, 2009).

Dialogue and discussion are two slightly different processes. Some groups mistakenly engage in discussion in which members share their own views with minimal attempts at true understanding. This can lead to debate, which may only beat down opposing views or lead to a deterioration of relationships that can unravel a group. Groups that value learning together will establish true dialogue methods, the goals of which are to learn together while engaging in change. Dialogue is built into the processes of reflection, which involves thinking together. Perhaps the best lesson for dialogue is, "Don't just do something, stand there" (Isaacs, as cited in Senge et al., 1994, p. 375). Your obligation as a listener is to understand and connect. Dialogue encourages you to clarify your points, not prove them. We encourage you to refer to Chapter Five to review how different individuals learn to truly listen to each other.

Understanding and Applying Strengths in Teams

In chapter Four, you learned the importance of knowing and applying your individual strengths. Maximizing the strengths of team members also increases productivity and engagement. Rath and Conchie (2008) identified four domains of leadership based on research of how the 34 signature strengths from Gallup's StrengthsFinder assessment cluster in these four broader categories: executing, influencing, relationship building, and strategic thinking. Table 8.4 shows how each of the strengths themes relate to one of the four domains of leadership. In their study of effective teams and what made them great, they found that leaders intentionally capitalize and build on each other's

Table 8.4 **Domains of Leadership Strength**

Executing	Influencing	Relationship Building	Strategic Thinking
Achiever	Activator	Adaptability	Analytical
Arranger	Command	Developer	Context
Belief	Communication	Connectedness	Futuristic
Consistency	Competition	Empathy	Ideation
Deliberative	Maximizer	Harmony	Input
Discipline	Self-assurance	Includer	Intellection
Focus	Significance	Individualization	Learner
Responsibility	Woo	Positivity	Strategic
Restorative		Relator	

Source: Rath & Conchie (2008).

strengths. They also discovered that the most successful teams had broader groupings of strengths in each of these four domains.

The executing domain of strengths includes behaviors that make things happen and that can assist in bringing plans to action. Executing strengths such as focus and achiever allow the group to move closer to accomplishing a task or goal. The influencing domain of strengths helps the team make progress in advocating for a new policy or advocating for a new initiative. Team members who have woo or communication in their top five profile can be helpful in advocating for the group. Individuals who possess strengths in the relationship building domain bring cohesion to the group by establishing relationships inside and outside of the organization. Individuals who have harmony are valuable in groups when there is conflict or low levels of engagement with others. The fourth domain of leadership strengths is strategic thinking that allows the group to think about the future and assist the group in making long-term decisions. Strengths such as futuristic and input can help the team chart a future direction.

Rath and Conchie (2008) argue that it is far better to have well-rounded teams by maximizing everyone's strengths than to attempt to be well-rounded individuals that could result in mediocrity—trying to be good at everything is humanly impossible. Individuals in groups and teams bring greater diversity of strengths. The domains of leadership in a group and team context discredits the notion that one leader needs to have all of the strengths and skills to do everything by placing greater emphasis on using the talents and strengths of all members across the four domains of leadership.

Leadership Implications

"In a productive work community, leaders are not commanders and controllers, bosses and big shots. They are servers and supporters, partners and providers" (Kouzes & Posner, 1993, p. 7). Leaders in teamwork settings are also facilitators of team learning. Facilitating team learning requires individual participants to understand their motivations, to advocate for their own interests while being open to hearing others' points of view, and to find common ground (Ross, 1994b).

Participants and leaders must all share the responsibility of processing any shared group experience to make it a conscious process as a team. Successes need to be understood as well as failures. Too often, groups do not reflect on why something worked really well but spend hours and hours finding errors in failures.

Team Leadership

Team performance and team development are two critical functions of leadership. The Relational Leadership Model underscores the importance of both of these functions, with its emphasis on process-oriented (team development) and purpose (team performance). Team performance means accomplishing the group's goals, making decisions and plans, achieving results, and solving problems. Team development includes establishing effective relationships, creating an environment in which individuals feel valued, and facilitating cohesion within the team. Research conducted on teams shows that productivity, innovation, creativity, decision making, quality, problem solving, and use of resources are all increased or enhanced as a result of people working in team structures.

While balancing the ongoing activities of the team or group, leaders also face both internal and external demands. Leaders shift between the behaviors of monitoring, taking action, and paying attention to internal and external group issues. Team members can also take on these functions, which is typically the case with more experienced and mature groups. In these cases, leaders would do well to step aside and let the team take on those responsibilities and tasks. It is a delicate balancing act of determining which problems to intervene in and which to let team members resolve as a whole.

Several researchers and scholars on team leadership have found the following characteristics of team leadership (Larson & LaFasto, 1989 in Hill, 2013, p. 299):

1. Clear, elevating goal—the group believes the goal is worth-while and it is clear enough to tell when the objectives have been met

2. Results-driven structure—the group's purpose needs to drive the structure of the team

3. Competent team members—the group members must possess appropriate technical knowledge and interpersonal skills to work collaboratively as a team

4. Unified commitment—the group has a sense of identity and level of team spirit that has been intentionally facilitated and developed

5. Collaborative climate—all individuals contribute collectively to the success of the project and individual accomplishments are integrated into the whole team's efforts

6. Standards of excellence—standards of excellence are established and clearly understood by the team with the emphasis
   on everyone performing at the highest levels

STUDENT ESSAY

In my three years as Project Leader for the first University of Manitoba student-designed nano-satellite, I faced many challenges coordinating more than 100 undergraduate and graduate students from
six different faculties and collaborating with more than 50 advisors
from academia and industry. In the beginning, my focus was on the
spacecraft itself and the technical issues surrounding the design.
However, as the project evolved, so did my role as a leader. I adopted
the philosophy, "always put people before purpose" as the driver
for all my endeavors. This change allowed me to focus on the team,
secure the necessary resources, learn more about each member,
and do my best to accommodate their needs. Some of the changes
included selecting meeting times and locations to better accommodate the team and celebrating major personal accomplishments
whenever possible (e.g., successful thesis defenses, graduations,
and engagements). I noticed the results within a matter of weeks,
with a sense of empowerment, increased confidence, enthusiasm,
and ownership throughout the team as they became more focused on
designing the satellite. Some may say these changes were not revolutionary, but changing my own mindset helped all of us reach our
goal of building a satellite.

Dario Schor is completing his masters of computer engineering at the University
of Manitoba. He has served as the project leader for the University of Manitoba
Space Applications and Technology Society, president of the University of Manitoba Amateur Radio Society, vice chair of the IEEE Winnipeg Section Education,
Management, and Communications joint chapter, and an active member of another
half-dozen committees in the Canadian province of Manitoba.

7. Principled leadership—the leader establishes priorities and helps team members stay focused on the goals, sustains collaborative environments for the team, and manages performance
8. External support—the team is provided resources (money, equipment, supplies) to accomplish its goals and is given recognition for its successes

Team leaders are tasked with monitoring the group's progress and relationships and taking action when appropriate. Leaders are often called upon to take action when the group is stuck and unable to move forward or when internal conflict takes place that the team itself cannot resolve. It may require the leader to mediate conflict, assist the group in focusing on its goals, or coach the group on interpersonal skills. In some cases, the leader facilitates an external role for the team by networking with other alliances or sharing information from external sources with the team.

> Chapter Summary

Groups are the building blocks of communities of practice. We function in many different kinds of groups that are at different stages of development. This chapter presented group development models and principles of group dynamics, including aspects of decision making, conflict resolution, and team learning that inform group practices. It is important to note the differences between groups and teams and the intentional process of developing working groups into effective teams. Understanding and applying the diverse strengths of team members allows groups to be more well-rounded, more productive, and more engaged in facilitating change.

> What's Next?

Organizations are made up of multiple groups and teams. The next chapter explores how formal organizations function, the unique role of leadership in the organizational context and how to promote the renewal of complex organizations.

> Chapter Activities

1. Analyze several groups of which you are a member according to the key dimensions of purpose, structure, and time. How are the groups similar? How are they different?
2. Think of a group of which you were a member. Using Tuckman's model as a framework, describe what it was like to be a member of the group in each of the four stages. Did the group experience any problems? In which stage? What did you do to resolve the problems? Have you ever known a group to dissolve itself? If yes, what were the situations surrounding this decision? Identify a group that should dissolve itself. Why do you think they do not take this final step?
3. Think about your personal style in conflict situations. Now read the descriptions that follow and assign a percentage to each conflict style based on how often you use it. Your total percentages should add up to 100%.

Style 1: I avoid conflict and stay away from issues involving conflict.

Style 2: I want to be the winner in conflict situations.

Style 3: I want to be liked, so I avoid conflict.

Style 4: I believe in compromise.

Style 5: I view conflict as an opportunity to identify and solve problems.

What are the advantages and disadvantages of each style? Consider your most preferred styles and identify circumstances in which these styles are most and least effective for you.

4. Identify a team that you are or have been affiliated with (sports, within an organization, class project, and so on). Analyze the leadership of that team using Hill's eight characteristics of team leadership. How well did your team perform on each of those eight dimensions? What improvements could be made to strengthen the effectiveness of your team?

5. Think of the best team of which you have ever been a member. This could be any kind of team (newspaper staff, student government, club or organization, scouts, 4-H, sports team). What made this team special? Was there ever a time when this team had to learn something? Describe that experience.

6. Using the SMART rubric for establishing clear goals, create a goal statement using each of the five elements of SMART. Check your goal statement to ensure that it meets the SMART test.

7. Think of a group you have been a member of since it began. Turn to Exhibit 8.1 and reflect on how this group has changed over time. Place a B on each item of the scale reflective of how the group functioned at the beginning; place an M to reflect

the middle as the group began to mature; and place a T for where it is today.

8. Identify a group or team you that you are involved in and have the most experience. Turn to Table 8.4 and highlight the strengths you believe are most prominent in this group. How can you work as a team to more effectively maximize everyone's and your strengths?

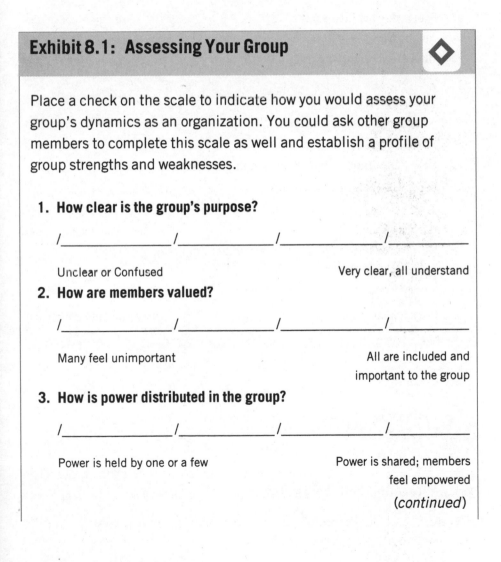

Exhibit 8.1: Assessing Your Group

Place a check on the scale to indicate how you would assess your group's dynamics as an organization. You could ask other group members to complete this scale as well and establish a profile of group strengths and weaknesses.

1. How clear is the group's purpose?

/_____/_____/_____/_____

Unclear or Confused   Very clear, all understand

2. How are members valued?

/_____/_____/_____/_____

Many feel unimportant   All are included and
                                             important to the group

3. How is power distributed in the group?

/_____/_____/_____/_____

Power is held by one or a few   Power is shared; members
                                             feel empowered

                                             (continued)

4. How is leadership handled in the group?

/_____/_____/_____/_____

Leadership comes only from the top   Leadership is shared among
most participants

5. Is an ethical climate sustained in your group?

/_____/_____/_____/_____

People do what they want   Principles are valued
with no regard for others

6. How are decisions made in this group?

/_____/_____/_____/_____

A few people decide everything   Decisions are not final until
with little group input   consensus is reached

7. How concerned is the group about process?

/_____/_____/_____/_____

Pays no attention to process   Very intentional about process

8. How purposeful is this group about accomplishing change?

/_____/_____/_____/_____

Often floundering   Very clear and intentional

ADDITIONAL READINGS

Hill, S.E.K. (2013). Team leadership. In P. G. Northouse (Ed.), *Leadership: Theory and practice* (6th ed, pp. 287–318). Thousand Oaks, CA: Sage.

Howard, V. A., & Barton, M. A. (1992). *Thinking together*. New York, NY: Morrow.

Johnson, D. W., & Johnson, F. P. (2008). *Joining together: Group theory and group skills* (10th ed). Boston, MA: Allyn & Bacon.

Kotter, J. P., & Cohen, D. S. (2002). *The heart of change: Real-life stories of how people change their organizations*. Boston, MA: Harvard Business School Press.

Parker, G. M. (2003). *Cross-functional teams: Working with allies, enemies, and other strangers*. San Francisco, CA: Jossey-Bass.

Rath, T., & Conchie, B. (2008). *Strengths-based leadership: Great leaders, teams, and why people follow*. New York, NY: Gallup Press.

Schirch, L., & Campt, D. (2007). *The little book of dialogue for difficult subjects: A practical hands-on guide*. Intercourse, PA: Good Books.

Chapter 9

Understanding and Renewing Complex Organizations

Consuela and Martin are newly elected leaders of the new multicultural student union. Both are second-year students who had a great deal of leadership experience in high school and in various community organizations. As they meet to begin developing a plan for the coming months, Consuela and Martin begin to feel overwhelmed. Their university is huge and their organization is new and small. The questions come quickly: How do we get others excited about the mission of our new organization? How are we going to recruit new members? What do we want our meetings to be like? What other officers will we need to make this work? How are we going to make decisions and handle conflict that we know is going to emerge? They end their first meeting with more questions than answers but they are excited about the challenges ahead.

You, as a student, see and experience numerous organizations every day. You may get up in the morning and read the campus newspaper or tune in to the student radio station—both are important student organizations. You have undoubtedly visited some campus administrative office and had the frustrating experience of trying to work with a bureaucratic organization.

Different types of student government organizations represent student views and help protect student rights. Student programming boards work closely with administrative offices to provide educational, cultural, social, and recreational activities for the campus. Campus service organizations like Habitat for Humanity or Circle-K are local branches of larger, international organizations; they provide opportunities for students to help those in need. ROTC units contain student organizations, are an academic unit in a college, and are a part of a bigger governmental military structure. Various forms of business organizations provide opportunities for students to make money by working on and off campus. Other organizations provide fellowship, programs, and support for students who are members of different cultural groups. Organizations of all kinds exist everywhere in and around campus and add to the quality of life for everyone. Leadership in organizations is both prevalent and common in our everyday lives, both on and off campus.

Learning to work successfully in organizations gains you a skill set you will use throughout your life. Teachers work in schools; engineers and lawyers work in firms; social workers operate in human service agencies and interact with the legal system. We live in towns with governance processes, worship in religious institutions, and have surgery in hospitals. No matter what your major, you encounter organizations on a regular basis.

> Chapter Overview

In the previous chapter, we explored leadership within team and group settings. In this chapter, we expand the scope of the environment and discuss leadership in an organizational context. In this context, the importance of focusing on the five aspects of the Relational Leadership Model (purpose, inclusivity, empowerment, ethics, and process) becomes even more evident.

> Groups and Organizations

It can be difficult to differentiate between groups and organizations. Some of the differences are obvious; some are more subtle. One way to get a sense of the difference can be shown by answering the who, what, when, where, how, and why questions (Table 9.1). Organizations are large collections of groups of people that interact in a continuous manner within a complex structure to accomplish a specific purpose. Organizations are inherently social entities. Although proximity of location has traditionally been a determining factor for organizations, we will see that this is not always the case.

Organizations have many participants. Remember when you were growing up and you played with your best friend? Although you sometimes had problems or difficulties with each other, it was relatively easy to work them out. As your friendship group expanded, things got more difficult. All of a sudden, you realized that not everyone wanted to play the same game you did or that they wanted to play the game differently. Then your world expanded even further to your high school or

Table 9.1 **Groups and Organizations**

	Groups	Organizations
Who?	Small-to-medium (3+ participants)	Large (20+ participants)
What?	Collection of individuals	Collection of groups
When?	Continuous interactions	Continuous interactions
Where?	Close proximity	Proximity unimportant (ranges from close to far away)
How?	Simple structures	Complex structures
Why?	Purpose	Purpose

places of employment. Being associated with more and more people meant being exposed to different values, ideas, and ways of doing things. This probably made life more interesting, as well as more complicated. As Goldstein, Hazy, and Lichtensten (2010) point out, with an eight-person organization you have 56 possible connections, which seems pretty manageable, but if your organization reaches 100 members, you jump to 9900 possible connections—"Any number of which can come together to influence the outcome" (p. 5).

Again, think about organizations as collections of groups of people. Imagine a college or university with students, professors, administrators, alumni, parents, a board of trustees, legislators, and others, all working together in entities such as offices, departments, or divisions to try to accomplish basically the same thing: to educate students. Yet each of these groups views the education of students in a different way. What groups participate in the life of your organization?

Interactions within organizations are continuous. The success of any organization depends on the various groups within it staying connected so they can work together easily and effectively. Becoming isolated or separated can have a negative impact not only on the specific group that has become separated but also on the entire organization.

Proximity—being physically close to other participants—is certainly helpful but not absolutely necessary in today's organizations. This is contrary to our conception of an organization as people working in the same room or at least in the same building. As we discuss later in the section on virtual organizations, there are a growing number of organizations that are physically separated yet remain connected through technology and the strong belief in a mission or purpose. You may already have experienced being part of a state or regional planning committee that never meets face-to-face, instead using Skype or other technologies to stay connected.

Organizations are complex in their structures. There are usually many layers and departments in the organizational structure and many people involved in leadership and decision making. Think again of the college or university example. To successfully involve all of the different groups in the educational process, different roles, policies, and procedures must be in place. There will also be a number of different leadership positions.

Organizations exist to accomplish a specific purpose. We have all been participants (and possibly leaders) in numerous organizations throughout our lives, but we probably have never stopped to ask, "I wonder how this organization got started?" Unless you were part of the core group that started an organization, it was probably just "always there." Your participation began with you showing up at a meeting and either continued or ended based on how your needs were met by the organization. If we try to formulate an answer to the question, Why do organizations exist? we probably come up with this: they exist to accomplish a specific purpose. This would be the correct response.

STUDENT ESSAY ◇

Leading an organization involves more than what meets the eye. Leading an organization entails not only being aware of your subordinates, but self-awareness as well. A leader of an organization must know what motives their subordinates, as well as what motivates themselves. This is a trait that must not be overlooked, especially in organizational leadership, where transparency of individuals is very evident. Another important aspect of organizational leadership involves empowering subordinates, in an attempt to minimize the hierarchical gap between leader and follower(s). The above description gives a quick glimpse into the world of organizational leadership.

Clay Comerford is a graduate of St. Norbert College, where he majored in business administration and minored in leadership studies. He enjoys sports and the outdoors.

> Organizations as Complex Systems

"It is important to note that organizations have always been complex" (Goldstein, Hazy, & Lichtensten, 2010, p. 5). Organizations are also systems. A system is defined as an environment in which each interaction between members produces outcomes that affect each individual and subsequent interactions and outcomes (Tubbs, 1984). With more people and groups in the organization, interactions become more frequent, and life within the organization becomes more complicated because everything affects everything else.

In *Out of Control*, Kevin Kelly (1994) introduces "The Nine Laws of God," which he describes as "the organizing principles in systems as diverse as biological evolution and SimCity" (p. 468). Depicted in Table 9.2, these "laws" also apply to organizations

Table 9.2 **The Nine Laws of God—Organizations as Systems**

Distribute being	Essence of the organization exists in all of its connected members.
Control from the bottom up	Empower members at all levels of the organization.
Cultivate increasing returns	Focus on what your organization does well and do it even better.
Grow by chunking	Organizations grow, not one piece at a time, but in bunches.
Maximize the fringes	Honor your creative members and their ideas, even if they're really "out there."
Honor your errors	It is only through trial and error that learning happens.
Pursue no optima, have multiple goals	There is no one "right" answer to complex problems; there are only many partial solutions.
Seek persistent disequilibrium	Disequilibrium brings energy into the organization.
Change changes itself	Change leads to more change, which changes the initial change.

Source: Adapted from Kelly, 1994, pp. 468–472. Copyright 1994 by Kevin Kelly. Reprinted by permission of Basic Books, a member of Perseus Books, LLC.

as systems. These qualities relate closely to the new paradigm material covered at the end of Chapter Two, yet they also apply directly (and indirectly) to organizational life. We believe that these qualities really describe life, both in and out of organizations, and will become even more visible to us in the coming century. Look at Kelly's list of principles (Table 9.2): which ones resonate with you? Which ones have you seen operate in your life or in your organizations?

Organizations are tremendously challenging places in which to participate and lead. They are also places of great potential because of the large number and variety of talented people who are members with you. As a leader, you may find yourself wanting to return to the time in your life when things seemed simpler and less complicated. Try not to worry. You will probably find that those qualities that helped you be successful in your youth—enthusiasm, energy, honesty, willingness to work hard, and character—will serve you well as a leader in a complex organization.

Organizational Leadership

In the previous sections, we addressed the questions: What are organizations? Why do they exist? It is also interesting to ask, Why does leadership exist in an organization? Because organizations are widely considered to be structures in which a set of groups can engage with each other over time, leadership in an organization exists to help these groups work together to accomplish a specific purpose. Although this seems simplistic, how could leadership be anything else? Regardless of how it comes

STUDENT ESSAY ◆

As President of my sorority, I have learned that leading an organization does not only require confidence in your own leadership capabilities, but it is also important to have confidence in your members' abilities to lead. Members frequently want to help sustain and improve the organization if given the chance. For those that joined the organization because they were passionate about it and have leadership qualities, it is an obligation of the President to encourage those members to reach their full potential. It is the President's job to ensure all tasks are distributed amongst members who are eager to participate because Presidents are not simply exceptional leaders; they help others become great leaders too. When Presidents entrust their members with tasks, they will hopefully help them learn and grow. Members should learn from failure and success; these experiences will help shape members to eventually become well-rounded leaders. Leaders of organizations do not simply demonstrate the "right way" to do something, rather they help others gain confidence in their own leadership capabilities through mistakes and accomplishments so the organization can continue to evolve and improve to become the organization everyone wants it to be.

Melissa Zissman is a senior at the University of Maryland, College Park where she majors in family science and minored in human development and leadership studies. She is president of Alpha Delta Pi Sorority, vice president of Phi Upsilon Omicron Honor Society, she is a Sexual Health And Reproductive Education (SHARE) peer educator, she is a member of Order of Omega Leadership Honor Society for Members of Greek Organizations, a member of the Maryland Council on Family Relations (MCFR), and a caregiver for a girl with special needs.

into being, leadership exists for only one reason: to help an organization accomplish its stated purpose. This purpose may shift over time, but leadership must always honor its inherent commitment to keep the organization on track to pursue its mission.

By maintaining this focus on the mission, leadership helps make the organization sustainable—to exist over the long term. This is a critical function of leadership. We believe that the Relational Leadership Model provides a usable framework from which leaders can work to accomplish an organization's purpose. By being inclusive, empowering, ethical, and process-oriented while helping all of the organization's members be purposeful and work toward positive purposes, leaders and members can work together successfully to accomplish significant change.

Organizational Structures

Just as all organizations exist for some purpose, they also have a structure that makes their day-to-day operations easier. Max Weber (1924/1947) created the classic bureaucratic model for organizations, featuring a hierarchical structure, "divisions of labor," and clearly articulated rules and regulations to govern how the organization should operate. This structure was designed to promote order and accountability within the organization. In Figure 9.1 this structure has been adapted to show how it might look for a typical student organization. In this model, the power, authority, and responsibility for leading the organization is at the top, with the president, and flows downward in the structure through the other officers and committee chairs. This power and authority are delegated as needed.

The "rules of the game" in the traditionally structured organization are that the members have little power, authority, or responsibility. They simply do as they are told and have little,

Figure 9.1 **The Traditional Organizational Structure**

if any, input into the decision-making process. But things are changing. There is a call for organizations to be collaborative (Berry, 2004), compassionate (Hill & Stephens, 2003), and empathetic (Lei & Greer, 2003). Rather than the old "command and control" functions, leadership within these structures is being asked to connect people across the entire environment by involving the wants, needs, and talents of the organization's membership (Allen & Cherrey, 2000).

One new way of conceptualizing the organization proposed that the traditional pyramid be flipped upside down so that the members are at the top and the president is at the bottom (Figure 9.2). This reconceptualization means that the work of the president is to support the efforts of the other officers and committee chairs so they can better meet the needs and wishes of the members. This can be a powerful exercise for any organization. Turn your organizational pyramid upside down. How well does your leadership help the other members of the organization work toward achieving the purposes for which the organization exists? Who are your members, and what are you as a leader doing to meet their wants and needs? How are you using the talents of your members?

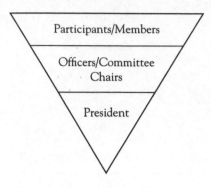

Figure 9.2 **Inverted Organizational Structure**

Another organizational structure that has been proposed is the concept of a web (Allen, 1990; Helgesen, 1990, 1995). The web is defined both by its pattern (similar to a spider's web) and by the idea that the shape and pattern of the web will vary over time (this is called series processes) (Helgesen, 1995). New members easily connect to the structure at its outer edges where the web is looser and more permeable (Helgesen, 1995). This structure works well in an environment filled with change, as the pattern is "continually being built up, stretched, altered, modified, and transformed" (Helgesen, 1995, p. 20).

Our conceptualization of the web is shown in Figure 9.3. As you can see, common purpose is at the center of the web. We believe that the purpose of the organization—the reason it exists—is more important than its leadership and is the reason people become participants. The RLM (see Figure 3.1) also places purpose at the center of the model. This is a different interpretation than Helgesen's (1995), which has the leader at the center of the web—surrounded by other participants and at the center of the organization's activities.

Helgesen (1995) outlines six important processes that define these webs more clearly than the patterns define them. Within the web, communication is open and happens across and among

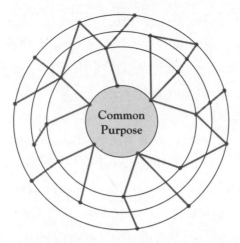

Figure 9.3 **The Web Structure**

all levels of the organization. Thinking of what to do and actually doing it are not separated, because information and expertise are distributed all over the web. The strands of the web distribute the power throughout the network, so those who come up with creative ideas feel they have both the responsibility and the authority to follow through on implementation. Reorganization is easy, as the web can tighten around its center or become looser, and there is less emphasis on who is in what position or who holds how much power. The strands radiating out from the leader provide points of connection to the outside environment and allow new members to latch onto the organization. Finally, the web organization constantly reinvents itself through a process of trial and error. Processes that are successful continue and strengthen the entire web, whereas those that are not successful change into something new. This change is more easily accomplished because communication and decision-making power are distributed throughout the web (Helgesen, 1995).

One final form of organizational structure is labeled nonhierarchical. In nonhierarchical organizations, power and authority are shared throughout the membership. This organizational

structure is flat with no levels. Decisions are often made by consensus, and leadership roles are shared by all. Many organizations
use a nonhierarchical structure for philosophical reasons—the
members believe in true equality.

A note of caution: whichever organizational structure
you have already in place, it is important to remember that
the structure is not the organization. The organization is the
membership—the people—who have come together for certain
purposes. The structure was created to help the membership
achieve the purposes for which the organization was developed.
Organizations also exist to connect people to each other. When
the structure ceases to do either of these things, it must be
changed. It is easy to convince yourself that a change in structure
will remedy an organization's problems. We have found that this
is not always the case. Changing your organization's structure
may simplify things or make them operate more efficiently. It
will not solve profound issues that exist between people.

Organizational Mission, Vision, and Core Values

Organizations exist for a specific purpose: to represent the
views of the membership, to produce some product, to provide
activities or services for its members, or for countless other reasons. This is what causes people to want to join and participate
in organizations. A critical aspect of the success or failure of any
organization will be how its purpose (or mission) comes to life
in its vision and actions. The importance of mission, vision, and
core values of an organization cannot be overestimated.

The mission of the organization is, quite simply, why
it exists. Jones and Kahaner (1995) collected the mission
statements of 50 corporations; these make for interesting

reading. Checking out the websites of most major corporations, it is easy to find their mission statements on their web page. Southwest Airlines vows, "The mission of Southwest Airlines is dedication to the highest quality of Customer Service delivered with a sense of warmth, friendliness, individual pride, and Company Spirit" (http://www.southwest.com/html/about-southwest/index.html). Google sets an incredibly high standard with their mission statement, "Google's mission is to organize the world's information and make it universally accessible and useful" (http://www.google.com/about/company/). Amazon's vision or mission statement reads, "Our vision is to be the earth's most customer centric company; to build a place where people can come to discover anything they might want to buy online" (http://phx.corporate-ir.net/phoenix.zhtml?c=97664&p=irol-faq#14296). Coca Cola's mission is

- To refresh the world . . .
- To inspire moments of optimism and happiness . . .
- To create value and make a difference.

Apple, well known for its innovative products, has typically included a mission-related statement in all of its press releases. The following is its most recent iteration:

> Apple designs Macs, the best personal computers in the world, along with OS X, iLife, iWork and professional software. Apple leads the digital music revolution with its iPods and iTunes online store. Apple has reinvented the mobile phone with its revolutionary iPhone and App Store, and is defining the future of mobile media and computing devices with iPad. (http://www.apple.com/pr/library/2012/07/30Mountain-Lion-Downloads-Top-Three-Million.html)

An organization's mission statement should answer the question, Why does this organization exist? The mission statement must be written in clear, concise language and include input gathered from throughout the organization so that it reflects the personality of the organization. Once written, the statement should be shared widely in as many forms as possible so that it can be used to truly guide the actions of the organization (Jones & Kahaner, 1995).

The mission statement should do something else. It should offer a compelling reason for the organization's existence. The contribution the organization makes to the campus, community, or world needs to be articulated in a way that is enticing to potential participants and motivational to those who have already joined the organization. The mission of your organization could be social, service-related, programmatic, political, or any combination, but the effectiveness of your organization will be determined by how well it moves toward its mission.

As you might imagine, many definitions could describe the vision of an organization. Kouzes and Posner (2008) call a vision "much like a literary or musical theme. It's the broad message that you want to convey, it's the primary melody that you want people to remember, and whenever it's repeated it reminds the audience of the entire work" (p. 106). Albrecht (1994) terms it "an image of what the people of the enterprise aspire for it to be or become" (p. 150). The vision answers the questions, "What do we want to be? What is the best we can be?" (Jaffe, Scott, & Tobe, 1994, p. 146). We believe that the vision answers the question, What is the ideal future for this organization? As such, it must motivate and inspire, be a stretch, be clear and concrete, be achievable, reflect high values, and be simple (Jaffe, et al., 1994). The vision that the organization embraces challenges both the leader and the membership to do their very best—sometimes even more than believed possible—to move toward the mission for which the organization exists.

Getting the members of your organization to share this vision can be very challenging, but unless it is shared and owned by the members, nothing of significance will ever happen. The vision must tap into the motivational systems of the people in your organization. This is why it is so important for the mission and vision statements to be clearly stated and inspiring. It is also the reason why these two statements must constantly be in front of all leaders and members and used to guide the actions of the organization. As Margaret Wheatley (2006) notes, "in creating a vision, we are creating a power, not a place, an influence, not a destination" (p. 54). In other words, the mission and vision need to come alive and be kept constantly alive through the actions of the leaders and members of the organization.

The final concept we explore in this section is that of core values. Without core values, any behavior would be justifiable as long as it moved the organization toward its mission or vision. We have all seen examples of this when people say that the ends justify the means. In their examination of visionary companies, Collins and Porras (1994) described core values as "The organization's essential and enduring tenets—a small set of general guiding principles; not to be confused with specific cultural or operating practices; not to be compromised for financial gain or short-term expediency" (p. 73). These core values are small in number (usually three to six values) and "so fundamental and deeply held that they will change or be compromised seldom, if ever" (p. 74). Core values answer the question, How do we, as organization members, agree to treat ourselves and others as we pursue our mission and vision? Although core values are important to the success of any organization, they are seldom discussed or shared among the membership. We encourage you to take some time, both individually and as a group, to reflect on the core values for which your organization stands. It will be time well spent.

Organizational Culture

Many people believe that organizations are so powerful and influential that they take on a culture of their own. Edgar Schein (2010) in his classic work, *Organizational Culture and Leadership*, notes that, "Culture is an abstraction, yet the forces that are created in social and organizational situations deriving from culture are powerful" (p. 7). He goes on to define this form of organizational culture as

> a pattern of shared basic assumptions learned by a group as it solved its problems of external adaptation and internal integration, which has worked well enough to be considered valid and, therefore, to be taught to new members as the correct way to perceive, think, and feel in relation to those problems. (p. 18)

James Carse (1986) defines culture in a slightly different manner. "Culture . . . is an infinite game. Culture has no boundaries . . ." (p. 53) and "for this reason it can be said that where society is defined by its boundaries, a culture is defined by its horizons" (p. 69).

Schein (2010) proposes that culture has three levels. The most visible level is the artifacts—the "structures and processes" of the organization. The espoused beliefs and values of the organization make up the next level. These are the "ideals, goals, values, and aspirations" that the organization claims it embraces. At the final, deepest level are the underlying assumptions. These are the "unconscious beliefs and values" that are assumed to be true by members of the organization. These underlying assumptions drive the values and actions of the organization. He asserts that "the central issue for leaders is to understand the deeper levels of a culture, to assess the functionality of the assumptions made at that level, and to deal with the anxiety that is unleashed when those assumptions are challenged" (p. 33).

Terrence Deal and Allan Kennedy (2000) offer a different framework from which to examine organizational cultures. They stress the importance of the organization's values, heroes, rites and rituals, and communications network. Values are important because they provide the core of the organization and a guide for the behaviors of the members. Ordinary individuals who are heroic in their actions are critical because they make success more possible to achieve, provide role models, symbolize the organization to outsiders, preserve what makes the organization special, set a standard of performance, and motivate members (Deal & Kennedy). Rites and rituals provide the formal and informal guidelines for how the everyday occurrences within the organization are to proceed. They include how members should communicate, socialize, work, and play, as well as what actions should be recognized and how they will be rewarded. The rites and rituals also govern the intricacies of how the organization operates—for example, how its meetings are conducted. Finally, Deal and Kennedy analyze the organization's communications network by examining how information is gathered and disseminated, both formally and informally. As they note, "The whole process depends on people, not on paper" (p. 87).

Deal and Kennedy (2000) describe various characters within the organization and outline how they contribute to the communications network. Storytellers interpret what is going on in the organization; what they say may or may not be the truth, because it reflects their perception of what is happening. Priests see themselves as guarding the values of the organization's culture; another of their roles is to keep the membership of the organization together. Whisperers work behind the scenes and have power because of their close connection to the leadership of the organization. Gossips can provide detailed information about what is currently happening within the organization; sometimes the facts they provide are correct, sometimes they are not. Administrative support sources can tell members what is really going on in the organization because of their access to important information. Spies are loyal to the leaders of the organization and provide information to them about what is happening. Finally, cabals are groups of two or more people whose main purpose in joining together is to advance themselves within the organization; their alliance is often kept secret.

Another way to view organizations is offered by Bolman and Deal (2007) who use four "frames" of organizations: structural, human resource, political, and symbolic. As you might imagine, the structural frame focuses on formal processes like organizational charts, roles, and job descriptions. The human resource frame emphasizes the people in the organization—their feelings and motivations. The political frame operates from the perspective that there will always be a scarcity of resources, so organizations are inevitably in conflict with each other and must operate in ways, such as forming coalitions, that will enable them to gain more. The symbolic frame focuses on the ceremonies, stories, and heroes that help define the organization and reveal or reflect its values. Paying attention to how these different frames are operating within your organization can provide clues to why some parts may be doing well while other aspects are struggling.

Geert Hofstede (2003) adds to our understanding of organizations and cultures through his studies of societies around the world. He proposes that people differ in five broad dimensions: the Power Distance Index (the degree to which the particular society supports inequality or equality), Individualism (how much individual work is emphasized over collective action), Masculinity (the degree to which traditionally male values are embraced over traditionally female values), Uncertainty Avoidance Index (the degree to which ambiguity and uncertainty are tolerated), and Long-Term Orientation (how much a long-term perspective is favored over a short-term view).

Compare this work with the dimensions of culture identified by Project GLOBE that appeared in Chapters Two and Five. Considering Hofstede's dimensions can help us understand our own organizations by reminding us that people have different beliefs and preferences for how the world should work. For example, imagine that a group of students wants to join your organization and that they believe strongly in equality and that all opinions should be given equal consideration (Power Distance). Unfortunately, for them at least, your organization has a long history of being hierarchical, with preference given to the ideas of long-standing members (Long-Term Orientation). This is simply how you operate, and you've been effective with this method of operation. As a leader in such a situation, you may have a difficult time convincing the group of students that they will be able to make a contribution to your organization.

It is important to have a sense of the culture of your organization because it provides insight into how your organization
really operates. This may seem trivial because we all think
we know how it operates. But veteran members' experiences
in an organization can be very different from those of new or
prospective members. Consider the general concept of change.
In some organizations, "If it ain't broke, break it" could define
the culture, whereas in other organizations, "If it ain't broke,
don't worry about it" may be the way things operate. Being a new
member of a change-oriented organization can be very exciting
because your opinions may be listened to more closely than in
the organization that embraces the status quo. Veteran members,
however, may think things are just fine the way they are now
and see no need for much change at all.

An organizational culture can also negatively affect life
within an organization. As Stacey (1992) notes, "Strongly shared
cultures inevitably block new learning and cut down on the
variety of perspectives brought to bear on an issue" (p. 143). In
other words, "The more norms we strongly share, the more we
resist changing them" (p. 143). Although the development of a
culture that supports the pursuit of the organization's mission,
values, and goals is very important, everyone must be aware
of how the culture may also be inhibiting the organization.
People must also realize that trying to change the mission, vision,
and values of the organization without paying attention to
changing the culture may meet with resistance. Think about how
something as "simple" as eliminating hazing from the initiation
process of an organization should be. Hazing is against the law,
causes harm, and does little to benefit the organization. Yet the
culture of many organizations strongly embraces the need for

such rites of passage in order for new members to show their dedication to their new organization. Changing the mission and values of the organization to embrace nonhazing principles is often relatively easy. Changing the culture of the organization so that individuals in it do not haze is often more difficult. Planning a rewarding substitute activity to celebrate the transition of new members to full membership can enrich the culture.

Organizational Networks

The importance of networks has received much attention in recent years (Barabási, 2002; Fisher, 2009, Watts, 2003). Networks even made it into the popular culture when people played the game "Six Degrees of Kevin Bacon." How many links would it take to connect Kevin Bacon to Will Smith? Probably two links. Bacon was in *JFK* with Tommy Lee Jones, who was in *Men in Black* with Will Smith—get the idea? Jessica Lipnack and Jeffrey Stamps (1993) define networks as "where disparate groups of people and groups 'link' to work together based on common purposes" (p. 7). These groups of people may be participants in your organization and may also include others from outside the organization. The keys are that they work together and have a common purpose. Networks are important because they provide the chance to bring together a wide range of individuals. The network either may address a specific issue, such as when a wide range of students, faculty, and staff members are brought together to plan an institution's one-hundredth birthday celebration, or it may work on an ongoing concern like student retention. Student ethnic or cultural groups may network for diversity programs on campus or take on advocacy issues. Key issues in the formation of a network include agreement on the network's purpose, creating as many links as possible among members of the network, and making sure that multiple leaders exist within the network (Lipnack & Stamps).

As you think of your organization as a network or group of networks, consider the following questions:

- What must the networks accomplish?
- Who needs to be connected to whom and for what purpose?
- What linkages can you construct to reduce the average length of pathways in the network?
- How will the network be maintained? That is, how can the organization keep its networks robust?
- How will you enhance interaction resonance across the network? (Goldstein, Hazy, & Lichtensten, 2010, p. 169)

Life Cycles of Organizations

Although the emerging paradigm described in Chapter Two would suggest that organizations cannot be controlled, we believe that a critical point in the success of any organization is its ability to adapt to change—changing conditions, changing membership, and changing leadership. This ability to adapt enables an organization to renew itself and maintain its vibrancy. A small group of skilled and determined individuals can move an organization into greatness by their focused actions.

This sometimes happens with new organizations. A group of students gets excited about an idea and, with the help of a few other students, forms an organization dedicated to a specific purpose. The energy, excitement, and dedication of this small group often helps them accomplish powerful outcomes. However, this success can be short-lived unless the organization makes plans for what will happen next—specifically, who will be recruited as new members and who will be groomed for future leadership positions. This is one of the most critical, and often overlooked, responsibilities of leadership—to identify, recruit, prepare, and mentor the future leaders of the organization. Feeling this obligation to sustain the organization into the future is called generativity.

John W. Gardner (1990) and Ichak Adizes (1988) present the concept of "lives" of organizations. Gardner uses the terms *infancy* and *maturity* to differentiate organizations that are in their early lives from those that have evolved into something more orderly and with more of a sense of direction. Adizes goes into more detail and uses the terms *courtship, infancy, go-go, adolescence, prime, stable, aristocracy, early bureaucracy, bureaucracy,* and *death* to describe a similar change process. As Gardner notes, "At each stage something is gained and something is lost" (p. 122). When organizations are young, they are very flexible and motivated, are willing to try new things, and have the ability to respond quickly to new challenges. Yet they may expend much energy to accomplish relatively little. As organizations mature, this flexibility lessens, and they become more orderly and are more satisfied with slow, steady advances (Gardner). These stages in the life of organizations are similar to the stages of group development presented in Chapter Eight.

It has been said that when asked about the early days of the Peace Corps, Sargent Shriver, its director, noted that the leadership of the organization didn't meet—they were too busy doing things. This dedication is often felt early on in new organizations and is exciting—even intoxicating—but it will always end. The model of Adizes (1988) is critical for student leaders to understand because of its focus on how an entire organization changes. Take a hard look at your organization. How would a random sample of students on your campus describe the student government? Would they be positive? Negative? Indifferent? Could they identify any recent accomplishments of the group?

Your organization needs to ask itself two questions on a regular basis:

What have we accomplished recently?
How does what we've accomplished reflect our organization's mission?

If you are having trouble formulating answers to either of these questions, you may need to reexamine what you are doing and how you are doing it. Remember that the purpose of meetings and standard operating procedures is to help your organization do things in the most expedient manner. They are not designed to become ends unto themselves. As a leader, you must identify and describe significant accomplishments that you helped your organization achieve—not the fact that you attended or ran a lot of meetings.

Multicultural Organizational Development

To remain vibrant and viable over an extended period, an organization needs to be willing to remake itself. One way to approach organizational transformation is through the concept of multicultural organizational development (Armour & Hayles, 1990; Jackson & Holvino, 1988; Pope, 1993; Wall & Obear, 2008). This process emphasizes the full participation of members from all cultural and social groups and a commitment to end all forms of social oppression that may exist within the organization that blocks the meaningful, inclusive involvement of all members.

This emphasis on diversity and social justice offers a fresh perspective from which to approach organizational transformation. Because the Relational Leadership Model emphasizes being inclusive and empowering, it is essential to understand how an organization might transform itself to be multicultural. What do you think the impact would be if every organization on your campus made a commitment to end all forms of social oppression? This would clearly be a transformation, and the campus would become a better place for all its students, faculty, and staff.

Armour and Hayles (1990) and Jackson and Holvino (1988) offer similar models for multicultural organizational development. Their models show the organization moving from a perspective that is monocultural and exclusionary to one that is compliant and nondiscriminatory, through a redefinition process, and finally to a multicultural perspective.

Of particular importance in Jackson and Holvino's (1988) work is their elaboration of the assumptions that change agents make, depending on whether they come from a monocultural, nondiscriminatory, or multicultural perspective (Table 9.3). Whereas those coming from a monocultural perspective view society as basically harmonious and doing all right, those having a multicultural perspective see society as filled with conflict and in need of radical change. You may already see examples of these two opposing perspectives on your campus. Learning to understand, respect, and work effectively with others who have strongly held views that differ from your own is one of the great

Table 9.3 **Change Agent Assumptions in Multicultural Organization Development**

	Monocultural	Nondiscriminatory	Multicultural
Nature of Society	Harmonious		Conflict
	Similar interests		Different interests
	Needs to improve, but basically OK		Oppressive, alienating, needs radical change
Oppression	Dominance	Desegregation	Pluralism
Liberation Model	Assimilation	Integration	Diversity
Self-Interest in Change	Survival and social acceptability	Adaptation and full use of human resources	Equity, empowerment, collective growth
Values and Ideology	Basic rights of individual		Interdependence
	Best person is rewarded		Ecological survival
	Efficiency and economic survival		Development of human and societal potential

Source: Adapted from Jackson & Holvino (1988), p. 18.

challenges of being a leader. It is also absolutely necessary as you work to make your organization and campus a better place for all people.

Learning in Organizations

Continuous learning by leaders and participants within organizations continues to be of critical importance. It is only through ongoing learning that organizations can improve how they operate, improve, and grow. In Exhibit 9.1, Yukl (2009) offers a number of ways that leaders can encourage this learning.

Exhibit 9.1: Ways Leaders Can Enhance Organizational Learning ◆

- Encourage people to question traditional methods and look for innovative new approaches that will be more effective.
- Articulate an inspiring vision to gain support for innovative changes from members of the organization.
- Encourage and facilitate the acquisition of skills needed for collective learning by individuals and teams.
- Strengthen values consistent with learning from experience and openness to new knowledge, thereby helping to create a learning culture in the organization.
- Encourage social networks that will facilitate knowledge sharing, collaborative development of creative ideas, and the acquisition of political support for innovations.
- Help people recognize when important learning has occurred and to understand the implications for the team or organization.
- Encourage teams to conduct after-activity reviews to identify effective and ineffective processes.

(continued)

- Encourage people to acknowledge when a new initiative is failing and should be aborted rather than continuing to waste resources on it.
- Develop, implement, and support programs and systems that will encourage and reward the discovery of new knowledge and its diffusion and application in the organization.

(Adapted from Yukl, 2009, p. 50)

Peter Senge (1990), Watkins and Marsick (1993), and others have proposed a way to conceptualize organizations that will help them operate successfully in the chaotic world described in Chapter Two. They used the label "learning organizations" to describe organizations that have the capacity to grow, change, and develop in order to adapt to the challenges of their constantly changing environments. In his conceptualization of the learning organization, Senge et al. (1994) included the modules of personal mastery, mental models, shared vision, and team learning. These modules make up a framework of systems thinking; each is interrelated with the others. We believe that the concept of the learning organization and its guiding principles of the primacy of the whole, the community nature of the self, and the generative power of language have much to offer in our discussion of organizations.

Personal mastery involves individuals doing the best possible job. For a treasurer in an organization, this might include knowing how to use new financial software, being able to follow the steps needed to purchase something, and having budgeting skills. For a vice president, this might include skills in working with committee chairs so that their respective groups can get organized and be productive. Everyone in an organization—officers and members—has skills and abilities that can be contributed to the organization. It is important for leaders to work with the group's membership, not only so that individuals can gain the skills needed to be effective in their current roles within the organization, but also as a way of preparing them for future positions. When members are skilled and empowered to use these skills, the whole organization benefits.

Mental models are the assumptions that people make about the various aspects of the world. For instance, when someone says the words *leader, conflict, diversity,* or *meeting,* what images pop into your head? These mental models are often difficult to grasp and, therefore, are sometimes difficult to change. But these models must be changed if any real positive change is to occur in the world. Disagreements sometimes arise because these differing mental models are not brought to the surface so they can be examined and, if necessary, changed. Consider for a moment the concept of adviser. If your organization has an adviser, you may assume that this person will make sure details do not fall through the cracks when you are planning a big event. When this turns out not to be true, everyone loses. It is important to compare the mental models that you have with others in your organization. In this way, false assumptions can be minimized. Mental models can also be empowering for a whole organization. Consider what would happen if, when members thought about your organization, the concepts of inclusion, empowerment, process, ethics, and common purpose immediately came to mind. These images could do a lot to guide the organization in a way that would help make it strong and successful.

Shared vision focuses on the idea that the mission, vision, and purpose of an organization must be shared by all members. Shared vision—or common purpose—is especially important given the current emphasis on empowerment. People can be empowered and their personal mastery level high, yet without some shared sense of direction, everyone will be pushing hard in different directions. The result will be an organization that moves haphazardly, if at all. Although vision is certainly important, Helgesen (1990) notes that feeling confident in one's "voice" may be just as critical because this is how the vision is related and shared with others.

The concept of team learning is also vital in any learning organization. As Senge (1990) and others (Kline & Saunders, 1993; Watkins & Marsick, 1993) note, learning at the individual level (Senge's concept of personal mastery) must be supplemented by learning at the team, organizational, and societal levels if any true learning is to occur. This might include learning how to make decisions, how to really communicate, and how to disagree—aspects of organizational life that we usually take for granted, yet perform very poorly. The concept of team learning also underscores the need to consider leadership as an ongoing process rather than an end result or product. Just as team members are constantly engaged with each other in learning new approaches or methods, leaders must be continually engaged in dialogue with members of their organizations.

Finally, a systems approach governs the thinking in a learning organization. When people think systematically, they share responsibility for the good and bad things that are happening. Rather than looking for someone else to blame, members of a learning organization hold up the mirror and ask what they have done to contribute to the problem. Think of how many problems we blame on someone or something else rather than accepting responsibility for them ourselves and working toward a solution. Senge (1990) calls this specific "learning disability" a belief that "the enemy is out there." As in our earlier example of the organization as a weather system, all aspects of a system are constantly working together to create the reality of the system. All of these aspects—personal mastery, mental models, shared vision, team learning, and systems thinking—combine to create a learning organization.

We have gone into so much detail about the learning organization because the capacity for an organization to continuously learn enables it to continuously recreate itself as it faces new challenges. Consider the following example: A student government organization needs to appoint a student member to its college's board of trustees. What qualities should such a representative have? How should that person be selected? What issues should this representative bring to the board? All of a sudden, the student government has moved from being an organization that may have a programming emphasis to one that gives students a voice in the group that makes the major decisions regarding campus life. This is a major change in focus. To take advantage of this opportunity, the organization must be able to learn how the board operates, what issues will be of most interest to the board, and what approaches will be most successful. Much of this learning will have to be "on the hoof" (Stacey, 1992). Only an organization that is truly open to and embracing of learning new approaches will make optimal use of this opportunity.

STUDENT ESSAY

One concept that I have learned as a leader and have come to appreciate is the power of learning from failures. Unfortunately, the emphasis on this notion has been very weak in regards to communicating with students that failure is not a bad feature if you learn from the experience.

I started an organization on campus midway through my college tenure and it failed miserably. I learned from my mistakes and used my experience to start a more productive organization two years later, which is now in works of expanding onto other campuses. The challenges and adversity have been high, but learning from mistakes has been tremendously helpful in moving forward.

Don't be afraid of failing; rather be afraid of not trying. Failure equals experience and it can be a wonderful teacher, but one has to be smart on duplicating it into success. As a leader it is crucial to understand why certain concepts did not go as planned, and implement changes by using your expertise in order to avoid the same results. Malcolm Forbes once said, "Failure is success if we learn from it." You have to learn about yourself first before you can learn how to lead others, and if you don't learn from previous failures, you will lead your constituents in the same direction.

Shawhin Mosadeghzad is a graduate of the University of Tennessee where he majored in management. He was the founder of the It's Not About Me Foundation and a brother of the Kappa Sigma Fraternity.

> Virtuality and the Impact of Technology

Understanding the essential role of technology and its impact on organizational life is crucial (see Oblinger & Oblinger, 2005; Postman, 1992). The growth of virtual teams and organizations has been chronicled in a number of publications (for example, Avolio & Kahai, 2003; Mockaitis, Rose, & Zettnig, 2012; Zigurs, 2003; Zofi, 2012). Charles Handy (1996) defines virtual organizations as "organizations that do not need to have all the people, or sometimes any of the people, in one place in order to deliver their service. The organization exists but you can't see it. It is a network, not an office" (p. 212). Zigurs notes that we should think in terms of "virtuality" as a continuum. The more the team is separated in terms of geography, time, or culture, or organizationally, the more virtual it is.

So what will these virtual organizations be like? Handy (1996), Zigurs (2003), and Zaccaro and Bader (2003) believe that trust will be extremely important—and very difficult to develop when people do not often see each other face-to-face. He also stresses the need for a common purpose and values to be shared by all the organization's members. Davidow and Malone (1992) note that organizations will certainly be flatter (multiple layers of hierarchy will be a thing of the past) and built on the need for the organization's members to believe and trust in each other, and that they will involve members at all levels more and more in the decision-making process.

Leadership within these virtual environments is described by Avolio and Kahai (2003). "At its core, leadership is about the development of relationships. Whether connected via information technology or not, leaders have to build relationships in order to lead effectively" (p. 331). Among the associated "major changes and future trends" identified by Avolio and Kahai are the following: "leaders and followers have more access to information and each other . . . leadership is migrating to lower and lower organizational levels . . . [and] leadership creates and exists in networks" (p. 333). Kissler (2001) identifies a number of e-leadership attributes for success; among other traits, successful leaders "revel in complexity, ambiguity, and uncertainty; [and are] incredibly curious and insatiable life-long learners; courageous due to deeply-held values and unwavering beliefs; able to build and retain talent" (p. 132). Zaccaro and Bader (2003) note a number of e-team leader roles that lead to e-team effectiveness, including "enhancing cohesion, nurturing trust, promoting sharing of information and ideas, moderating team conflict, facilitating team coordination and integration, and developing social and human capital" (p. 382).

Your organization may already seem a lot like a virtual organization, with members coming and going at all hours of the day or night and spending very little time together in the same place. You may already be involved in other examples of virtual organizations on your campus. Your student government organization may also be a member of a state, regional, or national coalition with other student government groups. You might plan a leadership conference with students on other campuses via e-mail, phone, and fax and never actually meet face-to-face in the same room until the conference begins. On your campus, you may find that you communicate more often with the members of your own organization through the use of cell phones, e-mail, text messaging, Yahoo! or Google Groups, or other technologies than in face-to-face meetings.

The impact of all this technology cannot be overstated. We now have the ability to communicate and share information with anyone, anytime, anywhere. So what does this mean for your organization? What will it mean for organizations in the future? We have already seen how this technology can be used to organize people (Rheingold, 2003). In what other ways will it fundamentally change how organizations operate? Does more communication always make better organizations? At what point does having access to all this information become overwhelming? At this point, we cannot predict how organizations will change as a result of the use of technology. All we know is that they will change.

> New Paradigm Leadership in Conventional Paradigm Cultures

One of the most challenging results of reading a book like this is realizing that you might embrace the principles of new paradigm leadership but find yourself mired in a conventional culture. This can present a dilemma, but you can take actions toward continuing to use this information. First of all, share what you know with other leaders, members of your organization, advisers—anyone who will listen. By sharing, you do two things: you learn the information better yourself, and you may find some other interested people with whom you can continue to connect. Accept personal responsibility for finding ways to use the information rather than always saying, "Well, so-and-so won't let me do that." Maintain a positive outlook and try to find areas in which you can use this information rather than focusing on areas that seem out of bounds. Continue to try new things, even in small ways. You will find a number of different exercises and thought pieces in *The Fifth Discipline Fieldbook* (Senge, Kleiner, Roberts, Ross, & Smith, 1994) that you can use in a variety of settings, both in and outside of your organization. Volunteer to do programs or activities with other organizations or to be a guest speaker or teacher. Finally, continue to read and explore. A number of resources are listed in this book. Continue to develop your own leadership library. It will serve you well for your entire life (Allen, 1990).

❯ Organizational Renewal

Organizations typically exist over long periods of time and can get rigid and stale. Gardner (1990) notes that continuous renewal is necessary in groups and organizations in order to renew and reinterpret values, liberate energies, reenergize forgotten goals or generate new goals, achieve new understandings, and foster the release of human potential. Gardner notes further that "leaders must understand the interweaving of continuity and change" (p. 124). Continuity means taking the best of how the group or organization is currently and carrying it forward under conditions that require new approaches.

According to Gardner (1990), the most critical step in the renewal process is "the release of talent and energy" (p. 136) from within the members. As he notes, "Nothing is more vital to the renewal of an organization than the arrangements by which able people are nurtured and moved into positions where they can make their greatest contribution" (p. 127). This process begins with the recruitment of new members and continues with their ongoing development. What do you do to tap into the talents and energy of the members of your groups, organizations, and communities? How could you do this even better?

Gardner (1990) makes a number of other suggestions that can help the renewal effort for organizations. We believe these suggestions can also apply to groups and communities. Groups, organizations, and communities can reassign their leaders to expose them to new challenges; take steps to increase the motivational level of leaders and participants alike; foster at least some diversity and dissent to encourage the development of new ideas; refocus on the original reasons that the groups and organizations were formed; ensure that both internal and external communication are easy and open; keep focused on the vision of a desired future; and, finally, reorganize. Some of these

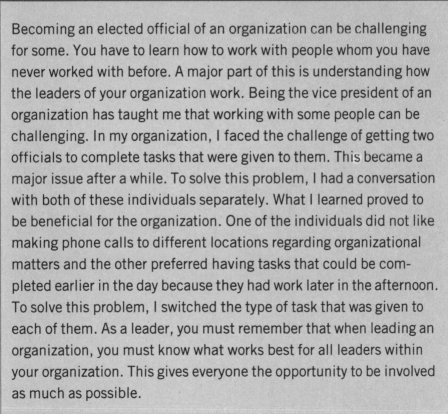

STUDENT ESSAY

Becoming an elected official of an organization can be challenging for some. You have to learn how to work with people whom you have never worked with before. A major part of this is understanding how the leaders of your organization work. Being the vice president of an organization has taught me that working with some people can be challenging. In my organization, I faced the challenge of getting two officials to complete tasks that were given to them. This became a major issue after a while. To solve this problem, I had a conversation with both of these individuals separately. What I learned proved to be beneficial for the organization. One of the individuals did not like making phone calls to different locations regarding organizational matters and the other preferred having tasks that could be completed earlier in the day because they had work later in the afternoon. To solve this problem, I switched the type of task that was given to each of them. As a leader, you must remember that when leading an organization, you must know what works best for all leaders within your organization. This gives everyone the opportunity to be involved as much as possible.

Reginald J. Horace is a sophomore at Florida Atlantic University where he majors in biology with hopes of becoming a medical doctor. He has served as the Campus Action vice chair in the House of Representatives under student government, vice president of the Council for Scholarship and Inquiry, Orientation and Welcome leader, and currently serves on the Relay for Life Committee.

steps may require the use of an outside evaluator, because people become used to the status quo and can find themselves resistant to any significant change efforts.

Gardner's ideas are important because they give us some ideas about where we need to go when things are going poorly. His work also reflects the relevance of the basic concepts of the Relational Leadership Model. By paying more attention to issues of purpose, inclusion, empowerment, ethics, and the process orientation, groups, organizations, and communities can remain productive places for all members. When things are going poorly, returning to these basic principles can provide an excellent starting point for efforts aimed at renewal.

Another way to maintain a focus on organizational learning is an exercise called The Five Whys, developed by Rick Ross (1994a, p. 108). Ask yourself the most simple of questions, such as, Why does your organization (or group or community) exist? This question is relevant whether it is asked about student government, a service organization, the chess club, a residence hall floor or house government, a fraternity or sorority, or a club related to your major. Probe deeply. Now take the reason you have given and ask why that answer is important. Take the answer to that second Why? and ask Why? again. Do this until you have asked Why? a total of five times. Doing this helps you get closer to the essence of why the group exists. See Table 9.4 for an example of the way this technique would apply to an organization.

Although the final line in Table 9.4 about working for the development office is humorous, the conversation does get us to a deeper understanding of why we have campus entertainment—to retain students. With this as a reason for the

Table 9.4 **The Five Whys**

Consider this imaginary conversation with the chair of a campus entertainment committee:	
Why does your organization exist?	To provide campus entertainment for students.
Why is that important?	So they'll have something to do and have fun.
Why is that important?	So they'll enjoy going to school here and stay out of trouble.
Why is that important?	If they like going to school here and stay out of trouble, they'll stay in school and hopefully graduate.
Why is that important?	If they graduate, hopefully they'll go out and be successful, make a big salary, and contribute money to the school.
So you really work for the Development Office?	I guess so!

Source: Adapted from Ross (1994a), pp. 108–112. Used with permission of Rick Ross.

existence of such an organization, the activities they sponsor must appeal to a broad range of students.

Consider the differences between a student government group whose primary reason for existence is to provide social, recreational, and physical activities for the campus community and another student government group whose purpose is to be the voice of student opinion to the campus administration. These two groups have very different focuses. No one group or organization can be all things to all people. Decide what is at the core and return to this core at every opportunity. The core defines why your group or organization exists. It is why people originally started it and why others decided to join. As leaders and active participants, it is your duty to help make this core come alive for the membership.

> When Things Go Wrong

In Chapters Ten and Eleven we will focus on change—the process of change and strategies for going about making change in organizations. In this chapter, however, we did want to provide some thoughts on what you might notice when things have gone off track in your organization. Exhibit 9.2 describes some of the conditions of which you should be aware. As with any list, use this as a guide, not as an absolute measure of how things are going.

Exhibit 9.2: Conditions in an Organization That Signal a Critical Period

- An increasing sense that what we had been doing is no longer working or appropriate.
- A sense of urgency begins to enter planning sessions and executive meetings.
- Well-crafted plans for expansion are not working out, expectations are continuously reframed, and the pace of internal change increases rapidly.
- Performance declines due to changing environments—the organization's traditionally reliance on specialized activities or offerings is no longer effective.
- Concern that all of the small changes will never add up to what is needed, that something really big is necessary.
- Competing interpretations and passionate disagreements about the meaning of external events for the organization, including which

events are relevant to the organization and what should be done to address them.

- Increased interpersonal conflict—constructive and destructive—puts line employees and supervisors on edge.
- Increased individual anxiety, and a growing divergence of organizational goals and the individual's best interest. This can show up as higher turnover or generalized questioning: "Should I stay or should I go?"
- Conditions of uncertainty which persist even in the face of attempted changes, or when normal efforts to reduce their significance or credibility are resisted. Sometimes, extraordinary means such as coercion begin to be used or threatened.
- The future of the organization is called into question; calls to "break-up or disband the organization" are heard.

(Adapted from Goldstein, Hazy, & Lichtensten, 2010, p 50)

> Chapter Summary

In this chapter we have discussed complex organizations. We have discussed why organizations exist and how they are structured. We have stressed the importance of mission, vision, and core values.

As Plowman, Solansky, Beck, Baker, Kulkarni, and Travis (2007) note:

> ... in complex systems leaders enable rather than control the future. While traditional views of leadership focus on the leader's responsibility for determining and directing the future through heavy reliance on control mechanisms, we offer empirical support for a different view of

leadership based on a complexity perspective of organizations. Our findings show that as enablers, leaders disrupt existing patterns of behavior, encourage novelty, and make sense of emerging events for others. (p. 341)

We also have presented what the virtual organization of the future might be like. Throughout this chapter the importance of the Relational Leadership Model has been evident. It is only by being inclusive that an organization can creatively use the talents and abilities of all of its membership. By being empowering and process-oriented, the organization encourages all members to take an active role in the life of the organization. By being ethical, the organization ensures that members can hold each other to a higher standard of behavior that is more closely aligned with the organization's mission, vision, and core values. Finally, it is only when this vision or common purpose is truly shared by the entire membership that an organization can reach its potential and be purposeful.

Organizational life need not be an endless series of meetings run by Robert's Rules of Order. There can and should be excitement and energy there. We hope you will find it.

> What's Next?

In the next chapters we shift gears and begin our discussion about change—understanding it and strategies for implementing it. The book concludes with the chapter, Thriving Together.

> Chapter Activities

1. Groups and Organizations. Identify a group and organization in which you are currently a participant. Now look at Exhibit 9.1. How do your experiences support the way we differentiated among these three concepts? How do your experiences differ from our framework?

2. Organizational Mission. Find your organization's mission statement or an example of a mission statement not described in this chapter. Does it meet the criteria suggested by Jones and Kahaner? What are your statement's strengths? Where does it fall short? How could you change it to make it more reflective of both the purpose and the personality of your organization? How compelling is it? If you don't have a mission statement, write one now. How did you do? Would you be inspired by your statement if you knew nothing of your organization?

3. Organizational Vision. Imagine an ideal future for your organization. Try to capture this image on paper. Be creative. You can make a collage or a drawing or use words—whatever works for you. When you are finished, look at your image. Is it inspiring? Would it motivate your members? How could it be improved?

4. Core Values. Reflect for a couple of minutes on the core values of your organization. Write down what these values are. Do not worry about the number you have, but try to come up with at least ten. Do not worry about putting them into any order. Once you have your list, pick the top five—the five

most important core values. Again, do not worry about prioritizing your choices. From this list of five, pick the three most important values. Finally, pick the most important core value for your organization. Repeat this exercise with all members of your organization.

5. Organizational Culture. Answer the following questions about your organization: Values—What basic values do the members of your organization embrace? Heroes—Who are the heroes of your organization? Why are they famous or infamous? What qualities do they exemplify?

6. Rites and Rituals. How do members of your organization work together? How do members of your organization play together? What actions or behaviors are recognized? How are they rewarded?

7. Four Frames of Organizations. Identify an organization of which you are a member. Describe your organization using each of the four frames of organizations in the four-frame theory of Bolman and Deal.

8. Multicultural Organizational Development. Think about the concept of multicultural organizational development. How committed is your organization to full participation by members of all cultural and social groups? How committed is your organization to ending all forms of social oppression that might exist within the organization? What could you do to increase this commitment?

9. Virtual Organizations. Think about your organization. How virtual are you? How do you use technology to interact? If you use technology in your organization, how do you use it? What has been the effect of its use? What have been the benefits and challenges associated with its use?

ADDITIONAL READINGS

Allen, K. A., & Cherrey, C. (2000). *Systemic leadership: Enriching the meaning of our work.* Lanham, MD: University Press of America.

Collins, J. (2001). *Good to great: Why some companies make the leap . . . and others don't.* New York, NY: HarperCollins.

Fisher, L. (2009). *The perfect swarm: The science of complexity in everyday life.* New York, NY: Basic Books.

Goldstein, J., Hazy, J. K., & Lichtensten, B. B. (2010). *Complexity and the nexus of leadership: Leveraging nonlinear science to create ecologies of innovation.* New York, NY: St. Martin's Press.

Schein, E. (2010). *Organizational culture and leadership* (4th ed). San Francisco, CA: Jossey-Bass.

Wall, V., & Obear, K. (2008). *Multicultural organizational development (MCOD): Exploring best practices to create socially just, inclusive campus communities.* Paper presented at the American Association of Colleges and Universities Conference, Oct. 17, 2008. http://www.aacu.org/meetings /diversityandlearning/DL2008/Resources/documents/AACUMCOD handouts2008-ObearandWall.pdf

PART IV

Making a Difference with Leadership

This final section of *Exploring Leadership* focuses on making a difference—through the change process and by using a strengths-based approach to help you and others thrive as leaders.

Over 40 years ago, futurist Alvin Toffler (1970) observed that "change is the process by which the future invades our lives" (p. 1). It is our assertion that leadership is the way we invade the future. Observing the trends around us, making meaning out of the perspectives of diverse shareholders and stakeholders on any topic, and seeking to continuously improve ourselves and our organizations leads us to be people who want to shape the future and not just have it happen to us.

Leadership is inherently about people working together toward change. People providing leadership are often called change agents; they seek to be effective in improving their organizations and addressing social issues. The first two chapters in this section explore the nature of change and the challenges for change agents. Chapter Ten, Understanding Change, explores processes for change. Chapter Eleven, Strategies for Change, examines the Social Change Model. This model advances a perspective on socially responsible leadership and the importance of collective action, coalitions, and civic engagement. This part focuses on the purpose element of the relational leadership model, illuminated by how the process orientation makes that purpose happen. It also introduces the Appreciative Inquiry process and other approaches to working with change.

Chapter Twelve, Thriving Together, focuses on how you can use a strengths-based approach to thrive as a leader and as a group, team, organization, and community. It also introduces the concept of positivity and how this perspective can be invaluable in working with others. Finally, the chapter presents various ways to stay renewed and offers reasons that this is important for leaders.

The leadership journey presented in this book started with the inward journey into yourself. Having consciousness of yourself is the most essential step toward relating effectively to others (Higher Education Research Institute, 1996). Throughout the pages of this book, you have explored leadership as a process engaging you and others in teams, communities, groups, and organizations.

It would be a mistake to end with something like "six steps to becoming an effective leader" or "ten principles of leadership for all times." Such postulates would be suspect, even ludicrous. Although we have promoted your thinking about relational leadership and strongly emphasized the importance of people working together, we encourage you to develop a personal philosophy of leadership grounded in the principles and values that will work for you in your uplifting relationships with others toward shared, positive purposes.

Heider (1985), in sharing the reflections of Lao Tzu, offers this:

Beginners acquire new theories and techniques until their minds are cluttered with options.

Advanced students forget their many options. They allow the theories and techniques that they have learned to recede into the background.

Learn to unclutter your mind. Learn to simplify your work.

As you rely less and less on knowing just what to do, your work will become more direct and more powerful. You will discover that the quality of your consciousness is more potent than any technique or theory or interpretation.

Learn how fruitful the blocked group or individual suddenly becomes when you give up trying to do just the right thing. (p. 95)

We want to end this journey by exploring how you are constructing a life you want to live, including how you view yourself working with others toward shared purposes. Engaging in leadership can be hard work. It can add pressure and stress and can require you to work hard to balance all aspects of your life. It will help you along in your journey if you can focus on the strengths and gifts you and those around you bring to whatever you are trying to accomplish. Finally, we all, as individuals, must connect our mind, body, and soul to stay renewed.

Renewal literally means to "make new again." To "re-new" through a process of individuals and their groups and organizations learning together is a dynamic undertaking. No matter how busy, no matter how stressed, no matter how discouraged, no matter how joyous, no matter how satisfied, no matter how happy, no matter how effective—individuals, groups, and organizations can thrive together by making renewal processes an essential focus.

Chapter 10

Understanding Change

Laura just took office as president of the Young Entrepreneurs Club, a student organization affiliated with the business school. She was excited to move this 300-member organization forward with an ambitious agenda of raising $100,000 to go toward student scholarships for entering business majors. Laura could see the benefits of such a scholarship in attracting academically talented students to the college. Laura wanted to use the mission of the club to make a difference in other students' lives. Applying what she learned in one of her courses, she put together a detailed business plan to share with other members at the first meeting of a new semester. Laura knew not every member would come to the first meeting, so she made only 150 copies of the business plan.

The first meeting drew only 30 members. After Laura presented her plan and asked for feedback, the members were silent and stared at Laura. Finally, a senior member spoke up and said that he doubted they would get enough of the membership to get behind this good idea because they had never done anything like this before. He feared that fewer members would come to meetings if they were expected to put this much time and energy into this plan. Another member added that she believed the college expected the club to carry out its traditional activities of sponsoring a car wash to raise money for the year-end banquet.

Laura was stunned at their reactions, because she'd expected the members to be excited about the new idea. After all, they were aspiring business majors who surely would want to gain this type of experience and successfully accomplish this goal.

> Chapter Overview

This chapter provides an overview of a major component of leadership—change. Understanding and facilitating change is a major task in the leadership process. Facilitating change is complex, fragile, exhilarating, and rewarding. This chapter provides a conceptual framework for understanding change and introduces various models of implementing change processes.

> Understanding Change

Much has changed since we wrote the last edition of this book. Change has seemingly been everywhere—from the national political happenings to the Arab Spring uprisings in the Middle East. Much of this change involved students. As the Center for Information & Research on Civic Learning & Engagement (2008) noted:

> An estimated 23 million young Americans under the age of 30 voted in the 2008 presidential election, an increase of 3.4 million compared with 2004. CIRCLE estimates that youth voter turnout rose to between 52 and 53 percent, an increase of four to five percentage points over CIRCLE's estimate based on the 2004 exit polls. The 2004 election was a strong one for youth turnout, reversing a long history of decline. If we compare 2008 with 2000, the increase in youth turnout is at least 11 percentage points. (p. 1)

We can see change all around us—we embrace some change, and we fear other types of change. In the scenario at the beginning of this chapter, Laura did not foresee or plan for the challenges of introducing change, including the resistance her idea might receive.

We no longer simply manage change, we now pursue change (Conner, 1992) and as Kotter (2008) notes, "We live in an age when change is accelerating" (p. 11). Today, change cannot be characterized along cultural dimensions—instead change strategies that are implemented in Hong Kong look very similar to change processes in Moscow. How individuals react to change may take on distinct cultural characteristics, but our ideas of how to facilitate change within organizations vary little across cultures (Conner, 1992). Losing control is a common fear of human beings and a common concern when change is introduced in organizational environments. A critical leadership task is to understand this tension and transform it into what Senge (1993) refers to as "creative tension" (p. 142).

Effective leaders approach change processes with sensitivity and the assumption that people may perceive even the smallest of changes to be monumental. Thomas Edison understood this human phenomenon well when he unveiled the electrical light bulb in 1879. He fashioned the look and intensity of these new lights after the familiar gaslights used in that era, diminishing people's fear of this unfamiliar invention (Conner, 1992, p. 101).

Change is a complex concept in the leadership process. Even the smallest of changes can be difficult to introduce and manage. Many people resist change or are fearful that a change in their work, their environment, their job, or their personal life will negatively affect them. Change disrupts the status quo—things will be different. Simply changing someone's office space can evoke feelings of uncertainty and resentment. Making personal transitions in your life can involve some type of change and often results in feelings of insecurity or disequilibrium. Moving away from home to go to college or changing your major can be exciting and scary at the same time. We often fear the unknown or are unsettled in changes to our patterns and way of life. Anthropologists who studied primitive tribes concluded that resistance to change was required to sustain social order and cohesion in groups (O'Toole, 1996). Facilitating change in the leadership process can trigger those same reactions. Healthy resistance can reveal important values and perspectives that should be honored or accommodated as change proceeds. Change can also bring about exciting possibilities, renewed energy and enthusiasm, and a deeper commitment to the goals and future of an organization.

To illustrate the complexities around change, even individuals or groups who are committed to making change might have an immunity to change due to hidden competing assumptions that become obstacles in the change process. These are moments in organizations when leaders are called upon to ask great questions around an immunity to change to help others see what is hidden and to help them learn and grow so that change can be possible. The concept of immunity to change will be explored later in this chapter.

STUDENT ESSAY

Being a leader is hard. It is the hardest thing I have ever had to do. The only thing harder than being a leader is being a leader for change. One thing that I have learned, and this might be the most important thing I have gained from this experience, is that there are two kinds of people in this world; you have your people who are catalysts for change, and your people who are roadblocks for change. You never want to be a roadblock. Be a catalyst. Be a force of action, an incredible energy that makes things happen. Change feels threatening to people, especially those who have held your position before you, so believe in yourself and nothing else matters...the roadblocks will come around.

Melanie Highbloom is a junior at University of Wisconsin-Madison and a social welfare major. She is president of her sorority, Sigma Delta Tau, a member of the Sports Business Club and a player on the UW-Madison Club Lacrosse Team.

Understanding Change from an Individual Perspective

To fully understand how organizations change, it is important first to explore how change is experienced by individuals. William Bridges (1980) and Nancy Schlossberg (1989a) offer models that are helpful in this regard. Bridges notes a difference between change and transition. A change occurs at a specific time and involves something beginning or ending. A transition cannot be pinpointed to a particular time and always begins with an ending. Transitions are much more difficult because they are psychological processes that take time to complete.

A commonly experienced example involves someone leaving an important leadership position, such as the presidency of an organization. There is a specific time when the change occurs—such as when the new president is elected or is ceremonially placed in office. For the outgoing president, the transition process of not being president any longer can be more difficult and lasts longer. This will be especially true if the person was very engaged in the leadership position. It is difficult to give up an office, especially one that has been important. The person may feel lost at first—unsure of how to spend free time, unsure of the new role in the organization, and missing the feeling of importance that goes along with being a leader.

This can be a difficult time, and the person needs to spend time there before being able to move on to a new beginning. The new beginning will also be difficult because it involves a great expenditure of physical and psychological energy. Likewise, members of the group have to get used to new leadership. They may regret the transition of the seasoned leader and be wary of new leadership. They may wait to see how the new position leader will fulfill the role before they fully engage in new directions.

Psychologist Nancy Schlossberg (1989a) notes that a life change is difficult because it impacts one's roles, relationships, routines, and assumptions about oneself. To illustrate, we will use the example of two students who care passionately about an issue and join a student organization to try to address this issue. Certainly their lives as students are impacted because this new activity has been added. New relationships are formed with other members of the organization, and their daily routines will be changed as they get more involved in the cause. Finally, their assumptions about themselves can change as they begin to make an impact.

Schlossberg (1989a) also identified four potential resources that can be used to help manage change—the situation (how you feel about the change, the timing), yourself (how you view change, your previous history of change, and so on), supports (people and resources that can be of assistance), and your strategies for coping (the steps taken to proactively engage the change). Understanding how change impacts you and others around you will help you be a more successful leader of change.

Every leader faces challenges and obstacles in facilitating and managing change, yet change processes are not rule bound, and there is no single tested approach that can guarantee successful change efforts. To understand how change is facilitated is to understand how human transformations take place (Bridges, 2003; Conner, 1992). As you prepare to facilitate change, you will be well served if you reflect on patterns of human behavior and how to respond to people's reactions to change. Understanding others is a primary step in any change management approach. Human beings, in general, want to control their environments, and some experience an even greater need to be in control of their surroundings. Connor (1992) comments that "the single most important factor to managing change successfully is the degree to which people demonstrate resilience: the capacity to absorb high levels of change while displaying minimal dysfunctional behavior" (p. 6).

Understanding those expectations is a part of understanding how to facilitate change. O'Toole (1996) offers a few hypotheses as to why people are resistant to change:

1. *Satisfaction*: Being satisfied with the status quo. You might hear this often in your organizations: "We've never done it that way before, so why do we need to change?" That is a clear sign of a change-resistant organizational response.

2. *Fear*: People fear the unknown. Risk-taking behaviors, like doubling your membership dues without knowing what impact that will have on recruiting new members, raises fear of unknown consequences or the fear of failure.

3. *Self-Interest*: Even if the change benefits others, it may alter their status or perks, so they resist. Sometimes change means giving up power or authority to achieve a particular result. For example, an individual interested in running for chair of an organization might resist a proposed change to create a cochair structure.

4. *Lack of Self-Confidence*: Change makes us vulnerable and requires confidence to inspire others to see the possibilities. Lack of confidence can deter a group from charting a new territory.

5. *Myopia*: Not being able to see beyond the present. Historian John Lukacs describes myopia this way: "when people do not see something, this often means that they do not wish to see it—a condition that may be comfortable and profitable to them" (as cited by O'Toole, 1996, p. 163).

6. *Habit*: Habits can be positive, but they can also inhibit change, causing groups to be driven by traditions, customs, and patterns. For example, it might be a habit for the Latino

Student Organization to recruit new members in the spring, but it might be a better practice, yielding more members, if recruitment took place in the fall.

How we learn and how we acquire information have changed dramatically over the last decade—with first the

STUDENT ESSAY ◆

In the words of Peter Senge, "people don't resist change. They resist being changed." Whether it is with an organization, job, leadership position, or personally, change is inevitable. But why is it so hard to do? As a graduate assistant within Student Involvement and Leadership, I have gained experience in leading change and accepting change. Within leading change, there are two things I feel that need to happen for it to be successful; trusting relationships should be built and individual input should be considered; in my opinion this promotes inclusiveness. In building trusting relationships, I have witnessed how people successfully cooperate with change. In regards to individual input, if people feel involved in decision making, they are included in the change process and are more likely to view the change positively. For example, a way that we encourage our students in leading change is through our post surveys for SIL programs. Students rate the program and give their input on what can make it better. Not only does it make SIL programs better, but it increases student participation, because students want to see the changes made.

Ashley Nicole Williams is a graduate of the University of Florida. She is currently a graduate assistant in the Student Involvement and Leadership office at Florida Atlantic University where she is pursing a masters in higher educational leadership. She is a proud member of Golden Key International Honour Society and Zeta Phi Beta Sorority, Incorporated.

Internet, then the advancement of websites and email communications, and now tweeting and blogs. Information is
instantaneous on the smart phone. These and other changes
have impacted how change is experienced by individuals and
how change is facilitated at organizational and community levels.

Immunity to Change

Understanding human behavior in the context of change is vital
in facilitating any type of change process. In addition to resistance
to change, some individuals have what Kegan and Lahey (2009)
refer to as, "immunity to change." It is not uncommon to encounter
situations in which team members commit to a change process, but
yet somehow still exhibit behaviors that prevent them from moving
the change process forward.

Unintentionally, some people might have a hidden block or
competing commitment that is an obstacle for making change
happen. For example, take the case of Alex, who is the public
relations coordinator for his group. Alex is excited about creating
a new program for his organization and is eager to implement the
plan, which includes involving members from the committee
he chairs. In the middle of implementing the group's plan, Joe
complained to the organization's president that a number of
his committee members stopped showing up to meetings. In
exploring with Alex some reasons why this was happening, the
president of the organization and Alex realized that Alex was
withholding information from the committee members and then
started doing most of the work himself. Alex's own immunity
to change was that he did not want to entrust his committee
members to carry out their parts of the project, so he stopped

communicating information and started to do the work on his own. Alex realized he was exhibiting this behavior because he feared that if he delegated some authority, autonomy, and power to the group he would lose control over the process.

This example of an immunity to change is one that opens up further growth and development in Alex's case and also provides deeper understanding and insights for leaders to explore with others who might openly support a change process, yet exhibit behaviors that prevent the group from moving forward (Kegan & Lahey, 2009). Kegan and Lahey (2009) use the immunity metaphor from the medical field to illustrate that personal and organizational strength and growth can emerge from an immunity to change. In the case of Alex, he realized his behavior was actually the obstacle in the change process that negatively impacted his committee members. Kegan and Lahey refer to this behavior as hidden competing commitments.

When taking notice of these hidden competing commitments, it opens Alex up for ways in which he can adapt his own behavior and be more open to trusting that his committee members will achieve results. Simply stated, sometimes it is necessary for individuals or a whole group to examine behaviors that might be inhibiting the group from accomplishing an intended change. Too often, groups dive right into a change process and only begin to analyze why the change process did not work after the fact, instead of asking others along the way about what was happening for them that prevented movement toward the organization's change. This is another example of the importance for leaders to sit back and ask great questions versus placing blame on others when goals are not accomplished or the group does not successfully implement a change initiative.

In addressing the immunity to change, there are three processes leaders and groups can use in uncovering hidden competing commitments (Kegan & Lahey, 2009):

1. Guide the group using questions to uncover the hidden commitments.
2. Ask individuals or members to identify what is at the core of their hidden commitments (in Alex's case, it was his assumption that work would not get done unless he completed it himself).
3. Engage the individual or group members to start the process of changing their own behavior so that the group can move toward facilitating the intended change for the organization.

The immunity to change process is complex and takes time. The power of this model is understanding hidden and competing commitments that can block change efforts. The following are questions you can use to help others uncover their competing commitments (Kegan & Lahey, 2001):

1. What would you like to see changed so that you can be more effective in this organization, team, or group? (Note: this will typically elicit complaints, which are useful to know about and use as a springboard toward personal growth and change.)
2. What commitments does your complaint imply? For example, if someone complains that information is not available to everyone to make good decisions, the commitment implies a belief in open and transparent community.

3. What are you doing, or not doing, that is keeping your commitment from being more fully realized? (these could be undermining behaviors that might be unintended—holding onto information or not open to receiving feedback). This question will allow you to understand why others are behaving in a way that undermines their success.

4. If you imagine doing the opposite of the undermining behavior (the response to question 3), do you detect in yourself any discomfort, worry, or fear? An example of a response from Alex might be fearing that committee members would not make good decisions on their own.

5. By engaging in this undermining behavior, what worrisome outcome are you committed to preventing? The response to this question is the competing commitment. In Alex's case, his response might be that he was protecting himself from making sure his committee did not make decisions that were not acceptable to him or would live up to his standards. (pp. 87–88)

These competing commitments should be viewed as opportunities for others to learn and grow and not has weaknesses. What often emerges under these competing commitments is a basic human response of self-protection. Kegan and Lahey (2009) refer to these responses as the big assumptions or "deeply rooted beliefs about themselves and the world around them" (p. 88). Big assumptions "may be true, and they may not be, but as long as we simply assume they are true, we are blind even to the question itself (Kegan & Lahey, 2009, p. 58).

Big assumptions are like rationalizations and competing commitments arise from these big assumptions. In the case of Alex, his big assumption is that his committee was not as experienced or as knowledgeable as he to fully execute a plan, so he assumed it would be best to do it himself and not waste others' time. Big assumptions are like perceptions that become people's realities. The key is to identify those big assumptions, begin understanding their complexities, and then assist others in making sense of those competing commitments so that they can overcome their own immunity to change.

The following are steps that can be used in questioning the big assumptions (Kegan & Lahey, 2001):

1. *Notice and record the current behavior*—be aware of actions in relation to your big assumptions; identify how these assumptions impact you.
2. *Look for contrary evidence*—identify experience that would question your big assumptions.
3. *Explore the history*—how and when did these assumptions first take place in your life? What were some of the critical turning points around these assumptions? (Understand the circumstance(s) that formed these assumptions.)
4. *Test the assumption*—pick one of your big assumptions and begin to identify behavior changes would give you accurate information about the validity of your big assumption.
   You might receive information that is counter to your big assumption. The point of testing your assumption is to start to get information about it if you started to make incremental changes.
5. *Evaluate the results*—identify ways to be more effective based on the results from testing your own assumption. (pp. 88–91)

Understanding why others, or even yourself, are immune to change can unleash obstacles in the change process and promote greater growth and learning for individuals and for groups as a whole. The immunity to change process is complex and takes time. In the long term, this process can position your group well to achieving its end goals in working to implement change.

Borrowing from the work of Kübler-Ross (1970), who studied human reactions to the death and dying process, we can understand people's reactions to negative change or to changes they cannot control, such as discontinuing a popular product, downsizing an organization, or changing the name or identity of an organization (Conner, 1992). Conner expanded Kübler-Ross's five-stage model by adding three phases:

Phase 1: *Stability*: the present state

Phase 2: *Immobilization*: shock or paralysis to initial change

Phase 3: *Denial*: change-related information is ignored or not accepted as reality

Phase 4: *Anger*: frustration and anger as a reaction to change and often directed to those most supportive of the change effort

Phase 5: *Bargaining*: negotiation to avoid pending change, signifying that the person can no longer deny the change process

Phase 6: *Depression*: a typical response to negatively perceived change, including disengagement and a decrease in physical and emotional energy

Phase 7: *Testing*: regaining a sense of control and seeking out new ways to redefine goals

Phase 8: *Acceptance*: change is responded to realistically, even though individuals may still be adverse to the change. (pp. 132–134)

Here's a scenario of a change effort with corresponding responses. The Liberal Arts School at State University decided that holding two commencements each year, one in December and one in May, was expensive and inefficient, so the dean announced a plan to eliminate the December ceremony. After all, twice as many students graduated at the end of the spring semester as at the end of fall semester. Alumni, parents of current students, the Liberal Arts Parents' Club, graduating students, and some faculty were stunned when they received the information about this change (immobilization). They wanted to see the fall graduation tradition continue (stability). Members of each of these groups emailed the dean saying that it would be impossible to expect the fall graduates and their families to come back to campus for the spring semester graduation after they had been gone for a semester (denial). Others wrote emails and letters in protest to the president (anger).

The Parents' Club banded together and offered to write other parents and alumni asking them to consider making financial donations to help pay for the fall graduation ceremony (bargaining). After several attempts to organize these and other efforts, the parents gave up because the dean's office was not responding to their proposals and they began to feel like they were wasting their time and energy (depression). Two months later, the leadership of the Parents' Club began to plan a separate fall reception for the graduates as a way to give those seniors special recognition at the time of their graduation (testing). The Dean's Office collaborated with the club members to sponsor the reception, which was less expensive and involved less staff effort. At the end of the first reception, several parents and graduating seniors commented on how they enjoyed the smaller, intimate environment while still having the opportunity to participate in the annual spring event (acceptance).

These eight phases represent human reaction to perceived negative changes. These phases are fluid and elastic—they are not lockstep and rigid. Effective change agents pay attention to the negative reactions to change and help others move through these stages to regain control and restore engagement and productivity.

Although it is normal to respond to negative change with phases that mirror a death and dying process, some may initially respond to a perceived positive change, then later resist this change. For example, some may initially perceive a company's merger with another as positive, based on little knowledge or facts. Then concern or doubt begins to emerge in the informed pessimism level. If this level of tolerance is exceeded, then "checking out" behavior begins to emerge and people withdraw from the change.

Conner (1992) offers five phases of positive response to change, illustrated in Figure 10.1:

Phase 1: Uninformed optimism
Phase 2: Informed pessimism
Phase 3: Hopeful realism
Phase 4: Informed optimism
Phase 5: Completion

Starting a new organization sometimes can evoke a positive response to change (uninformed optimism). Initially, individuals are excited about the possibilities of simply creating something new; then reality begins to sink in (informed pessimism) as

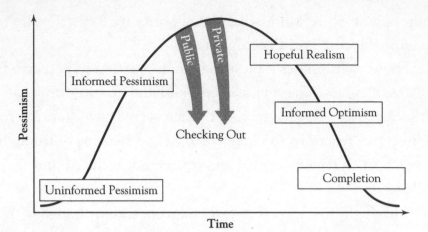

Figure 10.1   **Conner's Five Phases of Positive Response to Change**

Source: Managing at the Speed of Change by Daryl R. Conner, Copyright © 1992 by O. S. Resources, Inc. Used by permission of Villard Books, a division of Random House, Inc.

people begin to wonder if the idea will attract enough interest. Once individuals begin to see the opportunities and benefits this new organization can offer, they become more confident (hopeful realism). The founders of the group may begin to test the idea for launching the new entity by doing some focus groups and web surveys. The results show that a majority of people are interested and would join such an organization, motivating the founders to move forward with excitement and energy (informed optimism). The planning group remains focused on setting up the structure for the new organization and recruiting new members (completion).

Change also can be understood by examining the dimensions of depth and pervasiveness of the intended change (Eckel, Hill, & Green, 1998). As shown in Figure 10.2, "Depth focuses on how profoundly the change affects behavior or alters structures. The deeper the change, the more it is infused into the

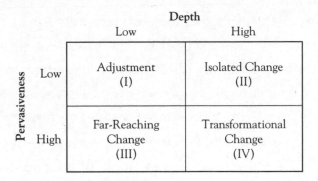

Figure 10.2 **The Typology of Change**

Source: Reproduced with permission of the American Council on Education from Eckel, Hill, & Green (1998), p. 5.

daily lives of those affected by it" (p. 4). A deep change results in changing patterns, behaviors, culture, and attitudes. When an organization decides to transform its mission from a social and recreational one to a service-based organization, deep change will follow. The values, patterns, behaviors, and culture will be transformed if the change effort is effective. "Pervasiveness refers to the extent to which the change is far-reaching within the institution. The more pervasive the change, the more it crosses unit boundaries and touches different parts of the institution" (p. 4). For example, if a university or college decides to require all professors and instructors to administer student course evaluations and also requires that those evaluation results be made public, pervasive change in the academic culture is a potential and expected outcome.

This matrix identifies four types of institutional change, which could overlap with each other: adjustment, isolated change, far-reaching change, and transformational change. Changes of the first type, in quadrant one, are described as adjustment changes, which are minor alterations. If an organization changed its membership requirement in its recruitment policy from a 3.0 GPA to a 3.1 GPA for prospective members, that would be an adjustment type change, just a type of tinkering. If a subcommittee of an organization wants to change its fundraising activity, which only the subcommittee participates in, that is a type of isolated change because it does not impact the rest of the organization. An example of a far-reaching change might be when an organization decides to change its name. The impact will be pervasive in that a new identity will develop, with marketing implications, but the name change most likely will not result in deep change. The fourth quadrant of transformational change is significant and includes both deep and pervasive changes. Transforming the Multicultural Student Organization into a Multicultural Student Union with a building, staff, strategic plan, and academic programs is an example of transformational change.

The Tipping Point

Some changes can be incremental, finite, and temporary; others are transforming, widespread, and monumental. Changes that usher in new fads, impact demographics, introduce new phenomena, or result in contagious behaviors can have a dramatic tipping effect. Malcolm Gladwell (2002) uses social epidemics to examine tipping points, which he defines as "that moment in an epidemic when everything can change all at once" (p. 9). The tipping point happens when something unique or unknown becomes common. Gladwell describes the tipping point of change using three characteristics: (1) the emergence of a trend, idea, a crime wave, and the like is contagious—these spread like viruses do; (2) little changes can have big effects; and (3) change happens in one dramatic moment rather than gradually. The term "Tipping Point" quickly became part of our common language, even becoming the name of a CD put out by The Roots in 2004.

Gladwell (2002) describes three agents of change that can tip an epidemic: (1) the law of the few, (2) the stickiness factor, and (3) the power of context. Often, student organization leaders reflect that 20% of the members do 80% of the work. You may think this same effect occurs in group projects in academic courses. This is the law of the few—a disproportionate number of people cause a tipping point change to occur.

Marketing messages illustrate the importance of the stickiness factor—how to create a lasting message so that people will buy your product. Jingles on the television or radio are designed to create the stickiness factor. Commercials during the Super Bowl game are dependent upon this to the point that they are now analyzed during postgame commentaries: Which commercial did you like the best? Universities and colleges create their own marketing messages—the University of Maryland at Baltimore Campus markets itself as an honors college, while New Century College at George Mason University uses the motto "Connecting the classroom to the world." They use this strategy as a way to brand their identity so that the general public will associate a motto with their institution, making that message unforgettable.

The power of context, Gladwell's (2002) third agent of change, points to understanding the smallest of details in people's immediate environment. Franklin D. Roosevelt's famous fireside chats are an example of the power of context. During that era, in the early 1930s, families valued gathering around the radio to listen to music and receive the news of the day. FDR understood that environment well and exploited it as a way to reach out to the American public and deliver his message. College and university websites offer that same common medium of disseminating information and messages to constituencies. Major renovations of student union buildings often are designed with the power of context in mind—a design that will consistently attract students to the building for educational, recreational, cultural, and social purposes.

Sudden change is at the core of the tipping point concept (Gladwell, 2002). The concept of "sudden change" was first introduced in the 1970s during White flight to the suburbs in the American Northeast. For example, sociologists predicted that a White neighborhood would tip when enough African Americans had moved into it to make up approximately 20% of households, causing Whites to begin moving out. "The tipping point is the moment of critic mass, the threshold, the boiling point" (Gladwell, p. 12). The tipping point is "where the unexpected becomes expected, where radical change is more than possibility" (p. 14).

Predicting the future is impossible and sometimes predicted tipping points do not occur. In 2006, the world was wondering whether or not the avian flu—originating in wild birds and spread to domesticated fowl, from which its mutations have infected humans—would reach a tipping point, causing a pandemic that could strike millions of people around the world. Luckily this did not happen and as of July 2006 only 131 people had died from this strain of flu (small event). In the meantime, as a precaution the U.S. Government Homeland

Security Council published a 233 page "National Strategy for Pandemic Influenza Implementation Plan" in May 2006 (http://www.flu.gov/planning-preparedness/federal/pandemic-influenza-implementation.pdf).

Technology is a powerful example for understanding the tipping point phenomenon. In recent years, cell phones have replaced land lines, laptop computers have replaced desktops, and in August 2012 the UK branch of Amazon reported selling more e-books than hardbacks and paperbacks combined. Television viewing has also changed dramatically in recent years, with viewers no longer locked into watching shows at the times they are offered instead using cable "On Demand" and services like Netflix and Hulu to watch almost anything when they want.

Change and Social Media

We could not have a chapter on Change without mentioning one of the greatest changes we have experienced in our society—the changes brought about by the use of social media. The profound role that social media has played, and continues to play in our lives has impacted leadership, organizations, and change around the world. Howard and Hussain (2011) discuss the profound role that social media had on the Arab Spring. Brionesa, Kucha, Liu, and Jin (2011) describe how the Red Cross uses a wide variety of social media to connect with and inform its various constituencies.

Consider the amazing changes we have experienced in the use of technology. Apple is now the single largest U.S. company with a vast international market. As we write this new edition,

Google and Apple control 85% of the global smartphone market. As the 2012 PEW Internet & American Life Project reports,

> As of September 2012, 85% of American adults have a cell phone, and 45% have a smartphone. As of early 2012, 58% have a desktop computer, 61% have a laptop, 18% own an e-book reader, and 18% have a tablet computer. (http://pewinternet.org/Static-Pages/Trend-Data-(Adults)/Device-Ownership.aspx)

Ownership of laptops passed that of desktops in approximately May 2011. Look around. When was the last time you or a fellow student purchased a desktop computer?

Sticking and Switching

In *Made to Stick*, Chip and Dan Heath (2007) offer reasons that some new ideas "stick" and remain in use while others disappear. They believe that new ideas must be Simple, Unexpected (able to get and hold attention), Concrete, Credible, Emotional (make people care), and use Stories (to get people to act). These ideas, although seemingly commonplace, are often overlooked when new ideas are introduced to a team, organization, or community. It pays to take the additional time needed to make your new idea as simple as possible and as concrete and specific as possible. If you can make others care through an emotional element, that helps an idea stick, as does being able to use Stories to motivate people to act.

In *Switch*, Heath and Heath (2010) offer three surprising ideas about change: "What looks like resistance is often lack of clarity . . . What looks like laziness is often exhaustion . . . What looks like a people problem is often a situation problem" (pp. 17–18). They also go on to expand on their ideas from *Made to Stick* and note that if you want to change behavior you must provide "crystal clear direction" and "engage people's emotional side," and "to change someone's behavior you've got to change that person's situation" (pp. 4, 17).

> Facilitating Change

Core values are a fundamental driving factor in leading successful change efforts. Social movement leaders focused on great values such as equality and freedom as the ultimate goal of effecting change (O'Toole, 1996). Their leadership was tied to deep beliefs in greater ideals, and their focus on change was founded on those same core values. Introducing change for the sake of change is contrary to facilitating change based on fundamental values. In the movie *Brubaker* an ambitious warden attempted to transform a corrupt prison by making deep changes that threatened internal and external political coalitions. He was met with resistance at every stage until finally his most trusted ally came to him with a proposition that if he stopped, he would get the resources to change the physical conditions inside the prison. Brubaker responded, "Every warden puts new paint on the walls" (Quinn, 1996, p. 122). He went on to argue that compromising on principles or core values would not lead to deep change for this troubled prison.

The same is true in student organizations. Organizations that struggle with retaining members think that if they change their logo, give everyone free T-shirts, or serve food at meetings that will result in a more committed membership. Following the

Brubaker example, members will want to stay involved in a group if they find meaning and purpose or feel a sense of affiliation beyond a T-shirt or free food at an event.

A challenge for leaders as they facilitate major change is to help others cope with their uncertainties and fears (Quinn, 2004). In attempting to facilitate change, the attitude of the leader(s) can have a huge impact. As Rubin, Dierdorff, Bommer, and Baldwin (2009) have found, if the leader(s) are cynical about change, participants in the organization will mirror these attitudes and be cynical about change. Leaders who were cynical about change were also viewed as less effective by supervisors. In a related finding, Kellerman (2004) notes that "Bad leadership falls into two categories: bad as in ineffective and bad as in unethical" (p. 32). This bad leadership takes the form of leaders being incompetent, rigid, intemperate, callous, corrupt, insular, or evil.

Facilitating deep change means helping people out of their comfort zones and supporting them as they try out new behaviors. It also requires leaders and members to provide support for each other as they make these transitions. Some will feel a sense of loss when a new change is introduced and an old practice or tradition is put to rest. Others may feel that they will lose status or will feel less significant as a result of a new arrangement. In Chapter Nine we presented similar concepts to support the concept of organizational renewal. Bridges (1991) offers seven approaches that can be used to assist organizations and people through transitions:

1. Explain that this is a time to think outside of the box and to let go of old assumptions and ways of thinking about the organization. Facilitators of change processes should model this

behavior by talking about how they too will be affected by changes and how they will think differently about their roles and practices.

2. Create opportunities or settings for everyone involved to engage in thinking differently about the organization or activity. Organize a retreat or focus group meetings to involve others in the initial stages of the change process before decisions are made.

3. Provide information or training on how to think outside of the box and how to facilitate innovation. Asking members or individuals to make changes does not assume that they are prepared for the creative process that follows.

4. Model and encourage risk taking and experimentation. People will need to feel secure and supported when they test new ideas or put new practices in place.

5. View mistakes and losses as learning opportunities and as a time for innovation. Facilitators of change will encourage people to stretch their thinking when they experience failure.

6. Encourage everyone to break through barriers or ruts by brainstorming new solutions, new ideas, or new ways of thinking about existing problems.

7. Persuade the group to be comfortable with ambiguity and uncertainty while explaining that they are in a temporary state until more clarity and direction can be achieved. Otherwise, people might have a tendency to move too quickly to solutions or closure in the process as a way to maintain their comfort zone of equilibrium and security. (pp. 43–44)

STUDENT ESSAY

Leading Change by Change is inevitable. Change is hard, but change is needed to make a difference. I came into a position of leadership where change was already is process and change needed to be instigated. Being a leader of change is never an easy task, in fact it presents opportunities for things to take a wrong turn, but nonetheless the risk of it being the catalyst to the beginning of something incredible is a risk I was willing to take. In turn, the change that occurred benefitted hundreds if not thousands of students within my position as Director of the Council of Student Organizations at my university. The creation of a Student Organization Club House went down in history as a momentous occasion and breakthrough for students on campus, providing them with resources galore. This was an example of a change that turned into something incredible. It was difficult at times, getting everyone on board, figuring out logistics and beginning the foundation of policies for the space, but in the end the result outweighed the difficulty and the change that occurred set up the entity of the Council of Student Organizations for future success.

Ella Bella Ariela Tepper is an undergraduate sociology major at Florida Atlantic University. She is a member of Sigma Kappa Sorority, Ballroom of FAU, and Sigma Alpha Iota Professional Women's Music Fraternity. She has served in many leadership roles within student government including house representative, director of the Council of Student Organizations, and currently serves as campus governor.

Any type of major or deep change does not come easy and does not happen overnight, at least in those changes where change has been successful. John P. Kotter, a management professor and scholar at Harvard Business School, has studied change processes in major companies and nonprofit organizations. Kotter (1996) formulated an eight-stage, sequential change model based on his research and insights of organizations who successfully achieved organizational transformations. Kotter's model is presented in Figure 10.3.

This model is sequential, but multiple phases can occur at the same time. The steps in this model build on one another, so it is important not to skip stages or phases when they become too time-consuming or challenging. Kotter and Cohen (2002) adapted this model based on new research about these eight stages. These researchers found that the core factor of organizational change is about changing people's behavior and not simply the structures, rules, systems, or culture. What they gleaned from their study of 130 organizations and 400 people is that "people change what they do less because they are given analysis that shifts their thinking than because they are shown a truth that influences their feelings" (p. 1). Here are the four major lessons learned:

1. Successful organizations know how to seize opportunities and avoid hazards. They recognize that taking bigger risks is associated with bigger wins and that small, gradual improvements are not enough.
2. Successful change processes flow in the eight-stage model until a culture is created that allows new behaviors to stick.
3. The core challenge and focus in each of the eight stages is changing people's behavior—what people do.
4. Change agents need to help others see and feel the emotions associated with a change effort. "The flow of see-feel-change is more powerful than that of analysis-think-change" (p. 2). This pattern of see-feel-change allows people to see the problems when they are presented vividly and visually, feel the

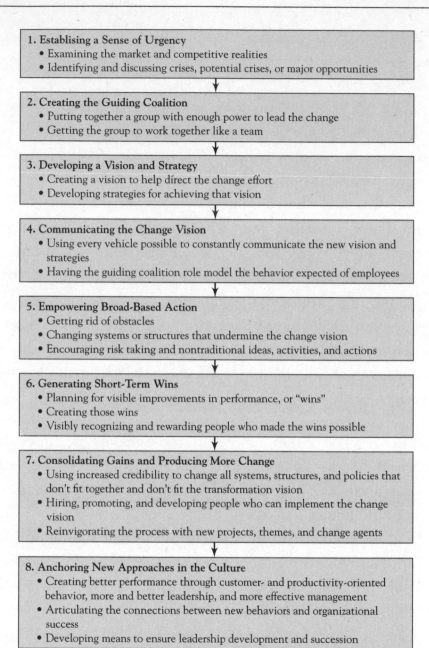

Figure 10.3 **The Eight-Stage Process of Creating Major Change**

Source: Reprinted by permission of *Harvard Business Review* from "Leading change: Why transformation efforts fail" by J. Kotter, 73, 1995. Copyright 1995 by the President and Fellows of Harvard College; all rights reserved.

negative emotions that are getting in the way and increase the positive feelings that change can create, and change or reinforce new behaviors (such as being less complacent, devoting more effort to achieve the vision, and so on).

The following chart of the eight-step model of change (Table 10.1) illustrates the importance of new behaviors at every stage (Kotter & Cohen, 2002, p. 7). These eight action steps are embedded in the dimensions of the Relational Leadership Model (RLM).

Before a change effort can be realized, it is critical to make a commitment to understand both change and the human responses to change. Too often, facilitators of change skip this important step and launch right into action. What can result from that omission is a chaotic state that may not allow an organization to achieve its results. The message is to be thoughtful and reflective as you plan a change effort. Anticipating and understanding human responses to change can lead to healthier and more meaningful processes. This approach calls for initiators of change to be empathetic, compassionate, and thoughtful while also acting with clarity, purpose, and vision.

A Sense of Urgency

No matter what approach you take to trying to implement change, you must first establish a sense of urgency. This makes complete sense. Change is hard. People generally like things the way they are so there must be compelling reasons to make changes in your life, in your organizations, in your communities.

Table 10.1   **The Eight Steps for Large-Scale Change Related to the Relational Leadership Model**

Step	Action	New Behavior
1	Increase urgency	People start telling each other, "Let's go, we need to change things!" (RLM—Purpose)
2	Build the guiding team	A group powerful enough to guide a big change is formed, and they start to work together well (RLM—Inclusive, Process)
3	Get the vision right	The guiding team develops the right vision and strategy for the change effort (RLM—Purpose and Ethical)
4	Communicate for buy-in	People begin to buy into the change, and this shows in their behavior (RLM—Purpose)
5	Empower action	More people feel able to act, and do act, on the vision (RLM—Empowering)
6	Create short-term wins	Momentum builds as people try to fulfill the vision, while fewer and fewer resist change (RLM—Process)
7	Don't let up	People make wave after wave of changes until the vision is fulfilled (RLM—Purpose)
8	Make change stick	New and winning behavior continues despite the pull of tradition, turnover of change leaders, and the like (RLM—Process)

As Kotter (2008) notes, "We are much too complacent. And we don't even know it" (p. 1). In order for this sense of urgency to really take hold you must engage not only the mind, but also the heart (Kotter, 2008). To be successful in establishing this sense of urgency, Kotter (2008) suggests the following in Exhibit 10.1 (pp. 60–61).

Exhibit 10.1: Increasing a True Sense of Urgency

1. Bring the Outside In
   - Reconnect internal reality with external opportunities and hazards.
   - Bring in emotionally compelling data, people, video, sites, and sounds.
2. Behave with Urgency Every Day
   - Never act content, anxious, or angry
   - Demonstrate your own sense of urgency always in meetings, one-on-one interactions, memos, and e-mail and do so as visibly as possible to as many people as possible.
3. Find Opportunity in Crises
   - Always be alert to see if crises can be a friend, not just a dreadful enemy in order to destroy complacency.
   - Proceed with caution, and never be naïve, since crises can be deadly.
4. Deal with the No-Nos
   - Remove or neutralize all the relentless urgency-killers, people who are not skeptics but are determined to keep a group complacent or, if needed, to create destructive urgency.

> Social Entrepreneurship and Social Innovation

Two concepts that have recently come into popularity as they describe social change and efforts to make the world a better place are social entrepreneurship and social innovation. Daniel Bornstein (2007) defines social entrepreneurs as "Transformative forces: people with new ideas to address major problems who are relentless in pursuit of their visions, people who will not take 'no' for an answer, who will not give up until they have spread their ideas as far as they possibly can" (pp. 1–2). He also notes, "Social entrepreneurship is not about a few extraordinary people saving the day for everyone else. At its deepest level it is about revealing possibilities that are currently unseen and releasing the capacity within each person to reshape a part of the world" (p. xvi). Social entrepreneurs are of all ages and are currently operating around the world in small rural areas and large cities. For example, Teach for America, founded by Wendy Kopp in 1990, has reached over 3,000,000 children through the efforts of its over 33,000 participants.

Bornstein (2007) has identified six qualities of social entrepreneurs (Exhibit 10.2).

Exhibit 10.2: Six Qualities of Successful Social Entrepreneurs

1. Willingness to self-correct
2. Willingness to share credit
3. Willingness to break free of established structures

4. Willingness to cross disciplinary boundaries
5. Willingness to work quietly
6. Strong ethical impetus

(Bornstein, 2007)

A related concept is social innovation, defined by Phills Jr., Deiglmeier, and Miller (2008) as "A novel solution to a social problem that is more effective, efficient, sustainable, or just than existing solutions and for which the value created accrues primarily to society as a whole rather than private individuals" (p. 34). Imagine a social problem or issue facing your campus, community, or region. What might be some creative ways to start to work on addressing these issues? At the University of Oregon and other institutions, students can apply for microgrants (often between $100-$1000) to be used to support community service projects.

We believe that these concepts, and the foundational beliefs behind them, offer much as we think about leadership, organizations, and change. They offer evidence that the world can be made better by people at all levels working together in a wide variety of ways. And they offer hope—hope that we are not powerless in the face of what can seem to be insurmountable challenges and difficulties.

> The world needs more social innovation—and so all who aspire to solve the world's most vexing problems—entrepreneurs, leaders, managers, activists, and change agents—regardless of whether they come from the world of business, government, or nonprofits, must shed old patterns of isolation, paternalism, and antagonism and strive to understand, embrace, and leverage cross-sector dynamics to find new ways of creating social value. (Phills Jr., Deiglmeier, & Miller, 2008, p. 43)

> What's Next?

The following chapter will describe various strategies for change, moving from understanding change to implementing change. You will learn about the importance of engaging others outside your organization through coalition building and how the Social Change Model of Leadership can influence change processes. We will also discuss the role of social media in the change process.

> Chapter Activities

1. Why is change important in the leadership process? What are the challenges of facilitating change?
2. What are some obstacles you might face in facilitating change? What are some reasons why some people are resistant to change?
3. Think of an experience in which a successful change effort took place. What factors in the organization or community environment led to successful change? What did the leaders and members do to prepare for change efforts? How were people aligned with the change?
4. Identify your own competing commitments outlined by Kegan and Lahey and respond to the five questions presented in this chapter on uncovering your competing commitments.
5. Consider an organization you're involved in. What one major change can be made and why? Describe how you could use each of the components of the RLM to facilitate change.
6. Why is it important for organizations to be flexible and open to change? What happens to organizations that are resistant to change?

7. What are the root causes of inertia in organizations?

8. Why is it that some ideas or behaviors or products start epidemics and others don't? What can you do to start a social epidemic of your own?

9. Consider the concepts of social entrepreneurship and social innovation. About what cause(s) are you passionate enough to consider working on them through these sorts of ways? How might you go about beginning?

ADDITIONAL READINGS

Bornstein, D. (2007). *How to change the world: Social entrepreneurs and the power of new ideas* (Updated edition). New York, NY: Oxford University Press.

Heath, C., & Heath, D. (2007). *Made to stick: Why some ideas survive and others die*. New York, NY: Random House.

Heath, C., & Heath, D. (2010). Switch: *How to change things when change is hard*. New York, NY: Random House.

Kegan, R., & Lahey, L. L. (2009). *Immunity to change: How to overcome it and unlock the potential in yourself and your organization*. Boston, MA: Harvard Business Press.

Kotter, J. P. (2008). A *sense of urgency*. Cambridge, MA: Harvard University Press.

Chapter 11

Strategies for Change

Meredith is a first-year biology major interested in environmental issues. She recently became concerned about how campus labs dispose of used chemicals. She began reading about the concept of "green biology," a more environmentally friendly approach to the discipline. She shared her concerns with a few classmates—some who were receptive and others who were not concerned at all. She approached her introductory biology course instructor about it, and he said that, although interested, he didn't have time to work on the issue. Meredith is becoming more and more concerned about this issue but is unsure what to do next. She's just a student—what can she do? Where can she go? Who can she talk to? How can she get others interested in this issue? Consider, too, any of the following situations:

- Jun and her suitemates have become concerned about a recent rise in the number of assaults against women on campus. One was in the parking lot behind their residence hall. They have decided to do something about it.

- Samuel decided to become active in the upcoming national election and has joined an on-campus group supporting the candidate of his choice.
- Tamela has worked twenty hours a week at the same accounting firm since she was a junior in high school. The firm is located a block from an elementary school with a growing proportion of children on the free or reduced-price lunch program and increasing numbers being raised by grandparents. She thinks the firm has an obligation, as a community neighbor, to partner with the school in some way to support those children.

In short, these students have gotten excited about an issue and want to do something to make the situation better. It could be an environmental issue, political issue, or social justice issue. What do you do? Where do you begin? How do you get others excited about this issue? What strategies might you use to make this change happen? What does it mean to be a change agent?

❯ Chapter Overview

In Chapter Ten you learned about the change process. In this chapter we will build on that change material and introduce strategies you can use to implement change. The chapter begins with a discussion of issues involved in individual change and moves on to present different perspectives on organizational change. The Social Change Model of Leadership Development is also presented in this chapter.

> Reflections on Change

The situations just described are examples of the many change efforts that are happening every day on campuses throughout the world. As Raelin (2003) notes, "An organization or a community is always in motion" (p. 155). Political issues, environmental issues, curricular issues, social justice issues, and numerous other issues are being engaged in from all sides; no single perspective has a monopoly on student support or action.

We believe that change is an essential part of leadership. Recall the definition from Chapter Three: Leadership is a relational and ethical process of people together attempting to accomplish positive change. From our perspective, maintaining the status quo is not leadership because it does not involve change or movement toward a shared purpose.

Yet, if we know anything about change, we know that change is difficult. Change is hard at any and every level— individual, team, organizational, institutional, societal. As labor organizer Saul Alinsky said, "Change means movement; movement means friction; friction means heat; heat means controversy" (Chambers & Cowan, 2004, p. 31). Teams, organizations, and institutions, like individuals, are the way they are for a number and variety of complicated reasons. These reasons may or may not make sense to persons within the groups and will make no sense at all to some outsiders. Leading change can seem impossible, yet it must be done. Raelin (2003) describes it this way:

> Change inevitably translates into letting go of old and safe ways of doing things. People and groups react differently to this tran. process, often depending upon their psychological security. H

people overcome the losses typically associated with change can serve as an important contribution on the part of change agents. (p. 160)

We explored some of those issues of transition in Chapter Ten. Anthropologist Margaret Mead said, "Never doubt that a small group of thoughtful, committed citizens can change the world; indeed it is the only thing that ever has" (cited in Mathews, 1994, p. 119). Individuals who decide to engage fully in their group or communities and join with others around common needs can make a difference. As Morton (1995) notes, "Change . . . comes about when otherwise ordinary people find way(s) to bring their values, their actions, and their world into closer alignment with each other" (p. 28). Making a difference may require that several groups form coalitions and work together toward shared outcomes. In this chapter we will outline strategies that will help you lead or participate in change processes.

> Students as Change Leaders

Students are involved in change efforts all over the country and the world. For example, Campus Compact—a national coalition of nearly 1,200 college and university presidents, representing some six million students—"promotes public and community service that develops students' citizenship skills, helps campuses forge effective community partnerships, and provides resources and training for faculty seeking to integrate civic and community-based learning into the curriculum" (http://www.compact.org/about/history-mission-vision/). On your campus, students may be involved in change efforts related

Strategies for Change

448

to campus life policies, curriculum initiatives, recyc[...]
various funding issues. In the community, students[...]
involved in change efforts in schools, agencies, an[...]
organizations.

The focus of each change may call for different change
agents—people who are able to facilitate the change. Consider
the following categories of change agents listed by Conner
(1992):

- Those who influence personal change: parents for their families, counselors for the troubled, individuals for friends in need
- Those who influence organizational change: executives, managers, and union leaders for work settings; administrators and teachers for educational systems; clergy for religious institutions; administrators, doctors, and nurses for health-care systems; students for the campus culture; consultants for their clients
- Those who influence large-scale social change: politicians for the general public; civil servants for government; political action groups for special interests; researchers for the scientific community; opinion leaders for the media (p. 9)

As a shareholder or a stakeholder in many arenas, purposeful participants can be change agents that do help accomplish shared goals.

Within any change efforts, there are those who are working directly with an issue, called advocates, and those who support those working directly with an issue, called allies (Edwards & Alimo, 2005). There are many lists of ally characteristics. Wijeyesinghe, Griffin, and Love (1997) offer one that includes

STUDENT ESSAY

"This is how it's always been done." A popular phrase that most change makers will often hear. This is a phrase I heard when I first joined my sorority. As a bold and eager new member I sought to create change in variety of ways. One of these changes that stands out most significantly in my memory is when I dared to implement a New Member program which would rid our organization entirely of hazing. Some sisters didn't agree, some actively fought against it, but as a leader I used my influence to create this positive change.

During my time as a leader in my sorority I felt an innate responsibility to redirect my organization onto the right track and leave behind a legacy by encouraging and inspiring positive change, which would remain even after I was gone.

What motivated me most of all was passion. When you think of great leaders who affected change; Dr. Martin Luther King Jr., Alice Paul, Harvey Milk, Gandhi, there is one quality they all share, passion. Their belief in what they sought to achieve was realized because they inspired the individuals around them to work towards the same change. Affecting change is about being an influential force filled with passion; a force which pushes past 99 "no's" to hear just one "Yes!"

Stephanie Hernandez is a graduate of William Paterson University where she majored in early childhood education, psychology, and women's and gender studies. She was president of her sorority Delta Phi Epsilon International Sorority, as well as president of Feminist Collective, a resident assistant, and actively involved in other campus clubs and committees.

"Acts against social injustice out of belief that it is in her/his own self-interest to do so" and "Is committed to taking action against social injustice in his or her own sphere of influence" (p. 108). In Exhibit 11.1, we offer a slightly different perspective, taken from *Real Change Leaders* (Katzenbach, Beckett, Dichter, Feigen, Gagnon, Hope, & Ling, 1996). We believe these attributes apply to advocates (those working directly with an issue) and allies (those who support those working directly with an issue). As Katzenbach et al. go on to say, "A critical mass of such leaders seems to be essential in every institution striving for major change" (p. 15).

Exhibit 11.1: Common Characteristics of Real Change Leaders

- Commitment to a better way. They share a seemingly inexhaustible and visible commitment to a better way.
- Courage to challenge existing power bases and norms. They develop the personal courage needed to sustain their commitment in the face of opposition, failure, uncertainty, and personal risk.
- Personal initiative to go beyond defined boundaries. They consistently take the initiative to work with others to solve unexpected problems, break bottlenecks, challenge the status quo, and think outside the box.
- Motivation of themselves and others. Not only are they highly motivated themselves, but they have the ability to motivate, if not inspire, others around them.
- Caring about how people are treated and enabled to perform. They really care about other people, but not to the extent of blind self-sacrifice . . . They do not knowingly manipulate or take advantage of others.
- Staying undercover. They attribute part of their effectiveness to keeping a low profile; grandstanding, strident crusading, and self-promotion are viewed as sure ways to undermine their credibility and acceptance as change leaders.

(continued)

• A sense of humor about themselves and their situations. This is
  not a trivial trait. A sense of humor is often what gets them through
  when those around them start losing heart.

This all sounds great, but trying to initiate change is very
difficult, challenging work that usually causes leaders to be filled
with self-doubt. It can be easy for students to come up with
many reasons to not get involved in change efforts, but it is not
just students who hesitate. In *Leadership Reconsidered: Engaging
Higher Education in Social Change*, Alexander Astin and Helen
Astin (2000) outline a number of beliefs that can both constrain
and empower students and faculty to action (see Table 11.1).
Notice how similar the beliefs are for these two groups—both
constraining and empowering. This can be helpful as you enlist
the assistance of faculty, staff, and administrators in your campus
change efforts.

In Chapter Ten, we explored the impact of the change process on individuals and some of the constraining and empowering beliefs you may be experiencing. The Social Change Model
of Leadership Development shows the relationship between the
individual and the group that is seeking a positive change to benefit the community.

Table 11.1 Constraining and Empowering Beliefs of Students and Faculty

Constraining Individual Internal Beliefs		Empowering Individual Internal Beliefs	
Students	Faculty	Students	Faculty
• I don't have time to get involved • Faculty don't value my contributions • I can't "lead" because I don't hold a formal leadership title	• I don't have time to get involved in change efforts • My colleagues will never change their way of doing things • I'm not a leader because I don't have a leadership position • My role is to transfer disciplinary knowledge • Students are not motivated, interested in, or capable of mature action • My role is to criticize, not to initiate	• I can manage multiple roles and tasks so that I can make a difference on campus • As a campus citizen, I have a responsibility to help shape matters that affect me • Individual students have the ability to shape their futures • Each student has the capacity to engage in leadership processes without formal titles	• I help create the institutional culture through my daily individual decisions • Leadership is not a separate activity; it is an integral part of what I do • Learning is an activity that I can model daily • I can model leadership in every class • I have the freedom and autonomy to initiate inquiry or action • Students have the capacity, and therefore should be given the opportunity, to engage in decision making that affects them

(continued)

Table 11.1 Constraining and Empowering Beliefs of Students and Faculty (*continued*)

Constraining Individual Internal Beliefs		Empowering Individual Internal Beliefs	
Students	Faculty	Students	Faculty
• This campus doesn't care about students	• Faculty expertise is not valued in running the institution	• Students are viewed as major stakeholders	• Faculty are the stewards of the institution
• Students do not have enough experience to lead major campus-change efforts	• Nothing can be changed because of administrative attitudes	• Students are viewed as change agents	• Everyone in the institution directly contributes to student development
• The senior campus leaders (president and vice president) are not responsible for making major decisions	• Faculty and administrators could never work together	• Student leadership can make a difference on campus	• Change initiatives can start with anyone
	• All learning occurs in the classroom		• We make change through collective action
	• Student Affairs can't be trusted in academic matters		
	• Faculty and staff have nothing in common		

Source: Astin & Astin (2000), pp. 25, 26, 42, 46. Used with permission.

> The Social Change Model of Leadership Development

In the mid-1990s, a group of college and university educators (including two of this book's authors, Komives and Lucas), supported by a grant from the Dwight D. Eisenhower Leadership Development Program of the U.S. Department of Education, met and developed the Social Change Model of Leadership Development (Astin, 1996; Higher Education Research Institute, 1996). The "7 Cs" model (see Exhibit 11.2), as it soon became known, describes the values that are necessary for a leader to embody as she or he works at the individual, group, and society or community levels. As you review the values embraced by the Social Change Model you will notice similarities with the Relational Leadership Model described in this book. (For examples of how the Social Change Model has been used, see *Developing Non-Hierarchical Leadership on Campus: Case Studies and Best Practices in Higher Education* by Outcalt, Faris, and McMahon, 2001; to read more about this model see *Leadership for a Better World* edited by Komives and Wagner, 2009).

Exhibit 11.2: The Social Change Model of Leadership

Personal (Individual) Values

Personal values are those that an individual strives to develop and exhibit at the group activity level. As personal qualities that support group functioning, they are essential in leadership for social change.

(continued)

Consciousness of Self. Consciousness of self means knowledge of yourself, or simply self-awareness. It is awareness of the values, emotions, attitudes, and beliefs that motivate one to take action. Self-awareness implies mindfulness, an ability and a propensity to be an observer of one's current actions and state of mind. A person with a highly developed capacity for consciousness of self not only has a reasonably accurate self-concept but also is a good observer of his or her own behavior and state of mind at any given time. Consciousness of self is a fundamental value in our model because it constitutes the necessary condition for realizing all the other values in the model.

Congruence. Congruence is thinking, feeling, and behaving with consistency, genuineness, authenticity, and honesty toward others. Congruent persons are those whose actions are consistent with their most deeply held beliefs and convictions. Developing a clear consciousness of self is a critical element in being congruent. Being clear about one's values, beliefs, strengths, and limitations, who one is as an individual, is essential.

Commitment. Commitment implies intensity and duration in relation to a person, idea, or activity. It requires a significant involvement and investment of self in the object of commitment and in the intended outcomes. It is the energy that drives the collective effort. Commitment is essential to accomplishing change. It is the heart, the profound passion that drives one to action. Commitment originates from within. No one can force a person to commit to something, but organizations and colleagues can create and support an environment that resonates with each individual's heart and passions.

Group Values

Group values are expressed and practiced in the group work of leadership activity. Group values are reflected in such questions as, How can the collaboration be developed in order to effect positive social change? What are the elements of group interaction that promote collective leadership?

Collaboration. Collaboration is a central value in the model that views leadership as a group process. It increases group effectiveness because it capitalizes on the multiple talents and perspectives of each group member, using the power of that diversity to generate creative solutions and actions. Collaboration underscores the model's relational focus. Collaboration is about human relationships, about achieving common goals by sharing responsibility, authority, and accountability. It is leadership for service.

Common Purpose. A common purpose develops when people work with others within a shared set of aims and values. Shared aims facilitate group members' engagement in collective analyses of the issues and the task to be undertaken. Common purpose is best achieved when all members of the group build and share in the vision and participate actively in articulating the purpose and goals of the group work.

Controversy with Civility. Controversy with civility recognizes two fundamental realities of any group effort: first, that differences in viewpoint are inevitable and valuable and, second, that such differences must be aired openly and with respect and courtesy. Disagreements are inherent in almost any social interaction or group process. They bring valuable perspectives and information to the collaborative group, but eventually, they must be resolved. Such resolution is accomplished through open and honest dialogue backed by the group's commitment to understand the sources of the disagreement and to work cooperatively toward common solutions.

A Societal and Community Value

Citizenship. A commitment to social change connects individuals and their collaborative groups to their communities. The societal and

community value of citizenship clarifies the purpose of the leadership. Toward what social ends is the leadership development activity
directed?

Citizenship names the process whereby the self is responsibly
connected to the environment and the community. It acknowledges
the interdependence of all involved in the leadership effort. Citizenship thus recognizes that effective democracy requires individual
responsibility as well as individual rights. Citizenship, in the context of the Social Change Model, means more than membership;
it implies active engagement of the individual and the leadership
group in an effort to serve the community. It implies social or civic
responsibility. It is, in short, the value of caring about others.

Adapted from Wagner, W. (2007). The social change model of leadership: A brief
overview. *Concepts & Connections,* 15(1), p. 9.

In Figure 11.1, the arrows show the feedback loops between
the various aspects of the model. Arrows a and b indicate
how the Individual and Group Values influence each other; c
and d, how the Group and Society/Community values impact
each other; and e and f indicate how the Society/Community
and Individual Values mutually shape each other. Each arrow
has specific meaning (Higher Education Research Institute,
1996).

Arrow a. Consciousness of self is a critical ingredient in forging a
common purpose for the group as its members ask, What are our
shared values and purposes? Similarly, the division of labor so basic
to true collaboration requires an understanding of each group member's special talents and limitations. Likewise, the civil controversy
that often leads to innovative solutions requires both congruence (a
willingness to share one's views with others even when those others

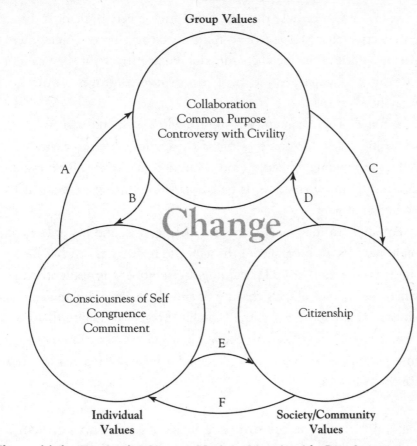

Figure 11.1 **The Social Change Model of Leadership Development**
Source: Reprinted with permission of the National Clearinghouse for Leadership Programs.

are likely to hold contrary views) and commitment (a willingness to stick to one's beliefs in the face of controversy).

Arrow b. Feedback from any leadership development group is most likely to enhance the individual qualities of consciousness of self, commitment, and congruence when the group operates collaboratively with a common purpose and accepts controversy with civility.

Arrow c. Responsible citizenship and positive change are most likely to occur when the leadership group functions collaboratively with a common purpose and encourages civility in the expression of controversy.

Arrow d. Conversely, the group will find it very difficult to be an effective change agent or to fulfill its citizenship or community responsibilities if its members function competitively, if they cannot identify a common purpose, or if they pursue controversy with incivility.

Arrow e. The community is most likely to respond positively to an individual's efforts to serve if these efforts are rooted in self-understanding, integrity, and genuine commitment. Responsible citizenship, in other words, is based on self-knowledge, congruence, and commitment.

Arrow f. An individual learns through service, and his or her consciousness of self is enhanced through the realization of what he or she is (and is not) capable of doing. Commitment is also enhanced when the individual feels that he or she can make a difference. Congruence is enhanced when the individual comes to realize that positive change is most likely to occur when individual actions are rooted in a person's most deeply held values and beliefs. (Higher Education Research Institute, 1996, p. 7)

Let's return to the opening scenario of Meredith's concern about green biology (commitment). She has become keenly aware that she does not want to dispose of chemicals in a harmful way (congruence). She is not sure how to go about making a change (consciousness of self) and knows she needs to reach out to others for assistance (consciousness of self, common purpose). Her lab instructor is too busy (consciousness of self), and although he has some sympathy for the cause (commitment), it does not seem to be enough to motivate him to get involved (lack of congruence). Meredith decides to approach the Society of Student Environmental Engineers (commitment, citizenship).

The president agrees to put the topic on the agenda of the next meeting (common purpose, collaboration) for the awareness raising (consciousness of self, commitment) and possible action of the group (common purpose).

At the meeting, Meredith knows she is nervous (consciousness of self), but the issue is important to her (congruence, commitment), so she brings a handout with information she has pulled from the Internet. The group has a lively discussion (common purpose, controversy with civility). One member even says, "This is the kind of thing we should have been talking about all year!" and there are nods of agreement from many members (commitment, common purpose). As the discussion proceeds, the president observes, "Seems like we want to take this on as an issue, right?" (common purpose, collaboration). The group discussed possible actions (common purpose, citizenship), like asking the department chair to come to the next meeting. Several members volunteer (commitment, collaboration) to check into different aspects of the issue (citizenship) for the next meeting. Meredith thanks the group and takes her seat, amazed that so much might now happen from bringing this to the meeting.

> Comparison of the Relational Leadership Model and Social Change Model

As you are undoubtedly seeing, the Social Change Model and the Relational Leadership Model have much in common, with a few important differences. Both view leadership as a relational and collaborative process. Both are values-focused, with an emphasis on being ethical and creating positive change for the greater good. The main difference between the models is their differing focus. Leadership, according to the Relational Leadership Model, involves the components of process and purpose by being ethical, empowering, and inclusive. The Social Change Model proposes a dynamic interplay between the sets of personal, group, and societal values. The models can be used together—in fact, we are encouraging you to do this, to help you better understand leadership in a given situation. Meredith, for example, knew she needed to involve others (inclusive) and that she had every right to raise this important issue (empowering). She wanted to address a problem that was causing harm to the environment (ethical, purpose). The way to do this was to find an advocate (process) or a group or coalition that would take on the issue with her (process). Educating the student group members was going to be critical (process) and she knew that the information would be compelling (empowering).

As you think about your own leadership development or the development of your organization and members, use the individual values portion of the Social Change Model in combination with the components of the Relational Leadership Model to identify areas of strength and areas you want to further strengthen. The connection between the two models is shown in Table 11.2.

To accomplish change, you must work with other individuals and groups of individuals. In the following sections, we will explore how to do that through the development of coalitions.

Table 11.2 **Comparison of the Relational Leadership Model and the Social Change Leadership Model**

Relational Leadership Model	Social Change Model
Purposeful	• Individual Values: Commitment • Group Values: Common Purpose • Societal Values: Citizenship
Ethical	• Individual Values: Congruence and Consciousness of Self • Group Values: Common Purpose and Controversy with Civility
Empowering	• Individual Values: Consciousness of Self and Commitment • Group Values: Collaboration and Common Purpose Societal Values: Citizenship
Inclusive	• Individual Values: Consciousness of Self and Commitment • Group Values: Collaboration and Controversy with Civility • Societal Values: Citizenship
Process-Oriented	• Individual Values: Commitment • Group Values: Collaboration and Common Purpose • Societal Values: Citizenship

❯ Building Coalitions for Community Action

Today's organizational and societal problems are complex and thus require community-based solutions. "If there is no sense of community, it stands to reason that it will be difficult to solve community problems ... People in a community have to have a public spirit and a sense of relationship" (Gudykunst, 1991, p. 128).

Whether these are campus community problems, problems in your apartment complex, or problems facing the athletics department, they need the involvement of several groups, not just one. Rarely is one group or one organization solely responsible or does it possess sufficient resources (including information) to create, implement, or sustain a complex change. This reality necessitates a commitment to coalition building. "Coalitions are often a preferred vehicle for intergroup action because they promise to preserve the autonomy of member organizations while providing the necessary structure for united effort" (Mizrahi & Rosenthal, 1993, p. 12). The approach to changing campus parking policies would not be nearly as meaningful if, for example, a residence hall government complained that change was needed instead of joining with the Commuter Student Union and Graduate Student Housing to work together toward that change.

Joining with other interested groups and organizations can create impressive change. "Through coalitions, separate groups can develop a common language and ideology with which to share a collective vision for progressive social change" (Mizrahi & Rosenthal, 1993, p. 12). They define a social change coalition as "a group of diverse organizational representatives who join forces to influence external institutions on one or more issues affecting their constituencies while maintaining their own autonomy. It is (a) an organization of organizations who share a common goal; (b) time limited; and (c) characterized by dynamic tensions" (p. 14).

STUDENT ESSAY

About a year ago, I was elected as president of the Associated Students of Boise State University (ASBSU) knowing that I would need to work with the team of new officers to direct large changes. The leaders the year before had wanted to revitalize ASBSU to serve students as best as possible. For them, this meant rebuilding relationships and spending their last months in office doing a constitutional revision that drastically changed the organizational structure of ASBSU.

The biggest challenge I faced being a "leader" through this transition was knowing when to consult others and seek feedback, and when to make a decision and keep moving forward. Reading through old documents, there were times when we thought "what was *ever* the purpose of this rule?" The vice president and I would discuss and come to a conclusion on our own, and we selectively sought input from officers and advisors on specific, individual issues. At times, it felt like we risked losing "buy-in" from others, but with the benefit of providing a firm plan that led to more immediate action. For our whole team, leadership meant that we consulted together about important decisions, trusted each other with smaller decisions, and presented a united front with all of our decisions.

Brandie VanOrder is a recent graduate from the political science program at Boise State University. She served as president of the Associated Students of Boise State University and was also involved in her sorority, Alpha Gamma Delta, the Honors College, and new student programming.

Mizrahi and Rosenthal (1993) have identified four distinct types of goals and time durations of coalitions: "specific goal, short-term groups (e.g. organizing demonstrations or forums); specific goal, long-term (e.g. banishing domestic violence,

Table 11.3 **Campus Coalitions**

Time Frame		
Goals	Short term	Long term
Specific	Homecoming; Thanksgiving canned food drive	Reducing incidents of date rape
General	Freshman community building	Diversity initiatives; revising general education requirements

housing court reform); general goal, short-term (fighting crime or drugs); and general goal, long-term (neighborhood improvement coalitions, anti-racist networks)" (pp. 14–15). Imagine some examples of what this might look like regarding campus issues (see Table 11.3).

Coalitions are not easy to build. Mizrahi and Rosenthal (1993) propose that each of these types of coalitions experiences a cooperation-conflict dynamic; four dynamic tensions arise to varying degrees.

1. The tension of mixed loyalties: this results from the dual commitment the members feel, to both their own sponsoring organization and the coalition. For example, a member of the Campus Safety Committee may come to learn the logistical and financial realities of improving campus lighting and see the need to have a phased program but be pressured from the women's group she is representing to make it all happen at once.

2. The tension between autonomy and accountability: the coalitions need the independence to act, yet each member needs to connect back to their organization to maintain organizational commitment and endorsement. The Campus

Environmental Action Coalition just discovered a state grant they can apply for, but they must set a focus for the grant and meet a one-week deadline. There is not time to fully consult with other organizations; this could cause those organizations to feel excluded.

3. The tension of determining the amount of emphasis to place on the coalition: should the group be seen as a means to achieve a specific goal or as a model of cooperation? Tension arises between those who support the coalition as a means for achieving desired results and those who want to preserve relationships regardless of the results. The coalition probably needs to be both. It needs to be the way in which some goal is actually addressed and also serve as a model of how various groups can work effectively together. For example, think of a coalition of Asian American Student Associations on campus who have come together to work for an Asian studies program. Some in the group will see the potential of working together for other purposes as well and be hopeful that the various Asian American student groups are in dialogue. Others in the group just want this one goal accomplished and see no need to preserve the coalition.

4. The tension between unity and diversity: members of the coalition need to find ways to act with common purpose, recognizing the differences they bring to the goal. "The more one favors strengthening communities . . . the more one must concern oneself with ensuring that they see themselves as parts of a more encompassing whole, rather than as fully independent and antagonistic" (Etzioni, 1993, p. 155). The homecoming committee might work hard to keep a balance among the athletic emphasis, social reunions, cultural events, current student celebrations,

and academic updates that are planned, even if those behind any one kind of event think it should be preeminent.

Bobo, Kendall, and Max (2001) note that "Coalitions are not built because it is good, moral, or nice to get everyone working together. Coalitions are about building power. The only reason to spend the time and energy building a coalition is to amass the power necessary to do something you cannot do through one organization" (p. 100). There are distinct advantages and disadvantages to working in coalitions (Table 11.4).

Coalitions face unique challenges when forming alliances between groups that differ in fundamentally different approaches or worldviews that are reflected in their sex, race, sexual orientation, or class. "Minority groups have many reasons to mistrust majority groups who have historically exploited, co-opted, and dominated them" (Mizrahi & Rosenthal, 1993, p. 31). Majority

Table 11.4 **Advantages and Disadvantages of Working in Coalitions**

Advantages	Disadvantages
Win what couldn't be won alone.	Distracts from other work.
Build an ongoing power base.	Weak members can't deliver.
Increase the impact of an individual organization's efforts.	Too many compromises.
Develop new leaders.	Inequality of power.
Increase resources.	Individual organizations may not get credit.
Broaden scope.	Dull tactics.

Source: Bobo, Kendall, & Max (2001), pp. 101–102. Used with permission.

groups (those who have been in the dominant culture) have
been used to being in control and have most often seen decisions
made and problems approached in ways they are comfortable
with. For marginalized group members to follow the methods
of the dominant culture, leadership may feel like it's being
co-opted; to bring up issues of interest may seem like having a
special agenda; and teaching the dominant culture about the
issues salient to those who have not been heard in the past takes
energy and can build resentment. The dominant culture may
be administrators, those with resources, or the White culture.
Marginalized culture may be students, lower socioeconomic
groups, or historically peripheral groups. Although this may not
be true of the group experiences of all those who have been
underrepresented, marginalization should be addressed as if it is
indeed a problem in the coalition. This will help build sensitive
coalitions. The RLM elements of inclusion, empowerment,
ethics, and process are all involved in building such coalitions.

Building effective coalitions among diverse members is
important to producing successful results. A critical question
is posed by Pascale, Millemann, and Gioja (2000, p. 203): "If
conversation is the source and soul of change, the first concern
is: Who should be included in it?" Mizrahi and Rosenthal (1993)
recommend that all coalition members (notably what they
identify as the minority groups) be involved in the design of the
coalition goals and methods from the beginning and not brought
in at a later point, which can be seen as tokenism. Further, the
coalition must continuously make it a top priority to enhance
diversity and must insist on the involvement of those who will
be affected by the change outcome. Relational leadership values
doing things with people, not to them.

> Civic Engagement

We all have a responsibility to be civically engaged in all the communities that matter to us. This engagement can take various forms and will exist to varying degrees. Association of American Colleges sand Universities vice president Caryn Musil (2003) shares the belief that "students need to be prepared to assume full and responsible lives in an interdependent world, marked by uncertainty, rapid change, and destabilizing inequalities" (p. 4). She envisions a range of different "expressions of citizenship" (summarized in Table 11.5). It is important to note that each face or phase describes a different form of campus engagement with the outside world and contains "different definitions of community, values, and knowledge" (p. 5).

The Relational Leadership Model—with its emphasis on the change process, purpose, empowerment, and being ethical and inclusive—relates directly to Musil's (2003) work, especially the Reciprocal and Generative Faces or Phases. Musil's view of citizenship is decidedly relational in nature—note how Musil defines community with the concepts of empowerment and interdependence. This theme is carried through in the "levels of knowledge" that are seen through "multiple vantage points." There are many examples of how this could work on campuses. When you say "We're going to do something," ask yourself "How big is our we?" (Bruteau, 1990, p. 510). Partnering with other organizations in forming coalitions expands your sense of perspective, especially if those organizations are ones with which you do not typically interact.

Table 11.5 **Faces or Phases of Citizenship**

Face or Phase	Community is . . .	Civic Scope	Levels of Knowledge	Benefits
Exclusionary	. . . only your own	Civic disengagement	• One vantage point (yours) • Monocultural	A few and only for a while
Oblivious	. . . a resource to mine	Civic detachment	• Observational skills • Largely monocultural	One party
Narve	. . . a resource to engage	Civic amnesia	• No history • No vantage point • Acultural	Random people
Charitable	. . . a resource that needs assistance	Civic altruism	• Awareness of depriva- tions • Affective kindliness and respect • Multicultural but yours is still the norm center	The giver's feelings the sufferer's immediate needs

(continued)

Table 11.5 Faces or Phases of Citizenship (*continued*)

Face or Phase	Community is …	Civic Scope	Levels of Knowledge	Benefits
Reciprocal	…a resource to empower and be empowered by	Civic engagement	• Legacies of inequalities • Values of partnering • Intercultural competencies • Arts of democracy • Multiple vantage points • Multicultural	Society as a whole in the present
Generative	…an interdependent resource filled with possibilities	Civic prosperity	• Struggles for democracy • Interconnectedness • Analysis of interlocking systems • Intercultural competencies • Arts of democracy • Multiple interactive vantage points • Multicultural	Everyone now and in the future

Source: Musil 2003 p. 8. Reprinted with permission from *Peer Review* vol. 5 no. 3. Copyright 2003 by the Association of American Colleges and Universities.

> Service as Change-Making

Service is one way in which many college students help bring about change in their communities and in the larger world. Service on a college campus can take many forms. It can be done because of an individual's commitment to a cause or program, or it can be part of an organizational effort to "give back" to the community. It can be one aspect of a course or can even be used as part of a conduct sanction. From volunteering for one-time service projects to being a participant in ongoing service efforts, you can learn a lot about yourself, about others, and about policies that inhibit or promote change through service of all kinds. Whether the service involves schools, hospitals, environmental agencies, or numerous other human services agencies or projects, good things generally happen.

For these good things to happen, the service program needs to contain certain factors. The program must place students within an agency or community that provides (1) real learning for students and a real benefit to the community, (2) an application of what students are learning in the classroom, (3) opportunities for reflection, and (4) chances for students to hear and experience the voice of the community (Eyler & Giles, 1999). It is important to remember that service does not benefit just those being served; it also benefits those doing the serving. Eyler, Giles, Stenson, and Gray (2001) summarize a number of studies in highlighting the benefits of service for students:

- Service-learning has a positive effect on interpersonal development and the ability to work well with others, leadership and communication skills.

- Service-learning has a positive effect on reducing stereotypes and facilitating cultural and racial understanding.
- Service-learning has a positive effect on sense of social responsibility and citizenship skills.
- Service-learning has a positive effect on commitment to service. (pp. 2–3) (Used with permission)

How someone engages in service makes all the difference. Although it might seem that the experience of service itself would be enough, this is not always the case. Imagine someone grudgingly participating in a service project as part of a course or because it is required of all members of an organization. How often have you heard someone say something like this: "I'm paying tuition to do this!? I don't know why we have to do this stuff—it doesn't make any difference. It's just glorified charity work. It's sure not academic. I could be spending my time studying." Contrast that with another student who is a willing participant: "I'm learning so much about myself from this experience—more than I ever learned in a class! I'm learning skills I can use in the real world. I'd rather do this than be stuck in a classroom." Certainly this student will have a different kind of experience. Still, without reflection, learning from the experience is minimized and, one could argue, personal growth as an individual and as a leader is limited.

Morton (1995) addresses this situation by describing service in terms of distinct paradigms: charity, project, and social change. Charity is "the provision of direct service where control of the service (resources and decisions affecting their distribution) remain with the provider" (p. 21). The project paradigm is a "focus on defining problems and their solutions and implementing well-conceived plans for achieving those solutions" (p. 22). The social change paradigm emphasizes "process: building relationships among or within stakeholder groups, and creating a learning environment that continually peels away the layers of the onion called 'root causes' " (p. 22–23). Using terminology taken from Geertz (1973), Morton goes on to note, "Each paradigm has 'thin' versions that are disempowering and hollow, and 'thick' versions that are sustaining and potentially revolutionary" (p. 24).

Morton (1995) sums up the potential of service in the following way:

> Certainly, students need to understand that several forms of service exist; that they can all be meaningful; and that they have choices about what they will do and how they will do it. And they need to be challenged to make those choices consciously, based on experience and reflection. The irony is that unless we can adequately describe the range of service that exists, students will continue to work with a narrow and artificial definition of service that polarizes into a limited domain of service and an expansive domain of non-service. (p. 29)

These paradigms of service offer much to help us broaden the concept of leadership. The critical nature of the "thin" and "thick" versions is important to keep in mind. The thin versions involve maintaining power and control of the processes, of doing things to and for others. The thick versions respect the agency of those populations with which the service group is working. Just as the Relational Leadership Model emphasizes empowering others, so does service when it is done in a thoughtful, respectful, reciprocal, reflective manner.

> Identifying Critical Issues

When you take a critical look at the organizations, institutions, communities, nation, and world in which you live, there is much that needs to be changed. But where to begin? This can be a very difficult question to consider because it can lead one to a sense of hopelessness—there is so much that needs to be changed, and you are only one person, so the task can seem overwhelming and impossible. One result is that we give in to that hopelessness and decide to not engage in any serious change efforts. Or we jump right into the fray—but once we have decided to try to make a difference, how do we select from the many areas that could use our attention? Here are some questions to ask yourself as you consider where to devote your leadership efforts and energy. You can relate these questions back to the Social Change Model.

- About what issues am I the most passionate? (Change takes energy.)
- Am I willing to take the time and make the sacrifices to work on this issue? (Change is not easy.)
- Am I willing to face the challenges associated with this issue? (Change takes courage.)
- For which issues am I most likely to be able to recruit others? Who are the shareholders or stakeholders who might join me in working with this issue? (Change involves others.)
- With which issues can I (and interested others) really make an impact? (We want our change efforts to accomplish something.)

Once you have answered these questions, you'll need to make the difficult choice of the one issue on which to focus. Although we all know students who have been able to juggle involvements in multiple change efforts, the time and energy needed for such efforts usually prohibits them from being successful. This can seem like a cop-out at first, but one successful change effort can lead to even more changes happening in the future. It is also important to remember the critical nature of working with others and being ethical while identifying critical issues. Without involving those stakeholders immediately in the situation, something important is being missed and the change efforts will have less chance of success. The ethical component of leadership also comes into play when working on important issues. Critical questions come to the forefront: To what lengths are we willing to go when working on this issue? Do the ends justify the means? The identification of critical issues can be a test of the leadership of a group, organization, or community. As Komives, Wager, and Associates (2009) note, "Social change addresses the root cause of problems" (p. 11) and "social change is collaborative" (p. 12). Are you willing to really work on the causes of the issues you are engaging? Are you enlisting the help of a wide range of others to help you work on this issue? Hopefully you are realizing one other important point made by Komives, et al., "Social Change is not simple" (p. 14).

> Joining with Others

Once you have identified a single issue, the challenge becomes joining with others to work on the change effort. Jeffrey Luke (1998) helps us with this next step by providing a set of common questions used to identify potential stakeholders (Bryson & Crosby, 1992; King, 1984):

- Who is affected by the issue?
- Who has an interest in or has expressed an opinion about the issue?
- Who is in a position to exert influence—positively or negatively—on the issue?
- Who ought to care? (Luke, 1998, p. 69)

Encouraging others to care about an issue as much as you do is difficult. Something that seems critical to you may seem like a nonissue to others. As you are considering different issues, it can be helpful to differentiate between a condition, a problem, and a priority issue (Luke, 1998) (see Table 11.6).

Luke (1998) also notes that issues rise to priority in the policy agenda due to the convergence of four elements, which do not necessarily occur in a predictable time frame or sequential order. The four elements are

1. Intellectual awareness of a worsening condition or troubling comparison
2. Emotional arousal and concern regarding the conditions
3. Sense that the problem is urgent
4. Belief that the problem can be addressed (p. 54)

In thinking about who you might be able to recruit for your change effort, some individuals may immediately come to mind.

Table 11.6 **The Issue Attention Cycle**

A "condition" (an existing situation or latent problem)	A "problem" (a problem captures the public's attention)	A "priority issue" (an issue rises to priority status for key decision makers)
• Not every condition will surface as a problem or be defined as a problem. • *Example:* Residential students complain that there is "nothing to do on the weekends."	• A societal concern becomes salient and important, and thus captures public attention through increasing awareness, visibility, and emotional concern. • *Example:* The student newspaper prints an article detailing the consumption of alcohol by under-age students at a student government retreat that was financed from student fees.	• The issue is felt as urgent and pressing, coupled with some optimism that it can be addressed, and thus displaces other problems on the policy agenda. • *Example:* Membership on key all-campus committees is composed of very similar students. You and a group of concerned peers decide to try to broaden this group to be more representative of the entire student body.

Source: Adapted from Luke (1998), p. 44. Used with permission.

These could be like-minded friends or acquaintances, peers who are members of organizations to which you belong, or others in groups that would be directly impacted by the changes you are interested in proposing. Luke (1998) offers questions to ask yourself as you consider who you might try to recruit:

- Who are the stakeholders, knowledge holders, and other resources?
- Who can make things happen in this issue area? Who can block action?
- Who are appropriate newcomers or outsiders with unique perspectives?
- What is an appropriate critical mass to initiate action?
- Who should be invited to participate in the effort to address the issue?
- How can core participants once identified, be motivated to join the collective effort?
- What other forms and levels or participation could generate quality ideas?
- How can first meetings be convened to create a safe space and legitimate process for problem solving? (p. 88) (Used with permission.)

Once you have brought the group together, Ospina and Foldy (2010) provide suggested actions that will help "bring diverse actors together and facilitate their ongoing ability for collaborative work" (Table 11.7).

Table 11.7 How to Bring Diverse Actors Together for Collaborative Work

Prompt cognitive shifts (to create a sense of shared interests)	From environmental degradation to human rights From another's problem to our problem
Name and shape identity (especially race and gender)	Celebrate identity Interrogate identity
Engage dialogue about difference	Deep, recurrent deliberations Ensure different voices in the circle Confront diverse ideas
Create equitable governance mechanisms	Fierce commitment to democratic governance Representative structures plus inclusive processes
Weave multiple worlds together through interpersonal relationships	One-on-one connections Personalized attention

Source: Adapted from Ospina and Foldy, 2010, pp. 297–301

STUDENT ESSAY

"Change:" if there was ever a word as simultaneously inspiring as it is potentially frustrating... I'd be hard pressed to find it. During my senior year at Hartwick College I served as Vice President of Student Senate after two years serving as Executive Secretary. As part of the administration's strategy, many new processes, policies, and plans were to be enacted in order to streamline our clubs' various

(continued)

requirements and to add a level of accountability; a system to track. This had never before been attempted and, as you would expect, garnered quite a pushback from some organizations under Senate who had been used to the old regime—the lawless society of vague deadlines, lost paperwork, and a toxic mentality of entitlement.

Through a masterful envisioning of a reformatted overall structure, our administration took a leap and began to make significant changes. With adjustments came frustration, naturally. I am of the mind that it is how a leader manages the reaction to change and steers those working within the team toward the goal, while respecting and acknowledging all viewpoints involved. Leaders drive peripheries; leaders strive to push themselves and their team to a place of uncertainty, for it is in that place we are forced to grow. Leaders enjoy viewing their evolution yet remember to question the reason for advancement before stepping through the event horizon. As John C. Maxwell stated, " . . . don't be afraid to break with tradition to achieve progress."

Peter Cody Fiduccia is a graduate of Hartwick College where he majored in business administration with a minor in finance. He was vice president of Student Senate, member of the Sigma Beta Delta Management Honors Society, and recipient of the Robert Houghton Award in Leadership; Peter is currently a first-year MBA candidate at Binghamton University in New York.

> Conflict

Conflict is inevitable, even among and between individuals who want to create similar changes. Dealing with conflict is one of the most challenging aspects of leadership. It is difficult to keep from labeling those who disagree with us as "bad," "wrong," or "not caring enough." As we have noted previously, groups that are able to work through the storming stage of group development find themselves stronger and better able to work together than they were before the conflict began. It is also important to remember that the Relational Leadership Model defines leadership as a process, and conflict is certainly one aspect of this process. As we noted in Chapter Eight The Relational Leadership Model encourages processes to handle conflict that will promote inclusivity and empowerment.

What is important to remember is the need to maintain focus on the purpose of what you are trying to accomplish as you also maintain the relationship with others who are involved. The Social Change Model presents the idea of "controversy with civility." Certainly disagreement is to be expected, and even invited, as you are trying to accomplish almost any sort of meaningful change. Luke (1998, p. 198) helps us understand this conflict and provides typical causes and possible interventions (see Table 11.8).

Conflict is almost inevitable when you are involved in change. Dealing, or not dealing, with that conflict can determine the success of the change effort. Conflict, in general, involves relationships and goals. When people are involved in a stressful change effort, our feelings become heightened, so anything can take on added importance. Obviously it is better to address conflict earlier rather than later and to do so in a respectful manner while maintaining an open mind. Working with conflict can be one of the most challenging aspects of leadership.

As you consider engaging in social change, there are a variety of possible pitfalls that can appear. Komives, Wager, and Associates (2009) identify several: paternalism, assimilation, a deficit-based perspective of the community, seeking a magic bullet, and ignoring cultural differences. These pitfalls can be avoided by focusing on being in community with others and on

Table 11.8 **Sources of Conflict on Action Strategies**

Source of Conflict	Typical Causes	Possible Interventions
• Underlying value differences	• Different ways of life ideology or religions • Strong emotional beliefs	• Rely on superordinate goal or outcome that all members share • Avoid defining criteria in terms of underlying values • Do not require the divergent strategies to adhere to the same underlying values • Seek shared interests not shared values
• Differing priorities	• Perceived or actual competing interests • "Zero-sum" or "fixed-pie" assumptions (additional allocation of resources for one cause/person means that another cause/person will receive less) • Scarce resources will force the selection of only a few strategies to pursue	• Facilitate interest-based bargaining • Agree on criteria for selecting strategies

Table 11.8 **Sources of Conflict on Action Strategies (*continued*)**

Source of Conflict	Typical Causes	Possible Interventions
• Relationship issues	• Historically created distrust • Stereotypes and misperceptions • Poor communication and listening	• Deal with past relationship issues • Control expression of negative emotions through procedural ground rules • Allow appropriate venting of emotions as part of strategy development process • Improve the quality and quantity of communications
• Data conflicts	• Lack of information • Different interpretations of data	• Agree on what data are important • Use third-party experts to gain outside opinion and clarify data interpretations

Source: Luke (1998) p. 198. Used with permission.

what you have in common rather than trying to "fix" or "help" them (p. 31–32).

Using a strengths based approach to conflict can be very helpful here as you focus on the positives of the situation rather then the negatives, on the strengths that your colleagues bring with them as opposed to what your group is lacking, and the helpful aspects that the surrounding environment can contribute (including people) rather than focusing on all that you are lacking. This can be a useful perspective as you try to work on what can seem to be overwhelmingly complex issues that defy your attempts to begin to remedy them.

> Navigating Environments

The college environment can be difficult to navigate. As in any complex hierarchical system, there are many layers. As with any bureaucratic organization, it can be tough to figure out who is responsible for what areas. You encounter deans, directors, coordinators, and all other levels of staff positions. Although there are similarities from campus to campus, each institution retains its own way of doing things. Figuring out who to contact in order to begin working for change is not always easy.

Some questions to ask yourself:

- What do I want to accomplish? Be able to state clearly and succinctly what you are trying to do. Try explaining this to someone who knows nothing about the particular topic or area. This will force you to state things in simple terms that are easy to understand.
- Who else might be interested in this project? What other individuals or organizations might I contact? No matter how committed or talented you are you cannot do it alone.
- Where can I begin? What person or office should I contact first? The key thing is to begin—starting any project may be frustrating at first.

- What persons or offices can this first contact refer me to? People are generally helpful—you will undoubtedly grow your list of contacts.

> Appreciative Inquiry

The process of Appreciative Inquiry has recently received attention from educators, organizational consultants, human resource professionals, and those who study organizational behavior (Whitney, 2005, 2008; Whitney & Trosten-Bloom, 2010; Whitney, Trosten-Bloom, & Cooperrider, 2003). Appreciative Inquiry is "a collaborative and highly participative, system-wide approach to seeking, identifying, and enhancing the 'life-giving forces' that are present when a system is performing optimally in human, economic, and organizational terms" (Watkins & Mohr, 2001, p. 14). Its basic premise is that every organization is doing something right, and the key to creating positive change is to identify and work from those positive aspects. Cooperrider and Whitney (2005) show the difference between Appreciative Inquiry and a more traditional Problem Solving Approach (Table 11.9)

This focus on what is already going well in the organization is shown further by Whitney and Trosten-Bloom (2010). This is shown in Table 11.10.

The Appreciative Inquiry process involves identifying a topic and then proceeding through four stages of inquiry—discover, dream, design, and destiny (Figure 11.2). The topic can be anything of importance to the organization—"anything the people of an organization

Table 11.9 **From Problem Solving to Appreciative Inquiry**

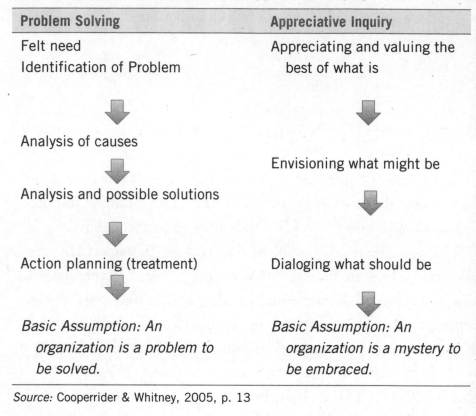

Problem Solving	Appreciative Inquiry
Felt need Identification of Problem	Appreciating and valuing the best of what is
Analysis of causes	Envisioning what might be
Analysis and possible solutions	
Action planning (treatment)	Dialoging what should be
Basic Assumption: An organization is a problem to be solved.	*Basic Assumption: An organization is a mystery to be embraced.*

Source: Cooperrider & Whitney, 2005, p. 13

feel gives life to the system" (Cooperrider & Whitney, 2000, p. 9).

Although using slightly different terminology, Charles Elliott (1999) offers succinct descriptions of the four stages of inquiry:

• Discovering periods of excellence and achievement. Through interviews and storytelling, participants remember significant achievements and periods of excellence.

• Dreaming an ideal organization or community. In this step people use past achievements to envisage a desired future . . . [I]mages of the community's future that emerge

Table 11.10 **The Shift from Deficit-Based Change to Positive Change**

	Deficit-Based Change	Positive Change
Intervention Focus	• Identified problem.	• Affirmative topics.
Participation	• Selective inclusion of people.	• Whole system.
Action Research	• Diagnosis of problem. • Causes and consequences. • Quantitative analysis. • Profile of need. • Conducted by outsiders.	• Discovery of positive core. • Organization at its best. • Narrative analysis. • Map of positive core. • Conducted by members.
Dissemination	• Feedback to decision makers.	• Widespread and creative sharing of best practices.
Creative Potential	• Brainstormed list of alternatives.	• Dreams of a better world and the organization's contributions.
Result	• Best solution to resolve the problem.	• Design to realize dreams and human aspirations.
Capacity Gained	• Capacity to implement and measure the plan.	• Capacity for ongoing positive change.

Source: Whitney & Trosten-Bloom, 2010, p. 17

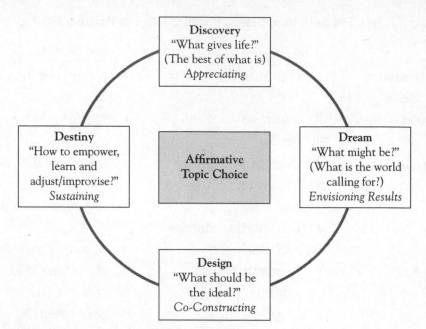

Figure 11.2 **Appreciative Inquiry 4-D Cycle**

Source: Cooperrider, Sorensen Jr., Whitney, & Yaeger (2000), p. 7. Reprinted with permission.

are grounded in history, and as such represent compelling possibilities.

- Designing new structures and processes. This stage is intended to be provocative—to develop, through consensus, concrete short- and long-term goals that will achieve the dream . . . Provocative propositions should stretch an organization or community, but they should also be achievable because they are based on past periods of excellence.

- Delivering the dream. In this stage, people act on their provocative propositions, establishing roles and responsibilities, developing strategies, forging institutional linkages and mobilizing resources to achieve their dream. (pp. 3–4)

Gervase Bushe (2000) describes an applicable use of an Appreciative Inquiry approach focused on teamwork. The group begins by talking about the best team experience they have ever had, with each member sharing his or her story while the rest of the group listens attentively, engaging in dialogue when appropriate. Working together, the group then creates a consensus list of attributes that would describe "best teams." Finally, members are asked to share any experiences they have had with other group members that embodied any of these attributes. Just imagine the power of this relatively simple experience.

Both of these process models have much to offer leaders. Rituals have been developed that encourage members to speak about what is in their hearts and minds and to share what they appreciate about their organization and its members. Groups may hold informal or formal sessions in which members share their thoughts and feelings about the group. Some organizations will periodically invite all members to form a circle and pass a candle or gavel around the group. When holding the candle or gavel, the member is free to say anything she or he wishes to say. Other organizations ask that members comment on one thing that is going poorly in the group and one thing that is going well. This is an excellent method of soliciting feedback from all members of the group, including those who are usually quiet. The following are simple questions you can use in your organization or team to begin an appreciative inquiry dialogue:

1. Describe your best moment or experience in this organization or team?
2. What made it a great experience?

3. What are the greatest strengths of the organization or team?
4. What would the organization look like if it maximized all of its strengths and positive attributes?
5. What has been the single greatest success of this organization?
6. What are your dreams for this organization?
7. What would the ideal future look like for this organization?
8. What would success look like three years from now?
9. How can the organization capitalize on its strengths in facilitating a change process?

Communities hold open forums or town meetings for a similar purpose. Whatever method is used, the leaders need to be sure that they know what the membership is thinking and feeling. They also need to strive to create an atmosphere in which members feel free to express their thoughts and feelings without fear of repercussions. Finally, they need to build on the positive things the organization is already doing. Whitney and Trosten-Bloom (2010) detail what needs to happen to apply Appreciative Inquiry to community settings (Exhibit 11.3).

Exhibit 11.3: Successfully Applying Appreciative Inquiry in Community Settings

1. "Communitize" your approach.
2. Prepare committed champions.
3. Be purposefully and radically inclusive.
4. Fan the affirmative flame.
5. Keep reaching out with information and opportunities.
6. Plan for continuity and transitions.
7. Invest the time, enjoy the return.

8. Be open to what emerges.
9. Provide ongoing training and education in AI.
10. Make Appreciative Inquiry a daily practice.

(Whitney & Trosten-Bloom, 2010, pp. 260–263)

Appreciative Inquiry is designed to maximize the positive potential of individuals and organizations, which is a powerful lever in facilitating change. Too often, strategies for change begin with a problem to solve or are prompted by a negative situation. A temptation is to immediately respond to and fix the problem through a change process. Using Appreciative Inquiry as a strategy for facilitating change will inspire others toward a greater future, maximize the assets of the organization, and create greater engagement among group members.

> Change and Cyberspace

We could not end a chapter on change without including some mention of cyberspace and the role of social media. Howard and Hussain (2011) describe in detail the role that digital media played in the Arab Spring:

There are many ways to tell the story of political change. But one of the most consistent narratives from civil society leaders in Arab countries has been that the Internet, mobile phones, and social media such as Facebook and Twitter made the difference this time. Using these technologies, people interested in democracy could build extensive networks, create social capital, and organize political action with a speed and on a scale never seen before. Thanks to these technologies, virtual networks materialized in the streets. Digital media became the tool that allowed social movements to reach once-unachievable goals, even as authoritarian forces moved with a dismaying speed of their own to devise both high- and low-tech countermeasures. (p. 35)

They go on to outline how this actually happened:

As we look back over the first quarter of 2011, the story of digital media and the Arab Spring seems to have unfolded in five or perhaps six parts or phases. The first was a *preparation* phase that involved activists using digital media in creative ways to find each other, build solidarity around shared grievances, and identify collective political goals. The second was an *ignition* phase involving an incident that the state-run media ignored, but which came to wide notice online and enraged the public. Then came the third phase, a period of *street protests* made possible, in part, by online networking and coordination. As these went on, there came the *international buy-in*, during which digital-media coverage (much of it locally generated) drew in foreign governments, international organizations, global diasporas, and overseas news agencies. Matters then built toward a *climax* as regimes, maneuvering via some mixture of concession and repression, either got the protesters off the street; failed to mollify or frighten them and began to crumble before their demands; or ended up in a bloody stalemate or even civil war as we are seeing in Bahrain, Libya, Syria, and Yemen. In some cases, such as those of Tunisia and Egypt, we are seeing an additional phase of *follow-on information* warfare as the various players left standing compete to shape the future course of events by gaining control over the revolutionary narrative. (pp. 41–42)

In another example, Brionesa, Kucha, Liu, and Jin (2011) describe how the Red Cross is "using a wide variety of tools such as websites, blogs, Twitter, and Facebook to develop relationships focused on recruiting and maintaining volunteers, updating the community on disaster preparedness and response, and engaging the media" (p. 410).

So while these cases may seem huge and world changing, social media can be used in smaller ways to encourage social change every day. These media connect people in ways that were previously thought to be almost unimaginable. They allow people to communicate in an intense, 24/7 manner. Finally, they can transmit information of all sorts almost instantaneously. Think about how your lives have changed with the advent of social media. Have your organizations changed in similar ways or are you still doing things as they were done in the days before Facebook and Twitter? How can you leverage these tools for your advantage?

> Conclusion

We began this chapter with a well-known quote by Margaret Mead, "Never doubt that a small group of thoughtful, committed citizens can change the world; indeed it is the only thing that ever has" (cited in Mathews, 1994, p. 119). We end it with a short but powerful quote by Paul Loeb (1999), who writes about a call to action in his book, *Soul of a Citizen:* "We can never predict the impact of our actions" (p. 1). When you engage in leadership in your organization, your community, your school, your neighborhoods, your state, your nation, and the world, you are working to make changes. Through these changes, the world becomes a better place for all of us.

> What's Next?

Your reactions to engaging with others to accomplish change
may signal how you have developed as a leader or how renewed
you feel to engage in new challenges. The concluding chapter
of the book examines how leadership can thrive by using a
strengths based approach and focusing on positivity. The
important topic of self-renewal is also be discussed.

> Chapter Activities

1. Revisit the Social Change Model. What personal values
   guide your leadership? How does your thinking, feeling, and
   behaving around these values show congruence? How do you
   demonstrate your commitment to those values?
2. Again, consider the Social Change Model as it relates to
   an organization in which you are a participant. What happens when you are faced with a difficult issue? How do you
   demonstrate "controversy with civility"? How might your
   organization improve in this area?
3. Consider a recent change you have made or tried to make
   within an organization. What role did conflict play in this
   change process? Who was involved in the conflict? What did
   you try that was unsuccessful in working with the conflict?
   What was successful?
4. Being an effective change agent means knowing key decision
   makers within the community (Kahn, 1991). What campus
   officials do you need to know better? How might you go about
   becoming better acquainted with them?

5. Identify an organization or group that you belong to and reflect on when the organization is at its best. What does it look like? How do people communicate with each other? How does work get accomplished? Imagine that your organization won the award as the Most Successful Organization of the Year. What is now different about the organization? What made it possible for the organization to achieve this award? What are others at your college or university saying now about your organization?

ADDITIONAL READINGS

Aaker, J. L., Smith, A., & Adler, C. (2010). *The dragonfly effect: Quick, effective, and powerful ways to use social media to drive social change*. San Francisco, CA: Jossey-Bass.

Alinsky, S. (1989). *Rules for radicals*. New York, NY: Vintage Books.

Komives, S. R., Wagner, W., & Associates. (2009). *Leadership for a better world: Understanding the social change model of leadership development*. San Francisco, CA: Jossey-Bass.

Loeb, P. R. (2010). *Soul of a citizen: Living with conviction in a cynical time* (Revised ed). New York, NY: St. Martin's Griffin.

Whitney, D., & Trosten-Bloom, A. (2010). *The power of appreciative inquiry: A practical guide to positive change* (2nd ed). San Francisco, CA: Berrett-Koehler.

Chapter 12

⌄

Thriving Together

◇

A number of leadership theories and concepts covered in this book emanate from psychology and the study of human behavior, personality, and organizations. We conclude this book with one of the newest areas in psychology to emerge, in 1998, positive psychology, which informs and influences the study and practice of leadership at individual and organizational levels.

This chapter includes an explanation of the science behind positive psychology and its relationship to leadership and practical applications for individuals and organizations. We will explore key concepts from positive psychology such as positivity using a theory to application approach. Models such as the Tipping Point (Fredrickson, 2007), Positive Leadership (Cameron, 2008), and PERMA (Seligman, 2011) are reviewed in this chapter with implications for leaders and leadership processes.

> Intersection of Leadership and Positive Psychology

Philosophers such as Aristotle, Plato, and Socrates initiated an examination of the good life thousands of years ago. This same question resonates well with our contemporary assumptions about leadership. Human beings yearn to live a satisfying life. People in organizations, groups, and communities want to live their lives with meaning and purpose through engagement with others. The Relational Leadership Model's components are designed to facilitate growth and learning for individuals and groups to achieve greater levels of meaning and purpose within the leadership process.

Psychologists and leadership scholars make the connection between positive psychology and leadership with the goal of positioning organizations and communities toward greater levels of flourishing. Researchers are addressing why some teams languish while others flourish and thrive together (Fredrickson, 2009). A central theme of this book is the importance of awareness of self and others. Using a positive psychology framework to understand leadership processes and to grow as a leader means starting with the strengths that you and your members already possess. Identifying and using everyone's strengths in a team or organization can maximize your productivity, increase satisfaction and engagement levels, and bring greater meaning and purpose to individuals and the group. Effective teams are inclusive and use the strengths of all of their members to accomplish goals and outcomes (Linley, Garcea, Harrington, Trenier, & Minhas, 2011). Teams that thrive engage meaningfully with each other while establishing positive relationships that endure over time.

❯ Positivity and the Tipping Point

Positivity in context of positive psychology does not mean the smiley face, bright yellow image that might come to your mind when you hear this term. Instead, it means the science and application of positive emotions and behaviors such as joy, gratitude, appreciation, curiosity, and resilience. Positivity "includes the positive meanings and optimistic attitudes that trigger positive emotions . . . and the long-term impact that positive emotions have on your character, relationships, communities, and environment" (Fredrickson, 2009, p. 6). In her study of emotions, Fredrickson (2009) developed the "broaden and build" theory of positive emotions: positive emotions open individuals to possibilities and spark interest and curiosity. Positivity transforms and allows people to discover new ways of being, learning, and acquiring new knowledge (Fredrickson, 2009). Parallel with one of the leadership assumptions associated with the Relational Leadership Model, positivity can be learned and developed. In leadership, positivity opens up new possibilities and can provide leaders and members with a more optimistic and hopeful perspective. Positivity also can cause a mind shift from seeing what is wrong with individuals and organizations to what is *right* about them. Neither people nor organizations are perfect, but often there is more that is right and can be appreciated than we realize.

Using mathematical modeling of group behaviors and the theory behind positivity, Barbara Fredrickson and Marcial Losada studied the characteristics of high-performing teams and those that were floundering (Fredrickson, 2009). In summary, they found that team members' connectivity to each other was related to higher levels of flourishing and greater performance.

They discovered the tipping point for human flourishing in team settings is three to one—three positive encounters for each negative encounter, which is called the positivity ratio. Fredrickson (2009) defines the tipping point as "that sweet spot in between where a small change makes a difference" (p. 11). In reference to positivity, Fredrickson further describes the tipping point as "a precise ratio to tip your life to the flourishing side" (p. 11). John Gottman, who studies the dynamics in marriages found the tipping point to be five to one for couples who were flourishing (cited in Fredrickson, 2009).

These researchers are careful to caution that too much positivity has negative effects. In the three to one tipping point, the one negative is just as important as the three positive inter-actions. Fredrickson (2009) describes this as the "appropriate negative" (p. 136). An appropriate negative allows for conflict to yield productive ends versus destructive ones. A negative response that is critical and destructive of another person would not factor into the three to one tipping point because that type of negativity does not promote learning and growth. A negative emotion such as guilt can be resolved for the betterment of a relationship, but an emotion like contempt can cause irreversible damage (Fredrickson, 2009). An appropriate negative allows for authenticity, learning, and growth, especially in having difficult conversations with group members.

The tipping point in leadership and in teams can lead to powerful outcomes, including enduring and meaningful relationships, greater productivity, and increased satisfaction. Fredrickson's (2009) research validated that positivity broadens minds, builds resources, fuels resilience, forecasts flourishing, and elevates languishing states to flourishing levels.

Using the science from her work on positivity, Fredrickson (2009) proposes tools to assist in raising levels of positivity. Here are some examples that can be applied in your leadership development and in teams (pp. 200–213):

Tool 1: Be open—cultivate curiosity and be aware of what you are experiencing in the moment.

Tool 2: Create high-quality connections—establish relationships that are life-giving, dynamic, energetic, and result in mutual appreciation.

Tool 3: Cultivate kindness—extend yourself to others who make a positive difference and positive connection while noticing the good feelings you experience.

Tool 4: Develop distractions—work intentionally to rid your mind of unhealthy distractions and catch yourself when you notice your negativity increasing or when you are about to engage in a potentially destructive behavior. Identify activities and thoughts that counter unhealthy distractions.

Tool 5: Dispute negative thinking—counter negative thoughts that lead to self-doubt or ill will with facts that dispute negative patterns of thinking.

Tool 6: Learn and apply your strengths—identify your strengths through assessments such as the Clifton StrengthsQuest and Values in Action (VIA) mentioned in Chapter Four. Reflect on the daily activities that energize you when you have opportunities to apply your strengths and develop strategies that can leverage your and others' strengths.

Tool 7: Ritualize gratitude—make it a habit to reflect upon what you are most grateful for each day. You might do this at the start or end of each day as a personal reflection or by keeping a daily gratitude journal. You can start or end meetings by asking members what they are most grateful for about the organization, the meeting, or each other.

Tool 8: Visualize your future—create a mental image of where you would like to be or where you would like your organization to be in the future. Think of what success would look like and what the experience would be like if you and all those in the organization reach your and their potential. Reflect on the purpose that drives you and your mission. You can use this reflection to help write a mission statement or multiyear plan for your organization.

> Positive Leadership

Kim Cameron (2008) used a powerful metaphor to frame his concept of positive leadership called the heliotropic effect (p. xi). Living systems tend to grow toward what gives life and grow away from what depletes life. Examples of the heliotropic effect include plants growing toward light and people learning faster and retaining more from positive information than negative. The same is true in leadership. People thrive on what is life-giving and are inspired by hope and optimism versus what depletes them. Kouzes and Posner (2003) also talk about the importance of bringing out the best in people in the leadership process as a way to both promote growth and strengthen trust between leaders and members. Cameron's concept of positive leadership includes three connotations (pp. 2–3):

1. Positive leadership facilitates positively deviant performance. Positive leaders assist members and organizations in achieving extraordinary performance and successes. Positively deviant performance means that a group significantly exceeded its performance expectations.

2. Positive leadership includes an affirmation bias that includes a focus on strengths and an affirmation of human potential. The orientation of positive leadership is on thriving together. Even in facing challenges and problems, positive leaders build on these obstacles to achieve positive outcomes and focus on strategies that provide positive energy to members and the organization that maximizes everyone's potential.

3. Borrowing from Aristotle's eudaemonist assumption that human systems are inclined toward achieving the best of the human condition, positive leaders have an orientation toward virtuousness—extracting the best of people by elevating them and encouraging virtuous behavior in others. They understand that each member of their team or organization has great worth and strengths.

Like other positive psychology scholars, Cameron cautions that negativity should not be ignored; positive leadership includes approaches and strategies that can build from the negative toward the development of positive outcomes. Cameron's model of positive leadership is grounded in social behavioral research on leaders and focuses on both performance expectations and cultivating individuals toward greater levels of thriving together in the leadership process.

Four strategies Cameron (2008) proposes for leaders and members that enable greater human potential (life-giving) and facilitate exceptional performance (positively deviant performance) are:

1. *Creating a positive climate*—referring to Fredrickson's positivity ratio, enabling positive emotions in the leadership process (joy, gratitude, appreciation); leaders set the tone by fostering compassionate and virtuous behaviors among all members and by modeling those same behaviors. Positive emotions and behaviors predominate over negative ones.

2. *Maintaining positive relationships*—establishing relationships that facilitate positively deviant performance and learning; experiencing relationships that are uplifting and result in quality connections with one another.

3. *Facilitating positive communications*—adopting strengths language and using language and words that convey possibilities, hope, advocacy, and curiosity (seeking others' views and having a curiosity about others). Leaders communicate a preponderance of positive statements compared to negative statements and use supportive communication when addressing concerns and shortcomings (giving negative feedback and suggesting alternative behaviors while still maintaining a healthy regard for one another).

4. *Enabling positive meaning*—leaders infuse a sense of meaning and purpose in the tasks and responsibilities of members using strategies that allow members to see personal value and long-term impact of their work; strategies of enabling positive meaning include building high-quality connections and community within the group and having participants see the impact of their work on others.

Table 12.1 **Domains of Leadership Strength**

Executing	Influencing	Relationship Building	Strategic Thinking
Achiever	Activator	Adaptability	Analytical
Arranger	Command	Developer	Context
Belief	Communication	Connectedness	Futuristic
Consistency	Competition	Empathy	Ideation
Deliberative	Maximizer	Harmony	Input
Discipline	Self-assurance	Includer	Intellection
Focus	Significance	Individualization	Learner
Responsibility	Woo	Positivity	Strategic
Restorative		Relator	

Source: Rath & Conchie, 2008.

Cameron (2008) proposes a checklist of behaviors that facilitate these four strategies of positive leadership. As a way to tailor these behaviors to your unique strengths, identify the behaviors in each of the four strategies that are natural to you and apply those in your interactions with others. See Table 12.1 for the checklist of positive leadership development behaviors.

Even using these positive leadership strategies, you most likely will encounter individuals who deplete energy from the group. Cameron calls these types of members, "negative energizers" (p. 42). Negative energizers bring down the group, reduce levels of morale, and cause unnecessary drama and distractions. Positive energizers bring the heliotropic effect to life—they move the group to greater levels of meaning and purpose while uplifting each other. Leaders tend to spend more time appeasing the negative energizers, which ironically ignores those who are doing good work and are meaningfully engaged. Pay careful attention to the behaviors of others you spend the most time on and consider investing the majority of your energy on the positive energizers. Teams that are thriving and performing at high levels have three times more positive energizers in their group than average teams (Cameron, 2008).

› PERMA Model of Well-Being

Building upon the work in positive psychology, including positive emotions and relationships, Martin Seligman (2011) proposes a model with five measurable dimensions that contribute to human flourishing and thriving called, PERMA (p. 24). Well-being is defined as subjective life satisfaction and one's assessment of what it means to live a good life (Diener, 2009). In a group and leadership context, flourishing is an essential construct in facilitating positive change, having impact, finding meaning and purpose, and living a life congruent with your values. Seligman's five dimensions of the PERMA model are

1. Positive emotion—expressing positive emotions with others that bring greater levels of vitality, resilience, and self-esteem
2. Engagement—being curious, seeking out learning, interacting with others
3. Relationships—caring about others and being cared for
4. Meaning and purpose—seeing value and worthiness in life's activities
5. Achievement—accomplishing something in service of a purpose larger than one's self interest

The PERMA model builds upon strengths-based leadership, positivity and the tipping point, and positive leadership. The five elements of the PERMA model contribute to individual and group flourishing.

Applying the elements of PERMA individually and in the leadership process will assist in achieving greater levels of human flourishing in groups and communities. These five components taken together help groups thrive to achieve greater meaning and purpose, goals, and high-quality connections with one another.

The concept of well-being is equally important for individuals and for organizations. On an individual level, advancing one's well-being tips a person toward greater levels of flourishing and happiness. In organizations, greater levels of well-being result in higher productivity, lower absenteeism in employment settings, and higher levels of engagement (Robertson & Cooper, 2011). In the context of leadership, it is a responsibility of leaders to assist in facilitating the well-being and growth of others.

> The Cycle of Renewal in Leadership Development

The health of a leader or participant is as important as the organization's goals and outcomes. A leader who is stressed, unbalanced, physically exhausted, or overwhelmed is not likely to be as effective as a leader who inspires through positivity. Being in leadership positions can be like living in a fishbowl—others seem to be watching what you do all the time. It is critical for all participants to pay attention to their mental and spiritual being. Leaders tend to take care of others and to put their personal needs aside as they advance the needs of their group and its members. Although this is noble, the leader's health is sometimes sacrificed or compromised for the good of others. A balanced approach would suggest that the leader's needs, such as personal time away from the organization without feeling guilty, time to reflect, and other opportunities for personal renewal, be balanced with organizational needs and priorities.

Personal or individual renewal can be viewed as a proactive strategy, in that a person works intentionally to bring new perspectives and energy into a task or role. Conversely, renewal can be approached in a reactive way or as a means to correct an already unhealthy or unbalanced lifestyle. Some students, unfortunately, realize too late that working 14 hours a day, six or seven days a week nonstop results in burnout, broken relationships, serious health problems, and ultimately a negative effect on their organizations. These cases have been chronicled in our daily newspapers by stories of university presidents, congressional leaders, or athletes who step down from their roles because they need to spend more time with family or to pursue other interests. They reflect that their jobs did not permit them to find balance in their lives.

Women and people of color may also feel pressure to work twice as hard to achieve the same recognition and credibility as their male or White counterparts (Morrison, 1996), and often are turned to as supports for others. While that adds to their impact, it also adds to their stress. This added stress can lead to burnout, dissatisfaction, or disappointment.

We also have positive role models in leaders and members whose lifestyles enable them to be productive in their roles. Perhaps they learned the hard way that there is more to life than a career on the fast track or working harder to get more recognition and material rewards. This realization might have come from a personal shipwreck in their lives—the sudden death of a family member or similar personal tragedies may cause leaders to reflect on what is most important in life.

STANDARD ESSAY

I have to be honest; college immediately greeted me with busy schedules and conflicting priorities. How could it not? From living a fairly compartmentalized life, I was thrown into a world where you lived, studied, worked, ate, slept, and socialized in the same building. It's an overwhelming task to blend every aspect of your life together, all the while trying to "find yourself" and figure out "meaning in your life." You'll hear anybody say it—"balance is the key to leadership." Not to pile on the cliché expressions all at once, but that seemed "easier said than done." I adversely hung from the extremes of the scale, tipping it in one way or the other—never initially finding a middle ground. This, obviously, took a toll on every aspect of my life. One week my grades were great at the expense of my sleeping and eating patterns. Another week I was sleeping and eating well, but my personal life got difficult to manage. All that time was spent trying to reconstruct that "compartmentalized" life that I had in the past and—cyclically—getting frustrated when it didn't work in my favor. I finally realized that a truly great leader knows how to integrate all aspects of their life. It sounds pretty basic, but once I merely informed my employers about school, or my friends about work, the idea of balance seemed exponentially more realistic and achievable.

Sukanya (Priya) Roychowdhury is a undergraduate of Michigan State University where she is pursuing a major in psychology with a minor in educational studies. She has been a resident mentor for two years and was also a choreographer for the university's largest cultural dance performance.

Some leaders possess a philosophy that they need daily or regular time for personal or spiritual renewal, and they work to avoid leading a stressful, unhealthy life that can lead to burnout. Dr. Freeman Hrabowski, president of the University of Maryland, Baltimore County, enjoys "reading 19th century British literature to get out of this fast-paced period" (Lucas, 1999, p. 179). Wilma Mankiller, former chief of the Cherokee Nation, had regular conversations with a confidant who understood her and with whom she could be open and honest (Lucas, 1999). Martin Luther King III, son of former civil rights leader Martin Luther King Jr. and former president of the Southern Christian Leadership Conference, "meditates and turns to God and prays as a way to gain strength" (Lucas, 1999, p. 181).

The relational leadership principles presented in this book emphasize being process-oriented, seeking common purpose with others, being inclusive, empowering, and ethical. As we noted earlier, being the kind of person who practices this philosophy of leadership is being what Covey (1991) calls a principle-centered leader. Covey relates values and beliefs to leadership by identifying characteristics of principle-centered leaders. They are continually learning. They are service-oriented. They radiate positive energy. They believe in themselves and in other people. They lead balanced lives. They see life as an adventure. They are synergistic. They exercise for self-renewal (pp. 33–39).

> Resonant Leaders and Renewal

Drawing from decades of research and work with leaders, Boyatzis and McKee (2005) talk about great leaders in terms of leaders who "are awake, aware, and attuned to themselves, to others, and to the world around them. They commit to their beliefs, stand strong in their values, and live full, passionate lives" (p. 3). In describing these types of great leaders, Boyatzis and McKee refer to them as resonant leaders. These types of leaders understand the value of developing practices that sustain their effectiveness by being able to manage the physiological and psychological ups and downs of leadership. They bring resonance to others and themselves by developing the competencies of self-awareness, self-management, social awareness, and relationship management (Boyatzis & McKee, 2005). They are able to effectively respond to the demands and pressures of leadership while maintaining hope and courage toward a positive future. Resonant leaders' emotions are contagious and inspire others through their passion, commitment, deep concern for others, and value on extraordinary performance.

Leaders who overextend themselves for others and sacrifice too much of themselves in the leadership process experience the opposite of resonance—*dissonance*. Boyatzis and McKee observe that leaders who are burned out, exhausted, and overextended experience dissonance, which like resonance, is contagious and but has a negative impact on others. Factors that cause dissonance in leaders include stress and lack of time for renewal. They get into what Boyatzis & McKee (2005) refer to as the Sacrifice Syndrome. Leaders in the Sacrifice Syndrome burn out completely or continue to act in unhealthy ways that might result in damaging relationships, frustration, and unawareness of their impact on others.

The reality is that leaders experience some level of sacrifice, but the key is not to tip too far when the effects of sacrifice are destructive. Boyatzis and McKee (2005) believe that resonant leaders are able to manage the Cycle of Sacrifice and Renewal.

In their work with executive leaders who they identified as resonant leaders, Boyatzis and McKee found three elements that were key in the Cycle of Sacrifice and Renewal: mindfulness, hope, and compassion (2005). They define mindfulness as "living in a state of full, conscious awareness of one's whole self, other people, and the context in which we live and work . . . being awake, aware, and attending—to ourselves and to the world around us" (pp. 8–9). Integrating all three elements together—mindfulness, hope, and compassion—can provide a source of renewal and resilience for leaders, especially when facing stressful situations or complex challenges.

STUDENT ESSAY

Vulnerability is not a sign of weakness, but a quality that can inspire and empower others. This revelation is quite the contrary to my beliefs when I first started college, but I have come to realize this from my peers who have inspired me to be a better person.

As an international student from Hong Kong, I was brought up in a family that truly values respect, especially those who are more experienced than I am. Respect is, undeniably, a great virtue, but I can sometimes come off as being too reserved in the U.S. Fortunately, my drive to learn has allowed me to overcome this barrier to be proactive in forming new relationships. However, there is one thing that I could not quite surmount—self-expression. Talking about my feelings seems almost unnatural, so I usually just listen to others talk about theirs.

It wasn't until the end of freshman year (at a retreat for newly elected execs of a student group) when I decided to give sharing about who I am a try. We first talked about the aspects of ourselves that we are happy to share with others. Then, we were asked to take a risk and reveal the things that we are normally too insecure to share. That was the first time I ever talked about my sexual orientation—-this moment of vulnerability has changed my life for the better ever since.

My "leap of faith" and the support of my friends helped me gain confidence to open up to more people. As I began to share more with the people I trust, I became much more willing to talk about my struggles and experiences with a wider audience. This in turn has helped me better connect with others and instill a sense of empowerment in some of my younger peers. For example, I have had some deep conversations with a few of my residents who identify as LGBTQIA [lesbian, gay, bisexual, transgender, queer, intersex, and asexual] to help with their adjustment in college.

My transformation allowed me to discover this revelation about leadership: to amplify your positive influence in your community, you should strive to understand and accept yourself. After I became more comfortable with who I am and more open in revealing my sensitivity, I have become more empathetic and patient. It has permitted me to be better at voicing my opinions, challenging my peers respectfully, and instilling a sense of self-assurance in others. All in all, I can see that I have grown to be a better facilitator to help my peers reach their potential.

I attribute a major part of my growth in the last four years to the many heroes who have shared their vulnerable side and inspired me to be myself, and I hope to continue their footsteps to develop my fellow schoolmates to become better leaders.

Monatrice Lam graduated from Washington University in St. Louis in 2012 with a bachelor's degree in chemistry and physics. She was a freshman resident advisor for the Liggett Koenig Residential College, and an executive board member of the St. Louis Area Dance Marathon that raises money for the Children's Miracle Network.

Being in a cycle of renewal requires intentionality and willingness to try new behaviors, such as mindfulness practices, and new approaches to how you manage your life. Boyatzis and McKee (2005) assert that leaders "need to focus deliberately on creating resonance within ourselves—mind, body, heart, and spirit—and then channel our resonance to the people and groups around us" (p. 9–10).

Consider several interventions or practices to keep you engaged in the opportunities of leadership while keeping yourself renewed:

1. *Stretch yourself to learn and to do new things.* Learning and confidence are built by experiencing new situations that require you to use your skills and values to adapt or to make changes. Fear of failure is an obstacle to your growth. The first woman commandant of the U.S. Naval Academy was asked about her experience and her advice to others in a similar situation. In describing how she best learned, her reply was "to find your comfort zone, and then stay out of it." Think of all the exciting possibilities for you and your organization with "a healthy disregard for the impossible" (LeaderShape Institute, 1996).

2. *Develop the realization that what you are doing matters.* People who know that their contributions make a difference somehow or that there is value in their work have a sense of purpose and confidence that sustains them through many difficult times. In a classic study of 60,000 Americans, Gail Sheehy (1981) sought to identify characteristics of well-being and life satisfaction. She found the ability to say "My life has meaning and direction" was the most salient factor distinguishing happy adults from those who were not.

3. *Engage in renewal as a holistic process that involves your mind, body, soul, and spirit* (Boyatzis & McKee, 2005). Leadership can be consuming and result in self-sacrifices that might impact you physically and mentally. Tending to yourself in the leadership process, seeking ways to reduce your stress, and paying attention to your physical and mental energy is key in your leadership development. Boyatzis and McKee (2005) reflect that "renewal can be a conscious process that actually invokes physiological and psychological changes that enable us to counter the effects of chronic stress and sacrifice" (p. 8).

4. *Make time for peaceful reflection and centering.* Reflect on what is actually happening and identify all your possible alternatives for action. On a personal level, constant reflection is needed to stay in touch with your inner core and to stay centered with your values and principles and with knowing what is really important to you. Many practices can bring you to peaceful reflection and centering, such as mediation, yoga, taking a walk to clear your mind while taking in the surrounding environment, and journaling, to name a few.

5. *Maintain healthy, supportive relationships.* This means relationships within your group and outside of your group. Develop relationships with mentors. Leaders often mentor others in the organization. Leaders also need the rich support and empowerment that can be derived from a mentor, someone who has your best interests at heart and can help you stay centered, renewed, and balanced while leading others. "Pity the leader who is caught between unloving critics and uncritical lovers. Leaders need reassurance, but just as important they need advisors who tell them the truth, gently but candidly." (Gardner, 1990, p. 135). Maintaining personal relationships that support your growth and

provide you with insights about your leadership and impact on others will assist in your leadership development, while giving you a source of renewal. Enlisting a mentor, friend, or advisor to serve as your thought partner can help you make personal transformations.

STUDENT ESSAY ◆

As a student at the University of California, Merced, the best experiences were from peer interactions. One particular student who made a positive influence on me is a student named Johnny Moua. His work ethic and knowledge inspired me to be like him. Throughout my two years here at UCM, Johnny encouraged my friends and me to take on leadership roles. He helped me connect with many other inspiring individuals, such as Maynard Medefind, a legendary Yosemite National Park Ranger. Johnny was a great mentor who saw potential in me and led me to many different resources. He challenged me by offering leadership opportunities such as nominating me to take an officer position for the Hmong Student Association. Many of the leadership skills I possess are due to Johnny. I was very fortunate to encounter an amazing individual like him. From the people I met and the involvement I had, I became more confident and outspoken. I pushed myself to take on responsibilities that will make me a better person or leader. Along the way, I made sure gain knowledge because learning is a lifelong process.

Nou Lee is a third year undergraduate at the University of California, Merced where she is studying human biology and doing research with faculty and the community. She was an orientation leader and is currently a peer instructor as well as a member of the Project Prevention Coalition, the Pre-pharmacy Club, and the Hmong Student Association.

Your personal leadership development can be a source of renewal-seeking opportunities to develop new skills and to find various avenues (careers, community service, recreational activities, and so forth) for exercising your leadership.

> Spirituality and Renewal

In Chapter Six, we discussed Johnson (2012), who uses the metaphor of casting shadow or casting light in describing the ethical dimensions of leadership. Parker Palmer (2000) uses this same analogy of shadow and light in describing the relationship between spirituality and leadership. Leaders can "shine a light that allows new growth to flourish, while others cast a shadow under which seedlings die" (p. 78). Paying attention to both the shadow and light sides of leadership (e.g., the criticisms leaders often receive) brings an understanding of their interplay versus compartmentalizing them. It is a danger to have the shadows go unchecked. "Leaders need not only technical skills to manage the external world but also the spiritual skills to journey inward toward the source of both shadow and light" (p. 79). Casting more light and fewer shadows is a renewal strategy for personal benefit and for those in relationship with you.

Giving and receiving love in all kinds of relationships, not just personal, are characteristics of self-renewed individuals (Gardner, 1981). "They are capable of depending on others and of being depended upon. They can see life through another's eyes and feel it through another's heart" (p. 15).

Positive leadership and the construct of well-being have a spiritual quality attached to them with a focus on wholeness, connectedness, meaning, purpose, inspiration, and transcendence. Spirituality is not synonymous with religion. Astin, Astin, and Lindholm (2011) define spirituality as having

> to do with the values that we hold most dear, our sense of who we are and where we come from, our beliefs about why we are here—the meaning and purpose that we see in our work and our life—and our sense of connectedness to one another and to the world around us. (p. 4)

They conclude that spiritual individuals possess qualities such as love, compassion, and equanimity. Equanimity is defined as "a general sense of psychological or spiritual well-being and optimism, coupled with a demeanor reflecting composure and calm" (p. 50). Being in a state of equanimity is an important condition of self-renewal for leaders, providing a capacity to redirect negative emotions such as anger and frustration in productive ways (Astin, Astin, & Lindholm, 2011). Leaders such as Nelson Mandela and the Dali Lama displayed high levels of equanimity in responding to injustices brought about from their respective country's leaders. Being able to bounce back from disappointment or loss, responding to negativity with careful diplomacy, and seeing the goodness of each day can keep leaders in a continuous state of self-renewal.

The five components of the Relational Leadership Model connect well with many of the concepts from the field of positive psychology. Positive emotions, positive relationships, and meaning and purpose from positive psychology are integral concepts throughout the Relational Leadership Model. Table 12.2 shows how various positive psychology concepts relate to the five components of the Relational Leadership Model.

Table 12.2 **Connections of the Relationship Leadership Models with Positive Psychology Concepts**

Relational Leadership Model	Positive Psychology Concepts
Purposeful	Meaning and purpose (PERMA Model); enabling positive meaning (positive leadership) achievement (PERMA); spirituality
Ethical	Maintaining positive relationships (Positive Leadership) (how you treat others); virtues in action (VIA); strengths; mindfulness
Empowering	Positivity and the tipping point; resonant leadership; creating high-quality connections (positivity); ritualize gratitude (positivity); positive emotions (PERMA); strengths
Inclusive	Creating a positive climate (Positive Leadership); engagement (PERMA); relationships (PERMA); strengths
Process-oriented	Strengths; resonant leadership; positivity and the tipping point

> Chapter Summary

Chapter One raised a few essential questions: What is your purpose? Who are you? What do you stand for? These questions are central for advancing a leadership approach of thriving together. Thriving together means that everyone in the leadership process has outlets and opportunities to achieve higher levels of flourishing and well-being. Understanding yourself, being aware of your inner core, paying attention to the signals your mind, body, and soul give you, and being comfortable with yourself are elements of self-renewal. Your journey to self-renewal will have no end destination. The process of renewal is cyclical.

Be careful not to fall victim to thinking that you are renewed when in fact you are not. Renewal affects your entire being. On your journey to renewal, make sure your mind, body, and soul together benefit from this process. Gardner (1990) observes, "The consideration leaders must never forget is that the key to renewal is the release of human energy and talent" (p. 136). When your mind, body, and soul are in harmony, you can thrive together with others and become a greater asset to your organization and to yourself.

> Chapter Activities

1. Identify examples of individuals in your organization who are negative energizers. What impact do they have on the group? Identify examples of positive energizers. What impact do they have on the group? How can you maximize the contributions of positive energizers?
2. In reviewing Fredrickson's tools for promoting positivity, which ones resonate the most for you? How can these tools enhance your leadership impact? How can you apply these in your organizations or communities?
3. Identify your top five strengths. In thinking the PERMA Model of Well-Being, what connections can you make among all five components and how these can be applied in groups?

4. The title of this chapter is Thriving Together. What would your organization or university look like if it was *thriving together*?

5. Reflect on the following questions: What does self-renewal mean to you? Right now, do you feel renewed? Why or why not?

6. What role does equanimity play in your leadership?

7. Think of an individual who you would identify as a resonant leader. Someone how is mindful, hopeful, and compassionate and who intentionally seeks ways to stay renewed. What does this person do that brings resonance to others and to himself or herself? (If possible, arrange an interview to ask questions to explore this.)

8. Reflect on your aspirations and purpose in life. What is your calling? What brings greater meaning and purpose to your life?

9. What self-renewal strategies or techniques can you use to reach your full potential in life or in your leadership?

> A Final Reflection

Through eleven chapters, we have taken a journey through the world of leadership. A theme throughout this book has been our belief that leadership means change—change for the greater good of the people in your group, organization, community, and world. We hope that you have found the Relational Leadership Model to be a useful guide when you work with others to accomplish change.

We ended each chapter with a series of reflections and activities. The activities are over, but we did want to end with a few questions for you to reflect on as you consider what you have learned and what the future might hold for you as a leader.

- How have you been able to apply what you have learned about leadership?
- How are you more aware of yourself?
- What things do you now see differently? How are you changing?
- How will you continue your learning about leadership?
- What is your own philosophy of leadership?
- What purpose does your leadership serve?
- How can you see the goodness in others?
- How can you bring out the best in others and maximize their strengths?
- What does it look like and feel like when you are able to do what you are best at doing on a regular basis?

As Michael Sarich and Reena Meltzer, both students at the University of Maryland, College Park when we wrote the first edition of this book, noted, "While the theories and concepts included within this text do work, they are not a substitute for work." Now it is time for you to continue on this incredible journey—into your own world of people and ideas—into your own future. We hope you have been challenged and maybe even inspired to see how you can make a difference.

We wish you well in this hard work. We know there will be rough seas ahead, but we hope you will navigate these challenges with a sense of passion, joy, and wonder and with a commitment to the relationships you will have along the way.

ADDITIONAL READINGS

Boyatzis, R., & McKee, A. (2005). *Resonant leadership: Renewing yourself and Connecting with others through mindfulness, hope, and compassion.* Boston, MA: *Harvard Business School Press.*

Cameron, K. (2008). *Positive leadership: strategies for extraordinary performance.* San Francisco, CA: Berrett-Koehler.

Fredrickson, B. (2009). *Positivity.* New York, NY: Random House.

Kashdan, T. (2009). *Curious? Discover the missing ingredient to a fulfilling life.* New York, NY: Harper Collins.

Robertson, I., & Cooper, G. (2011). *Well-being: Productivity and happiness at work.* New York, NY: Palgrave Macmillan.

Seligman, M.E.P. (2002). *Authentic happiness: Using the new positive psychology to realize your potential for lasting fulfillment.* New York, NY: The Free Press.

Seligman, M.E.P. (2011). *Flourish: A visionary new understanding of happiness and well-being.* New York, NY: Free Press.

REFERENCES

Adizes, I. (1988). *Corporate lifecycles: How and why corporations grow and die and what to do about it.* Englewood Cliffs, NJ: Prentice Hall.

Alberti, R. E., & Emmons, M. L. (1974). *Your perfect right: A guide to assertive behavior.* San Luis Obispo, CA: IMPACT.

Albrecht, K. (1994). *The northbound train.* New York, NY: AMACOM.

Alinsky, S. (1989). *Rules for radicals.* New York, NY: Vintage Books.

Allen, K. E. (1990). Making sense out of chaos: Leading and living in dynamic systems. *Campus Activities Programming,* May, 56–63.

Allen, K. E., & Cherrey, C. (2000). *Systemic leadership: Enriching the meaning of our work.* Lanham, MD: University Press of America.

Andersen, P. A. (2003). In different dimensions: Nonverbal communication and culture. In L. A. Samovar & R. E. Porter (Eds.), *Intercultural communication: A reader* (10th ed, pp. 239–252). Belmont, CA: Wadsworth.

Angelou, M. (1994). *The complete collected poems of Maya Angelou.* New York, NY: Random House.

Armour, M., & Hayles, R. (1990, July). Managing multicultural organizations. Paper presented at the Summer Institute for Intercultural Communications, Portland, OR.

Astin, A. W., & Astin, H. S. (2000). *Leadership reconsidered: Engaging higher education in social change.* Battle Creek, MI: W. K. Kellogg Foundation.

Astin, A. W., Astin, H. S., & Lindholm, J. A. (2010). *Cultivating the spirit: How college can enhance students' inner lives.* San Francisco, CA: Jossey-Bass.

Astin, H. S. (1996). Leadership for social change. *About Campus,* July/August, 4–10.

Avolio, B. J., & Gardner, W. L. (2005). Authentic leadership development: Getting to the root of positive forms of leadership. *Leadership Quarterly, 16,* 315–338.

Avolio, B. J., Gardner, W. L., Walumbwa, F. O., Luthans, F., & May, D. R. (2004). Unlocking the mask: A look at the processes by which authentic leaders impact follower attitudes and behaviors. *Leadership Quarterly, 15,* 801–823.

Avolio, B. J., & Kahai, S. S. (2003). Adding the "E" to e-leadership: How it may impact your leadership. *Organizational Dynamics*, *31*(4), 325–338.

Avolio, B. J., Walumbwa, F. O., & Weber, T. J. (2009). Leadership: Current theories, research, and future directions. *Annual Review of Psychology*, 60, 421–449.

Bandura, A. (1977). *Social learning theory*. Englewood Cliffs, NJ: Prentice Hall.

Bar-On, R. (2007). The Bar-On model of emotional intelligence: A valid, robust and applicable EI model. *Organisations & People*, *14*, 27–34.

Barabási, A.-L. (2002). *Linked: The new science of networks*. Cambridge, MA: Perseus.

Bass, B. M. (1981). *Stogdill's handbook of leadership: Theory and research* (2nd ed). New York, NY: Free Press.

Bass, B. M. (1990). *Bass & Stogdill's handbook of leadership: Theory, research, and managerial applications* (3rd ed). New York, NY: Free Press.

Beauchamp, T. L., & Childress, J. F. (1979). *Principles of biomedical ethics*. New York, NY: Oxford University Press.

Beauchamp, T. L., & Childress, J. F. (1989). *Principles of biomedical ethics* (3rd ed). New York, NY: Oxford University Press.

Beck, L. G., & Murphy, J. (1994). *Ethics in educational leadership programs: An expanding role*. Thousand Oaks, CA: Corwin Press.

Benne, K. D., & Sheats, P. (1948). Functional roles of group members. *Journal of Social Issues*, *2*, 42–47.

Bennett, M. (1979). Overcoming the Golden Rule: Sympathy and empathy. In D. Nimmo (Ed.), *Communication yearbook 3* (pp. 407–422). New Brunswick, NJ: Transaction Books.

Bennett, M. J. (2004). From ethnocentrism to ethnorelativism. In J. S. Wurzel (Ed.) *Toward multiculturalism: A reader in multicultural education* (2nd ed, pp. 62–78). Newton, MA: Intercultural Resource Corporation.

Bennett, M. J. (rev. 2011). A developmental model of Intercultural Sensitivity. Retrieved from IDR Institute website http://www.idrinstitute.org (pdf).

Bennett, J. (2011). Developing intercultural competence: For international education faculty and staff. Paper presented at the 2011 AIEA Conference, Feb. 20–23, San Francisco.

Bennis, W. G. (1989). *On becoming a leader*. Reading, MA: Addison-Wesley.

Bennis, W. G., & Goldsmith, J. (1994). *Learning to lead.* Reading, MA: Addison-Wesley.

Bennis, W. G., & Nanus, B. (1985). *Leaders: The strategies for taking charge.* New York, NY: Harper & Row.

Bennis, W. G., & Thomas, R. J. (2002). *Geeks and geezers: How era, values, and defining moments shape leaders.* Boston, MA: Harvard Business School Press.

Berman, S., & La Farge, P. (Eds.). (1993). *Promising practices in teaching social responsibility.* Albany, NY: State University of New York Press.

Berry, L. L. (2004). The collaborative organization: Leadership lessons from Mayo Clinic. *Organizational Dynamics, 33,* 228–242.

Bird, F. B., & Waters, J. A. (1989). The moral muteness of managers. *California Management Review, 32*(1), 73–87.

Block, P. (1993). *Stewardship: Choosing service over self-interest.* San Francisco, CA: Berrett-Koehler.

Bobo, K. A., Kendall, J., & Max, S. (2001). *Organizing for social change: Midwest Academy manual for activists* (3rd ed). Santa Ana, CA: Seven Locks Press.

Bok, D. (1982). *Beyond the ivory tower: Social responsibilities of the modern university.* Cambridge, MA: Harvard University Press.

Bok, D. (1990). *Universities and the future of America.* Durham, NC: Duke University Press.

Bolman, L. G., & Deal, T. E. (2003). Reframing ethics and spirit. In *Business leadership: A Jossey-Bass reader* (pp. 330–350). San Francisco, CA: Jossey-Bass.

Bolman, L. G., & Deal, T. (2008). *Reframing organizations: Artistry, choice, and leadership* (4th ed). San Francisco, CA: Jossey-Bass.

Bonebrake, K. (2002). College students' Internet use, relationship formation, and personality correlates. *CyberPsychology & Behavior, 5,* 551–558.

Bornstein, D. (2007). *How to change the world: Social entrepreneurs and the power of new ideas* (Updated edition). New York, NY: Oxford University Press.

Bothwell, L. (1983). *The art of leadership: Skill-building techniques that produce results.* Englewood Cliffs, NJ: Prentice Hall.

Boyatzis, R., & McKee, A. (2005). *Resonant leadership: Renewing yourself and connecting with others through mindfulness, hope, and compassion.* Boston, MA: Harvard Business School Press.

Bridges, W. (1980). *Transitions: Making sense of life's changes*. Reading, MA: Addison-Wesley.

Bridges, W. (1991). *Managing transitions: Making the most of change*. Cambridge, MA: Perseus Books.

Bridges, W. (2003). *Managing transitions: Making the most of change* (2nd ed). Cambridge, MA: Perseus Books.

Briggs, J., & Peat, F. (1999). *Seven life lessons of chaos: Timeless wisdom from the science of change*. New York: HarperCollins.

Brionesa, R. L., Kucha, B., Liu, B. F., & Jin, Y. (2011). Keeping up with the digital age: How the American Red Cross uses social media to build relationships. *Public Relations Review, 37*(1), 37–43.

Broome, B. J. (1993). Managing differences in conflict resolution: The role of relational empathy. In D.J.D. Sandole & H. van der Merwe (Eds.), *Conflict resolution theory and practice: Integration and application* (pp. 97–111). New York, NY: Manchester University Press.

Brown, I. (1963). *Understanding other cultures*. Englewood Cliffs, NJ: Prentice Hall.

Bruteau, B. (1990). Eucharistic ecology and ecological spirituality. *Cross Current, 40*, 499–514.

Bryson, J. M., & Crosby, B. C. (1992). *Leadership for the common good*. San Francisco, CA: Jossey-Bass.

Buber, M. (1958). *I and thou*. New York, NY: Scribner.

Buckingham. M., & Clifton, D. O. (2001). *Now, discover your strengths*. New York, NY: Free Press.

Burns, J. M. (1978). *Leadership*. New York, NY: Harper & Row.

Bushe, G. R. (2000). Appreciative inquiry with teams. In D. L. Cooperrider, P. F. Sorensen Jr., D. Whitney, & T. F. Yaeger (Eds.), *Appreciative inquiry: Rethinking human organization toward a positive theory of change* (pp. 183–194). Champaign, IL: Stipes.

Cabrera, A., & Unruh, G. (2012). *Being global: How to think, act, and lead in a transformed world*. Boston, MA: Harvard Business Review Press.

Cameron, K. (2008). *Positive leadership: strategies for extraordinary performance*. San Francisco, CA: Berrett-Koehler.

Campus Compact. (n.d.). Retrieved July 28, 2006, from http://www.campuscompact.org/

Carnegie Foundation for the Advancement of Teaching. (1990). *Campus life: In search of community.* Princeton, NJ: Carnegie Foundation for the Advancement of Teaching.

Carse, J. (1986). *Finite and infinite games.* New York, NY: Ballantine.

Cartwright, T. (1991). Planning and chaos theory. *APA Journal,* Winter, 44–56.

Cathcart, R. S., Samovar, L. A., & Henman, L. D. (Eds.). (1996). *Small group communication: Theory and practice* (7th ed). Madison, WI: Brown & Benchmark.

Center for Army Leadership & Department of the Army. (2004). *The U.S. Army leadership field manual.* New York, NY: McGraw-Hill.

Center for Information & Research on Civic Learning & Engagement (December 19, 2008). Young voters in the 2008 presidential election. http://www.civicyouth.org/PopUps/FactSheets/FS_08_exit_polls.pdf

Chaleff, I. (1995). *The courageous follower: Standing up to and for our leaders.* San Francisco, CA: Berrett-Koehler.

Chambers, E. T., & Cowan, M. A. (2004). *Roots for radicals: Organizing for power, action, and justice.* New York, NY: Continuum.

Chickering, A. W., Dalton, J. C., & Stamm, L. (2006). *Encouraging authenticity and spirituality in higher education.* San Francisco, CA: Jossey-Bass.

Chrislip, D. D., & Larson, C. E. (1994). *Collaborative leadership: How citizens and civic leaders can make a difference.* San Francisco, CA: Jossey-Bass.

Ciulla, J. B. (1995). Leadership ethics: Mapping the territory. *Business Ethics Quarterly, 5,* 5–28.

Clifton, D. O., & Nelson, P. (1992). *Soar with your strengths.* New York, NY: Delacorte Press.

Cohen, M. D., & March, J. G. (1974). *Leadership and ambiguity* (2nd ed). Boston, MA: Harvard Business School Press.

Collins, J., & Porras, J. (1994). *Built to last: Successful habits of visionary companies.* New York, NY: HarperCollins.

Conner, D. R. (1992). *Managing at the speed of change: How resilient managers succeed and prosper where others fail.* New York, NY: Villard Books.

Cooperrider, D. L., & Srivastva, S. (1987). Appreciative inquiry in organizational life. In W. Pasmore & R. Woodman (Eds.), *Research in organization change and development* (Vol. 1, pp. 129–169). Greenwich, CT: JAI Press.

Cooperrider, D. L., & Whitney, D. (2000). A positive revolution in change: Appreciative inquiry. In D. L. Cooperrider, P. F. Sorensen Jr., D. Whitney, & T. F. Yaeger (Eds.), *Appreciative inquiry: Rethinking human organization toward a positive theory of change* (pp. 3–27). Champaign, IL: Stipes.

Cooperrider, D. L., & Whitney, D. (2005). *Appreciative inquiry: A positive revolution in change.* San Francisco, CA: Berrett-Koehler.

Cormier, S., & Hackney, H. (2005). *Counseling strategies and interventions* (6th ed). Boston, MA: Allyn & Bacon.

Covey, S. R. (1991). *Principle-centered leadership.* New York, NY: Summit Books.

Crum, T. F. (1987). *The magic of conflict.* New York, NY: Simon & Schuster.

Cullen, M. (2008). *35 dumb things well-intentioned people say.* Garden City, NJ: Morgan James.

Cullinan, C. (1999). Vision, privilege, and the limits of tolerance. *Electronic Magazine of Multicultural Education, 1*(2), n.p. Retrieved July 28, 2006, from http://www.eastern.edu/publications/emme/1999spring/cullinan.html

Davidow, W., & Malone, M. (1992). *The virtual corporation: Structuring and revitalizing the corporation for the 21st century.* New York, NY: HarperBusiness.

Davidson, M. N. (2012). The end of diversity: How leaders make differences really matter. *Leader To Leader, 64,* 51–56.

Davidson, R. J., & Begley, S. (2012). *The emotional life of your brain.* New York, NY: Hudson Street Press.

De George, R. T. (1986). *Business ethics* (2nd ed). New York, NY: Macmillan.

De Pree, M. (1989). *Leadership is an art.* New York, NY: Doubleday.

De Pree, M. (1992). *Leadership jazz.* New York, NY: Doubleday.

Deal, T., & Kennedy, A. (2000). *Corporate cultures: The rites and rituals of corporate life* (2nd ed). Reading, MA: Addison-Wesley.

Diener, E. (2009). Subjective well-being. In E. Diener (Ed.), *The science of well-being: The collected works of Ed Diener.* New York: Springer.

Donaldson, T. (1989). *The ethics of international business.* New York, NY: Oxford University Press.

Drath, W. H., & Palus, C. J. (1994). *Making common sense: Leadership as meaning-making in a community of practice.* Greensboro, NC: Center for Creative Leadership.

Dugan, J. P., & Komives, S. R. (2007). *Developing leadership capacity in college students: Findings from a national study.* College Park, MD: National Clearinghouse for Leadership Programs.

Dugan, J. P., & Komives, S. R. (2010). Influences on college students' capacities for socially responsible leadership. *Journal of College Student Development, 51,* 525–549.

Eagley, A. H., Karau, S. J., & Makhijani, M. G. (1995). Gender and the effectiveness of leaders: A meta-analysis. *Psychological Bulletin, 117*(1), 125–145.

Eckel, P., Hill, B., & Green, M. (1998). *On change I: En route to transformation.* Washington, DC: American Council on Education.

Edwards, K. E., & Alimo, C. (2005, April 3). Social justice educator competencies. Pre-Conference Workshop, ACPA National Convention, Nashville, TN.

Elliott, C. (1999). *Locating the energy for change: An introduction to appreciative inquiry.* Winnipeg, Manitoba, Canada: International Institute for Sustainable Development.

Eoyang, G. (1997). *Coping with chaos: Seven simple tools.* Cheyenne, WY: Lagumo.

Erickson, A., Shaw, J. B., & Agabe, Z. (2007). An empirical investigation of the antecedents, behaviors, and outcomes of bad leadership. *Journal of Leadership, 1*(3), 26–43.

Ethics Resource Center. (2012). *National business ethics survey of Fortune 500 employers: An investigation into the state of ethics at America's most powerful companies.* Washington, DC: Ethics Resource Center.

Etzioni, A. (1993). *The spirit of community.* New York, NY: Crown.

Eyler, J., & Giles, D. (1999). *Where's the learning in service-learning?* San Francisco, CA: Jossey-Bass.

Eyler, J. S., Giles Jr., D. E., Stenson, C. M., & Gray, C. J. (2001). *At a glance: The effects of service-learning on college students, faculty, institutions, and communities, 1993–2000* (3rd ed). Providence, RI: Campus Compact. (http://www.campuscompact.org/resources/downloads/aag.pdf)

Fairholm, G. W. (1994). *Leadership and a culture of trust.* New York, NY: Praeger.

Festinger, L. (1962). *A theory of cognitive dissonance.* Stanford, CA: Stanford University Press.

Fisher, L. (2009). *The perfect swarm: The science of complexity in everyday life.* New York, NY: Basic Books.

Fletcher, J. K., & Kaufer, K. (2003). Shared leadership: Paradox and possibility. In C. L. Pearce & J. A. Conger (Eds.), *Shared leadership: Reframing the hows and whys of leadership.* Thousand Oaks, CA: Sage.

Fredrickson, B. (2009). *Positivity.* New York: Random House.

French, J.R.P., & Raven, B. H. (1959). The bases of social power. In D. Cartwright (Ed.), *Studies in social power* (pp. 150–167). Ann Arbor, MI: Institute for Social Research.

Friedman, T. L. (2005). *The world is flat: A brief history of the twenty-first century.* New York, NY: Farrar, Straus & Giroux.

Gallup Organization. (2012). American's negativity about U.S. moral values inches back up. Retrieved from http://www.gallup.com/poll/154715/americans-negativity-moral-values-inches-back.aspx

Gallup Poll Social Series. (2012). Princeton, NJ: The Gallup Organization.

Gandhi, A. (1998). Lessons from Sevagram Ashram. In F. Hesselbein, M. Goldsmith, R. Beckhard, & R. F. Schubert (Eds.), *The community of the future* (pp. 83–90). San Francisco, CA: Jossey-Bass/The Drucker Foundation.

Gandossy, R., & Effron, M. (2004). *Leading the way: Three truths from the top companies for leaders.* Hoboken, NJ: Wiley.

Gardner, J. W. (1981). *Self-renewal* (rev ed). New York, NY: Norton.

Gardner, J. W. (1990). *On leadership.* New York, NY: Free Press.

Gardner, J. W. (1993). The antileadership vaccine. In W. E. Rosenbach & R. L. Taylor (Eds.), *Contemporary issues in leadership* (3rd ed, pp. 193–200). Boulder, CO: Westview Press. (Original work published 1965)

Gardner, J. W. (2003). *Living, leading, and the American dream.* San Francisco, CA: Jossey-Bass.

Gardner, W. L., Avolio, B. J., Luthans, F., May, D. R., & Walumbwa, F. (2005). "Can you see the real me?" A self-based model of authentic leader and follower development. *The Leadership Quarterly, 16,* 343–372.

Geertz, C. (1973). Thick description: Toward an interpretive theory of culture. In C. Geertz (Ed.), *The interpretation of cultures* (pp. 3–32). New York, NY: Basic Books.

George, B. (2007). *True north: Discover your authentic leadership*. San Francisco, CA: Jossey-Bass.

Gladwell, M. (2002). *The tipping point: How little things can make a big difference*. Boston, MA: Little, Brown.

Goldstein, J., Hazy, J. K., & Lichtensten, B. B. (2010). *Complexity and the nexus of leadership: Leveraging nonlinear science to create ecologies of innovation*. New York, NY: St. Martin's Press.

Goleman, D. (1998). *Working with emotional intelligence*. New York, NY: Bantam Books.

Goleman, D. (2004, January). What makes a leader? *Harvard Business Review*, pp. 1–11.

Goodman, N. (1992). *Introduction to sociology*. New York, NY: HarperCollins.

Gozdz, K. (1993). Building community as a leadership discipline. In M. Ray & A. Rinzler (Eds.), *The new paradigm in business: Emerging strategies for leadership and organizational change* (pp. 107–119). Los Angeles, CA: Tarcher/Perigee.

Greenleaf, R. G. (1977). *Servant leadership: A journey in the nature of legitimate power and greatness*. New York, NY: Paulist.

Greenwood, R. G. (1993). Leadership theory: A historical look at its evolution. *The Journal of Leadership Studies, 1*(1), 4–19.

Gudykunst, W. B. (1991). *Bridging differences: Effective intergroup communication*. Thousand Oaks, CA: Sage.

Haas, H. G., & Tamarkin, B. (1992). *The leader within*. New York, NY: Harper-Collins.

Handy, C. (1996). *Beyond certainty: The changing worlds of organizations*. Boston, MA: Harvard Business School Press.

Hanson, R. (2009). *Buddha's brain: The practical neuroscience of happiness, love, and wisdom*. Oakland, CA: New Harbinger.

Harriger, K., & Ford, M. (1989). Lessons learned: Teaching citizenship in the university. In S. W. Morse (Ed.), *Public leadership education: Preparing college students for their civic roles* (pp. 22–28). Dayton, OH: Kettering Foundation.

Hart, L. B., & Dalke, J. D. (1983). *The sexes at work: Improving work relationships between men and women.* Englewood Cliffs, NJ: Prentice-Hall.

Heath, C., & Heath, D. (2007). *Made to stick: Why some ideas survive and others die.* New York, NY: Random House.

Heath, C., & Heath, D. (2010). *Switch: How to change things when change is hard.* New York, NY: Random House.

Heider, J. (1985). *The tao of leadership: Lao Tzu's Tao Te Ching adapted for a new age.* New York, NY: Bantam.

Heifetz, R. A., & Linsky, M. (2002). *Leadership on the line: Staying alive through the dangers of leading,* Boston: Harvard Business School Press.

Heilbrunn, J. (1994). Can leadership be studied? *The Wilson Quarterly,* Autumn, 65–72.

Helgesen, S. (1990). *The female advantage: Women's ways of leadership.* New York, NY: Doubleday.

Helgesen, S. (1995). *The web of inclusion: A new architecture for building great organizations.* New York, NY: Currency/Doubleday.

Helms, J. E. (1992). *A race is a nice thing to have.* Topeka, KS: Content Communications.

Henderson, V. E. (1992). *What's ethical in business?* New York, NY: McGraw-Hill.

Hesselbein, F. (2002). *Hesselbein on leadership.* San Francisco, CA: Jossey-Bass.

Hesselbein, F., & Shinseki, E. K. (2004). *Be-know-do: Leadership the army way.* (Adapted from the *Official Army Leadership Manual*). San Francisco, CA: Jossey-Bass.

Hesselbein, F., Goldsmith, M., Beckhard, R., & Schubert, R. F. (Eds.). (1998). *The community of the future.* San Francisco, CA: Jossey-Bass/The Drucker Foundation.

Higher Education Research Institute (HERI). (1996). *A social change model of leadership development: Guidebook version III.* Los Angeles, CA: University of California Los Angeles Higher Education Research Institute. (Guidebooks are available from the National Clearinghouse for Leadership Programs; http://www.nclp.umd.edu/)

Hill, R. P., & Stephens, D. L. (2003). The compassionate organization in the 21st Century. *Organizational Dynamics, 23,* 331–341.

Hill, S.E.K. (2013). Team leadership. In P. G. Northouse (Ed.), *Leadership: Theory and practice* (6th ed, pp. 287–318). Thousand Oaks, CA: Sage.

Hodgkinson, C. (1983). *The philosophy of leadership*. New York, NY: St. Martin's Press.

Hofstede, G. (2003). *Culture's consequences: Comparing values, behaviors, institutions and organizations across nations* (2nd ed). Thousand Oaks, CA: Sage.

Holland, J. (1998). *Emergence: From chaos to order*. Reading, MA: Helix/Addison-Wesley.

Hollander, E. P. (1993). Legitimacy, power, and influence: A perspective on relational features of leadership. In M. M. Chemers & R. Ayman (Eds.), *Leadership theory and research: Perspectives and directions* (pp. 29–47). San Diego: Academic Press.

Hoopes, D. S., & Pusch, M. D. (1979). Definition of terms. In M. D. Pusch (Ed.), *Multicultural education: A cross cultural training approach* (pp. 1–8). Chicago, IL: Intercultural Press.

Horwood, B. (1989). Reflections on reflection. *Journal of Experiential Education, 12*(2), 5–7.

House, R. J., Hanges, P. J., Javidan, M., Dorfman, P. W., & Gupta, V. (Eds.). (2004). *Culture, leadership, and organizations: The GLOBE study of 62 societies*. Thousand Oaks, CA: Sage.

Howard, P. N., & Hussain, M. M. (2011). The role of digital media. *Journal of Democracy, 22*(3), 35–48.

Howell, J. M. (1988). Two faces of charisma: Socialized and personalized leadership in organizations. In J. A. Conger, R. N. Kanungo, & Associates (Eds.), *Charismatic leadership: The elusive factor in organizational effectiveness* (pp. 213–236). San Francisco, CA: Jossey-Bass.

Howell, J. M., & Avolio, B. J. (1992). The ethics of charismatic leadership: Submission or liberation? *Academy of Management Executive, 6*(2), 43–54.

Hughes, R. L., Ginnett, R. C., & Curphy, G. J. (1993). *Leadership: Enhancing the lessons of experience*. Homewood, IL: Richard D. Irwin.

Hughes, R. L., Ginnett, R. C., & Curphy, G. J. (2012). *Leadership: Enhancing the lessons of experience* (7th ed). Homewood, IL: Richard D. Irwin.

Hurley, R. F. (2012). *The decision to trust: How leaders create high-trust organizations*. San Francisco, CA: Jossey-Bass.

Jackson, B., & Holvino, E. (1988). Developing multicultural organizations. *Journal of Religion and Applied Behavioral Science, 9*, 14–19.

Jaffe, D., Scott, C., & Tobe, G. (1994). *Rekindling commitment: How to revitalize yourself, your work, and your organization*. San Francisco, CA: Jossey-Bass.

Javidan, M., & House, R. J. (2001). Cultural acumen for the global manager: Lessons from Project GLOBE. *Organizational Dynamics, 29*, 289–305.

Johnson, C. E. (2012). *Meeting the ethical challenges of leadership: Casting light or shadow*. Thousand Oaks, CA: Sage.

Johnson, D. W., & Johnson, F. P. (1994). *Joining together: Group theory and group skills* (6th ed). Boston: Allyn & Bacon.

Johnson, D. W., & Johnson, F. P. (2006). *Joining together: Group theory and group skills* (9th ed). Boston, MA: Allyn & Bacon.

Johnson, D. W., Maruyama, G., Johnson, R., Nelson, D., & Skon, L. (1981). Effects of cooperative, competitive, and individualistic goal structures on achievement: A meta-analysis. *Psychological Bulletin, 89*(1), 47–62.

Jones, J. M. (Ed.). (2003). Issues facing state, local governments affect public trust. Gallup Poll Tuesday Briefing. Retrieved October 14, 2003, from http://www.gallup.com/poll/tb/goverpubli/20031014b.asp

Jones, P., & Kahaner, L. (1995). *Say it and live it: The 50 corporate mission statements that hit the mark*. New York, NY: Currency/Doubleday.

Jones, S. R., & Lucas, N. J. (1994). Interview with Michael Josephson. *Concepts & Connections: Rethinking Ethics & Leadership, 2*(3), 1, 3–5.

Kahn, S. (1991). *Organizing: A guide for grassroots leaders* (rev ed). Washington, DC: National Association of Social Workers.

Kanter, R. M. (1989). *When giants learn to dance*. New York, NY: Simon & Schuster.

Kanungo, R. N., & Mendonca, M. (1996). Ethical dimensions in leadership motivation. In R. N. Kanungo & M. Mendonca (Eds.), *Ethical dimensions of leadership* (pp. 33–51). Thousand Oaks, CA: Sage .

Katzenbach, J. R., Beckett, F., Dichter, S., Feigen, M., Gagnon, C., Hope, Q., & Ling, T. (1996). *Real change leaders: How you can create growth and high performance at your company*. New York, NY: Random House.

Kegan, R., & Lahey, L. (2001, November). The real reason people won't change, *Harvard Business Review, 79*(10), 84–93.

Kegan, R. & Lahey, L. L. (2009). *Immunity to change: How to overcome it and unlock the potential in yourself and your organization*. Boston, MA: Harvard Business Press.

Kellerman, B. (2004). *Bad leadership*. Cambridge, MA: Harvard Business School Press.

Kelley, R. E. (1988). In praise of followers. *Harvard Business Review*, 66(6), 142–148.

Kelley, R. E. (1992). *The power of followership: How to create leaders people want to follow and followers who lead themselves*. New York, NY: Currency/Doubleday.

Kelly, K. (1994). *Out of control: The new biology of machines, social systems, and the economic world*. Reading, MA: Addison-Wesley.

Kennedy, D. (2009). How to put our differences to work. *Leader To Leader, 52*, 49–55.

Kets de Vries, M.F.R., & Florent-Treacy, E. (2002). Global leadership from A to Z: Creating high commitment organizations. *Organizational Dynamics, 30*, 295–309.

Kidder, R. M. (1995). *How good people make tough choices: Resolving the dilemmas of ethical living*. New York, NY: Fireside.

Kidder, R. M. (2005). *Moral courage: Taking action when your values are put to the test*. New York, NY: William Morrow.

Kiefer, C. F., & Senge, P. M. (1984). Metanoic organizations. In J. D. Adams (Ed.), *Transforming work: A collection of organizational transformation readings* (pp. 68–84). Alexandria, VA: Miles River Press.

Kimmel, M. (2008). *Guyland: The perilous world where boys become men*. New York. NY: HarperCollins.

Kimmel, M. S., & Ferber, A. L. (Eds.). (2003). *Privilege: A reader*. Boulder, CO: Westview.

King, W. R. (1984). Integrating strategic issues into strategic management OMEGA: *The International Journal of Management Science, 12*, 529–538.

Kissler, G. D. (2001). e-Leadership. *Organizational Dynamics, 30*, 121–133.

Kitchener, K. S. (1984). Intuition, critical evaluation and ethical principles: The foundation for ethical decisions in counseling psychology. *The Counseling Psychologist, 12*(3), 43–55.

Kline, P., & Saunders, B. (1993). *Ten steps to a learning organization*. Arlington, VA: Great Ocean.

Knowles, M., & Knowles, H. (1959). *Introduction to group dynamics*. New York, NY: Association Press.

Koestenbaum, P. (2002). *Leadership: The inner side of greatness: A philosophy for leaders*. San Francisco, CA: Jossey-Bass.

Kohn, A. (1992). *No contest: The case against competition* (rev ed). Boston, MA: Houghton Mifflin.

Kolb, D. A. (1981). Learning styles and disciplinary differences. In A. W. Chickering & Associates (Eds.), *The modern American college: Responding to the new realities of diverse students and a changing society* (pp. 232–255). San Francisco, CA: Jossey-Bass.

Kolb, A.Y., & Kolb, D. A. (2005). Learning styles and learning spaces: Enhancing experiential learning in higher education. *Academy of Management Learning & Education, 4*(2), 193–212.

Komives, S. R. (1994). Increasing student involvement through civic leadership education. In P. Mable & C. Schroeder (Eds.), *Realizing the educational potential of college residence halls* (pp. 218–240). San Francisco, CA: Jossey-Bass.

Komives, S. R. (2000). Inhabit the gap. *About Campus: Enhancing the Student Learning Experience, 5*(5), 31–32.

Komives, S. R. (2010). Leadership. In J. Schuh, S. R. Jones, & S. Harper (Eds.) *Student services: A handbook for the profession* (5th ed, pp. 353–371). San Francisco, CA: Jossey-Bass.

Komives, S. R. (2011). Advancing leadership education. In S. R. Komives, J. P. Dugan, J. E. Owen, C. Slack, W. Wagner, & Associates (Eds.), *The handbook for student leadership development* (2nd ed, pp. 1–32). San Francisco, CA: Jossey-Bass.

Komives, S. R., & Dugan, J. P. (2010). Contemporary leadership theories. In R. A. Couto (Ed.) *Political and civic leadership: A reference handbook* (pp. 111–120). Thousand Oaks, CA: Sage.

Komives, S. R., Owen, J. E., Longerbeam, S., Mainella, F. C., & Osteen, L. (2005). Developing a leadership identity: A grounded theory. *Journal of College Student Development, 46*, 593–611.

Komives, S. R., Wagner, W., & Associates. (2009). *Leadership for a better world: Understanding the social change model of leadership development.* San Francisco, CA: Jossey-Bass.

Kotter, J. P. (1996). *Leading change.* Boston, MA: Harvard Business School Press.

Kotter, J. P. (2008). *A sense of urgency.* Cambridge, MA: Harvard University Press.

Kotter, J. P., & Cohen, D. S. (2002). *The heart of change: Real-life stories of how people change their organizations.* Boston, MA: Harvard Business School Press.

Kouzes, J. M., & Posner, B. Z. (1987). *The leadership challenge.* San Francisco, CA: Jossey-Bass.

Kouzes, J. M., & Posner, B. Z. (1993). *Credibility: How leaders gain and lose it, why people demand it.* San Francisco, CA: Jossey-Bass.

Kouzes, J. M., & Posner, B. Z. (2002). *The leadership challenge* (3rd ed). San Francisco, CA: Jossey-Bass.

Kouzes, J. M., & Posner, B. Z. (2008). *The leadership challenge* (4th ed). San Francisco, CA: Jossey-Bass.

Kübler-Ross, E. (1970). *On death and dying.* New York, NY: Macmillan.

Lappé, F. M., & Du Bois, P. M. (1994). *The quickening of America: Rebuilding our nation, remaking our lives.* San Francisco, CA: Jossey-Bass.

Latour, S. M., & Rast, V. J. (2004). Dynamic followership: The prerequisite for effective leadership. *Air & Space Power Journal, 18*(4), 102–114. Retrieved April 14, 2006, from http://www.airpower.maxwell.af.mil/airchronicles/apje.html

LeaderShape Institute Manual (1996). Champaign, IL: LeaderShape.

Lei, D., & Greer, C. R. (2003). The empathetic organization. *Organizational Dynamics, 32*(2), 142–164.

Leppo, J., & Lustgraaf, M. (1987). *Student government: Working with special constituencies.* Programming, Leadership & Activities Network, Memorial Union. Grand Forks, ND: University of North Dakota.

Levine, A. (1993). A portrait of college students in the 90s: Taking responsibility for educational management. Paper presented at the Annual Conference of the National Association of Student Personnel Administrators, Boston.

Levoy, G. (2000). *Character: Courage to follow your calling.* The Inner Edge, 3(3), 22–23.

Lewin, K. (1958). Group decision and social change. In E. E. Maccoby, T. M. Newcomb, & E. L. Hartley (Eds.), *Readings in social psychology* (pp. 197–211). New York, NY: Holt, Rinehart & Winston.

Lewin, R., & Regine, B. (2000). *The soul at work: Listen . . . respond . . . let go.* New York: Simon & Schuster.

Lewis, H. A. (1990). *A question of values.* New York, NY: Harper & Row.

Lichtenstein, B. B., Uhl-Bien, M., Marion, R., Seers, A., & Orton, J. D. (2006). Complexity Leadership theory: An interactive perspective on leading in complex adaptive systems. *Emergence: Complexity and Organization, 8*(4), 2–12.

Linley, P. A., Garcea, N., Harrington, S., Trenier, E., & Minhas, G. (2011). Organizational applications of positive psychology: Taking stock and a research/practice roadmap for the future. In K. M. Sheldon, T. B. Kashdan, & M. F. Steger (Eds.), *Designing positive psychology: Taking stock and moving forward*. New York: Oxford University Press.

Lipman-Blumen, J. (1984). *Gender roles and power*. Englewood Cliffs, NJ: Prentice Hall.

Lipman-Blumen, J. (2005). *The allure of toxic leaders*. New York, NY: Oxford University Press.

Lipnack, J., & Stamps, J. (2000). *Virtual teams: People working across boundaries with technology*. New York, NY: John Wiley & Sons.

Lippitt, G. L. (1969). *Organizational renewal: Achieving viability in a changing world*. New York, NY: Appleton-Century Crofts.

Lippitt, G. L. (1973). *Visualizing change: Model building and the change process*. Fairfax, VA: NTL-Learning Resources.

Loden, M., & Rosener, J. B. (1991). *Workforce America!* Homewood, IL: Business One Irwin.

Loeb, P. R. (1999). *Soul of a citizen: Living with conviction in a cynical time*. New York, NY: St. Martin's Griffin.

Loeb, P. R. (2010). *Soul of a citizen: Living with conviction in a cynical time* (rev ed). New York, NY: St. Martin's Griffin.

Lucas, N., & Anello, E. (1995). Ethics and leadership. Unpublished paper. Salzburg Leadership Seminar, Salzburg, Austria. November 11–18.

Lucas, N., & Koerwer, V. S. (2004). Featured interview: Sherron Watkins, former vice-president for corporate development of Enron. *Journal of Leadership and Organizational Studies, 11*(1), 38–47.

Lucas, N. J. (1999). Lives of integrity: Factors that influence moral transforming leaders. Unpublished doctoral dissertation, University of Maryland, College Park, MD.

Luke, J. S. (1998). *Catalytic leadership: Strategies for an interconnected world*. San Francisco, CA: Jossey-Bass.

Lussier, R. N., & Achua, C. F. (2004). *Leadership: Theory, application, skill development* (2nd ed). Eagan, MN: Thomson-West.

Luthans, F., & Avolio, B. (2003). Authentic leadership development. In K. S. Cameron, J. E. Dutton, & R. E. Quinn (Eds.), *Positive organizational scholarship: Foundations for a new discipline* (pp. 241–258). San Francisco, CA: Berrett-Koehler.

Luthans, F., & Slocum, J. (2004). Special issue: New leadership for a new time. *Organizational Dynamics, 33*(3), 227.

Manz, C. C., & Sims Jr., H. P., (1981). Vicarious learning: The influence of modeling on organizational behavior. *Academy of Management Review,* 6(1), 105–113.

Manz, C. C., & Sims Jr., H. P., (1989). *SuperLeadership: Leading others to lead themselves.* New York, NY: Berkley Books.

Mathews, D. (1994). *Politics for people.* Urbana, IL: University of Illinois Press.

Matusak, L. R. (1996). *Finding your voice: Learning to lead . . . anywhere you want to make a difference.* San Francisco, CA: Jossey-Bass.

May, D. R., Hodges, T. D., Chan, A.Y.L., & Avolio, B. J. (2003). Developing the moral component of authentic leadership. *Organizational Dynamics, 32*(3), 247–260.

McFarland, L. J., Senn, L. E., & Childress, J. R. (1993). *21st century leadership: Dialogues with 100 top leaders.* Los Angeles, CA: The Leadership Press.

McGill, M. E., & Slocum, J. W. (1993). Unlearning the organization, *Organizational Dynamics,* Fall, 67–79.

McIntosh, P. M. (1989, July/August). White privilege: Unpacking the invisible knapsack. *Peace and Freedom,* 10–12.

McMahon, T., Kochner, C., Clemetsen, B., & Bolger, A. (1995). *Moving beyond TQM to learning organizations: New perspectives to transform the academy.* Paper presented at the annual meeting of the American College Personnel Association, Boston, March 18–22.

Meadows, D. (1982). Whole earth models and systems. *Co-Evolution Quarterly,* Summer, 98–108.

Mizrahi, T., & Rosenthal, B. S. (1993). Managing dynamic tensions in social change coalitions. In T. Mizrahi & J. Morrison (Eds.), *Community organization and social administration: Advances, trends and emerging principles* (pp. 11–40). New York, NY: Haworth Press.

Mockaitis, A. I., Rose, E. L., & Zettnig, P. (2012). The power of individual cultural values in global virtual teams. *International Journal of Cross Cultural Management, 12*(2), 193–210.

Morrison, A. M. (1996). *The new leaders: Leadership diversity in America.* San Francisco, CA: Jossey-Bass.

Morse, S. W. (1998). Five building blocks for successful communities. In F. Hesselbein, M. Goldsmith, R. Beckhard, & R. F. Schubert (Eds.), *The community of the future* (pp. 229–236). San Francisco, CA: Jossey-Bass/The Drucker Foundation.

Morton, K. (1995). The irony of service: Charity, project and social change in service-learning. *Michigan Journal of Community Service Learning, 2,* 19–32.

Murrell, K. L. (1985). The development of a theory of empowerment: Rethinking power for organizational development. *Organizational Development Journal, 34,* 34–38.

Musil, C. M. (2003). Educating for citizenship. *Peer Review, 5*(3), 4–8.

Nanus, B. (1992). *Visionary leadership: Creating a compelling sense of direction for your organization.* San Francisco, CA: Jossey-Bass.

Nash, L. L. (1990). *Good intentions aside.* Boston, MA: Harvard Business School Press.

Nathan, R. (2005). *My freshman year: What a professor learned by becoming a student.* Ithaca, NY: Cornell University.

National Invitational Leadership Symposium. (1991). *Proceedings from the 1991 National Invitational Leadership Symposium.* College Park, MD: National Clearinghouse for Leadership Programs.

Neilson, R. P. (1990). Dialogic leadership as ethics action method. *Journal of Business Ethics, 9,* 765–783.

Nicoll, D. (1984). Grace beyond the roles: A new paradigm for lives on a human scale. In J. D. Adams (Ed.), *Transforming work: A collection of organizational transformation readings* (pp. 4–16). Alexandria, VA: Miles River Press.

Northouse, P. G. (2004). *Leadership theory and practice* (3rd ed). Thousand Oaks, CA: Sage.

Northouse, P. G. (2013). *Leadership: Theory and practice* (6th ed). Thousand Oaks, CA: Sage Publications, Inc.

Oblinger, D. G., & Oblinger, J. L. (Eds.) (2005). *Educating the net generation.* Educause. http://www.educause.edu/content.asp?PAGE_ID= 5989&bhcp= 1#copyright

O'Neill, N. (2012). *Promising practices for personal and social responsibility: Findings from a national research collaborative.* Washington, DC: Association of American Colleges & Universities.

O'Toole, J. (1996). *Leading change: The argument for values-based leadership.* New York, NY: Ballantine Books.

Ospina, S., & Foldy, E. (2010). Building bridges from the margins: The work of leadership in social change organizations. *The Leadership Quarterly, 21*, 292–307.

Outcalt, C. L., Faris, S. K., & McMahon, K. N. (Eds.). (2001). *Developing non-hierarchical leadership on campus: Case studies and best practices in higher education.* Westport, CT: Greenwood Press.

Palmer, P. J. (1981). *The company of strangers: Christians and the renewal of America's public life.* New York, NY: Crossroad.

Palmer, P. J. (1998). *The courage to teach: Exploring the inner landscape of a teacher's life.* San Francisco, CA: Jossey-Bass.

Palmer, P. J. (2000). *Let your life speak: Listening for the voice of vocation.* San Francisco, CA: Jossey-Bass.

Parker, G. M. (2003). *Cross-functional teams: Working with allies, enemies, and other strangers.* San Francisco, CA: Jossey-Bass.

Parks, S. D. (2005). *Leadership can be taught: A bold approach for a complex world.* Boston, MA: Harvard Business School Press.

Parr, J. (1994). Foreword. In D. D. Chrislip & C. E. Larson, *Collaborative leadership: How citizens and civic leaders can make a difference* (pp. xi–xiii). San Francisco, CA: Jossey-Bass.

Pascale, R., Millemann, M., & Gioja, L. (2000). *Surfing the edge of chaos: The laws of nature and the new laws of business.* New York, NY: Crown Business.

Pearce, C. L., & Conger, J. A. (2003). *Shared leadership: Reframing the hows and whys of leadership.* Thousand Oaks, CA: Sage.

Peck, M. S. (1987). *The different drum: Community-making and peace.* New York, NY: Simon & Schuster.

Pedersen, P. (1988). *Handbook for developing multicultural awareness.* Alexandria, VA: American Association of Counseling and Development.

Peters, T. (1989). Foreword. In C. C. Manz & H. P. Sims Jr., *Superleadership: Leading others to lead themselves* (pp. xiii–xiv). New York, NY: Prentice Hall.

Peterson, C., & Seligman, M.E.P. (2004). *Character strengths and virtues: A handbook and classification.* New York, NY: Oxford University Press.

PEW Internet & American Life Project. (2012). http://pewinternet.org/Static-Pages/Trend-Data-(Adults)/Device-Ownership.aspx

Phillips, J. M. (1995). Leadership since 1975: Advancement or inertia? *The Journal of Leadership Studies, 2*(1), 58–80.

Phills Jr., J. A., Deiglmeier, K., & Miller, D. T. (2008). Rediscovering social innovation. *Stanford Social Innovation Review, 6*(4), 34–43.

Piper, T. R., Gentile, M. C., & Parks, S. D. (1993). *Can ethics be taught? Perspectives, challenges, and approaches at Harvard Business School.* Boston, MA: Harvard Business School Press.

Plowman, D. A., Solansky, S., Beck, T. E., Baker, L., Kulkarni, M., & Travis, D. E. (2007). The role of leadership in emergent, self-organization. *The Leadership Quarterly, 18,* 341–356.

Pocock, P. (1989). Is business ethics a contradiction in terms? *Personnel Management, 21*(11), 60–63.

Pope, R. (1993). Multicultural-organization development in student affairs: An introduction. *Journal of College Student Development, 34,* 201–205.

Porter, E. H., Rosenbach, W. E., & Pittman, T. S. (2005). Leading the new professions. In R. L. Taylor & W. E. Rosenbach (Eds.), *Military leadership* (5th ed, p. 149). Boulder, CO: Westview Press.

Postman, N. (1992). *Technopoly: The surrender of culture to technology.* New York, NY: Knopf.

Potter, E. H., III, & Fiedler, F. E. (1993). Selecting leaders: Making the most of previous experience. *Journal of Leadership Studies, 1*(1), 61–70.

Putnam, R. D. (1995). Bowling alone: America's declining social capital. *Journal of Democracy, 6*(1), 65–78.

Quinn, R. E. (1996). *Deep change: Discovering the leader within.* San Francisco, CA: Jossey-Bass.

Quinn, R. E. (2004). *Building the bridge: A guide for leading change as you walk on it.* San Francisco, CA: Jossey-Bass.

The quotable woman. (1991). Philadelphia: Running Press.

Radostina K., Purvanova, R. K., & Bono, J. E. (2009). Transformational leadership in context: Face-to-face and virtual teams. *Leadership Quarterly, 20,* 343–357.

Raelin, J. R. (2003). *Creating leaderful organizations: How to bring out leadership in everyone*. San Francisco, CA: Berrett-Koehler.

Rath, T., & Clifton, D. O. (2004). *How full is your bucket: Positive strengths for work and life*. New York, NY: Gallup Press.

Rath, T., & Conchie, B. (2008). *Strengths-based leadership: Great leaders, teams, and why people follow*. New York, NY: Gallup Press.

Raven, B. H., & Kruglanski, W. (1975). Conflict and power. In P. G. Swingle (Ed.), *The structure of conflict* (pp. 177–219). New York, NY: Academic Press.

Rayner, S. R. (1996). *Team traps: Survival stories and lessons from team disasters, near-misses, mishaps, and other near-death experiences*. New York, NY: Wiley.

Rheingold, H. (1993). *The virtual community: Homesteading on the electronic frontier*. New York, NY: HarperCollins.

Rheingold, H. (2003). *Smart mobs: The next social revolution*. New York: Basic Books.

Riggio, R. E., Chaleff, I., & Lipman-Blumen, J. (Eds.). (2008). *The art of followership: How great followers create great leaders and organizations*. San Francisco, CA: Jossey-Bass.

Roberts, L. M., Spreitzer, G., Dutton, J., Quinn, R., Heaphy, E. & Barker, B. (2005). How to play to your strengths. *Harvard Business Review, 83,*(1), 75–80.

Robertson, I., & Cooper, G. (2011). *Well-being: Productivity and happiness at work*. New York: Palgrave Macmillan.

Rogers, J. L. (1996). Leadership. In S. R. Komives, D. B. Woodard Jr., & Associates, *Student services: A handbook for the profession* (3rd ed, pp. 299–319). San Francisco, CA: Jossey-Bass.

Rosenthal, T. L., & Zimmerman, B. J. (1978). *Social learning and cognition*. New York, NY: Academic Press.

Ross, R. (1994a). The five whys. In P. M. Senge, A. Kleiner, C. Roberts, R. Ross, & B. Smith (Eds.), *The fifth discipline fieldbook: Strategies and tools for building a learning organization* (pp. 108–112). New York, NY: Currency/Doubleday.

Ross, R. (1994b). Skillful discussion: Protocols for reaching a decision—mindfully. In P. M. Senge, A. Kleiner, C. Roberts, R. Ross, & B. Smith (Eds.), *The fifth discipline fieldbook: Strategies and tools for building a learning organization* (pp. 385–391). New York, NY: Currency/Doubleday.

Rost, J. C. (1991). *Leadership for the twenty-first century.* New York, NY: Praeger.

Rost, J. C. (1993). Leadership development in the new millennium. *Journal of Leadership Studies, 1*(1), 91–110.

Rubin, R. S., Dierdorff, E. C., Bommer, W. H., & Baldwin, T. T. (2009). Do leaders reap what they sow? Leader and employee outcomes of leader organizational cynicism about change. *The Leadership Quarterly 20,* 680–688

Salzburg, S. (2011). *Real happiness: The power of meditation.* New York, NY: Workman Publishing.

Schein, E. (2010). *Organizational culture and leadership* (4th ed). San Francisco, CA: Jossey-Bass.

Schlossberg, N. K. (1989a). *Overwhelmed: Coping with life's ups and downs.* Lexington, MA: Lexington.

Schlossberg, N. K. (1989b). Marginality and mattering: Key issues in building community. In D. C. Roberts (Ed.), *Designing campus activities to foster a sense of community* (pp. 5–15). New Directions for Student Services, No. 48. San Francisco, CA: Jossey-Bass.

Seligman, M.E.P. (2002). *Authentic happiness: Using the new positive psychology to realize your potential for lasting fulfillment.* New York, NY: Free Press.

Seligman, M.E.P. (2011). *Flourish: A visionary new understanding of happiness and well-being.* New York, NY: Free Press

Senge, P. M. (1990). *The fifth discipline: The art and practice of the learning organization.* New York, NY: Currency/Doubleday.

Senge, P. M. (1993). The art and practice of the learning organization. In M. Ray & A. Rinzler (Eds.), *The new paradigm in business: Emerging strategies for leadership and organizational change* (pp. 126–137). Los Angeles, CA: Tarcher/Perigree.

Senge, P. M., Kleiner, A., Roberts, C., Ross, R., & Smith, B. (1994). *The fifth discipline fieldbook: Strategies and tools for building a learning organization.* New York, NY: Currency/Doubleday.

Shamir, B., & Eilam, G. (2005). "What's your story?" A life-stories approach to authentic leadership development. *Leadership Quarterly, 16,* 295–417.

Shankman M. L., & Allen, S. J. (2008). *Emotionally intelligent leadership: A guide for college students.* San Francisco, CA: Jossey-Bass.

Shaw, W., & Barry, V. (1989). *Moral issues in business* (4th ed). Belmont, CA: Wadsworth.

Shea, G. F. (1988). *Practical ethics: AMA Management Briefing*. New York, NY: AMA Membership Publications Division.

Sheehy, G. (1981). *Pathfinders*. New York, NY: Bantam.

Simons, G. F., Vázquez, C., & Harris, P. R. (1993). *Transcultural leadership*. Houston, TX: Gulf.

Sims Jr., H. P., & Lorenzi, P. (1992). *The new leadership paradigm: Social learning and cognition in organizations*. Thousand Oaks, CA: Sage.

Sims Jr., H. P., & Manz, C. C. (1981). Social learning theory: The role of modeling in the exercise of leadership. *Journal of Organizational Behavior Management, 3*(4), 55–63.

Smith, B. L., MacGregor, J., Matthews, R. S., & Gabelnick, F. (2004). *Learning communities: Reforming undergraduate education*. San Francisco, CA: Jossey-Bass.

Smith, M. K. (2005). Bruce W. Tuckman—Forming, storming, norming, and performing in groups. *The encyclopaedia of informal education*. Retrieved April 29, 2006, from www.infed.org/thinkers/tuckman.htm

Spears, L. C. (1995). *Reflections on leadership: How Robert K. Greenleaf's theory of servant-leadership influenced today's top management thinkers*. Hoboken, NJ: Wiley.

Spence, J. T. (Ed.). (1983). *Achievement and achievement motives: Psychological and sociological approaches*. San Francisco, CA: Freeman.

Stacey, R. (1992). *Managing the unknowable*. San Francisco, CA: Jossey-Bass.

Stogdill, R. M. (1974). *Handbook of leadership: A survey of theory and research*. New York, NY: Free Press.

Sue, D. W. (2003). *Overcoming our racism: The journey to liberation*. San Francisco, CA: Jossey-Bass.

Sue, D. W. (2010). *Microaggressions in everyday life: Race, gender, and sexual orientation*. Hoboken, NJ: Wiley.

Talbot, D. M. (1996). Multiculturalism. In S. R. Komives, D. B. Woodard Jr., & Associates (Eds.), *Student services: A handbook for the profession* (3rd ed, pp. 380–396). San Francisco, CA: Jossey-Bass.

Tannen, D. (1990). *You don't understand me: Women and men in conversation*. New York, NY: Morrow.

Taylor, H. L. (1989). *Delegate: The key to successful management.* New York, NY: Warner Books.

Terry, R. (1993). *Authentic leadership.* San Francisco: Jossey-Bass.

Thomas Jr., R. R. (2006). Diversity management: An essential craft for leaders. *Leader To Leader, 41,* 45–49.

Tichy, N. W., & Devanna, M. A. (1986). *The transformational leader.* Hoboken, NJ: Wiley.

Tjosvold, D., & Tjosvold, M. M. (1991). *Leading the team organization.* New York, NY: Macmillan.

Toffler, A. (1970). *Future shock.* New York, NY: Random House.

Toffler, B. L. (1986). *Tough choices: Managers talk ethics.* Hoboken, NJ: Wiley.

Trevino, L. K., Weaver, G. R., & Brown, M. E. (2007). It's lonely at the top: Hierarchical levels, identities, and perceptions of organizational ethics. *Business Ethics Quarterly, 18*(2), 233–252.

Tubbs, S. (1984). *A systems approach to small group interaction* (2nd ed). Reading, MA: Addison-Wesley.

Tuckman, B. W. (1965). Developmental sequence in small groups. *Psychological Bulletin, 63,* 384–399.

Tuckman, B. W., & Jensen, M. C. (1977). Stages of small group development revisited. *Group and Organizational Studies, 2,* 419–427.

Uhl-Bien, M., Marion, R., & McKelvey, B. (2007). Complexity leadership theory: Shifting Leadership from the industrial age to the knowledge era. *The Leadership Quarterly, 18,* 298–318.

Ulrich, D. (1998). Six practices for creating communities of value, not proximity. In F. Hesselbein, M. Goldsmith, R. Beckhard, & R. F. Schubert (Eds.), *The community of the future* (pp. 155–165). San Francisco, CA: Jossey-Bass/The Drucker Foundation.

Vaill, P. B. (1991). *Permanent white water: The realities, myths, paradoxes, and dilemmas of managing organizations.* San Francisco, CA: Jossey-Bass.

Van Fleet, D. D., & Yukl, G. A. (1989). A century of leadership research. In W. E. Rosenbach & R. L. Taylor (Eds.), *Contemporary issues in leadership* (2nd ed, pp. 65–90). Boulder, CO: Westview Press.

Wagner, W. (2009). What is social change? In S. R. Komives, W. Wagner, & Associates. *Leadership for a better world: Understanding the social change model of leadership development* (pp. 7–42). San Francisco, CA: Jossey-Bass.

Wagner, W. (2007). The social change model of leadership: A brief overview. *Concepts & Connections, 15*(1), p. 9.

Wall, V., & Obear, K. (2008). Multicultural organizational development (MCOD): Exploring best practices to create socially just, inclusive campus communities. Paper presented at the American Association of Colleges and Universities Conference, Oct. 17, 2008. http://www.aacu.org/meetings/diversityandlearning/DL2008/Resources/documents/AACUMCOD handouts2008-ObearandWall.pdf

Walton, C. C. (1988). *The moral manager.* New York, NY: Harper & Row.

Watkins, J. M., & Mohr, B. J. (2001). *Appreciate inquiry: Change at the speed of imagination.* San Francisco, CA: Pfeiffer.

Watkins, K. E., & Marsick, V. J. (1993). *Sculpting the learning organization.* San Francisco, CA: Jossey-Bass.

Watts, D. J. (2003). *Six degrees: The science of a connected age.* New York, NY: Norton.

Weber, M. (1947). *The theory of social and economic organization* (A. H. Henderson & T. Parsons, Trans.). Blencoe, IL: Free Press. (Original work published 1924)

Webster's Ninth New Collegiate Dictionary. (1986). Springfield, MA: Merriam-Webster.

Weick, K. E. (1979). *The social psychology of organizing* (2nd ed). New York, NY: Random House.

Wheatley, M. J. (1999). *Leadership and the new science: Learning about organization from an orderly universe.* San Francisco, CA: Berrett-Koehler.

Wheatley, M. J. (2003). *Change: The capacity of life. In Business leadership: A Jossey-Bass reader* (pp. 496–517). San Francisco, CA: Jossey-Bass.

Wheatley, M. J. (2006). *Leadership and the new science: Discovering order in a chaotic world* (3rd ed). San Francisco, CA: Berrett-Koehler.

Wheatley, M. J., & Kellner-Rogers, M. (1996). *A simpler way.* San Francisco, CA: Berrett-Koehler.

Whitney, D. (2005). *Appreciative inquiry: A positive revolution in change.* San Francisco, CA: Berrett-Koehler.

Whitney, D. (2008). *Appreciative inquiry handbook: For leaders of change.* San Francisco, CA: Berrett-Koehler.

Whitney, D., & Trosten-Bloom, A. (2010). *The power of appreciative inquiry: A practical guide to positive change* (2nd ed). San Francisco: Berrett-Koehler.

Whitney, D., Trosten-Bloom, A., & Cooperrider, D. L. (2003). *The power of appreciative inquiry: A practical guide to positive change*. San Francisco, CA: Berrett-Koehler.

Wijeyesinghe, C. L., Griffin, P., & Love, P. (1997). Racism curriculum design. In M. Adams, L. A. Bell, & P. Griffin (Eds.), *Teaching for diversity and social justice: A sourcebook* (pp. 87–109). New York, NY: Routledge.

Willie, C. V. (1992). Achieving community on the college campus. Paper presented to the Annual Conference of the American College and University Housing Officers-International, Boston College, Boston.

Wood, D. J., & Gray, B. (1991). Toward a comprehensive theory of collaboration. *Journal of Applied Behavioral Science, 27*(2), 139–162.

Wood, J. T. (2004). *Interpersonal communication: Everyday encounters* (4th ed). Belmont, CA: Wadsworth.

Wren, T. (1994). Interview: H. Norman Schwarzkopf, General, USA. *Journal of Leadership Studies, 1*(3), 1–6.

Yukl, G. A. (1989). *Leadership in organizations* (2nd ed). Englewood Cliffs, NJ: Prentice Hall.

Yukl, G. A. (1994). *Leadership in organizations* (3rd ed). Englewood Cliffs, NJ: Prentice Hall.

Yukl, G. A. (2009). Leading organizational learning: Reflections on theory and research. *The Leadership Quarterly, 20*, 49–53.

Zaccaro, S. J., & Bader, P. (2003). E-Leadership and the challenges of leading e-teams: Minimizing the bad and maximizing the good. *Organizational Dynamics, 31*, 377–387.

Zaleznik, A. (1977). Managers and leaders: Are they different? *Harvard Business Review, 55*(5), 67–78.

Zigurs, I. (2003). Leadership in virtual teams: Oxymoron or opportunity? *Organizational Dynamics, 31* (4), 339–351

Zofi, Y.S. (2012). *A manager's guide to virtual teams*. New York, NY: AMACOM.

AUTHOR INDEX

SUBJECT INDEX

Command and control leadership, 11

Commitment: to change, 435; to community, 35, 288–289, 302; description of, 454e; immunity to change and, 414–417, 418; in Social Change Model, 457, 458; of team members, 344; as trait of allies and advocates, 449

Common Cause, 45

Common good: in ethical decision-making models, 271–272; leadership's purpose regarding, 23; local heroes and, 25

Common purpose: description of, 455e; in Social Change Model, 457, 458, 459

Commonality, in understanding others, 189–192

Communication: assertiveness in, 223–225; chaos and, 300–301; culture and, 216–218; in dialogic leadership, 263–265; difficult dialogues and, 225–226; empathy in, 220–223; facilitating positive types of, 504; importance of listening in, 219–220; inclusiveness and, 110, 111; technology for, 388

Communities: Appreciative Inquiry in, 490–491e; central practices of, 293–294; comfort of, 286; commitment to, 35, 288–289, 302; culture of, 289; description of, 283, 287, 288, 293; development of, 298–305; diversity in, 290; elements of, 288–299; ethical dilemmas involving, 269, 270; example of, 285–286; global nature of, 305; importance of, 287–288; of practice, 294–299; in Relational Leadership Model, 303t; shared values of, 293–294; traditional views of, 290

Community action, coalitions for, 461–467

Community organizations, 292

Community service movement, 25

Community values, 455–456e, 457f

Competence, of team members, 344

Competition: in American structures, 134; versus cooperation, 135; Social Change Model and, 458

Complementary partnerships, 171

Completion phase, 421, 422

Complexity leadership theory, 73–74

Computers, 427

Concrete experience, 32

Conditions, 476, 477t

Confidence, 157–160

Confidentiality, 267

Conflict resolution: civility and, 481; diversity and, 218–219; in group dynamics, 326–329; strengths-based approach to, 483–484

Conflicts: advantages and liabilities of, 327t; challenges of, 480–481; description of, 481; source of, 326, 482–483t

Congruency: description of, 454e; mindfulness and, 162; in Social Change Model, 456, 457f, 458

Connections, importance of, 85

Consciousness of self: description of, 454e; example of, 44; in Social Change Model, 456, 457f, 458, 459

Consensus, 218–219, 331–333

Consideration, 63

Constituents, 20

Contemplation, 141–142

Contingency theories, 64

Continuity, 390

Continuous learning, 381

Contrary evidence, 408

Contributive justice, 297

Controversy, 326–327

Controversy with civility: description of, 455e; disagreements and, 481; in Social Change Model, 456, 457f, 458, 459

Cooperation: benefits of, 136; versus collaboration, 135–136; versus competition, 135; example of, 136